P9-DHJ-187

YOSEMITE
NATIONAL PARK

KURT WOLFF

AMY MARR

DAVID LUKAS

CHERYL KOEHLER

LONELY PLANET PUBLICATIONS
Melbourne · Oakland · London · Paris

Yosemite National Park
1st edition – March 2003

Published by
Lonely Planet Publications Pty Ltd ABN 36 005 607 983
90 Maribyrnong St, Footscray, Victoria 3011, Australia

Lonely Planet Offices
Australia Locked Bag 1, Footscray, Victoria 3011
USA 150 Linden St, Oakland, CA 94607
UK 10a Spring Place, London NW5 3BH
France 1 rue du Dahomey, 75011 Paris

Photographs
Many of the images in this guide are available for licensing from
Lonely Planet Images.
W www.lonelyplanetimages.com

Front cover photograph
Half dome in the fall,
Yosemite National Park (Chris Mellor/Lonely Planet Images)

ISBN 1 74104 117 1

text & maps © Lonely Planet Publications Pty Ltd 2002
photos © photographers as indicated 2002

Printed through Colorcraft Ltd, Hong Kong
Printed in China

All rights reserved. No part of this publication may be reproduced,
stored in a retrieval system or transmitted in any form by any means,
electronic, mechanical, photocopying, recording or otherwise, except
brief extracts for the purpose of review, without the written permission
of the publisher.

Lonely Planet, the Lonely Planet logo, Lonely Planet Images, CitySync
and eKno are trade marks of Lonely Planet Publications Pty Ltd.
Other trade marks are the property of their respective owners.

**Although the authors
and Lonely Planet try
to make the informa-
tion as accurate as
possible, we accept
no responsibility for
any loss, injury or
inconvenience sus-
tained by anyone
using this book.**

YOSEMITE CONTENTS

YOSEMITE AUTHORS

Kurt Wolff

Born and raised in Ohio, Kurt has traveled and lived all over the USA, from Waterville, Maine, to Kenai, Alaska. He first visited Yosemite at the age of eight, when he floated the Merced River, saw his first black bear, and took way too many photos of Half Dome. He settled in San Francisco in the late 1980s and has since been back to Yosemite many times. When he's not meandering hiking trails, exploring mountain byways, or scouring junk stores for old Johnny Paycheck records, he works as a freelance writer and editor. He wrote the Rough Guide's *Country Music* and *Country: 100 Essential CDs*; for Lonely Planet, he contributed to *Out to Eat – San Francisco* and coauthored both the second edition of *USA* and the third edition of *California*.

Amy Marr

Boston-born Amy's first camping trip was to Yellowstone when she was two. Her inaugural night in a tent was interrupted by a mama bear and her cubs pawing through the family cooler. After studying at Williams College and in Italy, she worked as a business writer and PR director before leading biking and hiking trips. In 1998 she moved to Santa Fe, where she managed *Outside Online*. Now a freelance writer and editor, she is firmly rooted in Marin County, California, but still exhibits signs of restlessness, which she tempers with a healthy regimen of Mt Tam biking and hiking, and cooking for large groups of friends.

David Lukas

David has been an avid student of the natural world since he started memorizing field guides at age five. This same love took him around the world for 10 years to study animals and ecosystems. He has had dangerous encounters with cobras and orangutans in Borneo, been charged by a caiman while swimming in the Amazon, backed against a cliff by bear cubs, mauled by an enraged chimpanzee, and once stumbled in the pitch black over a deer killed seconds before by a mountain lion. Somehow along the way he managed to eke out an English degree from Reed College. Now living in the Sierra Nevada and working as a professional naturalist, David leads natural history tours, conducts biological surveys, and writes on a wide range of natural history topics. His articles have appeared in *Audubon, Orion, Sunset,* and many other national magazines. His most recent book is *Wild Birds of California,* and he just completed revising the classic guidebook *Sierra Nevada Natural History.*

Cheryl Koehler

Cheryl Koehler makes her home in Oakland, California, but dreams of living in a forgotten corner of the far northern Sierra, in a town she happened upon while doing research. She started out her career as a performing artist but made a midlife escape into writing, finding publishing opportunities for her deviant ideas with the *East Bay Express,* Compass American Guides, KQED radio, and the *Castro Valley Forum.* She previously contributed to Lonely Planet's *Out to Eat – San Francisco* and *World Food Morocco.*

From the Authors:

Kurt Wolff Kurt would like to thank all who went out of their way to offer vital information, a helping hand, and kind words of encouragement during the long days (and even longer nights) he spent fretting and sweating to finish this project, including Amy Ventura, Kathleen Munnelly, Kate Hoffman, Mariah Bear, Amy Marr, David Lukas, Cheryl Koehler, Martha VanAman, Barbara Taylor, John Mock, Kimberley O'Neil, Margaret Eissler, Gary Koy, Gerry Caputo, Jim Flanagan, and Elgy Gillespie.

Amy Marr I'm grateful to the many individuals who offered advice, kindness, hospitality, regional insights and answers. Special thanks to Doug Skiba, Doug Kerr, and Karen Hales

(Yosemite); Dan Braun (Evergreen); Sharon Harvey and Joani Lynch (Mammoth); Michael Ninos and River Klass (Murphys); Matt Eoff (Convict Lake); Shirley Rizzo and Kelly (Bishop); Aaron Johnson (Bear Valley); and Ruggero and Gina Gigli (Markleeville). A warm thanks you to Kurt Wolff for his kindness and humor, project manager Kathleen Munnelly for her unfailing excitement, cartographer Bart Wright for his creative talent, and all for their support and patience. Appreciation and thanks to Pete Wheelan and Kate Hoffman. Thanks and love to my home team posse: Johanna & Jim, Heather, Drew, Lele, Ken, Ben D, Sarah, Dylan, Markos, Hannah & Tom, Claire & Markham, Kay, Daryl, Jim K, Doug C, and Peter & Catherine. Grazie to Stephanie & Katie, my best vado pazzo cohorts, for the always-good vibes from NM. Lastly, a huge thank you to my parents, for the early introduction to Yosemite and for early on stirring a love for the outdoors, passion for adventure, and respect for forging one's own trail. You are both shining examples of steadfast love, enthusiasm, integrity and kindness.

David Lukas Thanks to Stephen Botti for introducing me to Yosemite's stupendous alpine flora, and to Tim Laman for his company on a breathtaking tour of Yosemite's higher peaks. Maya and Ishan were a great help in reading the text, and Ishan added levity to my first formal Lonely Planet meeting by bringing a squishy ball that was a huge hit.

Cheryl Koehler Cheryl Koehler would like to thank her Yosemite traveling companions Robin Hathaway, Mark Middlebrook, Beth Burleson, Kit Robberson, Charmaine Koehler-Lodge, Jera Lodge, Paul Koehler and Angelina Koehler. Also to be thanked are Kit and Dick Duane, Howard Weamer, and Dr Bill Bowie for their insight into recent Yosemite history, Jim Snyder at the Yosemite Museum for verifying certain esoteric facts, Kate Hoffman for creating the vision for this book, Kathleen Munnelly and Valerie Sinzdak for finding the potholes in the writing, and Ben Greensfelder for revealing the mysteries of LP.

YOSEMITE THIS BOOK

The first edition of *Yosemite National Park* was researched and written by Kurt Wolff, Cheryl Koehler, David Lukas, and Amy Marr. Coordinating author Kurt Wolff researched and wrote the majority of the book. Amy Marr contributed the Surfing the Net section, non-hiking activities within the park, general activities information, and portions of the Beyond Yosemite and Excursions chapters. Cheryl Koehler wrote the History chapter, while David Lukas wrote the Geology and Ecosystem chapters. Michaela Klink shared her memories of the bunny slopes. Lonely Planet's Global Travel Editor Don George composed the inspiring preface.

From the Publisher

This book would not have been possible without the tireless and visionary work of Kate "John Muir" Hoffman, who developed the National Parks series, devised the structure for the launch titles, and commissioned and created *Yosemite National Park*. Project Manager Kathleen Munnelly stepped into Kate's hiking boots to complete the project, under the steadfast leadership of Head Ranger and US Publisher Mariah Bear.

Valerie "Half Dome" Sinzdak was the main editor on the book, and David "El Capitan" Lauterborn pitched in with final edits and proofreading. Cartographers Annette "Merced" Olson and Bart "Tuolumne" Wright expertly mapped each dome and river in the park and beyond. Ken DellaPenta indexed the book.

Design Manager Ruth "Ansel Adams" Askevold created the awesome template and cover, while Candice Jacobus added her design flair to the layout and color wraps. Hayden Foell drew the cute critters and majestic trees that grace the wildlife gallery.

A special shout goes out to the Lonely Planet Images crew, especially Glenn Beanland, who searched high and low to find us a bear. The historical photographs in this book appear courtesy of the National Park Service and the US Library of Congress.

Andreas Schueller provided invaluable technical assistance in translating tricky code. Amy Willis cheerfully helped research the illustrations.

Thanks also to Lindsay Brown, who supplied us with material from the award-winning *Hiking in the Sierra Nevada*, and to Global Publisher Simon Westcott for supporting the series.

Acknowledgments

Grateful acknowledgment is made to the Library of Congress and to the National Park Service for the use of their historic photos.

Dedication

This book is dedicated to nature photographer Galen Rowell (1940–2002), whose inspiring images of Yosemite are truly a national treasure.

Foreword

ABOUT LONELY PLANET GUIDEBOOKS

The story begins with a classic travel adventure: Tony and Maureen Wheeler's 1972 journey across Europe and Asia to Australia. There was no useful information about the overland trail then, so Tony and Maureen published the first Lonely Planet guidebook to meet a growing need.

From a kitchen table, Lonely Planet has grown to become the largest independent travel publisher in the world, with offices in Melbourne (Australia), Oakland (USA), London (UK) and Paris (France).

Today Lonely Planet guidebooks cover the globe. There is an ever-growing list of books and information in a variety of media. Some things haven't changed. The main aim is still to make it possible for adventurous travelers to get out there – to explore and better understand the world.

At Lonely Planet we believe travelers can make a positive contribution to the countries they visit – if they respect their host communities and spend their money wisely. Since 1986 a percentage of the income from each book has been donated to aid projects and human rights campaigns, and, more recently, to wildlife conservation.

Although inclusion in a guidebook usually implies a recommendation, we cannot list every good place. Exclusion does not necessarily imply criticism. In fact, there are a number of reasons why we might exclude a place – sometimes it is simply inappropriate to encourage an influx of travelers.

UPDATES & READER FEEDBACK

Things change – prices go up, schedules change, good places go bad and bad places go bankrupt. Nothing stays the same. So, if you find things better or worse, recently opened or long-since closed, please tell us and help make the next edition even more accurate and useful.

Lonely Planet thoroughly updates each guidebook as often as possible – usually every two years, although for some destinations the gap can be longer. Between editions, up-to-date information is available in our free, quarterly *Planet Talk* newsletter and monthly email bulletin *Comet*. The *Upgrades* section of our website (W www.lonelyplanet.com) is also regularly updated by Lonely Planet authors, and the site's *Scoop* section covers news and current affairs relevant to travelers. Lastly, the *Thorn Tree* bulletin board and *Postcards* section carry unverified, but fascinating, reports from travelers.

Tell us about it! We genuinely value your feedback. A well-traveled team at Lonely Planet reads and acknowledges every email and letter we receive and ensures that every morsel of information finds its way to the relevant authors, editors and cartographers.

Everyone who writes to us will find their name listed in the next edition of the appropriate guidebook and will receive the latest issue of *Comet* or *Planet Talk*. The very best contributions will be rewarded with a free guidebook.

We may edit, reproduce and incorporate your comments in Lonely Planet products such as guidebooks, websites and digital products, so let us know if you don't want your comments reproduced or your name acknowledged.

How to contact Lonely Planet:
Online: e talk2us@lonelyplanet.com.au, W www.lonelyplanet.com
Australia: Locked Bag 1, Footscray, Victoria 3011
UK: 10a Spring Place, London NW5 3BH
USA: 150 Linden St, Oakland, CA 94607

YOSEMITE PREFACE
by DON GEORGE

Sunlight skeins through the mesh panel of the tent. Peering out, I see fog wisping in the high branches of the evergreens, feel the chill of early-morning air. The mingled scent of fog, firs, wet pine needles and coffee tendrils through the campsite. Twenty feet away, two deer prance delicately by a fallen trunk, then stop – ears twitching – to study me. Another day in Yosemite.

I first visited this sacred, sensuous place two decades ago, on a whirlwind cross-country tour that allowed only a quick drive through the Valley. On first encounter, Yosemite seemed overwhelmingly huge, raw, old, a vast and self-contained world of peaks and trees and waterfalls and meadows like nothing I'd seen before. It was exhilarating and tantalizing.

Since then, it has become a place of pilgrimage for me. I go at least once every year to cleanse my soul, open my pores, refresh my eyes and drink in great lungs-full of mountain air. I go to scuffle through dust and pine needles, to scrape my knees and knuckles on rocks, to eat fruit bars on boulders, to lose myself in a waterfall's roar.

There are countless ways to savor the riches in and around Yosemite. For the last few years, my favorite has been to hike with my family from Yosemite Valley to the top of the park's great granite icon: Half Dome. Sometimes we switchback along the John Muir Trail, following in the dusty footsteps of that legendary explorer/writer whose life and words are so deeply embedded here. Other times we take the shorter and more precipitous Mist Trail, pulling ourselves up steep stony steps slicked by Vernal Fall's spray.

Whichever route we take, we reach the campsite in Little Yosemite Valley by late afternoon. The kids choose a site and pitch the tents while my wife and I go to the Merced River to gather water. The river is always different and always the same: an astonishing, assuring, ever-shifting mirror of mottled earth, rock, tree and sky. I wade a couple of feet into the stream, wiggle onto a suitably stable perch and begin the laborious process of pumping water through the purifier into our container. The pumping purifies me too. I slow down and notice the way the stream wrinkles around rocks, how lightning has charred one trunk since my last visit and age has toppled another, how the patch of black-veined boulders on the far bank endures seemingly unchanged. Last year two bear cubs gamboled onto that patch and proceeded to chase each other over tree trunks and around bushes for a half hour until mama lumbered in and led them away.

By the time we get back to camp, the kids have set out the stove, spoons and bowls. As the first stars prick the sky, we take beef stroganoff, spaghetti, cocoa, and tea out of the bear canisters and arrange ourselves on tree-stump stools. We cook and laugh and exclaim anew at how everything tastes better under the evergreens and stars. At some point a hush comes over us and we simply listen to the breeze rustling the branches.

We fall asleep on Earth's prickly, poking mattress. During the night, a coyote wails in the distance and bears snuffle by, sniffing for stray snacks. Over the years, birds, squirrels and deer have been regular visitors, and we've encountered rattlesnakes a few times. Each time we remind ourselves that we are guests in their home.

The next morning we set off early, winding though fairy-tale stretches of forest and past great quilts of purple and yellow wildflowers. We climb hard over a series of zigzagging boulder steps that lead to the base of Half Dome itself, then don thick gloves and haul ourselves up the cabled walkway that rangers reconstruct each spring to the summit of the peak. After an electrifying, exhausting 40 minutes of step-by-step ascent – eyes fix straight ahead, boots scratch the rock for a secure sole-hold, arms extend and pull! – we reach the top of the world.

It doesn't get any better than this. Yosemite stretches all around us – pristine stands of deep green trees, ribboning silver rivers, grand gray-stone peaks proceeding as far as the eye can reach. The wonder of this natural, national treasure rises through us – bigger, older, wilder than we can comprehend.

Now I sit on that recollected peak and think: Yosemite puts us in touch with truths that are so fundamental and so powerful that we almost never have a chance to touch them. It gives us a sense of place and perspective, of smallness and connection. It offers the gift of discovery and vulnerability. It allows us to confront and stretch our limits, to embrace wildness, and perhaps most important of all, to immerse ourselves in mystery made palpable.

Most wonderfully, Yosemite offers these gifts to all. You don't have to make a multiple-day trek into its backcountry to receive them. On my first visit, I had time for only a quick drive through Yosemite Valley. And look where it got me.

Don George is Lonely Planet's Global Travel Editor.

One of the world's most celebrated natural preserves, Yosemite National Park is an awe-inspiring place. Massive granite cliffs, peaks, and domes, roaring waterfalls, towering forests, shimmering lakes, and lush meadows all mingle here on a monumental scale. It's one of those places people go out of their way to see at least once in their lifetime, then can't wait to revisit. The topography, flora, and fauna are so varied, there's so much to see and do, that a few days or even a week or two just isn't enough.

YOSEMITE INTRODUCTION

The centerpiece of the park is Yosemite Valley. Most visitors enter the Valley from the west, threading past green meadows and forests criss-crossed by the meandering Merced River. What lends the scene such drama, though, are the sheer 3000ft granite walls that ring the Valley, a cathedral of rock that glorifies the natural world. Cascading from these cliffs are some of the country's tallest waterfalls, adding an ethereal, life-affirming grace to the scene. A series of grand peaks and domes tower above the north and south rims, while the east end is anchored by mighty Half Dome, the park's powerful icon.

But Yosemite's natural wonders stretch well beyond its spectacular Valley. Venture farther afield to the meadowy oasis of Wawona and gaze up in disbelief at the giant sequoias of the Mariposa Grove. Choose a high-country hike amid the craggy peaks, polished domes, and emerald subalpine lakes surrounding Tuolumne Meadows. Climb the jagged Clark Range in the park's southeastern quadrant. Or explore the rugged back-country north and east of the dam at Hetch Hetchy. You'll arrive with visions of Half Dome and Yosemite Falls and leave with a deeper appreciation of the park's breadth of beauty.

Native Americans have lived amid these wonders for nearly 4000 years. Naturalist John Muir spent perhaps more time in the park and environs than anyone since nonnatives first caught sight of the Valley in 1851. His relentless advocacy was crucial in securing Yosemite's national park status in 1890. Muir never tired of the place – perhaps because it was impossible, even for him, to see it all.

Some eager visitors still *try* to pack in all they can. But while glimpsing the sights from a bus or car window is all well and fine, you really need to get out and walk a mile or two to experience the place. Pad down trails, feeling the weight of granite beneath your feet. Dip into a chill mountain lake. Charge off into the backcountry on horseback or, in winter, on a pair of skis. Or simply soak up the sights and sounds of the meadows as the sun falls and the evening glows warm and golden.

Using this Guidebook

The heart of this book is the Yosemite National Park chapter, which details the park's primary regions: Yosemite Valley, Glacier Point & Badger Pass, Wawona, Hetch Hetchy, Big Oak Flat Road/Crane Flat, Tioga Road, and Tuolumne Meadows. You'll learn about the major sights, featured hikes, and other activities, many of which go untapped by the average visitor. That's a shame, because raft rentals, horseback rides, and rock climbing classes are among the many rewarding ways to expand the scope of your visit.

The Highlights chapter delves into the park's "don't miss" attractions and includes suggested itineraries and other tips for enjoying your trip. Explore options for outdoor fun in Activities. Planning the Trip is filled with such practical information as when to go, how to get there, what to bring, and how to reserve a campsite online. Gateway Corridors outlines the four main routes to Yosemite and suggests things to see and do along the way, while Places to Stay and Places to Eat give you the lowdown on accommodations and dining both inside and outside the park.

WORLD HERITAGE SITE

In 1972 the United Nations Educational, Scientific, and Cultural Organization (UNESCO) adopted an international treaty titled the Convention Concerning the Protection of the World Cultural and Natural Heritage. By identifying so-called World Heritage Sites, member countries aim to protect natural and cultural properties of outstanding universal value against the threat of damage in our rapidly developing world. With this in mind, Yosemite National Park was named a UNESCO World Heritage Site in 1984. For more information, visit UNESCO on the web at whc.unesco.org.

If you'd like to explore beyond the park borders, check the Beyond Yosemite chapter for sights and activities in surrounding public lands. We've also included an Excursions chapter filled with worthwhile detours for those with more time to roam.

Curious how glaciers carved the Valley, what birds you'll likely spot, or who the heck John Muir was? The Geology, Ecosystem and History chapters will fill you in, providing background on the fascinating natural and human history of the region. Nature lovers will soon dog-ear the wildlife photo gallery, which introduces some of the plants and animals that make the park their home.

There's no "one right way" to approach a trip to Yosemite. Each person's needs and desires are unique. This book will help you focus your itinerary, with advice on the best times to visit, key sights, how to avoid the crowds, activities to engage your kids, and much more. Of course, the whole point is to have a great time – something you'll find easy to do while visiting this remarkable corner of the world.

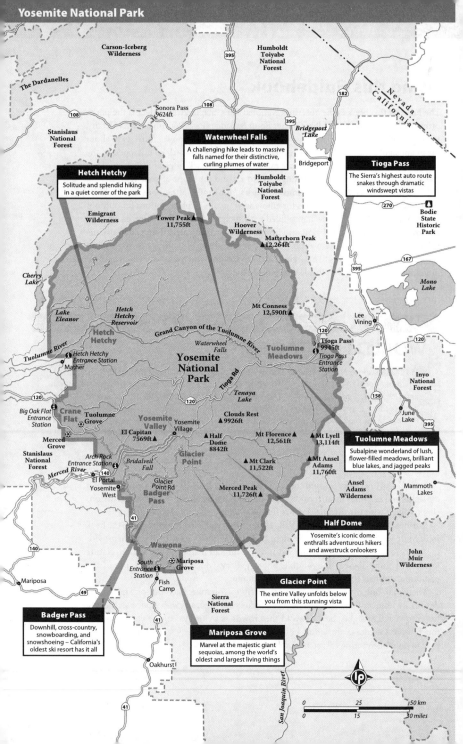

Yosemite National Park

Waterwheel Falls
A challenging hike leads to massive falls named for their distinctive, curling plumes of water

Hetch Hetchy
Solitude and splendid hiking in a quiet corner of the park

Tioga Pass
The Sierra's highest auto route snakes through dramatic windswept vistas

Tuolumne Meadows
Subalpine wonderland of lush, flower-filled meadows, brilliant blue lakes, and jagged peaks

Half Dome
Yosemite's iconic dome enthralls adventurous hikers and awestruck onlookers

Glacier Point
The entire Valley unfolds below you from this stunning vista

Badger Pass
Downhill, cross-country, snowboarding, and snowshoeing – California's oldest ski resort has it all

Mariposa Grove
Marvel at the majestic giant sequoias, among the world's oldest and largest living things

Awesome, majestic, inspiring – no matter how many superlatives are used to describe Yosemite National Park, no words can really do it justice.

YOSEMITE **HIGHLIGHTS**

Photographs do a better job of capturing its magnificence, but they're no substitute for experiencing the place for yourself – the sweeping vistas, enormous granite domes, thundering waterfalls and meadows blanketed in summer wildflowers. Tunnel View (above, photo: Thomas Winz) provides a panorama of Yosemite Valley's most lauded features: imposing El Capitan on the left, lovely Bridalveil Fall on the right, the green Valley floor and incomparable Half Dome in the very center.

Whether this is your first visit to Yosemite or your fiftieth, the splendors of this natural wonderland are endlessly enthralling. For more highlights, plus suggested itineraries and favorite activities, read on …

YOSEMITE FALLS Alpine waters cascade from Yosemite Falls and rush downstream in a torrent of whitewater. Its combined tiers make this the tallest waterfall in North America. [Photo: Thomas Winz]

KAYAKING A thrilling ride on the Merced River at El Portal, just outside Yosemite National Park. [Photo: Corey Rich]

YOSEMITE **HIGHLIGHTS**

YOSEMITE VALLEY Facing east into Yosemite Valley, a luscious landscape of green and granite that has wowed visitors for more than 150 years. [Photo: John Elk III]

JEFFREY PINE The twisted trunk of a dead Jeffrey pine soaks up the sunset from its lonesome, picturesque perch atop 8122ft Sentinel Dome. [Photo: John Elk III]

BEAR Frequently feared but also revered by almost every Yosemite visitor, the black bear is the superstar of the park's ecosystem. [Photo: Shannon Nace]

SENTINEL DOME One of Yosemite's most spectacular panoramas, the view from Sentinel Dome takes in practically every corner of the park, including the distinctive face of Half Dome. [Photo: John Elk III]

BADGER PASS Founded In 1935, Yosemite's Badger Pass Ski Area is the oldest ski resort in California. [Photo: Thomas Winz]

SNOWSHOEING An invigorating way to explore the park in winter, snow-shoeing is fun, easy, and growing in popularity. [Photo: Lee Foster]

EL CAPITAN One of the world's largest granite monoliths, El Capitan is Yosemite Valley's steadfast gatekeeper. Its sheer face withstood the force of glaciers and now lures serious rock climbers. [Photo: Lee Foster]

YOSEMITE **HIGHLIGHTS**

COYOTE Yosemite's coyote population is widespread and active during daytime. [Photo: John Mock]

TIOGA LAKE Snow lingers until summer around Tioga Lake, which lies just east of Tioga Pass and is a popular fishing spot. [Photo: Richard I'Anson]

SEQUOIA Giant sequoia trees, such as this colossus in Mariposa Grove, are the world's largest living things.
[Photo: Judy Bellah]

ROCK CLIMBING Climbers come from around the world to scale Yosemite's numerous granite domes, peaks, and walls.
[Photo: Corey Rich]

YOSEMITE **HIGHLIGHTS**

HALF DOME No landmark better symbolizes Yosemite National Park than Half Dome, which dominates the east end of Yosemite Valley. The view here is from Sentinel Bridge at sunset.
[Photo: John Elk III]

WILDFLOWERS After the snow melts, wildflowers, like this Pacific dogwood, bloom throughout the park. [Photo: John Mock]

AHWAHNEE HOTEL Perhaps the only manmade structure in Yosemite to rival its natural features is this 1927 architectural masterpiece. [Photo: Curtis Martin]

BRIDALVEIL FALL Lush, willowy, and wild, 620ft Bridalveil Fall is one of Yosemite Valley's most graceful features. [Photo: Richard I'Anson]

JOHN MUIR TRAIL A backpacker readies a quick breakfast before getting back to the John Muir Trail, which runs along the Sierra Crest between Yosemite and Sequoia National Parks.
[Photo: Woods Wheatcroft]

SWIMMING If you can stand brisk water, Yosemite offers plenty of spots for a dip, including this swimming hole along the Tuolumne River. [Photo: Lee Foster]

TUOLUMNE MEADOWS One of John Muir's favorite spots, Tuolumne Meadows (8600ft) is the largest subalpine meadow in the Sierra Nevada. It bursts into life for only a few brief months each summer. [Photo: Richard I'Anson]

With so much to see and do in Yosemite, the real question is where to begin? This chapter suggests some options, though no matter which attractions and activities you choose as your focus, you really can't go wrong.

YOSEMITE HIGHLIGHTS

If you arrive in Yosemite for the day on a package tour or by public transit and have only a few hours of sightseeing time, you're best off taking the two-hour Valley Floor Tour (see p 86). For those with limited time, this is the best way to take in the Valley's major natural features and classic viewpoints.

Suggested Itineraries

The following itineraries mainly focus on warm-weather sights and activities within Yosemite National Park. If you have plenty of time, consider exploring beyond the park borders; see our Beyond Yosemite and Excursions chapters for ideas.

ONE DAY

Concentrate on Yosemite Valley, where you'll find the most famous features.

- Drive along Northside and Southside Drives (p 27), stopping at **Bridalveil Fall, Lower Yosemite Fall, Valley View** and viewpoints for **El Capitan** (or take the two-hour Valley Floor Tour)
- Take snapshots from **Tunnel View** (p 92)
- Hike the Mist/Muir trail to the footbridge below **Vernal Fall** (p 98)
- Drive to **Glacier Point** (p 103)
- Visit **Yosemite Museum** and the **Indian Village** (p 92)
- Have a drink at the swanky **Ahwahnee Hotel** (p 187)

THREE DAYS

Widen your perspective somewhat. In addition to the above, you can:

- Spend a day hiking in **Tuolumne Meadows** (p 131)
- Rent rafts and spend an afternoon on the **Merced River** (p 102)
- Attend an evening **campfire program** (p 49)
- Take a **ranger-led hike** (p 50)
- Rent **bicycles** and ride Yosemite Valley's bike path (p 102)
- Relax with a book by the **Tuolumne River** (p 150)
- Marvel at the giant sequoias in **Mariposa Grove** (p 113)
- Dine at the lovely **Wawona Hotel** (p 187)

With five days at your disposal, you have time to stretch out a bit. Consider all of the above, plus:

- Hike up the **Four-Mile Trail** (p 98) and down the **Panorama Trail** (p 108)
- Take a half-day **horseback ride** (p 46)
- Hike to **Sentinel Dome** and **Taft Point** (p 107)
- Attend a **sunrise photo walk** (p 52)
- Hike to **Lukens Lake** (p 124)
- Visit the Yosemite **Pioneer History Center** (p 114)
- Hike to the **Lembert Dome** summit (p 136)
- Relax on the beach at **Tenaya Lake** (p 131)

All of the above, plus:

- Walk the **Yosemite Valley Loop** (p 95)
- Attend a **rock-climbing** class (p 42)
- Hike to **Wapama Falls** in Hetch Hetchy (p 119)
- Spend a night **camping** in the backcountry (p 84)
- Hike to **Mono Pass** (p 141)
- Attend a free class at the **Art Activity Center** (p 95)
- Hike from **Tioga Rd** down to Yosemite Valley (p 128)
- Take a side trip to otherworldly **Mono Lake** (p 202)

All of the above, plus:

- Hike overnight to **Waterwheel Falls** (p 148)
- Climb **Half Dome** (p 99)
- Hike around **20 Lakes Basin** east of Tioga Pass (p 201)
- Backpack two or three nights around **Vogelsang** (p 144)
- Take a full-day **horseback trip** (p 46)
- Bicycle along **Glacier Point Rd** (p 109)
- Attend a photography seminar at the **Ansel Adams Gallery** (p 52)
- Consider an excursion to **Mammoth Lakes** (p 219) or **Kings Canyon & Sequoia National Parks** (p 227)

Driving Tours

There are a limited number of roads in Yosemite, and only one (Tioga Rd) that bisects the park between its eastern and western borders. All park roads are lined with beautiful scenery, so basically you can't go wrong. Be sure to pick up a copy of the Yosemite Association's booklet *Yosemite Road Guide* ($3.95), a near-essential companion on any driving tour. It has descriptions that coincide with the little roadside markers you see along each of Yosemite's roads.

You'll find gas stations at Crane Flat, Wawona, and Tuolumne Meadows, the latter open in summer only. Gas is also available outside the park in El Portal, Fish Camp, and Lee Vining. There are no gas stations in Yosemite Valley.

YOSEMITE VALLEY

The most popular driving tour is the loop that follows the only two roads in and out of Yosemite Valley, **Northside Dr** and **Southside Dr**. Each is (mostly) one-way, and as their names suggest, they sit on either side of the Merced River. The roads lead to great viewpoints of many of the Valley's best-known natural features. You can easily drive this loop in less than an hour, but budget more time, as you'll want to stop frequently.

Starting in Yosemite Village, head west on Northside Dr, which leads past Yosemite Falls, the Three Brothers and El Capitan to **Valley View** (roadside marker V11), a great viewpoint along the Merced River. To complete the loop, turn left (south) just past Valley View, cross the Merced River and then head east on Southside Dr back toward Yosemite Village. From that road you get wider views of Yosemite Falls and El Capitan on the north rim and a closer look at south rim features such as Cathedral Rocks, Sentinel Rock, and Bridalveil Fall. You also drive by the old site of Yosemite Village, near where the chapel

FIVE FANTASTIC DAY HIKES

✔ Elizabeth Lake
✔ Cathedral Lakes
✔ Mono Pass
✔ Vernal and Nevada Falls
✔ Panorama Trail

TOP 10 WINTER ACTIVITIES IN YOSEMITE

✔ **Overnight skiing trip** to Ostrander Ski Hut or Glacier Point Hut
✔ **Ice skating** at Curry Village
✔ **Snowshoeing** along the John Muir Trail
✔ Drinking a fireside **hot toddy** at the Ahwahnee
✔ **Backcountry ski touring** near Tioga Pass
✔ **Downhill skiing** at Badger Pass
✔ Winter **bicycling** through the valley
✔ Learning **winter camping** and survival skills
✔ **Cross-country skiing** through Mariposa Grove

now sits. The road dead-ends just past Curry Village, or you can turn at Sentinel Bridge back toward Yosemite Village.

ELSEWHERE IN THE PARK

Another satisfying driving tour follows **Tioga Rd** from Crane Flat past Tuolumne Meadows to Tioga Pass (and, for those with enough time and inclination, all the way down the eastern side of the Sierra Crest to gorgeous Mono Lake). The subalpine scenery (peaks, domes, forests, lakes) is mind-bogglingly beautiful, and the road has far fewer cars. It's only open during summer and fall however, usually from mid-June to late October. From Yosemite Valley, it's about a 90-minute drive to Tuolumne Meadows, but that's not including stops for views (Olmsted Point is a must), hikes, or snacks at the Tuolumne Meadows Store. From Tioga Pass, it's another half hour east to Hwy 395 and Mono Lake. The road is etched into the side of Lee Vining Canyon as it descends some 3500ft. It's a spectacular drive on a smooth road, although the cliffs above and below are rugged and the drop-off steep.

TOP FIVE EFFORTLESS ROADSIDE VIEWS

From these spots you get big, juicy views just by stepping out the door of the car.

- ✔ **Tunnel View** (Wawona Rd)
- ✔ **Valley View** (Northside Dr)
- ✔ **Olmsted Point** (Tioga Rd)
- ✔ **Washburn Point** (Glacier Point Rd)
- ✔ **Poopenaut Valley** (Hetch Hetchy)

Wawona Rd (Hwy 41) runs south from Yosemite Valley to Wawona and Mariposa Grove, taking about an hour. **Tunnel View** is one of the park's most popular viewpoints; from there, you can take in dense woods, meadows, and the Valley's great granite walls.

Glacier Point Rd (open summer and fall only) runs east from Hwy 41 to Washburn Point and Glacier Point. The road is also lined with dense woods, although there are glimpses of the San Joaquin Valley to the west and the Clark Range to the east.

The drive to **Hetch Hetchy** (daylight hours only), which begins just west of the Big Oak Flat Entrance, traverses lush meadows and forest before climbing the cliffs above the Tuolumne River (and Poopenaut Valley) toward the reservoir.

Watching Wildlife

The Yosemite region is rich in wildlife, from bears and deer to birds and lovely little butterflies. This wealth of birds, mammals, insects and reptiles is widely scattered over a vast area, rarely congregating in large numbers or within easy view of most visitors. In other words, don't come expecting a zoo-like display right off the highway or trail. On the other hand, if you remain patient and stay alert, you never know what sort of creature you might encounter. Just remember, it's illegal to feed the wildlife, and often dangerous to even approach animals too closely.

Birdwatchers visiting Yosemite are in for a real treat, as the region boasts more than 300 species, from the Nashville warbler to the great gray owl, Yosemite's most famous and sought-after bird. These majestic owls have been seen at Ackerson Meadow and Crane Flat, where they hunt around large meadow systems in the late afternoon. At Mono Lake, a large and picturesque desert lake about a half hour east of the park's Tioga Pass Entrance, one of North America's great birding events takes place during late summer: the arrival of nearly two million eared grebes.

Yosemite's most common large mammal is the **mule deer**, found just about anywhere below the tree line throughout the Sierra Nevada. The park's deer are remarkably unconcerned about the people who often crowd around them, snapping photos like crazy when they wander near a trailhead or parking area. Even for visitors who see deer on a regular basis in their own backyards, there's still something sublime about seeing them up close or watching them graze away in one of the park's spacious meadows. If you're on the lookout, keep your eyes trained on open grassy areas from late afternoon to sunset.

The animal that gets star billing at Yosemite is unquestionably the **black bear**. Some visitors come hoping to get a glimpse of one, even if just rummaging through a Dumpster; others go to bed nightly fearing one will come lumbering unannounced through their campsite – or that, during a day hike, one of the furry beasts will be waiting around the next bend. Many bears do lose their fear of humans and want nothing more than to get inside your backpack or food locker, but for the most part bears in the park shy away from people. For that reason, catching sight of a bear is mostly a matter of luck.

Another elusive park inhabitant is the solitary **mountain lion**. Few park visitors will ever see one of these big cats, although they are certainly out there, roaming the park's forested regions below the tree line. They pose little threat to humans, being more interested in dining on deer. Hikers are more likely to see the handsome **bobcat**, which looks like a scaled-up version of the domestic tabby, with a brown-spotted, yellowish-tan coat and stubby tail.

As to wild members of the dog family, both the **coyote** and its much smaller cousin the **gray fox** are found throughout the park. Coyotes are readily

FIVE BEST HIKES FOR WILDFLOWERS

- ✔ Tuolumne Meadow
- ✔ McGurk Meadow
- ✔ Lukens Lake
- ✔ Lyell Canyon
- ✔ Wapama Falls

SURE SHOTS

It's hard *not* to get a great snap from these enticing, photo-friendly viewpoints.

✔ **Glacier Point**
✔ **Panorama Trail**
✔ **Sentinel Dome**
✔ **Olmsted Point**
✔ **Lembert Dome**

observed during the daytime, especially around meadows, where they come to feed on rodents, while foxes mainly emerge at night and are seen crossing trails or roads. Coyotes are widespread throughout the region, but foxes are mainly limited to the low foothills of the west slope.

Living above the timberline, but restricted to a handful of remote slopes, are magnificent **bighorn sheep**, perhaps the rarest animal in North America. The rams, with their thick, curled horns and massive, muscular bodies, are a spectacular sight if you're lucky enough to see one of the maybe 100 individuals left.

For a much more detailed discussion of the park's wildlife, including specific information on many of the trees, wildflowers, birds, and mammals found here and the varied environment that supports them, see the Ecosystem chapter.

Rocks, Cliffs & Domes: Yosemite's Geology

The Sierra Nevada is one of the world's premier granite landscapes, and even visitors who had never given much thought to geology before often find themselves fascinated by its features and interested in learning more about how they came to be.

Much of Yosemite's majestic landscape, including its famous U-shaped valleys, was created by **glaciers**. Between about two million and 10,000 years ago, these rivers of ice covered portions of the Sierra Nevada, flowing down from high elevation icefields and scouring out rugged river canyons and valleys. Evidence of the glaciers' mighty force is often right at your feet, in areas where granite surfaces were worn down to a smooth, shiny finish by the ice's relentless grinding. Along Tioga Rd near Tenaya Lake, look for granite shelves that are so polished they glisten.

Glaciers have the funny effect of rounding out landscape features that lie below the ice, while sharpening features that rise above it. The same grinding force that smoothed out the valleys also quarried rocks from the base of peaks, resulting in undercutting that formed high towering spikes. For a fascinating contrast, compare the smooth domes such as Lembert and Pothole in Tuolumne Meadows to the sheer spires of nearby Cathedral and Unicorn Peaks.

An additional geological factor at work is the granite's tendency to crack and separate on a massive scale. At Olmsted Point along Tioga Rd, visitors have a surrealistic view of vast granite walls peeling off like onion layers below Clouds Rest. This **exfoliation** is the result of massive rock formations expanding and cracking in shell-like layers as the pressure of overlying materials erodes away. Over time, sharp angles and corners are replaced by increasingly rounded curves that leave us with distinctive landmarks like Half Dome.

For more details on the forces that shaped this region's stunning landmarks, see the Geology chapter.

Seeking Solitude

If you've come to Yosemite looking for peace and solitude, there are plenty of places to find it. Sure, the park gets packed every summer, but with a little effort you can find near-empty trails, quiet riverside hangouts and other hideaways tucked throughout the park. One main rule to remember is that most visitors never stray too far from roads or developed areas; head away from the cars, hotels and ice-cream stands and you're off in the right direction.

If solitude – or something close to it – is a priority, avoid summer (especially August weekends) and try coming off season. Fall is beautiful, with many high-country points still open, but for true quiet, visit during winter, when people are few (except around Badger Pass) and the snow forms a thick blanket over the entire landscape.

Another good rule is to get up and on the trail just after sunrise. This works well when visiting hot spots like Glacier Point and the Mariposa Grove; or try late in the day, when the big crowds have all gone to supper.

Yosemite Valley is where most visitors throng, and roads, campgrounds, and popular trails (such as that to Vernal Fall) are predictably packed. Even in summer, though, you may find peace and quiet along the Yosemite Valley Loop, a trail few Valley visitors even know about.

ESCAPING THE CROWDS

You can certainly get away from it all by taking a serious backpacking trip into the wilderness – that's our obvious top choice. But here are a few places for a little peace that don't require so much sweat and strain. You may not be *miles* from your fellow humans, but they won't be in your face, either.

✔ South (far) shore of **Tenaya Lake**

✔ **Yosemite Valley Loop** (especially early morning)

✔ **Lukens Lake** (late in the day)

✔ **Inspiration Point** (1000ft above Tunnel View)

✔ Yosemite Valley in **winter**

Even better, make the effort to explore the park's less-frequented areas, including Hetch Hetchy and Tuolumne Meadows. The latter involves a 90-minute drive from the Valley, which is part of the reason it's less crowded. Sights like Lembert Dome and Soda Springs are popular, but as soon as you hit the trail, the mountains can seem practically empty. Not ready to hike? If you don't mind a little company, there's also the main meadow itself, loaded with cozy spots along the river from which to fish, read, or simply soak up the sights. Sink down in the grass and the world drops away.

Cool Stuff for Kids

Yosemite has no shortage of activities that kids will dig, including swimming, rafting, cycling, hiking, and horseback riding; standing underneath the giant sequoias in Mariposa Grove; taking a rock-climbing class from the Yosemite Mountaineering School (ages 10 and up); learning to watercolor at the Art Activity Center; and peering 3000ft down into the Valley from Glacier Point. Further ideas are discussed in the Activities chapter.

One place not to miss is the **Nature Center at Happy Isles**, which has great hands-on exhibits and dioramas depicting various natural environments and including numerous stuffed animals. You may not encounter a porcupine, owl, or coyote in the wild during your trip, but kids can get a close-up view of what they look like here. They can also learn about pinecones, rub their hands across some granite, check out different animal tracks, and even snicker a bit at the display on animal scat. Out back is an exhibit explaining the 1996 rockfall that happened nearby, which some kids find mighty cool.

The **LeConte Memorial Lodge** has a great children's activity corner and a good nature-book library that will please parents. The **Yosemite Museum** and the **Indian Village** out back are worth a look, as are the great old buildings, stagecoaches, and the covered bridge at the Yosemite **Pioneer History Center** in Wawona. You can even take a 10-minute stagecoach ride.

Children ages 7 to 13 can earn a patch and become a **Junior Ranger**, one of the park's most popular kids programs. To get the patch, they have to attend a guided program (see *Yosemite Today* for schedule), collect a bag of trash, and complete a self-guided activity booklet, the

(see *Yosemite Today* for schedule)

FIVE KID-FRIENDLY HIKES

A selection of hikes that little tykes can handle without much trouble:

✔ **Yosemite Valley Loop**

✔ **Lukens Lake**

✔ **Vernal Fall** (footbridge below the falls)

✔ **Soda Springs**

✔ **Mariposa Grove**

Junior Ranger Handbook ($4.95), available from the Nature Center at Happy Isles or any of the park's visitor centers.

The younger set (ages 3 to 6) can earn a **Little Cubs** button by completing a different self-guided booklet ($3). Both booklets are published by the reputable Yosemite Association, so it's not just a purely commercial activity.

Peruse *Yosemite Today* for various children's programs, including an hour of nature stories, a photo walk geared just for kids, and a "Wee Wild Ones" program of stories and activities for those 6 and under. Other events such as the evening campfires and the "Stars Over Yosemite" astronomy talk at Glacier Point are great for kids and families, too.

Shopping

While you probably didn't come to Yosemite to shop, there are plenty of opportunities to do so. A standard assortment of T-shirts, key chains, and postcards are sold at just about every retail outlet in the park, including visitor centers and grocery stores.

There aren't a huge number of stores in the park (thankfully), but you'll find the best choices in and around Yosemite Valley. The Ansel Adams Gallery is one of the nicest, selling prints and posters of the great photographer's famous works. The Ahwahnee Hotel has a nice gift shop with upscale items.

Popular souvenirs include the Yosemite Mountaineering School's "Go Climb a Rock" T-shirt and a bevy of bear-themed coffee mugs. If you're looking for a classier memento, here are some of our favorite keepsakes from the park and surrounding areas:

- John Muir's **The Yosemite**, featuring Galen Rowell's photography ($24.95)
- A special edition **Ansel Adams photograph** ($175)
- **Jamestown Olive Oil** ($15), in Jamestown (near Sonora)
- **Chatom's Sauvignon Blanc** ($11) or **Stevenot's Cabernet** ($16), both from Calaveras County vineyards

Anyone with a passion for the outdoors will find an unbeatable playground of near limit-less possibilities in and around Yosemite. Between Yosemite's incredible offerings and the wealth of national forests and designated wilderness areas encircling the park, you could easily spend months in these parts and never tread the same trail twice. If you're an outdoor enthusiast planning a visit to Yosemite, your only real concern should be not where and how but what – the sheer abundance of options for experiencing this region's scenic riches can be overwhelming.

YOSEMITE ACTIVITIES

Hiking is the most popular activity, with literally hundreds of miles of trails to choose from. Hikes range from easy sightseeing strolls to challenging climbs. And if you're feeling adventurous and have more time to roam, there's a full range of backcountry ambles offering solitude. Look to the comprehensive trail chart to help select a hike that's well suited for you.

Those interested in **rock climbing** congregate in Yosemite Valley, lured by legendary peaks like Half Dome and El Capitan. While you're in the Valley, **biking** is a particularly enjoyable way to get around. **Horseback riding**, a family-friendly activity, offers a terrific opportunity to stay away from car traffic and explore some of Yosemite's backcountry.

With plenty of lakes, creeks, and fast-moving streams, Yosemite is an ideal place for **fishing** and **swimming**. There's just one caveat: You'd best be able to tolerate cold water. Midsummer you'll find the warmest waters (and air temperatures) in the Valley, where there are plenty of swimming holes fringed with sandy beaches along the Merced. For fast white water, head to the west, where a bevy of Class III to IV+ rapids make great spots for **rafting** once the runoff begins in late spring.

Although summer is undoubtedly the high season, more and more visitors are heading to Yosemite during the winter months to enjoy the stunning snowscapes and in-vigorating activities. For **downhill and cross-country skiing**, head to Badger Pass or enjoy Yosemite's tranquil beauty by **snowshoeing** and **ice skating** in the Valley.

While the majority of activity within the park centers around Yosemite Valley, Tuolumne Meadows is the high-country hub for alpine activities. In the park's southern reaches, most of the action revolves around Wawona and the nearby grove of giant se-quoias. The Hetch Hetchy area makes a fantastic jumping-off place for long hikes into the quiet northern reaches.

On all sides, the park boundaries literally flow into neighboring national forests, state parks, and wilderness and recreation areas, forming a vast and varied area for exploration. Just a short distance from Yosemite, you'll find less-visited trails and wilderness access points, campgrounds with available sites, interesting historic towns, and no end of activities to compliment your in-park experience.

This chapter offers general planning information for activities within Yosemite and beyond. Use the lists and charts to decide what activities you want to do and where. More specific details are covered within the main Yosemite National Park chapter under the corresponding regions (Yosemite Valley, Wawona, etc). Look to the Beyond Yosemite and Excursions chapters for additional information on activities surrounding the park.

Gauging Your Physical Fitness

Any outdoor activity, but particularly those in mountain and wilderness areas, carries inherent risks. The most common reasons visitors to Yosemite get into trouble are lack of proper planning and overzealous exertion. The first and foremost safeguard against these problems is knowing one's physical fitness level – then sticking within it.

In and around Yosemite, elevation is a constant factor and can be a huge variable when it comes to exerting yourself outdoors. Add to that the constant threat of changeable and extreme weather, which can in turn cause heat exhaustion, dehydration, hypothermia, or even stroke. With the extra challenge of thin air and heightened exposure, doing an 8-mile hike or 20-mile bike ride becomes a whole different beast in the mountains. So even if you're extremely fit, always keep the elevation factor in mind when choosing an activity. If you plan on being super-active, start out with some easier hikes and gradually work up to the more challenging full-day excursions. Go easy on your body for the first couple of days to acclimatize properly, particularly if you'll be in the higher parts of Yosemite like Tuolumne Meadows.

A word of warning: If you're planning on seriously exerting yourself in Yosemite and have suffered from heart or serious respiratory problems in the past, be sure to check with your doctor. Ultimately, it's crucial to know your body and learn to hear and heed its signs. The more aware you are of your personal fitness level, the more you'll enjoy every activity you undertake while visiting Yosemite.

Gauging Your Skill Level

Having a basic sense of your skills will help you make educated – and hence safer – decisions about activities. For hiking and biking, it's simply a question of knowing your comfort level and maximum threshold when doing these activities at home, then taking into consideration Yosemite-specific factors such as altitude, weather, terrain, and access to help if needed. If a 4-mile hike at lower elevations wears you out, a 2-mile hike at a higher altitude might be plenty. And if you're comfortable riding 25 hilly miles on your bike at home, chances are you'll be fine pedaling up Glacier Point Rd.

When it comes to horseback riding in Yosemite, in general the shorter rides are geared toward beginners; the longer rides should be comfortable for those who have already logged long hours sitting on the back of a horse.

In rafting and rock climbing, there are more-specific criteria for gauging your skill level. White-water rapids are rated by difficulty on an open-ended multiple-level scale, with Class I the easiest and Class V for experts only (Class VI does exist, for water that's considered unrunnable without risk of death). Class II to III rapids are standard novice and intermediate runs, while Class IV to V tend to be better suited to rafters with some experience. Most of the rafting on the Merced is rated Class III+ and is perfect for intermediates.

Similarly, rock climbers use the Yosemite Decimal System, an elaborate means of rating all climbs from 5.0 to 5.13, with grades from "a" to "d" at each level signifying even more specific degrees of difficulty. Adding to the complexity, climbs from 5.8 to 5.10 may sometimes be rated with a + or -, indicating more or less difficulty within the specified range. Both El Capitan and Half Dome have climbs rated at the hardest of the 5.13 levels; the Direct Northwest Face route on Half Dome, for example, is rated 5.13 c/d.

Keep in mind that different countries have different ways of assessing and rating both climbs and white water (for climbing, at least eight different classification systems are used around the world), so make sure you understand the US scales if you're from abroad.

Outfitters offering climbing and rafting excursions in and near Yosemite will help you determine what level you're at, then direct you to a climb, class, or adventure that's a good fit. Climbing guides will ask about your climbing history in order to select comparable terrain in the park. Ditto for rafting. The raucous Cherry Creek area rapids aren't for beginners – so outfitters are going to make sure you can swim a certain distance comfortably, and have prior experience on a certain level of rapid, before allowing you to hop aboard. It goes without saying that answering skill level and activity experience questions honestly and completely is imperative for safety reasons. You don't want to engage in any activity over your skill level, and no guides or outfits want to put you, themselves, or other clients at risk.

It goes without saying that answering skill level and activity experience questions honestly and completely is imperative for safety reasons.

Hiking

The 800 miles of trails crisscrossing the park offer hikes of all sizes and lengths to match any desire and ability. You can spend a half-hour on a gentle half-mile stroll, take a full day to reach lakes above the tree line in Tuolumne Meadows, or strap on a 60lb pack and head into Yosemite's 700,000 acres of wilderness (which actually constitute nearly 95% of the entire park) on a multiday backcountry excursion.

Some of the park's most famous hikes start from **Yosemite Valley**, many of them involving steep ascents, including the trails to the top of Yosemite Falls and Glacier Point. Most famous (and popular) of all is the 17-mile roundtrip trek from Happy Isles to the top of Half Dome, a journey that thousands attempt every summer despite its steep climb and grueling nature. There are, though, gentler options in the Valley, including a long and meandering trail around the Valley floor that many visitors don't even know exists.

The highest concentration of Yosemite hikes lie in and around the subalpine high country of **Tuolumne Meadows**. This part of the park is only fully open three to four months every summer, but when the snow melts, the place jumps to life, with green meadows growing at the base of craggy peaks and colorful swatches of blossoming wildflowers poking from wherever they can. It's a magnificent destination no hiking enthusiast should miss, even beginners. Hikes such as those to Dog Lake and down Lyell Canyon make fine choices for families and stone-cold novices.

You can find excellent hikes in every other corner of the park, too, leading to such premier sights as the often-overlooked Chilnualna Fall in **Wawona**; the gushing torrent of Wapama Falls in **Hetch Hetchy**; the awe-inspiring 360-degree views from the easily reached summit of Sentinel Dome, off **Glacier Point Rd**; and the gorgeous, wide-screen look at classic Yosemite scenery on the **Panorama Trail**, as you meander from Glacier Point to the top of Nevada Fall.

FIVE HIKES FOR ASTOUNDING VIEWS

Half Dome is the obvious choice for stupendous vistas, but here are some other hikes to consider:

- ✔ **Sentinel Dome & Taft Point**
- ✔ **Panorama Trail**
- ✔ **Clouds Rest**
- ✔ **North Dome**
- ✔ **Mt Dana**

For spectacular hikes beyond park borders, head to the 20 Lakes Basin, east of Tioga Pass near Saddlebag Lake; Hite Cove, along Hwy 140, known for its awesome wildflower displays each spring; and The Minarets in the Ansel Adams Wilderness.

DIFFICULTY LEVEL

There are hikes suitable for everyone from the novice to the pro in Yosemite and around. The hikes in this section are organized into four levels of difficulty to help you better gauge which is right for you:

Easy – These gentle hikes with little elevation gain are accessible to just about everyone, including kids and those with no hiking experience.

Moderate – Hikes have a modest elevation gain, usually in the range of 500ft to 1000ft, and may be longer and take you farther from the road than those rated "easy." Still, don't be deterred – these are generally fine for most hikers.

Difficult – Now we're getting into the territory for the more experienced. Expect a significant amount of elevation gain and longer, more complex routes.

Very Difficult – Been going to the gym on a regular basis? You better have, because these hikes are the toughest, involving serious amounts of climbing and a long, grueling day (or days) on the trail.

Keep in mind that many Yosemite hikes do involve some elevation gain, from just a meager few hundred feet to (gulp) several thousand. Pay attention to the "elevation gain" listed under each hike.

Another important factor to consider is altitude, which can slow you down and sap your strength quickly – if you're wondering why you're feeling exhausted only a half-hour into your hike, it's a good chance altitude is to blame. Tuolumne Meadows, for instance, lies above 8000 feet, and many hikes in the area take you much higher. The difference may not be noticeable when you're setting up a tent or strolling to the restroom, but start puffing your way 1000ft up the Cathedral Lakes Trail, and even hardy hikers may feel like they haven't exercised in months. The trick is to acclimate yourself by taking shorter hikes at first, slowly working your way up to longer ascents involving greater elevation gains.

HIKING IN YOSEMITE

NAME	TYPE	LOCATION (STARTING)	DISTANCE (R/T)	DURATION	CHALLENGE	ELEVATION GAIN	FEATURES	FACILITIES	DESCRIPTION	PAGE
Cathedral Lakes	Day Hike	Tuolumne Meadows	7.6mi	4–6 hrs	Moderate	1000ft			One of Yosemite's finest day hikes to subalpine lakes with numerous surrounding peaks.	138
Chilnualna Fall	Day Hike	Wawona	8.6mi	4–5 hrs	Moderate-Difficult	2240ft			Uncrowded trail along cascading creek to top of waterfalls over Wawona Dome's shoulder.	115
Clouds Rest	Day Hike	Tioga Rd	14.4mi	6–7 hrs	Difficult	2205ft			Yosemite's largest expanse of granite; arguably its finest panoramic viewpoint.	126
Dog Lake	Day Hike	Tuolumne Meadows	2.8mi	2 hrs	Moderate	600ft			Short hike to small lake, very popular in summer.	137
Elizabeth Lake	Day Hike	Tuolumne Meadows	4.8mi	3–4 hrs	Moderate	900ft			Steep but short hike to superb subalpine lake.	138
Four-Mile Trail to Glacier Point	Day Hike	Yosemite Valley	9.2mi	4–8 hrs	Difficult	3200ft			Tough but satisfying hike to the park's best viewpoint; can also bus up and walk down.	98
Gaylor Lakes	Day Hike	Tuolumne Meadows	3mi	2–3 hrs	Moderate	560ft			Short but steep hike to high country and lakes above Tioga Pass.	140
Glen Aulin	Day Hike	Tuolumne Meadows	11mi	6–8 hrs	Moderate	600ft			Follows the Tuolumne River past numerous waterfalls to one of the High Sierra Camps.	139
Half Dome	Day or Overnight Hike	Yosemite Valley	17mi	10–12 hrs	Very Difficult	4800ft			The park's most difficult day hike to the summit of its most famous natural icon.	99
Inspiration Point	Day Hike	Yosemite Valley	2.6mi	1.5–2.5 hrs	Moderate-Difficult	1000ft			Short, steep hike above Tunnel View with great Valley views.	96
Lembert Dome	Day Hike	Tuolumne Meadows	2.8mi	2 hrs	Moderate	850ft			Short hike to summit of dome above Tuolumne Meadows.	136
Lukens Lake	Day Hike	Tioga Rd	1.6mi	1 hr	Easy	200ft			Quick hike to small but attractive lake; lots of wildflowers.	124
Lyell Canyon	Overnight Hike	Tuolumne Meadows	17.6mi	2 days	Moderate	200ft			Hike a relatively flat portion of the John Muir Trail through this gorgeous canyon.	143
Mariposa Grove to Wawona	Day Hike	Wawona	6.5mi (one-way)	2–3 hrs	Easy	2000ft descent			Woodsy, downhill alternative to shuttle bus.	115
May Lake & Mt Hoffmann	Day Hike	Tioga Rd	6mi	4–5 hrs	Moderate	2004ft			Short steep hike to May Lake High Sierra Camp, with option to summit nearby peak.	125
McGurk Meadow	Day Hike	Glacier Point Rd	1.6mi	1 hr	Easy	150ft			Short, flat walk to lush meadow, lots of wildflowers.	106
Merced Grove	Day Hike	Crane Flat	3mi	1.5–2 hrs	Easy-Moderate	600ft			The park's least-visited sequoia grove; the hike in is downhill, ascent is on the return.	122

NAME	TYPE	LOCATION (STARTING)	DISTANCE (R/T)	DURATION	CHALLENGE	ELEVATION GAIN	FEATURES	FACILITIES	DESCRIPTION	PAGE
Mirror Lake & Tenaya Canyon Loop	Day Hike	Yosemite Valley	4.5mi	2 hrs	Easy	100ft		🚻	Quick, flat hike close to Valley campgrounds.	96
Mono Pass	Day Hike	Tuolumne Meadows	7.4mi	4 hrs	Moderate	915ft		🚻	Excellent, moderately paced day hike into high country near Tioga Pass.	141
Mt Dana	Day Hike	Tuolumne Meadows	5.8mi	6–7 hrs	Very Difficult	3108ft		🚻	Hike to the top of the park's second-highest peak.	142
North Dome	Day Hike	Tioga Rd	8.5mi	4.5–5 hrs	Moderate	422ft			Astounding views of Yosemite Valley, Half Dome, and Tenaya Canyon; includes 1000ft descent.	127
Panorama Trail	Day Hike	Glacier Point Rd	8.5mi (one-way)	5 hrs	Moderate-Difficult	760ft		🚻 ▲ 🚻	Includes 3200ft descent from Glacier Point to Valley floor, with postcard views the whole way down.	108
Pohono Trail	Day Hike	Glacier Point Rd	13.8mi (one-way)	7–9 hrs	Moderate-Difficult	2800ft descent		🚻	Passes numerous Valley viewpoints; requires car shuttle.	109
Sentinel Dome	Day Hike	Glacier Point Rd	2.2mi	1 hr	Moderate	370ft		🚻	Easiest hike to top of a dome with amazing 360° views.	107
Taft Point & the Fissures	Day Hike	Glacier Point Rd	2.2mi	1 hr	Easy	250ft		🚻	Major Valley viewpoint with interesting geological features.	107
Tenaya Lake	Day Hike	Tioga Rd	2mi	1 hr	Easy	50ft		🚻	Back-and-forth hike along south side of a lovely subalpine lake.	124
Tenaya Lake to Yosemite Valley	Overnight Hike	Tioga Rd	17.2mi (one-way)	2 days	Difficult	2205ft		🚻 ▲ 🚻	Includes 6321ft descent from Tioga Rd to Yosemite Valley, with option to summit Clouds Rest.	128
Tueeulala & Wapama Falls	Day Hike	Hetch Hetchy	5.4mi	2.5–3 hrs	Easy	400ft		🚻	Easy, hot (in summer), and mostly flat trail to two waterfalls (Tueeulala seasonal only).	119
Tuolumne Grove	Day Hike	Crane Flat	2mi	1.5 hrs	Moderate	500ft		🚻	Descend along portion of Old Big Oak Flat Rd to small but less-crowded sequoia grove.	121
Vernal & Nevada Falls	Day Hike	Yosemite Valley	6.5mi	4–7hrs	Moderate-Difficult	1900ft		🚻	Popular hike, spectacular waterfalls, often crowded.	98
Vogelsang	Overnight Hike	Tuolumne Meadows	27mi	3 days	Moderate-Difficult	3852ft		🚻 ▲ 🚻	Exceptional multi-day high-country backpack trip.	144
Waterwheel Falls	Overnight Hike	Tuolumne Meadows	18mi	2 days	Difficult	2260ft		🚻 ▲ 🚻	Splendid series of waterfalls at head of Grand Canyon of the Tuolumne River.	148
Wawona Meadow	Day Hike	Wawona	3.5mi	1–1.5 hrs	Easy	200ft		🚻	Loop around meadow is shaded and flat, but has lots of horse manure.	114
Yosemite Falls	Day Hike	Yosemite Valley	6.8mi	5–6 hrs	Difficult	2400ft		🚻	Steep, hot (in summer) hike to top of Yosemite's highest waterfall.	97
Yosemite Valley Loops	Day Hike	Yosemite Valley	Varies	Varies	Easy	330ft		🚻	Meander quietly through the Valley for as long as you wish.	95

🐾 Wildlife Watching   📷 Views   👨‍👩‍👧 Great for Families   🚌 Public Transportation to Trailhead   ▲ Backcountry Campsites   🚻 Restrooms

Prior to setting out, get a good Yosemite map, read through the hiking descriptions in this guidebook and establish concrete ideas of where you want to go *before* you start. The various visitor centers can help with ideas.

TYPES OF HIKES

All the hikes included in this book – from day hikes to backcountry treks – follow marked, established trails, and the distance listed in each hike description is for a roundtrip journey unless it says otherwise. The estimated duration listed in each hike description will vary a bit depending on the hiker's ability.

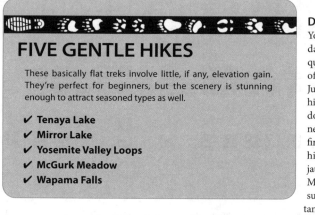

FIVE GENTLE HIKES

These basically flat treks involve little, if any, elevation gain. They're perfect for beginners, but the scenery is stunning enough to attract seasoned types as well.

- ✔ **Tenaya Lake**
- ✔ **Mirror Lake**
- ✔ **Yosemite Valley Loops**
- ✔ **McGurk Meadow**
- ✔ **Wapama Falls**

Day Hikes

Yosemite's abundance of day hikes range from a quick hour's stroll to treks of eight hours or more. Just because some of these hikes are short, however, doesn't mean you don't need to prepare. Water is first on the agenda for any hike, even a quick, easy jaunt to a destination like Mirror Lake. Hats and sunscreen are also important. In the higher elevations, it may feel warm when you start out, but take an extra shirt, as breezes can quickly bring a surprising chill, especially in the late afternoon. And carry something to eat. The journey may seem brief, but once you arrive and start taking in the scenery, you may wind up staying awhile … and wishing you'd packed that peanut-butter sandwich after all.

Some day hikes can be combined to create multi-day excursions; a few examples are noted in the hiking descriptions.

Backcountry Hikes

Anyone who loves being out in the countryside, away from the crowds, noise, and craziness of modern life, stands to gain a lot by planning a backcountry hike. The wilderness here is immense, beautiful, and surprisingly accessible. Even those with only a modest amount of experience can easily handle trips to locales such as Lyell Canyon and Rancheria Falls.

You will need a wilderness permit to stay overnight (see p 84). And trips also require decent equipment, along with some basic camping and hiking skills. If you feel you need some guidance in this department before setting out, though, there are educational group outings available – see Taking a Class, p 52.

Long-Distance Trails

Several long-distance trails pass through Yosemite, including the **John Muir Trail**, which follows the Sierra Crest between Yosemite and Sequoia National

✔ BACKCOUNTRY TIPS

These few simple rules – some official, others just plain common sense – should help you (and the wilderness) survive your backcountry experience:

✔ Filter or boil all water, including water from springs.

✔ Carry food in a bear-resistant canister – hanging food bags in trees rarely works anymore.

✔ Don't put any soap in the water (even biodegradable soap pollutes); discard it 100ft from water sources. Or try washing with just hot water.

✔ Carry out all trash and toilet paper; do not burn it.

✔ Don't start any campfires over 9600ft or above the tree line.

✔ Collect only dead and downed wood, or better yet, avoid campfires altogether.

✔ Yield to pack animals on the trail.

✔ Stay on the trail – don't make shortcuts.

✔ Camp at least 100ft from water and, if possible, the trail.

Parks, and the daunting **Pacific Crest National Scenic Trail**, which extends from Canada to Mexico. The province of experts, these trails can be a lifetime achievement for those who manage to hike their entire distance; many people choose to hike them in smaller, more manageable sections. You'll cross parts of them while hiking shorter local trails in several areas of Yosemite.

John Muir Trail The 211-mile John Muir Trail links Yosemite Valley and Mt Whitney, traveling through three national parks and two wilderness areas and offering what many consider to be very best mountain hiking in the US.

Uncrossed by any roads, the trail is a spectacular and pristine route through continual wilderness. It crosses 11 mountain passes, half of which are higher than 12,000ft and all but one of which are above 10,000ft. As it traverses the timberline country of the High Sierra, the trail passes thousands of lakes and numerous granite peaks between 13,000ft and 14,000ft and takes in the Sierra's highest peak. The trail frequently descends from the Sierra Crest into forested areas of the western Sierra, with 5000ft deep canyons.

The trail begins in Yosemite Valley at Happy Isles (4035ft) on the Merced River, continuing over Cathedral Pass (9700ft) to Tuolumne Meadows (8600ft). Traveling along the Lyell Fork of the Tuolumne River, it then climbs out of the national park and into the Ansel Adams Wilderness at **Donohue Pass** (11,056ft) before covering the John Muir Wilderness Area, Kings Canyon, and Sequoia National Park to reach Mt Whitney.

An average through hiker covering 12 miles per day needs 19 or 20 days to complete the trail. Faster backpackers might take as few as 12 days.

Pacific Crest Trail The Pacific Crest National Scenic Trail (PCT) stretches 2650 miles from Campo, California, on the Mexican border to Manning Provincial Park in British Columbia, Canada. It hugs the crest of the glacially carved Sierra Nevada range in California and the volcanic Cascade Range in northern California, Oregon, and Washington, crossing seven national parks, three in the Sierra Nevada and four in the Cascades. Most of this mountainous terrain lies within 24 national forests and 33 roadless wilderness areas, with the longest unbroken stretch extending more than 200 miles; the wilderness of the High Sierra is crossed by only five roads.

The trail skirts the Mojave Desert along the Tehachapi Range and then enters the southern Sierra, where it joins the John Muir Trail in Sequoia National Park, just west of Mt Whitney (14,496ft). Leaving the park via Forester Pass (13,120ft), the trail's highest point, it continues through Kings Canyon National Park, where imposing peaks rise above the deep canyons of the Kings River. After passing Devils Postpile National Monument, the path enters Yosemite National Park at Donohue Pass and diverges from the John Muir Trail at Tuolumne Meadows. It crosses Dorothy Lake Pass as it exits Yosemite, then travels over Sonora Pass, Ebbetts Pass, Carson Pass, and Echo Summit. Entering the popular Desolation Wilderness Area west of Lake Tahoe, the trail passes Alpine Meadows and Squaw Valley ski resorts en route to Donner Summit. It undulates through deep river valleys in the northern Sierra and continues to Lassen Volcanic National Park, marking the southern extent of the Cascade Range.

As a through hike, the entire trail takes 175 days (six months) to complete. For more information, contact the Pacific Crest Trail Association (☎ 916-349-2109; W *www.pcta.org*).

Rock Climbing & Bouldering

Blessed with 3000ft supreme granite monoliths, sheer spires, near-vertical walls like El Capitan and Half Dome, and a temperate climate, Yosemite has long been a climber's utopia, home to a mind-boggling array of difficult and legendary ascents. The main climbing season runs from April to October.

During spring and fall, climbers flock to Yosemite Valley and boulder-strewn Camp 4, which enjoys an international reputation as a hangout for some of climbing's legendary stars. Come summer, base camp relocates to the gentler and quieter Tuolumne Meadows Campground, where temperatures tend to be a good 15° to 20° cooler than in the Valley and where there's an abundance of glacially polished granite domes.

People looking for partners or equipment post notices on bulletin boards at both campgrounds, and the Tuolumne rangers sometimes host climbing coffees on Sunday mornings. **Yosemite Mountaineering School** (☎ 209-372-8344; W *www.yosemitemountaineering.com*), regarded as the country's best, offers top-rate instruction throughout the park.

For detailed information about specific routes, climbers unanimously recommend any of the books by Don Reid, especially *Yosemite Climbs: Free Climbs, Yosemite Climbs: Big Walls,* and *Rock Climbs of Tuolumne Meadows,* written with Chris Falkenstein.

With so much glacial debris scattered about, Yosemite is also a perfect place for bouldering, or practicing rock climbing moves close to the ground; you'll find many primo playgrounds, particularly throughout the Valley.

Even if you have no desire to haul yourself up a craggy rock face, it's thrilling to see – and sometimes hear – climbers dangling from granite throughout the park. Look for the haul bags first – they're bigger and more colorful and move around more than the climbers, making them easier to spot.

To the north of Yosemite, there's good climbing near Bear Valley and Sonora Pass. Beyond the park's east boundary, the Owens River Gorge and the Buttermilks just outside of Bishop are top areas.

HISTORY OF ROCK CLIMBING IN YOSEMITE

Post World War II, rock climbing in the United States lagged far behind Europe, where climbers during the 1930s had dazzled the world with their accomplishments in the Alps. Yet Yosemite remained virtually untouched, and the park's monolithic granite, vertical cracks, and sheer walls posed entirely new challenges for climbers. Although technical rock climbing had started to take hold – in 1933 a few climbers using simple equipment reached Lunch Ledge, just opposite Half Dome – tackling Yosemite would ultimately require a new style of climbing, specialized equipment, and bold visionaries to lead the way.

Climbing with hand-forged steel pitons, Swiss climber John Salathé was one of the early pioneers, putting up numerous technically demanding aid routes for future climbers. In 1947, his first ascent of Lost Arrow Chimney was regarded as the most difficult climb of the day. As equipment became tougher and more lightweight, climbers began focusing on conquests that were previously thought to be unattainable. Following Salathé's path came a team of illustrious climbers, including Royal Robbins, who was the first to scale the northwest face of Half Dome, then viewed as the toughest climb in North America. Later, Robbins was instrumental in refining hauling techniques, allowing for longer climbs. In 1958, big-wall expert Warren Harding claimed Yosemite's last great climbing prize – the Nose on El Cap, which he mastered with a brilliant 13-day single-push ascent.

The 1960s marked the golden age of climbing in Yosemite, and legions of the world's best climbers and newbies alike flocked to Camp 4. During this formative era, all the major walls and hundreds of minor routes were completed. Later, purists began to eschew aid ascents, giving rise to a free-climbing renaissance led by Chuck Pratt, Bob Kampe, and others. Lynn Hill's free ascent of the Nose in 1993 is still regarded as one of the most impressive such climbs ever made. These days, climbers continue to up the ante by doing longer aid-free routes and by completing both long aid and free routes in shockingly short amounts of time, with "quicker and lighter" being the mantra.

The first person to climb a new path (a "first ascent") gets the honor of coming up with a name and rating the climb for difficulty. Some of Yosemite's more interestingly named climbs include: Half Dome's Snake Dike, Renus Wrinkle, Stroke My Erect Ear Tufts, Crotch Cricket, and Great White Book (a climb on Tuolumne's Stately Pleasure Dome).

For an entertaining account from an insider who spent 10 years immersed in Yosemite's climbing world, check out Steve Roper's *Camp 4: Recollections of a Yosemite Rockclimber*.

Rafting, Canoeing, & Kayaking

Two rivers descend from Yosemite, the Merced and the Tuolumne, and runoff from typical early-season snowmelt creates massive flows and lots of big rapids. Later in the season, lower flows and river levels often result in more technical white water. During the summer months, floating the Merced makes a good way to beat the heat. But with the exception of gentle river floating, all the real watery action happens just outside the park's boundaries.

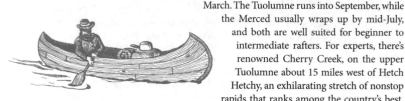

Most of the white water lies to the west, where a collection of Class III to IV+ rapids are ideal for rafting once the runoff starts, sometime in mid-March. The Tuolumne runs into September, while the Merced usually wraps up by mid-July, and both are well suited for beginner to intermediate rafters. For experts, there's renowned Cherry Creek, on the upper Tuolumne about 15 miles west of Hetch Hetchy, an exhilarating stretch of nonstop rapids that ranks among the country's best. Also farther afield, the North Fork of the Stanislaus River offers the most continuous white water of any river in California (Class IV, May to September); trips run out of both Sonora and Arnold.

Several outfitters offer one- to three-day excursions. For information on specific trips and outfits, see the Beyond Yosemite and Excursions chapters.

Within Yosemite, canoe and kayak enthusiasts will be happiest on Tenaya Lake, a sparkling sapphire beauty off Tioga Rd. The many good paddling options to the north include Lake Alpine, near Bear Valley on Hwy 4; and Spicer Reservoir and Pinecrest Lake, both off Hwy 108; you can rent all types of boats in Sonora, Arnold, and Bear Valley. To the east, Tioga and Saddlebag Lakes have easy put-ins and are both resplendent. Beyond there are many other fine places to paddle, including Mono Lake, Lundy Lake, June Lake, and the several small lakes above Mammoth.

Road & Mountain Biking

Tooling around on two wheels is a great way to explore Yosemite Valley. Twelve miles of mostly flat paved bike trails weave past popular sights and up to Mirror Lake; you can pick up simple but decent maps at the visitor center and hotels. Just be sure to ride defensively – the path is not always clearly marked, and there are lots of people paying more attention to gawking than steering. You can rent bikes all year, weather permitting, from a stand at Yosemite Lodge and during the summer at Curry Village.

For other good rides in the park, you might want to plan on bringing your own bike – unless you've got steel thighs or are a glutton for pain, you'll need more than a single-speed rental for the hills. For more information on riding in Yosemite, pick up a copy of David Story's detailed *Bicycling America's National Parks*.

Mountain bikes are not allowed on any dirt trails within Yosemite. That said, there are plenty of terrific places to ride in recreation areas surrounding the park, including excellent trails throughout Calaveras County and the Stanislaus National Forest. To the north, Bear Valley has lots of great single-track, and to the southeast is Mammoth, a mecca for downhill riders, with its top-to-bottom mountain bike park.

MOUNTAIN-BIKING MECCAS

Fat-tire riders will find lots of single-track terrain and fire roads in these three spots beyond Yosemite:

✔ **Bear Valley** – lots of gorgeous, aspen-lined trails for all levels of riding

✔ **Stanislaus National Forest** – plenty of piney terrain for two-wheel exploring

✔ **Mammoth** – volcanic steeps that make you feel like you're riding on a hilly moon

Swimming & Soaking

Of all the stellar spots for swimming, Lake Tenaya tops the list. The slightly warmer Merced and Tuolumne Rivers feature numerous swimming holes, sandy inlets, and creeks for all types of swimmers. During the summer, jumping in the Merced is a cool way to immerse your hot self in Yosemite's grandeur.

Beyond the park, there's no shortage of places for a quick cold plunge, a lakeside lounge, or even a hot-tub soak. To the north are gems like Lake Alpine, just east of Bear Valley on Hwy 4, and the popular-with-locals Pinecrest Lake, on Hwy 108 west of Dardanelle. Along the eastern Sierra, there's June Lake, Lundy Lake, and Lake Sabrina, near Bishop (see the Beyond Yosemite and Excursions chapters). Thanks to major underground runoff from the Sierra Crest, the east side is also full of hot springs. See the boxed text "Eastern Sierra Hot Springs" (p 224).

Fishing

While not exactly a primary park activity, fishing in Yosemite can certainly be fun and fruitful. Stocking officially ended in 1991, but anglers can still find five types of trout in several of the streams and lakes: native rainbow, brook, brown, golden, and cutthroat. The fishing season for streams and rivers runs from the last Saturday in April through mid-November, except for Frog Creek (near Lake Eleanor), which opens in mid-June; fishing is permitted year-round on the reservoirs and lakes.

To fish Yosemite's waterways, you must get a valid California fishing license (two-day permits $11/30 for a California resident/nonresident) if you're over the age of 16. These can be purchased at Tuolumne Meadows (summer only), Wawona, and Crane Flat general stores, at the Curry Village Mountain Shop, and the Yosemite Village Sport Shop, which also has the best selection of rental equipment. You must obey all California state fishing laws (☎ 559-222-3761; 🔲 www.dfg.ca.gov), as well as park-specific regulations, such as no fishing from bridges, a strict catch-and-release policy for rainbows, and a five-fish-per-day limit on brown trout caught between Happy Isles and Pohono Bridge. You can pick up a list of regulations from any visitor center. For current water levels, talk to a ranger or call the updated recording (☎ 800-952-5530).

Exactly where to find the stealthy fish hinges on water runoff, access points, weather patterns, and the finicky preferences of the trout themselves. Rainbows tend to favor swift-moving streams and lakes, while brook trout like waters above 7000ft. Browns prefer slower, warmer waters at lower elevations, and goldens seem to pop up over 8000ft. The South Fork of the Merced, and the Lyell and Dana Forks of the Tuolumne offer some of the best stream fishing in the park. For good tips, pick up a copy of Hank Johnson's *Yosemite Trout* or attend the frequently offered "How to Catch a Fish in Yosemite" interpretive talk (check *Yosemite Today* for a schedule). Online, you'll find some interesting tidbits at [W] www.yosemitefun.com/fishing.htm.

For customized fly-fishing excursions throughout the park, try **Yosemite Guides** *(☎ 209-379-2231, 877-425-3366)*, which charges up to $175 for a half-day, including lunch and tackle. **Southern Yosemite Mountain Guides** *(☎ 800-231-4575; [W] www.symg.com)* also leads one-day and weekend trips ($330-385 per person).

If fishing really is your thing, you'll find the best waters for trophy trout just beyond the park. North, Carson River and the 30 lakes and hundreds of miles of streams along the eastern Sierra offer some of the best fishing in the state. A long list of legendary trout-filled waters have long lured anglers, including Virginia Lakes, Twin Lakes, June Lakes and Crowley Lake.

> *Exactly where to find the stealthy fish hinges on water runoff, access points, weather patterns, and the finicky preferences of the trout themselves.*

Horseback Riding & Packing

Three different stables within the park offer daily two-hour to full-day trips ($40-80) from late spring through mid-fall. Though no experience is necessary, riders must be at least seven years old and 44in tall and weigh less than 225lb. During the summer months, reservations are advised, particularly for the longer rides from the Valley.

Pack trips are a multiday option for getting deeper into the wilderness; those that go to Yosemite's High Sierra Camps are hugely popular.

If bringing your own pack animals, you can use the stock camps at Tuolumne Meadows, Wawona, Bridalveil Fall, and Hetch Hetchy (one-night stay only). Each site ($20) accommodates six people and six animals. You can reserve sites up to five months in advance via the campsite reservation system.

Beyond the park, the eastern Sierra is particularly well suited for horse-back adventuring, with its Sierra Crest vistas, collection of lakes, sweeping valleys, and easily accessible wilderness. Numerous outfitters run trips for all levels out of Mammoth and Bishop, where riders are within easy reach of the gorgeous terrain of the Ansel Adams and John Muir Wilderness Areas.

Winter Activities

Some argue there's no better time than winter to experience the tranquil and otherworldly beauty of Yosemite. Indeed, the park transforms itself into a winter sports playground for skaters, skiers, and snow-shoers, with most activity revolving around the Valley, Glacier Point Rd, and Crane Flat.

Winter tends to arrive in full force by mid-November, though summer snow is not unheard of in Yosemite. Once the snow hits for good, Hwys 41 and 120 usually stay open, and Hwy 140 is almost always passable, conditions permitting. Tioga Rd, though, closes with the first snowfall. It's a good idea to bring snow chains with you, as conditions can change rapidly and chain prices double once you hit the foothills. If you find yourself in a bind, you can pick up some chains at the Wawona Chevron gas station, where prices start at $56 plus $13 for installation.

DOWNHILL SKIING & SNOWBOARDING

Badger Pass is Yosemite's long-adored ski mountain, where multiple generations have learned the sport at the excellent ski school. Gentle slopes and consistent snow make it a good spot for snowboarders as well.

Beyond the park, snug **Bear Valley** is a local's favorite, with some good steeps and even better cruisers. To the south lies mighty **Mammoth**, currently undergoing a transformation into an international ski destination. A top-rate mountain with excellent terrain for all levels, Mammoth is known for its sunny skies, vertical chutes, airy snow, and laid-back feel.

CROSS-COUNTRY SKIING

Yosemite's a fantastic spot for cross-country skiers of all levels, with options ranging from scenic half-mile loops to challenging 20-mile trails. Nordic skiers can take their pick from more than 350 miles of trails, many near **Badger Pass**; from there, you can schuss out to the Clark Range Vista and Glacier Point, an invigorating 21-mile round trip. Badger's excellent cross-country ski school offers a wide range of instruction, packages, and tours, including guided overnights to Yosemite's two cozy and incredibly scenic backcountry huts.

You'll find additional trails at **Crane Flat** and the **Mariposa Grove**. Most trails are well marked and easy to follow, and you can pick up ski and topo maps at the visitor centers and ranger stations.

Beyond the park, **Bear Valley** boasts an excellent ski school and network of trails, plus many ski workshops and a telemark festival. **Mammoth**, too, has some top-rate cross-country skiing, particularly in the areas accessed by Lake Mary Rd and around Devils Postpile.

ICE SKATING

One of the more delightful and certainly most popular winter activities in Yosemite is skating on Curry Village's open-air rink, which is open daily from mid-November through March. Regular session rates are $6.50 for adults and $5 for kids 12 and under. Rental skates are available at the ice rink for $3.25 per session.

BADGER PASS MEMORIES

My family wintered in Yosemite when I was growing up, for a week at Christmastime and, some lucky years, a second week in March. My mom had decided it was time for the kids to learn to ski, but was wary about her two speed demons heading off into the wild, snowy yonder. She was relieved to discover the Mid-Week Ski Package at Yosemite's ski area, Badger Pass. The program, now called the "Learn to Ski" package, included lift tickets, rental equipment, two ski lessons per day, and evening entertainment. Dad was onboard, as he wanted to sharpen his own rusty skills. Mom was sold when she learned there were only 10 runs, all rolling into a central basin, making it hard for my brother and me to get lost in the snow.

We still managed, between lessons, to get lost in the trees hunting for the perfect "whoopie trail" (trail with jumps) with our new ski school pals. But we always found our way back, emerging from the trees and charging down the mountain, answering the call of the brass school-bell rung by the charming ski program director, Nic Fior. Nic has taught at Badger Pass for 50 years, and his many former students remember him with delight. It is comforting for me to report that he is still there, sharing his infinite knowledge of the sport

and his love of the park with the next young batch of skiers.

After a full day of skiing (and pizza everyday for lunch!), we returned to the valley for the evening events. From ranger talks and Warren Miller ski films, to ice skating under Half Dome, the nighttimes were as fun as the days.

This year, I visited Yosemite in autumn and for the first time saw the waterfalls without ice and the grassy meadows minus the snow. The weather was gorgeous and the hiking perfect, but the park was not the wonderland I knew and adored. I was overcome with the desire for another winter romp. Perhaps I will call the family, to see if they want to come along.

— **Michaela Klink**

For more information on the "Learn to Ski" program and the "Badger Pups" ski lessons for younger children (four to six years old), call Yosemite's Badger Pass Ski & Snowboard School Desk at (209) 372-8430 or visit their website at http://www.yosemiteparktours.com/winter/activities_downhill_skiing.htm.

BACKCOUNTRY TOURING

For the most part, the same backcountry regulations apply in winter as in summer. If organizing a trip for yourself, make sure you have plenty of backcountry experience – ill-prepared travel in Yosemite's wilderness can always be dicey, but it can be downright deadly in winter. So if you doubt your ability to build a snow cave, you might want to head to either the **Glacier Point Hut** or the **Ostrander Lake Ski Hut**, both very popular and reachable by a day's ski from Glacier Point Rd. Another good, safe option is organizing a customized backcountry trip through **Sierra Guides Alliance** (☎ 209-379-2231; W *www.yosemiteguides.com*).

To Yosemite's east, the **Ansel Adams Wilderness**, **Saddlebag Lake** basin, and the peaks encircling **Mt Dana** offer lots of exploring opportunities for backcountry skiers. If you're determined to carve up the surrounding peaks on your own, pick up a copy of Paul Richin Jr.'s *50 Classic Backcountry Ski & Snowboard Summits*.

SNOWSHOEING

One of the easiest ways to explore the winter wilderness is to step into a pair of snow-shoes and head out on any of the hiking or cross-country skiing trails – for good karma's sake, just don't tramp directly in the ski tracks themselves. Provided there's adequate snow, you can snowshoe anywhere. Some excellent choices include the **John Muir Trail** and **Mariposa Grove**. You can rent snowshoes at Badger Pass and explore on your own or join one of the popular and fun ranger-led excursions.

SNOW CAMPING

Within Yosemite, winter camping is limited to four campgrounds: Upper Pines, Camp 4, Wawona, and Hodgdon Meadow. Outside the park, the more temperate and often sunny Eastern Sierra is spectacular for winter camping, with some of the campgrounds in and around Bishop open year-round.

Joining a Group

Joining a group is an excellent way to explore a very large and multifaceted park. Group activities provide knowledge and insight for both first-time visitors and those seeking to learn something new. They can also be a great opportunity to make friends and have fun.

CAMPFIRES & PUBLIC PROGRAMS

There's something almost universally enjoyable about group campfire programs, no matter how cynical you might think you are. Pull a bench around a roaring bonfire, with stars above, big trees behind you, and lots of friendly folks all around, and it's as if you've left the world's troubles behind.

During the summer, free campfire programs are held at the following Yosemite campgrounds: Tuolumne Meadows, Wawona, Bridalveil Creek, Crane Flat, White Wolf, and Lower Pines. Check *Yosemite Today* for that week's programs and times. Rangers, naturalists, and other park staff lead the programs, and topics include the history, ecology, and geology of the local region, a few tips on dealing with bears, and maybe some stories and songs. They're geared toward families and people of all ages.

Similar evening programs are also held at amphitheaters behind Yosemite Lodge and Curry Village – even in the absence of an actual campfire, the mood remains the same. These programs include general talks about the area, with occasional slide shows and films.

FUN FOR THE KIDS

Yosemite offers a wealth of kid-friendly activities, with some outdoor endeavors easier for kids to master than others. Youngsters can learn paddling skills and begin cross-country skiing fairly early, around age three or four. Children four and up can enroll in downhill skiing lessons at Badger Pass, a popular wintertime option. Horseback riding and bicycling are good summertime choices, and there are plenty of pleasant hikes easy enough for little legs. Climbing and rafting, on the other hand, require a higher level of dexterity and endurance and are best left to teens and adults.

Glacier Point rangers lead weekly programs at a lovely stone amphitheater near the snack bar, and sometimes also offer sunset talks along the railing overlooking the Valley. Over at Tuolumne Meadows, talks take place during the afternoons at Parsons Memorial Lodge, reachable via an easy half-mile hike.

The Sierra Club's LeConte Lodge hosts programs each week. A little more in-depth than the average campfire talk, these cover such topics as the founding of the John Muir Trail and the history of Hetch Hetchy.

Theater and storytelling events also occasionally pop up in the auditorium behind the visitor center or in the Curry Village amphitheater. These usually involve a small fee, with tickets available from the tour desk at Yosemite Lodge.

The busiest time is, of course, during the summer, usually June to September; limited programs are, however, offered in the off-season, and they're held during cold weather at indoor locations such as Yosemite Lodge and the Ahwahnee Hotel.

Glacier Point rangers lead weekly programs at a lovely stone amphitheater.

GROUP HIKES

If you haven't done much hiking before – or even if you have – taking a ranger-guided hike with a group of fellow travelers is a great way to get to know this massive park better. Rangers lead hikes year-round, most often in the summer. Check *Yosemite Today* for the schedule and take note of any directions given there – if the description says to pack a lunch and wear sturdy shoes, do it. And always bring water. Like most ranger programs, the hikes are generally free and require no reservations.

Hikes take place in all major areas of the park and range from mild (walks to Mirror Lake or through the Mariposa Grove) to moderately strenuous (out to Mono Pass or up to Vernal Fall). *Yosemite Today* offers an idea of the hike's degree of difficulty, as well as an approximate time frame. Short hikes may be just an hour or two – including sunrise photo walks that kick off at 6:30am in summer – while longer excursions can last all day.

Science & Nature

Science programs are plentiful in the park, both for the younger set (such as the Junior Ranger program – see p 32) as well as for grownups.

You'll find interesting **exhibits** on the park's natural history – including its glacial formation – at the Yosemite Valley and Tuolumne Meadows visitor centers (the Valley center also shows a free film, *The Spirit of Yosemite*, that's worth checking out). For more science displays, head to the Happy Isles Nature Center in Yosemite Valley. Its many hands-on exhibits are geared toward kids, but adults will likely learn something as well – such as how to tell one sort of pinecone from another and how to differentiate a wolf track from that of a mountain lion. Another good place to gather knowledge is the small library of books and brochures inside the historic LeConte Memorial Lodge.

To get a firsthand account of the local environment, attend one of the free **ranger-led programs** throughout the park. Rangers and naturalists take on subjects such as bears, birds, and wildflowers and also lead educational **walks** in various areas of the park – exploring the riparian ecosystem of Tuolumne Meadows, for instance, or discussing details about sequoia trees on a jaunt through Mariposa Grove. Check *Yosemite Today* for specific programs.

Astronomy buffs and budding stargazers will likely dig the evening "Stars Over Yosemite" programs. Free programs take place weekly (usually on Saturday night) at the amphitheater at Glacier Point, and the talks on constellations and stars are often accompanied by free telescope viewing courtesy of various California astronomy clubs, who volunteer their time. "Starry Skies" programs also happen in the Valley at Yosemite Lodge and Curry Village, though these usually involve a reservation and a modest fee; sign up at the tour desk at Yosemite Lodge. You can also go to a "Starry Skies" program at Wawona (sign up at the hotel there); those in Tuolumne Meadows should check the campfire program for a special ranger talk on stars.

Talks on constellations and stars are often accompanied by free telescope viewing.

Arts & Crafts

Free art classes happen each summer in Yosemite. They're very informal and geared toward all levels and abilities; the media change each week, from watercolor to pastel and so on. For more information, stop by the **Art Activity Center** in Yosemite Village.

Special art programs are occasionally held in other parts of the park, too, such as Tuolumne Meadows. Check *Yosemite Today* or stop by any of the visitor centers for details. The Yosemite Association's **Yosemite Outdoor Adventures** program offers college-level art and photography classes which may be taken for UC Berkeley credit.

Photographers looking for both guidance and good company can head out on one of the free **sunrise photo walks**, held most mornings in summer (at 6:30am) and on a more limited basis (weather permitting) in winter. Check *Yosemite Today* for the current schedule and starting point. You'll need to sign up in advance for these, too, as space is usually limited.

The **Ansel Adams Gallery** also offers photographic **seminars** for experienced photographers seeking more in-depth instruction. Subjects include crafting classic black-and-white photographs, working with color at Mono Lake, and exploring the world of digital photography; seminars run from several days to a week in length and cost several hundred dollars. Stop by the gallery in Yosemite Village or check out the website W www.anseladams.com.

Children's photo walks take place at various times during the week; look at *Yosemite Today* for specific dates and meeting points.

Taking a Class

The Yosemite Association sponsors a series of nature seminars in the park under the name **Yosemite Outdoor Adventures**. These classes are college-level educational opportunities for adults and, in some specific cases, teenagers 16 and up. Hiking is often involved, so participants need to be able to handle varying degrees of physical activity. Some classes last just for the day, including snowshoe jaunts at Badger Pass and "Map and Compass for Beginners." Longer trips involve overnights, including wildflower explorations, beginning backpackers' trips, rafting excursions on the Merced River, and outdoor survival classes for women. You can also join writing, drawing, photography, and natural history seminars. Quite well respected, the program has been active since 1971. For information, call ☎ 209-379-2321 or check W www.yosemite.org/seminars.

The **Yosemite Institute** (☎ *209-379-9511;* W *www.yni.org/yi)* is a private nonprofit group that has run its own educational programs in the park since 1971. The institute operates cabins in the Valley as well as a center on Tioga Rd near Crane Flat. Trips combine hiking with environmental education.

TIPS FOR TEACHERS

Educational and scientific groups who want to study in the park can get their entrance fees waived if they apply in advance and provide the proper documentation. The trip must be for educational purposes, not simply recreation. For details, check the park's website at W www.nps.gov/yose/trip/waivers.htm or call ☎ 209-372-0206.

The park also runs a couple of educational programs set up specifically for teachers who wish to bring their students to study in Yosemite. Teachers can contact the park's education center at ☎ 209-375-9505 or online at W www.nps.gov/yose/learn/visits.htm.

Volunteering

Many folks get even more satisfaction from their visit if they've lent a hand cleaning, sweeping, weeding, or in some way helping support the understaffed park. There are many ways to volunteer in Yosemite, whether you're simply an individual with a desire to do good or a large corporate group willing to spend a weekend picking up trash or cleaning fire pits. For information, contact the volunteer office at ☎ 209-379-1850.

The Yosemite Association also runs an established volunteer program for its members that includes restoration and revegetation projects, as well as staffing information stations. Long-term volunteers receive free camping, a small stipend, and bookstore discounts. To find out more, visit W www.yosemite.org/helpus/volunteer.html or call ☎ 209-379-2317.

Many folks get even more satisfaction from their visit if they've lent a hand cleaning, sweeping, weeding, or in some way helping support the understaffed park.

Working

The park's chief concessionaire is Yosemite Concession Services Corporation (YCS), which runs nearly all of the park's lodges, restaurants, shops, tours, shuttle buses, and recreation centers. During the summer, YCS employs about 1800 people – it's by far your best bet if you're eager to nab a job inside the park. Call ☎ 209-372-1236 or visit W www.yosemitepark.com/html/jobs.html for information on specific job types and application procedures.

If your heart is set on becoming a park ranger, you'll need to apply directly to the National Park Service. While competition can be fierce for permanent jobs, the NPS also hires seasonal workers; for more information, visit W www.nps.gov/personnel. Please note that you must be a US citizen to work for the NPS.

Planning may be a revolutionary concept to some vacationers. Traveling on the fly has that air of "outlaw" about it, and adventurous sorts will likely find their way through Yosemite no matter what they encounter. But be forewarned, you may quickly find yourself bogged down in unforeseen circumstances: tired and cranky because the campgrounds and hotels are full; bummed that you forgot your swimsuit though the weather and water are perfect; or feeling lost and silly because you're not sure which road to take (Tioga? Big Oak Flat? Wawona?). Even a small amount of preparation will make for a less stressful experience.

YOSEMITE PLANNING THE TRIP

Trip planning isn't just about drawing up a packing list – it's about plotting a strategy. The park is vast, the choices many, and likely as not, your time is limited. So ask yourself, what is it you *most* want to see and do?

Park veterans and repeat visitors probably have a general idea what they want from their next Yosemite visit. Those in need of guidance should first peruse the Highlights chapter. Once you have some destinations in mind, figure out exactly what it will take to get there (making reservations, buying and breaking in new hiking boots, spending a day getting acclimatized to higher elevations). It may sound simple, but a little advance planning really does make a difference.

When to Go

Summer is the best time to visit Yosemite, as everything (save Badger Pass Ski Area) is open, including campgrounds, trails, and facilities along Tioga Rd, Glacier Point Rd, and other high-country locales. Wildflowers bloom in the High Sierra, and the Merced River beckons swimmers to the Valley. Keep in mind, though, that it's also the driest time of year, when smog and smoke can clog the sky and waterfalls (including Yosemite Falls) often turn to trickles or dry up entirely. Temperatures in the Valley commonly reach into the high 80s and 90s Fahrenheit during the day, cooling to the 50s at night.

Fall foliage in Yosemite may never match New England's Technicolor displays, but leaves do flare into brilliant yellows and rusty, crunchy browns, creating a vibrant autumnal mood, especially in Yosemite Valley and Wawona. Daytime temperatures in the Valley remain in the low 70s through October, dipping into the 50s by November; nights are often in the 30s. Most high-country facilities and trails shut for the season by September or October, and Glacier Point and Tioga Rds close once snow starts falling. Until it does, this is a brilliant time to visit – the deep winter chill has yet to set in, many campgrounds remain open, and perhaps most appealing of all, the stifling summer crowds are gone, allowing the park and its patrons to breathe a bit easier.

Winter snows close the high-elevation roads, and most facilities shut down, even in the Valley. However, winter also means far fewer fellow travelers – good news for those seeking solitude. It's also one of the most serenely beautiful times of the year, as snow blankets the Valley pines and the air turns crisp and quiet. Half Dome and El Capitan are stunning anytime, but with a dusting of snow they feel, well, magical. When the snow stops falling, the sun offers respite from the biting cold (highs often in the 40s and 50s) – though nights do frequently dip back down into the 20s.

In spring, the waterfalls gush at full capacity, and the Valley's meadow grasses, oaks, and wildflowers come to life. Temperatures, though, stay plenty crisp – expect high 50s and 60s during the day, 30s and 40s at night – and some facilities remain closed until Memorial Day or even later. This is a good season to explore Hetch Hetchy's lower elevations.

COPING WITH THE CROWDS

There's no doubt about it: Yosemite is a popular park and can get very, very crowded. Millions of visitors jam into its borders each year, clogging the roads and trails and filling campgrounds and hotels to the bursting point. To avoid the worst throngs, visit the park in just about any season but summer. Winter is quietest (except during Christmas), with fall a close second. Spring is often quiet, too, as many trails, roads, and services stay closed through May.

If you do arrive on a weekend in July or August (by far the busiest times of the year), take the hordes in stride and practice a few crowd-avoidance techniques. For starters, visit major sights or hit the trails early in the morning – Bridalveil Fall is beautiful at sunrise. The same goes for evenings – popular spots like Mariposa Grove and Glacier Point often clear out by late afternoon. As a rule, hiking almost anywhere is a good bet, as most visitors never stray far from their cars. If solitude is your chief objective, avoid popular destinations like Vernal Fall, Mariposa Grove, and Glacier Point and roam beyond the Valley to such areas as Tuolumne Meadows or Wawona.

Roads and parking lots often fill up in summer. To eliminate driving hassles, park your car in one spot and get around via the free shuttle buses, which operate daily in Yosemite Valley and seasonally in Tuolumne Meadows and Mariposa Grove.

It's also a good idea – and rather crucial in summer – to make reservations for your accommodations as far in advance as possible, be it for a campground, tent cabin, or hotel.

To eliminate driving hassles, park your car in one spot and get around via the free shuttle buses.

SPECIAL EVENTS

Yosemite's best-known seasonal event is the **Bracebridge Dinner** at the Ahwahnee Hotel, a traditional Christmas pageant that's part grand feast and part Renaissance fair. During this evening spectacle, guests indulge in a multicourse meal while being entertained by more than 100 actors in 17th-century costume. The reservation process for this hugely popular event begins almost a year in advance; call ☎ 559-252-4848 for more information.

Gourmets are also drawn to the Ahwahnee for the annual **Vintners' Holidays**, held in November and December. Each of the eight sessions features four wine authorities, who lead seminars and discussions. The two- and three-day events culminate in a grand finale dinner in the Ahwahnee Dining Room. The Ahwahnee also hosts **Chefs' Holidays** in January and February, during which top American chefs lead cooking demonstrations, offer behind-the-scenes kitchen tours, and cook another sumptuous feast. For information on both events, call ☎ 559-253-2001.

Held in February at the Ahwahnee, the **Yosemite Winter Literary Conference** features seminars and discussions with an impressive selection of writers and poets. It's cosponsored by the Yosemite Association; call ☎ 209-379-2646 for details.

The internationally recognized **Mariposa Storytelling Festival** (☎ 209-966-3155, 800-903-9936; Ⓦ www.arts-mariposa.org/storytelling.html), takes place in late winter in Mariposa, with stories and performances for all ages. (Along Hwy 140, near the park.)

Another late-winter event, the **Yosemite Nordic Holiday Race** is held at the Badger Pass Ski Area. Events include a 17km trek that's California's longest-running nonprofessional cross-country ski race. For information, call ☎ 209-372-8444 or ☎ 209-372-1000.

Also held at Badger Pass is **Yosemite Springfest**, a winter carnival that falls on the last weekend of each ski season, usually in March or April. Events include slalom racing, costume contests, obstacle courses, a barbecue, and snow-sculpting. Call Badger Pass at ☎ 209-372-8430 for details.

Earth Day (April 22) celebrations in Yosemite feature chances to help out the park – including cleanup projects, tree planting, etc. – as well as kids' educational events, a vendors fair, and live music and poetry.

If you like country or folk music, head to Camp Mather for the biannual **Strawberry Music Festival** (☎ 209-533-0191; Ⓦ www.strawberrymusic.com), held each Memorial Day and Labor Day weekend. Owned by the City of San Francisco, the family camp is in Mather, about 10 miles northwest of the park's Big Oak Flat Entrance. The location may change in coming years, so call to confirm. Get tickets early to this popular event and expect to camp out, as lodging is limited.

The **Tuolumne Meadows Poetry Festival** alights in the meadows each August. Call the Yosemite Association (☎ 209-379-2646) for information.

Gathering Information

Have more questions? Below you'll find a wealth of places to look for answers, readily available to anyone with access to the Internet, the library, a bookstore, or a telephone.

SUGGESTED READING

For a thorough, fascinating account of the park and its history, start with *Yosemite: Its Discovery, Its Wonders & Its People* by Margaret Sanborn. *Discovery of the Yosemite* offers a firsthand record of early Yosemite history by Lafayette Houghton Bunnell, MD, medical officer of the Mariposa Battalion, while *Indian Life of the Yosemite Region* describes Yosemite's Native American culture, as recorded by SA Barrett and EW Gifford, anthropologists who worked with the Miwok people around 1900.

John Muir's *My First Summer in the Sierra* is the inspirational diary Muir kept while tending sheep in 1869, when he recognized his life calling. Another Muir title, *The*

SURFING THE NET

Online you can research specific hikes, find average temperatures and summer crowd counts, book hotel rooms, make campground reservations, and buy wilderness maps or anything else you may need.

This section offers a roundup of the best Yosemite-related sites. Lonely Planet's own website (W *www.lonelyplanet.com)* also makes a great resource; it's home to the Thorn Tree bulletin board, where you can ask fellow travelers for their tips and share your own when you return home.

GENERAL PARK INFORMATION

W **www.nps.gov/yose**
The official Yosemite National Park Service website contains the most in-depth information about almost everything you need to know, from bear updates to wilderness permit requirements. There's a nifty map of campgrounds with instructions on how to book via ParkNet (W www. reservations.nps.gov), the NPS' booking engine, plus links to other national parks and Yosemite's bookstore. Best of all, you can download current and archived issues of *Yosemite Today* for a rundown of daily park programs and schedules.

W **www.yosemite.org**
The nonprofit Yosemite Association site features class listings, membership news, and daily weather forecasts. It also operates Yosemite's primary online shopping site (W www.yosemitestore.com), which sells books, bear canisters, and other merchandise. And the good email newsletter can keep you abreast of things like new Yosemite book releases, featured naturalists, and general park news.

W **www.yosemitepark.net**
A general resource site that's updated monthly with FAQs, message boards, web cams, and lots of easy-to-skip junk in the shuffle. The links section is worthwhile, however, organized by subject matter and activity.

W **www.yosemitefun.com**
This personal website can be irreverent at times, but it's comprehensive and sometimes humorous, with lots of photos, discussions of local politics, and insider tips.

W **www.4yosemite.com/parkinfo.htm**
A little rough around the edges, this site is updated daily with park news and information. It's run by Yosemite Vacation Homes, which rents out private homes within the park.

W **www.yosemitesites.com**
This search engine crawls through a database and identifies available campsites. Go here to do your initial research, then reserve a site through the NPS ParkNet.

W **www.yosemitepark.com**
Make reservations at any park hotel through this online home for Yosemite Concession Services (YCS), which oversees virtually all park lodging, restaurants, tours, activities, and transportation. The site also features an email newsletter and more than 200 pages of general information.

SPECIAL INTEREST

W **www.yni.org/yi**
The nonprofit Yosemite Institute website describes its educational programs for elementary, middle, and high school students and provides post-visit information for educators.

W **www.sierraclub.org**
The official site of the Sierra Club addresses conservation issues and provides information on hiking and camping trips open to members and nonmembers alike.

W **www.highsierrahikers.org**
The nonprofit High Sierra Hikers Association tackles issues affecting hikers in the region, offering information, research papers, essays, and resource links.

W **www.supertopo.com**
An excellent resource for climbers, this site offers tons of information on climbing in Yosemite and throughout the High Sierra. The free, downloadable topo maps are tops.

W **www.terragalleria.com/mountain/info/yosemite/index.html**
Another good site for information on climbing in Yosemite, this one draws its content directly from climbers.

W **www.yosemite.ca.us/phorum**
Though it's hard to tell who's at the helm, this regularly updated site features forums on a wide range of subjects, from trip planning to rock climbing.

W **www.yosemite.ca.us**
This site provides direct answers to your questions. Though not much to look at, it's worth checking out if you'd like to pose queries to those who know Yosemite.

BEYOND YOSEMITE

W **www.yosemitegold.com**
This snappy, well-organized site includes information and news on the surrounding Gold Country. Its paid-advertising listings make it less than comprehensive or objective, but it's still worth a look if you're planning to explore the foothills region.

W **www.yosemite-sierra.org**
The official site of the Yosemite-Sierra Visitor's Bureau in Oakhurst, this offers loads of general information about Yosemite, Sierra National Forest, Bass Lake and other areas south of the park.

W **www.395.com**
This interesting eastern Sierra community site features local news, weather reports, and information on skiing and climbing in the region.

Yosemite, has been republished with accompanying photographs by the late Galen Rowell. The similarly titled *Yosemite* by Ansel Adams presents the famous photographer's finest images of the place closest to his heart.

Climbing enthusiasts should pick up a copy of *Camp 4: Recollections of a Yosemite Rockclimber* by Steve Roper, a definitive chronicle of the heyday of Yosemite climbing. For birdwatchers, *Birds of Yosemite and the East Slope* by David Gaines is the best reference, covering every known species in the Yosemite and Mono Lake region. To learn about Yosemite's plants, take a look at Stephen J Botti's *An Illustrated Flora of Yosemite National Park*.

For those in a contemplative mood, *The High Sierra of California* presents the haunting, Japanese-inspired woodcut prints of Tom Killion in collaboration with poet Gary Snyder, who offers spare Buddhist musings on High Sierra camping. Snyder studied Japanese sumi painting with University of California at Berkeley professor Chiura Obata. In *Obata's Yosemite – The Art and Letters of Chiura Obata from His Trip to the High Sierra in 1927*, Yosemite is rendered in traditional Japanese sumi brush and ink drawings, watercolors, and woodcut prints.

For in-depth detail on hiking and backpacking in Yosemite and the surrounding mountains, seek out Lonely Planet's *Hiking in the Sierra Nevada* by John Mock and Kimberley O'Neil. You can find broader statewide coverage in Lonely Planet's *California* guide.

MAPS

At the entrance gates, park rangers provide all visitors with a free Yosemite map that's acceptable, albeit limited. Additional maps of developed areas like Yosemite Village and Tuolumne Meadows appear in *Yosemite Today*.

Hikers and more serious sightseers, however, will definitely appreciate a better, more detailed map. The *Topographic Map of Yosemite National Park and Vicinity* \from Wilderness Press is our favorite for hikers. The National Geographic/Trails Illustrated *Yosemite National Park* topographic map offers similar coverage. The latter is printed on waterproof, tear-resistant paper, though trails aren't as detailed as on the Wilderness Press map.

For day hikers in Tuolumne Meadows, the Yosemite Association's *Guide to Yosemite High Sierra Trails* is a great help that includes trail descriptions and elevation charts. Serious backpackers should pick up United States Geological Survey (USGS) topographic quadrangle maps covering their planned routes.

If you plan to visit one of the national forests outside the park, the appropriate national forest map will show forest service roads, campgrounds, trailheads, and natural features.

USEFUL ORGANIZATIONS
Sierra Club

Founded by John Muir in 1892, the **Sierra Club** (☎ 415-977-5500; Ⓦ *www.sierra club.org; 85 Second St, San Francisco, CA 94105)* today boasts more than 700,000 members and remains an active and important environmental advocate. The club's ties to Yosemite have always been strong, and it continues to operate the LeConte Memorial Lodge in Yosemite Valley as an environmental education center. Outings, mostly led by informed volunteers, are a vital part of club activities, and the California chapters offer a busy schedule of hiking and camping trips that often include Yosemite and Sierra destinations; check Ⓦ california.sierraclub.org or Ⓦ www.sierraclub.org/outings for current notices. You

HIKING CLUBS

Hiking clubs offer a great introduction to the mountains, an opportunity to meet and exchange information with other hikers, and a way to share planning and transportation. Often associated with a large employer or a university, these clubs can be hard to find. Start at a local outdoor gear supply store, which may have club members on staff or an informative bulletin board.

usually don't have to be a member to participate, and costs are often very low.

Yosemite Association
The nonprofit **Yosemite Association** (YA; ☎ 209-379-2646; W www.yosemite.org) is an educational organization founded in 1923 with the specific purpose of supporting Yosemite National Park. Through membership dues, book sales, seminar fees, and donations, YA offers financial assistance directly to the park. YA also aids with visitor services, organizes volunteer work crews, supports scientific and educational research projects, publishes its own series of books, operates the Ostrander Ski Hut and the wilderness permit reservation system, and cosponsors programs such as free classes at the Art Activity Center and its own Yosemite Outdoor Adventures seminars. Pick up YA information at kiosks throughout the park or at the visitor center bookstores, which are operated by the association.

Bringing the Kids

Kids love Yosemite, and bringing them along – though it requires extra planning and keeping a sharp eye on their whereabouts – is definitely worthwhile. There's loads for kids to do here, from swimming, rafting (an excellent choice for kids 50lbs and up), biking, and hiking to wildlife watching, marveling at waterfalls, and peering over the edge of tall cliffs like Glacier Point (perhaps nerve-racking for parents but a thrill for adventurous young ones). In addition, Yosemite provides quite a few activities and programs geared specifically to kids; see the Activities and Highlights chapters for ideas, and be sure to check *Yosemite Today* for a current schedule of events.

CHOOSING WHAT TO DO
When planning what to do and see, try not to overdo things; packing too much into your trip can cause frustration and spoil the adventure.

When choosing activities, make sure they appeal to your kids as well. Balance a morning at the museum, for instance, with a swim in the Merced River or Curry Village pool. Or spend time at a place both adults and children might enjoy, such as LeConte Memorial Lodge or the Happy Isles Nature Center, which offers hands-on exhibits specifically for kids, as well as nearby areas for a picnic, short walk, or dip in the river.

Even better, include the kids in the trip planning from the get-go. If they have a hand in choosing activities, they'll be much more interested and excited when you arrive. For more information, advice, and anecdotes, pick up a copy of Lonely Planet's *Travel with Children* by Cathy Lanigan.

KEEPING IT FUN

Active, adventurous, and environmentally aware parents are often eager to share those interests with their kids. Take care, though, not to turn a diversion into a chore. For example, don't make your kids memorize 80 different kinds of rocks; that's no fun for anyone (adult family members included). Kids may be curious and eager to learn, but they also need time to play.

Consider participating in organized activities, such as junior ranger programs and nature walks, or visiting kid-friendly spots like the Happy Isles Nature Center – great ways to spark kids who seem lackluster about the whole "nature thing." Kids also usually like it when there are other kids around.

Kids may be curious and eager to learn, but they also need time to play.

Hiking is great exercise for kids, though parents should gauge their children's abilities and choose hikes carefully. If you're unsure, try hikes that don't require much elevation gain (Mirror Lake or Soda Springs, for instance). If the little ones handle that fine, work your way up from there. Kids often thrill at viewpoints such as Sentinel Dome, Lembert Dome, and Taft Point, all reachable via short, easy trails. Mariposa Grove is another magical place that will likely enthrall.

Let kids carry a backpack of some kind, too. Just don't overfill it, or they may never want to strap one on again. *Backpacking with Babies & Small Children* by Goldie Silverman is a useful resource for anyone planning a hike with the kids.

In Yosemite Valley, keep the free shuttle bus in mind when you're out and about. That way, if your kids get tired, you can simply hop the bus and head back to your car, campsite, or lodge.

KEEPING IT SAFE

When hiking, be sure your kids stay within earshot (if not sight) of the adults. They may want to rush ahead, but it's very easy to miss a necessary junction or take a wrong turn. As a precaution, dress them in brightly colored clothes, and have each one carry a flashlight and safety whistle. Make sure they know what to do if they get lost (for instance, stay put and periodically blow the whistle).

Whether you're hiking or just plain sightseeing, dress kids (and yourself) in layers, so they can peel off or pull on clothing when needed. And bring along lots of high-energy snacks and drinks, even on short outings.

If you're traveling in the high country such as Tuolumne Meadows, keep in mind that kids are just as vulnerable as adults to altitude sickness. They may not know what it is they're feeling, and they may not let you know. Familiarize yourself with the symptoms (headaches and nausea are common) and watch for them, especially during physical activities. If your child shows symptoms, descend to lower elevations.

Be extra cautious around viewpoints such as Taft Point, which has a railing at the cliff's edge but none around the periphery (including around the Fissures – giant cracks in the granite that plunge thousands of feet to the Valley floor). The same goes for the summits of any peaks or domes.

What's It Going to Cost?

At $20, the entrance fee to Yosemite may seem steep. But remember, that covers an entire carload of visitors, and it's good for seven days. Plus, once you're inside, you don't have to spend any money sightseeing, hiking, or attending ranger-led programs. With a wilderness permit, even camping in the backcountry is free.

Lodging and restaurants, however, can send expenses soaring. For example, the cost for two adults to share a hotel room in Yosemite Lodge and dine exclusively at park restaurants can approach $200 a day. Hotel rates start at just over $100 and go up – way up – from there. You can opt to stay in a motel

PETS IN THE PARK

Pets are allowed in Yosemite, though restrictions are pretty limiting. Pets are permitted on roads and paved trails, but you can't bring your dog (we assume you're not even *thinking* of bringing the cat) on nonpaved hiking trails or into any wilderness areas. The rules protect wildlife from your dog, and vice versa, and keep your dog from disturbing other hikers. However, there are a few exceptions to the nonpaved trail rule, including Wawona Meadow Loop and parts of Old Big Oak Flat Rd south of Hodgdon Meadow.

Dogs are not allowed on shuttle buses or inside lodge rooms. You can bring pets into most campgrounds, except Tamarack Flat, Porcupine Flat, and any of the walk-in campgrounds. Some campgrounds allot special sections for pet owners, so look for signs. Dogs must be on leashes (6ft or less) at all times and never left unattended. And it goes without saying that you must clean up after your dog.

A kennel in Yosemite Valley is open during summer months. For rules and fees, call ☎ 209-372-8348.

In other parts of the Sierra Nevada, dogs are often permitted, with the possible exception of USFS-administered wilderness areas. Ask at local ranger stations about any special regulations concerning pets.

outside the park, but even budget places run at least $60 to $70 a night in summer – many are even higher. Couple that with the $25 to $30 per day to eat at park restaurants, and you can see how things add up quickly.

Tent cabins bring the cost down some, but even they start at around $60. Bare site camping is the best option for bargain hunters, with Yosemite campsites ranging between $8 and $18 per night. Cooking your own meals and packing a picnic lunch also lowers costs, especially if you plan ahead and buy supplies at supermarkets *before* entering the park. You'll probably wind up with a better meal than what's offered at most park snack stands.

From Yosemite Valley, public transportation is limited to hiker/sightseer buses, which run in summer to either Tuolumne Meadows ($22 round-trip) or Glacier Point ($30 round-trip) – not exactly a bargain. Most visitors will probably wind up driving, though how much you spend on gas depends on whether you left the SUV at home. Shuttle buses in Yosemite Valley, Tuolumne Meadows, and Mariposa Grove, however, are free, as is the winter shuttle between the Valley and Badger Pass. The park entrance fee is waived for those choosing to visit Yosemite by bus – a nice bonus.

NATIONAL PARKS PASSES

If you plan to visit several national parks this year, the **National Parks Pass** ($50) is an excellent deal. It grants the holder and anyone else in the vehicle unlimited admission to any national park for one year from the month of purchase. You can buy one at the park entrance or in advance by calling ☎ 888-467-2757 or visiting Ⓦ www.nationalparks.org.

For an additional $15, a **Golden Eagle** hologram will be affixed to your National Parks Pass, extending coverage to all NPS sites (national monuments, seashores, and the like), plus those managed by the US Fish and Wildlife Service, the US Forest Service, and the Bureau of Land Management.

If you're a US citizen or permanent resident older than 62, you qualify for the **Golden Age Passport**, which costs $10 and offers unlimited free admission to all national parks, monuments, historic sites, recreation areas, and national wildlife refuges for the rest of your life. You also get a 50% discount on camping, parking, and other fees. The pass is only available in person at an entrance station to a federal recreation area. You must show proof of age.

Finally, there's the **Golden Access Passport**, available to citizens or permanent residents of the US who are blind or permanently disabled. It works the same way as the Golden Age Passport, except there is no age restriction and it's free.

Health & Safety

DISABLED TRAVELERS

At every national park, accessibility brochures and a services coordinator offer information on park and ranger-led activities. If you need to make arrangements in advance, call any park visitor center or contact the coordinator prior to your arrival.

To obtain Yosemite's accessibility brochure, visit Ⓦ www.nps.gov/yose/trip/access.htm; you can also pick one up in person at the park's entrance stations and visitor centers. You can rent **wheelchairs** from the bike stand at Yosemite Lodge (☎ 209-372-1208) or the Medical Clinic (☎ 209-372-4637). There are a few **paved trails**, such as those leading to the base of Bridalveil Fall and Lower Yosemite Fall. Note, however, these are not exactly a smooth ride and will likely require assistance.

For **deaf visitors** and those with hearing difficulties, a deaf services coordinator may be available during summer months to interpret information and even assist with park-led

✔ WHAT TO PACK

You probably don't need a reminder to bring a toothbrush and an extra pair of socks, but following are some useful items you may have overlooked. This checklist is designed primarily for car campers and day hikers, not hardcore backpackers, though it applies to nearly anyone who plans to stretch their legs for more than a few minutes. Don't worry if you forget a few items – many (including sandwich bags, wool hats, even sleeping bags) are available at stores inside the park.

✔ Day pack
✔ Hiking boots
✔ First-aid kit
✔ Flashlight (and/or a headlamp)
✔ Spare batteries
✔ Bandanna
✔ Insect repellent
✔ Sunscreen
✔ Sunglasses
✔ Wide-brimmed hat
✔ Shorts
✔ Swimsuit
✔ Towel
✔ Raingear
✔ Map (easily purchased in park stores)
✔ Matches (waterproof is best)

✔ Water bottles (at least one per person)
✔ Extra water (a gallon or two in the car)
✔ Pocket knife
✔ Watch
✔ Hand soap
✔ Toilet paper
✔ Resealable plastic bags (for food storage)
✔ Dishtowel
✔ Wool/stocking cap (cold nights even in summer)
✔ Sweater and/or long-sleeved shirt
✔ Warm jacket or fleece pullover
✔ Lightweight gloves
✔ Ground sheet (for tent)
✔ Portable chair

walks and talks. For information, contact the Valley visitor center or call ☎ 209-372-4726 (TTY) or ☎ 209-372-0296 (voice).

Easy Access to National Parks: The Sierra Club Guide for People with Disabilities by Wendy Roth and Michael Tompane is a carefully researched guide for intrepid travelers with physical limitations. Published in 1992, it's not fully up-to-date but is still quite useful.

EMERGENCY SERVICES

In an emergency, dial ☎ 911. The **Yosemite Medical Clinic** (*☎ 209-372-4637*) offers 24-hour emergency care. The hospitals nearest to Yosemite include the **John C Fremont Hospital and Clinic** (*☎ 209-966-3631; 5189 Hospital Rd*) in Mariposa; **Tuolumne General Hospital** (*☎ 209-533-7100; 101 Hospital Rd*) in Sonora; and **Doctors Medical Center** (*☎ 209-578-1211; 1441 Florida Ave*) in Modesto, the largest facility in the general region.

WATER PURIFICATION

If you drink snowmelt, stream, lake, or groundwater in the park, you risk coming into contact with the waterborne parasite *Giardia lamblia*, which causes giardiasis, an intestinal disease marked by chronic diarrhea, abdominal cramps, bloating, fatigue, and weight loss. Symptoms may take a week or so to manifest. Though not usually dangerous, it is unpleasant and requires treatment with antibiotics.

As a rule, don't drink *any* naturally occurring water without boiling it for several minutes, filtering it with a *Giardia*-rated water filter, or treating it with an iodine-based purifier. Also refrain from brushing your teeth or doing dishes with untreated water.

ALTITUDE SICKNESS

In the thinner atmosphere of the High Sierra, lack of oxygen may cause headaches, nausea, nosebleeds, shortness of breath, physical weakness, and other symptoms. These can lead to serious consequences, especially if combined with heat exhaustion, sunburn, or hypothermia. Most people adjust to altitude within a few hours or days. In mild cases of altitude sickness, everyday painkillers such as aspirin may relieve discomfort. If symptoms persist, descend to lower elevations.

SEASONAL CONSIDERATIONS

If you plan to stay in campgrounds, lodges, or the backcountry at high elevation, remember that temperatures can drop considerably at night, even in midsummer. Pack warm clothing, including a sweater or fleece pullover, coat, hat, gloves, and even long underwear. Remember, it can snow any season in Tuolumne Meadows. Be prepared for rain, too.

Hypothermia

Temperatures in the mountains can quickly drop from balmy to below freezing. A sudden downpour and high winds can also rapidly lower your body temperature. If possible, avoid traveling alone; partners are better able to avoid hypothermia. If you must travel alone, especially when hiking, be sure someone knows both your route and your schedule.

Seek shelter when bad weather is unavoidable. Woolen clothing and synthetics, which retain warmth even when wet, are superior to cottons. A quality sleeping bag is a worthwhile investment, although down loses much of its insulating properties when wet. Carry high-energy, easily digestible snacks like chocolate or dried fruit.

Symptoms of hypothermia include shivering, loss of coordination, slurred speech, and disorientation or confusion. These can be accompanied by exhaustion, numbness (particularly in toes and fingers), irrational or violent behavior, lethargy, dizzy spells, muscle cramps, and bursts of energy. To treat early stages of hypothermia, get victims out of the wind or rain, remove any wet clothing, and replace it with dry, warm clothing. Give them hot liquids – not alcohol – and high-calorie, easily digestible food. In advanced stages, it may be necessary to place victims in warm sleeping bags and get in with them. If possible, place them near a fire or in a warm (not hot) bath. Do *not* rub a victim's skin.

Sunburn

You face a greater risk from sun exposure when hiking in high elevations. Sunburn is possible on hazy or cloudy days and even when it snows. Use sunscreen and lip moisturizer with UV-A and UV-B protection and an SPF of 30 or greater. Reapply it throughout the day. Wear a wide-brimmed hat and sunglasses and consider tying a bandanna around your neck for extra protection.

Dangers & Annoyances

CRIME

Crime does happen in Yosemite, and it's no wonder, considering the park sees some three or four million visitors each year. However, the majority of crimes are small-time theft, vandalism, and public drunkenness.

Car break-ins are more often the work of bears than burglars, although signs at trailheads often warn not to leave valuables in the car. Chances are your car will be fine if parked for the day or even longer, but it's wise to take some precautions.

Ask at the nearest visitor center or ranger station about known problems at your trailhead, especially if you're heading out for several days. Carry your money and valuables with you. If you do leave anything in the car, put it in the trunk or other enclosed area.

When possible, avoid leaving your vehicle at an isolated trailhead and instead park in a more heavily used parking area within reasonable walking distance. Better yet, use shuttle buses or arrange a carpool. Park your vehicle facing in, so the trunk or rear access door remains visible. It's unlikely the vehicle itself will be snatched, but if you're feeling unlucky, consider temporarily disabling it (that is, if you know what you're doing). Never hide your vehicle's keys in, under, or near the vehicle.

UNPREDICTABLE WEATHER

Changeable weather, a given in the mountains, presents a small yet inherent risk. Before starting your hike – especially if you're heading to the top of an exposed peak or dome – check the forecast at a visitor center or ranger station, which post daily weather reports on bulletin boards. Regardless of the forecast, if you're planning a long hike, carry rain gear and be prepared for the worst. *Reading Weather: Where Will You Be When the Storm Hits?* by meteorologist Jim Woodmency explains how to anticipate storms by understanding clouds and weather patterns.

INSECTS

Much of Yosemite and the Sierra in general teem with annoying **mosquitoes**, especially in June and July. You're most likely to run across them anywhere there's standing water. If you're susceptible, bring lots of insect repellent and wear long-sleeved shirts and long pants. Backpackers should bring a lightweight tent or mosquito net for protection.

Present in brush, forest, and grassland, **ticks** may carry Lyme disease or relapsing fever (borelliosis), which are transmitted by bite. Early symptoms of both diseases are similar to the flu: chills, high fever, headache, digestive problems, and general aches. Check your clothes, hair, and skin after hiking, and your sleeping bag if it has been out beneath trees.

CLIFFS & WATERFALLS

Smooth granite beside Yosemite's many rivers, streams, and waterfalls is often slippery, even when dry. Tumbling over a fall is almost certain to be fatal. Despite warning signs in several languages and protective railings in many places, people have died. Approach any waterfall with caution, and above all, don't get into the water.

Use caution, too, when hiking to and around Glacier Point, Taft Point, Dewey Point, and other precarious viewpoints. Some of these overlooks have railings, but plenty of others don't.

WILDLIFE

There's one rule you'll hear time and again in Yosemite: Don't leave food in your car, on your picnic table, or anywhere else bears and other creatures can access it. It's also a bad idea to pose for pictures with wildlife. Yes, we're nagging, but please keep a safe distance. Snakes frequent areas below 5000ft, so keep your eyes on the trails in Hetch Hetchy and other areas at lower elevations.

Bear Facts

Bears are active day and night throughout the Sierra Nevada and are especially prevalent in Yosemite, thanks in large part to the presence of humans and the enticing smells we bring with us. Only black bears live in California. (Though a grizzly adorns the state flag, the species was long ago hunted out.) To many visitors, bears represent a mix of the fascinating and the frightening. It's not often we get to see such powerful, majestic animals in the wild – at the same time, many of us would just as soon *not* see one while in the park.

Bears elsewhere often flee at the sight, sound, or smell of people. Sadly, many of Yosemite's bears do the exact opposite and are notorious for regularly breaking into vehicles and raiding campgrounds and backcountry campsites in search of food. Though the bears rarely charge visitors, having one traipse through your campsite or make off with your food or backpack can leave you quite unnerved.

To keep the bears at bay, the park service insists that you remove all scented items from your car, including any food, trash (scour the car for those empty potato chip bags), and products such as gum, toothpaste, soap, and sunscreen. It's best, too, to cover anything in your car that even *looks* like a cooler or food. Place the items in bear boxes – large metal storage lockers found in most major parking lots, every Yosemite campsite, and a few popular backcountry campgrounds. In Yosemite, failure to use bear boxes can result in a fine – not to mention the possibility of your car windows being shattered and upholstery ravaged by a hungry beast. Elsewhere in the Sierra, you'll find bear boxes at national park trailheads and the most troublesome USFS trailheads.

At campsites, keep bear boxes shut and latched even while preparing dinner, as bears can appear out of nowhere and leave you no time to lock things up. Cook evening meals well before dusk and wash dishes immediately after eating. If a bear does visit your campsite, make lots of noise – yell, clap your hands, bang pots – and try to look big by raising your arms and opening your jacket. More than likely the bear will wander off. Whatever you do, don't corner the bear – give it room to escape. And never, ever, get between a mother bear and her cubs.

Backpackers should rent a bear-resistant food container ($5 per trip), available at wilderness centers, visitor centers, and

Sadly, many of Yosemite's bears are notorious for regularly breaking into vehicles and raiding campgrounds and backcountry campsites in search of food.

stores throughout the park. If confronted by a bear, don't drop your backpack – that's probably just what the bear wants, and it will only lead to more problems for other people (and, ultimately, the bear). Never run from a bear, either. You'll only trigger its instinct to chase, and you cannot outrun a bear.

You can and should fight back if a black bear attacks you. Use any means available – throw rocks and sticks or hit it with your gear. Fortunately, however, it's extremely rare for a bear to make an unprovoked attack on a human.

Getting There

Yosemite National Park is accessible year-round by road from the west side of the Sierra Nevada and in summer from the east side as well. There is no direct plane or train service, though connections by bus are available. The town of Merced, along Hwy 99 west of the park, is the main public transportation hub, linking Amtrak and Greyhound riders with the YARTS bus system, which serves the park. Frankly, however, despite the park service's desire to discourage cars, driving remains the easiest way to get to and travel about the park.

For information on transportation within Yosemite National Park, see Getting Around (p 84).

AIR

The major airports nearest to Yosemite are in Los Angeles (360 miles from the park), the Bay Area (San Francisco, Oakland, and San Jose, all about 200 miles away) and Reno (155 miles). You can also fly into Las Vegas (340 miles), Sacramento (191 miles), and the **Fresno-Yosemite International Airport** (☎ 559-621-4500; Ⓦ www.fly fresno.org), the closest airport served by major commercial airlines; it's only 90 miles from Yosemite. Mariposa, Merced, Modesto, and Lee Vining have small municipal and county airports.

TRAIN

Amtrak (☎ 800-872-7245; Ⓦ www.amtrak.com) runs several trains daily to the Central Valley city of Merced, where you can transfer to YARTS and VIA buses serving Yosemite Valley. For convenience, Amtrak offers a through-ticket to Yosemite, accepted by YARTS and VIA drivers – though it may be cheaper to purchase tickets separately. Prices below are fares to Merced only.

From most major airports, the first leg of Amtrak service is often by bus to the nearest train station. From San Francisco ($31 one-way) the bus goes to Emeryville, where you board a train to Merced; from Los Angeles ($32) the bus goes to Bakersfield; from Reno ($34) you transfer in Sacramento and/or Stockton (you can travel direct by train from Reno, but you must transfer in Martinez, and the cost rises to $101 one-way).

BUS

Buses represent the only public transportation into Yosemite, typically along Hwy 140. A one-way trip from Merced to the park takes 2.5 to three hours. Summer service is available from Mammoth Lakes east of Yosemite. Park admission is included in bus fare.

Public transportation is not available along Hwy 120 W or from Oakhurst, Fish Camp, or other points south of the park.

YARTS

The **Yosemite Area Regional Transportation System** (*YARTS*; ☎ *209-388-9589, 877-989-2787*; W *www.yarts.com*) operates two bus routes to Yosemite Valley: The most popular is the daily year-round service from Merced along Hwy 140; in summer there's also service along Hwy 120 E from Mammoth Lakes. Check with YARTS to confirm all fares, departure times, and stops listed below.

Reservations are not required, but it's best to obtain tickets before boarding. You can purchase tickets from area motels, the California Welcome Center in Merced, the visitor center in Mariposa, and the Yosemite Bug Lodge & Hostel in Midpines. Bus drivers also sell tickets. Bike racks are provided on most Merced buses. On the Mammoth route, those traveling with a bicycle or large backpack or requiring a child-protection seat or wheelchair lift or should call ahead.

Getting There **California & Nevada**

The route from Merced is managed by **VIA Adventures** (☎ 209-384-1315, 800-842-5463; W www.via-adventures.com), a private, Merced-based tour and charter bus company. Your bus may bear either a VIA or YARTS logo; either way, it's the same service and price. The route originates from the Merced Transpo Center (also the Greyhound terminal) at 16th St between N and O Sts. Buses depart daily at 7am, 8:45am, 10:30am, and 5:15pm, first stopping at the Merced Amtrak station at K and 23rd Sts. On the way to Yosemite Valley, buses stop at Mariposa, Midpines, El Portal, and other points. In the Valley, they stop at Yosemite Lodge, the visitor center, the Ahwahnee Hotel, and Curry Village. The 8:45am and 10:30am buses are most popular with tourists, and your driver may offer some narration. Return buses depart Yosemite Valley for Merced at 9:35am, 3:45pm, 4:20pm, 5:05pm, and 7:50pm. The round-trip fare from Merced to Yosemite is $20/14 adult/child; one-way tickets are half that, and prices are lower to and from closer stops.

YOSEMITE IN A DAY?

As crazy as it sounds, lots of people allot just one day to see Yosemite. Many depart the Bay Area on Amtrak or Greyhound and connect with the YARTS/VIA buses in Merced; they *can* actually make it to and from the park in a day, though the journey leaves them only about three or four hours in Yosemite Valley. We highly recommend you spend more time, but if that's all you've got, so be it. YARTS buses are timed to connect with Amtrak and Greyhound schedules and with a tram tour of Yosemite Valley.

Mammoth YARTS (☎ 800-626-6684), operated by Mammoth California Vacations, offers round-trip bus service between Yosemite Valley and Mammoth Lakes once daily in July and August and on Saturday and Sunday only in June and September. The bus departs Mammoth at 7am and Yosemite Valley at 5pm, stopping at June Lake, Lee Vining, Tuolumne Meadows, White Wolf, and Crane Flat. The round-trip fare from Yosemite Valley to Mammoth Lakes is $20/10 adult/child.

Greyhound

Greyhound (☎ 800-229-9424; W www.greyhound.com) buses run only as far as Merced, where passengers transfer to YARTS buses for the final leg into Yosemite. Buses travel to Merced from San Francisco ($28 one-way, five hours), Los Angeles ($32, seven hours), and many other locales.

Organized Tours

A handful of companies run bus tours from outside the park. Tour prices below include admission to Yosemite. For information on sightseeing tours inside the park, see p 85.

Yosemite Sightseeing Tours (☎ 559-877-8687; W www.yosemite tours.com) operates tours from Oakhurst, Fish Camp, and Bass Lake, all south of the park along Hwy 41. The "Deluxe Full-Day Tour" (adult/senior/child $66/62/33) is a nine-hour extravaganza that takes in Yosemite Valley, Glacier Point, and Mariposa Grove. The company also offers hiking tours.

VIA Adventures (☎ 800-842-5463, 209-384-1315; W www.via-adventures.com), which operates the YARTS buses along the Merced-Yosemite route, sells Yosemite tour packages as well. For $30, in addition to transportation costs (see YARTS section above), visitors get a narrated ride to the park, a box lunch, and a two-hour Yosemite Valley tour. VIA buses pick up and drop off passengers at Merced's Greyhound and Amtrak stations. For those staying overnight, VIA can also arrange lodging in the park, though at least 30 days notice is required.

Backpacker-friendly **Green Tortoise** (☎ 415-956-7500, 800-867-8647; W www.greentortoise.com; 494 Broadway, San Francisco, CA 94133) runs two-day ($130) and three-day ($170) trips to Yosemite from San Francisco. The price includes most meals. This is more adventure travel than standard bus tour: Travelers sleep on the converted bus or in campgrounds, cook collectively (that means pitching in to help), and choose among activities like hiking, swimming, or just hanging out. Schedules and prices change frequently, so call in advance to confirm trip details.

Incredible Adventures (☎ 415-751-7791, 800-777-8464; W www.incadventures.com), another San Francisco company with an adventure-travel focus, offers one-day ($93), two-day ($150), and three-day ($200) trips to Yosemite. Most meals are included, though help with preparation is required. You'll travel in large vans, and the company provides all cooking and camping gear (except sleeping bags).

CAR

Driving is by far the most popular way to get to and around Yosemite. This means lots of traffic, smog, and sometimes frustrating battles for parking spaces – woes of the urban world that, sadly, are not escapable here. A good compromise is to park in a central location and take advantage of free shuttle buses in Yosemite Valley, Tuolumne Meadows, and Mariposa Grove.

Gateway Corridors

Yosemite operates three entrance stations on the west side of the Sierra Nevada: the South Entrance on Hwy 41 (Wawona Rd) north of Fresno, convenient from southern California; the Arch Rock Entrance on Hwy 140 (El Portal Rd) east of Merced, convenient from northern California; and the Big Oak Flat Entrance on Hwy 120 W (Big Oak Flat Rd) east of Manteca, the quickest route from the Bay Area. Roads are generally kept open all year, though in winter (usually November to April), drivers may be required to carry tire chains.

The Tioga Pass Entrance, along Hwy 120 E (Tioga Rd) on the east side of the park, is open from about June to October, depending on when the snow is cleared. From Tioga Pass, drivers connect with Hwy 395 and points such as Reno and Death Valley National Park.

Car Rental

Rental cars are available in nearby cities and at all major airports, including those in the Bay Area, Los Angeles, Fresno, Las Vegas, and Reno. Prices fluctuate quite a bit with the seasons and varying demand. Ask about special weekend and weeklong rates, which often cut the daily cost considerably.

In Merced, you can rent from **Hertz** (☎ 209-722-4200, 800-654-3131; 1710 W Hwy 140) or **Enterprise** (☎ 209-722-1600, 800-736-8222; 1334 W Main St), both offering rates of about $30 a day.

Whether you're heading to Yosemite by car or bus, you'll travel along one of four primary approaches: Hwy 41 from Fresno, Hwy 140 from Merced, Hwy 120 W from the San Francisco Bay Area and Hwy 120 E from Lee Vining. Many of the old mining towns along these routes are worth a stop – they're great places to refuel your car and yourself or to stock up on groceries for your backcountry adventures. Towns closest to the park offer overflow accommodations and a variety of restaurant options. See our Places to Stay and Places to Eat chapters for listings.

YOSEMITE GATEWAY CORRIDORS

Highway 120 West
MAP 10

The drive from the San Francisco Bay Area to Yosemite Valley takes about 3.5 to 4 hours. Most Bay Area residents opt for this straightforward and relatively easy route.

Hwy 120 W begins at I-5 just west of Manteca, first crossing the farms, orchards and suburbs of the flat San Joaquin Valley. The road slowly enters the foothills before finally facing precipitous Priest Grade, which climbs some 1500ft over 2 miles and leads to the historic towns of Big Oak Flat and Groveland. At Priest Grade, you can choose the modern, circuitous route up or opt for Old Priest Grade Rd, a much steeper and narrower – though somewhat shorter – drive to the top.

Your best bet for finding last-minute camping supplies and a decent selection of groceries is Oakdale. Groveland, much cuter and closer to the park, is a nice place to spend the night in an old hotel, have a good sit-down dinner, or grab a quick shot of espresso before making your final run to the park border.

OAKDALE

Oakdale, the last bastion of cheap gas outside the park, features a good collection of chain stores and supermarkets. Most of the commercial establishments lie on the east end of town near Hwys 120 and 108, which join here. Downtown is older and offers a bit more character – mostly in the form of **antique shops**, of which you'll find about a dozen.

Along Hwy 120, **Big 5 Sporting Goods** (☎ *209-847-2537; 1596 F St; open 10am-9pm Mon-Fri, 9am-9pm Sat, 10am-7pm Sun*) can help if you forgot your sleeping bag, camp stove, or a clean pair of socks. It's about a mile east of downtown, near the well-stocked Richland Market and the Oakdale Rodeo grounds. The rodeo takes place every April; if you miss it, you can still visit the **Oakdale Cowboy Museum** (☎ *209-847-5163; 355 East F St; admission $1; open 10am-2pm Mon-Fri*).

KNIGHTS FERRY

This tiny, historic town, about a mile north of Hwy 120/108, sits alongside the Stanislaus River, its old buildings tucked beneath trees and hidden from the rush of the world. Though tourists have discovered the place, it's not overly quaint and still feels like a secret. Stop for drinks at the **Knights Ferry Resort** (☎ 209-881-3349) or even dinner and an overnight stay if you've got the time. Signs point the way about 11 miles east of Oakdale.

Aside from the river itself (which attracts boaters, anglers, and rafters), the main attractions here include a **Civil War reenactment** each spring and the 330ft-long **covered bridge** built in 1863. The bridge lies a short walk from a small riverside park that's good for a picnic. You'll also find several historic buildings and the **Knights Ferry Information Center** (☎ 209-881-3517; open 8am-4pm Mon-Fri, 10am-2pm Sat-Sun, closed daily noon-1pm), run by the Army Corps of Engineers.

GROVELAND

The old mining boomtown of Groveland lines both sides of Hwy 120, about 2 miles west of Yosemite. Together with nearby Big Oak Flat, it was originally called Savage's Diggings, after James Savage, who found gold here in 1848. Savage went on to tangle with local Indians over mining rights, in the process becoming one of the first white men to see Yosemite Valley. In 1875, the town name changed to Groveland.

The mining years were followed by a construction boom in the early 20th century. Workers poured into town to work on the dam and water project at Hetch Hetchy, staying at the Groveland Hotel and Hotel Charlotte, among other places.

THE "BIG OAK"

About a mile east of the top of Priest Grade, the rundown former mining town of **Big Oak Flat** doesn't have much to offer these days besides a few old buildings. But it does occupy a small place in history, as the source of the "big oak" that gave the town – and the historic road into Yosemite – its name. The tree itself is long gone, however, having suffered many trials and tribulations, including fire, storms, and damage from overeager miners.

Today the town is a major draw for tourists on their way to the park. Historic hotels, restaurants, espresso counters, and what's claimed to be the oldest continuously operating saloon in the state (the funky **Iron Door Saloon**) cluster together alongside Hwy 120, comprising Groveland's attractive old downtown.

About 8 miles east of Groveland, the USFS **Groveland Ranger Station** (☎ 209-962-7825; 24545 Hwy 120; open 8am-5:30pm daily in summer, reduced hours fall to spring) offers information on camping, rafting, fishing, and other activities in the surrounding Stanislaus National Forest and nearby Tuolumne Wild and Scenic River Area. If you arrive after hours, check the big national forest map posted outside for the location of local campgrounds.

Highway 140
MAP 11

Both Hwy 120 and Hwy 41 may be open during the winter, but Hwy 140 is Yosemite's "All-Year Highway," a nickname given when the road first opened to cars in 1926. Its lower elevation makes it easier to keep the road clear in bad weather, thus it remains the chief year-round route into the park.

The drive between Merced and Yosemite is very pleasant. The highway meanders past rolling foothills of gold and green, rich in the warm light of summer sunsets. It climbs to meet Mariposa, the last "real" town on the route, and tiny Midpines before dropping into the magnificent Merced River Canyon. From here, the highway follows the Merced River through El Portal to the park's Arch Rock Entrance. The route also parallels the bed of the long-defunct Yosemite Valley Railroad, which operated from 1907 to 1945.

A major transportation hub, Merced is the end of the line for Amtrak train and Greyhound bus passengers. From here, passengers can take the YARTS (Yosemite Area Regional Transportation System) bus along Hwy 140. See Getting There & Away under Merced, below.

MERCED

At the junction of Hwys 140 and 99 in the central San Joaquin Valley, Merced (population 63,893) is about two hours' drive from Yosemite – too far to qualify as a home base while visiting the park. That aside, it is a convenient stopover for those passing through by bus, train, or car, with plenty of cheap lodgings, including a good hostel. Hwy 140 heads east toward Yosemite from an exit off Hwy 99 about a mile south of downtown.

Downtown Merced lies east of Hwy 99 along Main St, between R St and Martin Luther King Jr Way. The **California Welcome Center** (☎ 209-384-2791, 800-446-5353; 710 W 16th St), adjacent to the bus depot, has local maps ($2), information on Yosemite, and coupon books offering local motel discounts.

While a little rundown on the edges, Merced's downtown can be quite pleasant during the day, with tree-lined streets, Victorian homes, a handful of movie theaters, and several antique shops. A popular **farmers' market** operates downtown every Thursday evening and Saturday morning from April to October.

The main attraction, though, is the 1874 **Merced County Courthouse**. Surrounded by a lovely parklike square, it's the town's architectural patriarch, the only survivor among eight county courthouses designed by Albert A Bennett. Inside is the excellent **Courthouse Museum** (☎ 209-723-2401; free admission; open 1pm-4pm Wed-Sun), well worth a quick peek.

If you have a little more time on your hands, check out the field full of restored military aircraft at the **Castle Air Museum** (☎ 209-723-2178; 5050 Santa Fe Dr; adult/child $7/5; open 10am-4pm daily) in Atwater, about 6 miles north of Merced.

Getting There & Away

YARTS (☎ 209-388-9589, 877-989-2787; W www.yarts.com) buses run between Merced and Yosemite Valley, stopping in most towns and key spots along the way. They depart daily from several Merced locations, including the **Merced Transpo Center** (16th St at N St) and the **Amtrak station** (24th St at K St). See p 68 for details and ticket information.

Greyhound (☎ 800-229-9424) also operates from the Transpo Center, while **Amtrak** (☎ 209-722-6862, 800-872-7245) passengers transfer in Merced to reach the park.

MARIPOSA

Before you enter the park, stop in the former gold rush settlement of Mariposa for any last-minute groceries or a full night's sleep in a comfortable, clean motel that's not terribly overpriced.

The largest of the state's original 27 counties, Mariposa County was founded in 1850. The town of Mariposa was named the county seat a year later. Today the town feels like a cross between a mountain community and a wannabe tourist haven. On the one hand, it's filled with antique shops, cute boutiques and upscale restaurants; yet it's also home to ragged muscle cars and colorful characters. But it's a safe and, for the most part, charming place – the down-to-earth element helps to counterbalance a touristy vibe that might otherwise get too cute too fast.

It's filled with antique shops, cute boutiques and upscale restaurants; yet it's also home to ragged muscle cars and colorful characters.

Hwy 49 joins Hwy 140 at the south end of town, then splits off again at the north end, heading toward Coulterville and Sonora. At the intersection, the **Mariposa County Visitor Center** (☎ 209-966-2456; 5158 N Hwy 140; open 7am-8pm Mon-Sat, 8am-5pm Sun in summer, 8am-5pm Mon-Sat in winter) can supply a good county map ($1.50) and loads of brochures on both Yosemite and Mariposa.

The town straddles Hwy 140, though some historic buildings lie one block east on Bullion St, including the **Mariposa County Courthouse** (Bullion St at 8th St), a cute wooden building worth a quick look. Built in 1854, it's the state's oldest active courthouse.

Rock hounds should drive to the Mariposa County Fairgrounds, 2 miles south of town on Hwy 49, to see the 13-pound "Fricot Nugget" and other gems and machinery at the **California State Mining & Mineral Museum** (☎ 209-742-7625; admission $1; open 10am-6pm daily in summer, 10am-4pm Wed-Mon in spring and fall, closed in winter).

MIDPINES

There's not much to see or do in Midpines, a rural community about 25 miles west of Yosemite's Arch Rock Entrance. The small **Midpines Country Store** marks the center of "town," which is actually spread thin over several miles along Hwy 140.

The best reason for travelers to stop is the popular **Yosemite Bug Lodge & Hostel**, a few miles east of the Midpines Store; it offers cheap guest rooms, Yosemite advice, mountain bike rentals, and the best meals you'll find anywhere along this highway. For more information, see our Places to Stay and Places to Eat chapters.

From Midpines, Hwy 140 drops down into the beautiful Merced River Canyon. On the north side of the road near the Merced River, you'll find the small **Briceburg Visitor Center** (☎ *209-379-9414, 916-985-4474; open 11am-6pm Fri, 9am-6pm Sat-Sun in summer only)*. The lovely granite building, originally a tavern and restaurant, dates from 1927 and now belongs to the Bureau of Land Management (BLM). Here you can get local camping, hiking, and recreation information.

EL PORTAL

Once the terminus of the Yosemite Valley Railroad, El Portal is now home to a collection of gateway services (motels, restaurants, a gas station, and small store) and NPS administrative offices. Just west of the Arch Rock Entrance and about 14 miles west of Yosemite Village, the town is curiously narrow and long, stretching 7 miles alongside the Merced River.

Adjacent to the store, El Portal Rd leads one block north to a **post office** (*open 8:30am-5pm Mon-Fri*) and a small outdoor **Yosemite Valley Railroad exhibit** that includes railcars and a locomotive.

In the parking lot of the Yosemite View Lodge, you'll find the **Gateway Visitor Center** (*open 8:30am-10:30am and 5pm-9:30pm daily)*, a combination gift shop, tourist resource center, and home base for **Yosemite Guides** (☎ *209-379-2231, 877-425-3366;* W *www.yosemite guides.com)*, a private company that hires local experts to lead a variety of guided hiking, birding, fly-fishing, and other tours of Yosemite. The sunset walk on Sentinel Dome is $55 per person, including a picnic dinner.

ROADSIDE ATTRACTIONS

On your way in or out, try one of these roadside highlights, which range from the historically significant to the down-right wacky. All are free or close to it.

✔ **Merced County Courthouse** (Merced)
✔ **Mariposa County Courthouse** (Mariposa)
✔ **Fricot Nugget** (Mariposa)
✔ **Yosemite Valley Railroad exhibit** (El Portal)
✔ **Teddy Bear Hospital** (Oakhurst)
✔ **Upside-Down House** (Lee Vining)

Highway 41
MAP 12

If you're heading up from Los Angeles (six hours away) or other Southern California points, this is the highway you'll likely wind up driving. From Fresno – where there's no shortage of restaurants, motels, and shopping malls – it's about a 60-mile drive north through busy Oakhurst to the park's South Entrance Station near Wawona. Hwy 41 is generally open year-round, though in winter you should be careful when nearing Oakhurst – as the highway descends into town, it can get quite slippery.

OAKHURST

Oakhurst is one of the least charming towns along any of the gateway corridors. But value and convenience, not charm, are its strong points. If you're on your way to Yosemite or other scenic points in the area – such as Bass Lake, the Nelder Grove of giant sequoias, or the Sierra Vista National Scenic Byway (see the Beyond Yosemite chapter) – it makes great sense to spend the night here, as you can stay in a (relatively) affordable motel and grab a halfway (but only halfway) decent dinner just down the street.

The town was first settled in 1873, when the area was known as Fresno Flats, now the name of a local historic park. It didn't grow into much until recently, though modern Oakhurst is still not much to look at. The town is basically a sprawl of tourist-oriented businesses along either side of Hwy 41, near the point where the road meets the southern terminus of Hwy 49, which heads north to Mariposa, Sonora, and the rest of the Gold Country.

The town was first settled in 1873, when the area was known as Fresno Flats.

A great place to gather information on Yosemite National Park, as well as the local area, is the **Yosemite Sierra Visitors Bureau** (☎ 559-683-4636; 41969 Hwy 41; open 8:30am-5pm Mon-Sat, 9am-1pm Sun), about a half-mile north of the Hwy 41/Hwy 49 intersection. Loaded with brochures, the place also sells maps of the area. The friendly staff issue wilderness permits (for points outside Yosemite only) and patiently dole out helpful advice to the seemingly endless stream of Yosemite tourists.

If you're in town for the night, there are a few diversions. Drives to Bass Lake (see p 207) or along parts of the Sierra Vista Scenic Byway (see p 206) are definitely worthwhile if you've got the time. You can also take a steam-train ride (see Fish Camp) or catch a movie at the **Met Cinema** (☎ 559-683-1234; 40015 Hwy 49), in Raley's shopping plaza at the corner of Hwys 41 and 49. If you've got kids ages two to 12, then the **Children's Museum of the Sierra** (☎ 559-658-5656; W www.childrensmuseumofthe-sierra.org; 49269 Golden Oak Dr; admission $2) can entertain them with its hands-on exhibits, including a Castle Room, a theater, and a **teddy bear hospital**, where kids can dress in scrubs and study x-rays.

Fresno Flats Historic Park is a collection of old buildings that were brought to this suburban setting beginning in 1975. It's a nice distraction if you like cute, pieced-together villages of restored historic buildings – and the folks do dress up in costume once in a while, parading about and giving the place some life. To reach the park from Hwy 41, head east on Rd 426, then turn left on Rd 427 (School Rd).

FISH CAMP

You won't find much at Fish Camp but a bend in the road, a small general store, a post office, and a handful of lodges and B&Bs. Many of the latter, however, boast loads more personality than the pedestrian motels found in Oakhurst, so it's actually a destination worth considering. Plus the town is only two miles from Yosemite's southernmost entrance, which means you can use Fish Camp as a base while visiting the park.

By far the biggest and boldest attraction in town is the **Yosemite Mountain Sugar Pine Railroad** (☎ 559-683-7273; W *www.ymsprr.com; 56001 Hwy 41)*, at the south end of Fish Camp next to the Narrow Gauge Inn. Tours on either the old "Logger" steam train or the Jenny railcar (adults $9-13, kids $5-6) take place several times daily between March and October. Call for reservations or just pop in. The Moonlight Special (adult/child $36/20), on selected Saturday and Wednesday nights, includes a steak dinner, live music, and a reenacted train robbery; reservations are essential.

Highway 120 East
MAP 13

Hwy 120 between Lee Vining and Tioga Pass is the most epic route in or out of Yosemite – and one of the most stunning anywhere in the Sierra. The roadbed is scratched into the side of steep, dramatic **Lee Vining Canyon**, with sheer drop-offs, rugged rock walls, and sweeping views. It's incredible to witness how quickly and significantly the scenery changes from one side of Tioga Pass to the other. Once you cross the pass heading east and start downhill, you'll leave behind the lush grasses and tall pines of Tuolumne and Dana Meadows for the dry, sagebrush-coated landscape of the Great Basin Desert.

Due to heavy snowfall, this magnificent drive is only open for several months a year. Most maps of California mark this route as "closed in winter," but winter is a loose term – the pass shuts down as early as October and doesn't reopen until late May or even June, depending on the length of the snow season.

Even if you don't arrive or depart along this route, it's worth a quick drive to see the change in landscape – and also

Hwy 120 between Lee Vining and Tioga Pass is the most epic route in or out of Yosemite – and one of the most stunning anywhere in the Sierra.

to catch a glimpse of Mono Lake, a massive expanse of saltwater at the very edge of the Great Basin Desert.

At its eastern terminus, Hwy 120 meets Hwy 395, a major north-south roadway along the eastern Sierra. There's lots to explore here (see Excursions), but if you're just looking for a quick spot to eat or spend the night, turn north into the tiny town of Lee Vining, which guards the west shore of Mono Lake.

LEE VINING CANYON

Tioga Rd was initially built in 1883 in order to supply a silver mine in Bennettville, near Tioga Pass. The mine, however, failed soon after, and the road never served its intended purpose. Decades later, with Yosemite becoming an increasingly popular tourist destination, the road was rehabilitated for the sake of tourism. It was finally rebuilt, rerouted, and widened in the 1960s. As you follow the road up or down, you'll find historical displays in the numerous turnouts along the way. Each is worth a stop, if only to gape at the impressive views (those with vertigo might want to stay in the car). Numerous campgrounds and one historic resort line Hwy 120 between Tioga Pass and Hwy 395.

LEE VINING

This small town along the western shore of Mono Lake comes fully alive during the summer, as it's geared heavily toward tourists. There's more than enough kitsch to go around, though there is something almost charming and old-fashioned about Lee Vining's souvenir shops, cowboy outfitters, and old roadside motels. You'll find several good lodging options, though they often fill up fast in summer. Gas stations, like local motel rooms, can be expensive – sometimes even higher than inside the park. You'll find ATMs at the Mono Market and inside the Mobil gas station at the corner of Hwys 395 and 120.

Lee Vining is a great base for exploring gorgeous Mono Lake (see p 202). For information on the lake and the eastern Sierra in general, stop by the excellent **Mono Basin Scenic Area Visitor Center** (☎ 760-647-3044; open 9am-4:30pm daily, reduced hours in winter), a half-mile north of town along Hwy 395.

In town, the **Mono Lake Information Center** (☎ 760-647-6595; W www.mono lake.org; Hwy 395 at 3rd St; open 9am-10pm daily in summer, 9am-7pm daily in spring and fall, 9am-5pm daily in winter) is another excellent resource, with a large bookstore, displays on the lake's history, and also public Internet access ($2 for 15 minutes).

Before you leave, take a quick look at the **Upside-Down House**, a kooky tourist attraction created by silent film actress Nellie Bly O'Bryan. Originally situated along Tioga Rd, it now resides in a park in front of the tiny **Mono Basin Historical Society Museum** (admission $1; 10am-5pm Mon-Tues and Thur-Sat, noon-5pm Sun in summer). To find it, turn east on 1st St and drive one block to Mattley Ave.

NPS PHOTOGRAPHS

Between three and four million people descend on Yosemite National Park each year. Most arrive with high expectations, and few leave disappointed. The park's 1169 square miles boast mighty scenery, comprising craggy peaks, sheer cliffs, massive granite domes, deep valleys, tall waterfalls, and trees that kiss the clouds.

EXPERIENCING YOSEMITE

Yosemite Valley is a wonder in itself, an oasis of river, groves, and meadows hemmed in on seemingly all sides by sheer cliffs that soar more than 3000ft overhead. Visitors stand in awe of such famous features as El Capitan, Yosemite Falls, and Half Dome. At dawn and dusk, many are drawn to Glacier Point, a spectacular viewpoint some 3200ft above the Valley floor.

Beyond the Valley, more than 800 miles of trails offer hikers a serene backcountry experience. To the northeast, Yosemite's high country is an alpine wilderness of flower-filled meadows, conifer forest, winding streams, and shimmering glacial lakes. Tuolumne Meadows, off Tioga Rd (open in summer only), is the high-country hub, sprawled out beneath the smooth domes and jagged peaks of the 13,000ft Sierra Crest. Like the air, the crowds up here are noticeably thinner, making it a great spot for those seeking solitude.

Anchoring the west side is the Hetch Hetchy Reservoir and O'Shaughnessy Dam, which holds back the Tuolumne River. This is the starting point for long hikes into the park's quiet northern reaches. Environmental controversies aside, it's an awesome sight and the least-visited of the areas reachable by car.

Activity to the south centers on Wawona, the park's historical heart, reflected in a lovely 1879 hotel and other restored buildings. Adjacent is the Mariposa Grove of giant sequoias. First-time visitors to the grove are astounded by these magnificent trees, among the world's largest living things.

When You Arrive

Yosemite's entrance fee is $20 per vehicle and $10 for people on foot, bicycle, or horseback; it's valid for seven contiguous days. A one-year pass to Yosemite is $40; a one-year pass to *all* national parks is $50. Either pass can be purchased at any park gate.

The park is open 24 hours every day of the year. If you arrive at night and the gate is unattended, simply pay the entrance fee when you leave. Keep your receipt, as you must show it every time you leave or reenter the park.

Upon entering the park, you'll receive an illustrated National Park Service map and copies of the *Yosemite Guide* (a biannual newspaper with park news, sightseeing tips, and useful background information) and the biweekly *Yosemite Today* (with current ranger programs, park activities, opening hours of visitor services, and a shuttle bus map and schedule). Save both – they come in handy.

For recorded park information, campground availability, and road and weather conditions, call the National Park Service's main Yosemite information line at ☎ 209-372-0200. The NPS also maintains an excellent, comprehensive website at Ⓦ www .nps.gov/yose. For reservations and information about lodging and other types of services (horseback riding, sightseeing tours, etc.), call Yosemite Concession Services (YCS) at ☎ 209-252-4848 or go to Ⓦ www.yosemitepark.com.

ORIENTATION

Though the park encompasses a vast swath of land, more than 94% of it is designated wilderness and, therefore, inaccessible by car. Elevations range from below 3000ft at Hetch Hetchy to 13,114ft atop Mt Lyell, the park's tallest peak.

The most popular (and crowded) region is Yosemite Valley, a small sliver at the heart of the park. Along with spectacular scenery, you'll find the largest concentration of visitor services, including lodges, campgrounds, stores, and restaurants.

About 55 miles northeast of the Valley, near the east end of Tioga Rd, is Tuolumne Meadows (elevation 8600ft), the focal point of Yosemite's high country and summertime home to a small hub of visitor services.

Crane Flat sits at the junction of Tioga and Big Oak Flat Rds. You'll find limited visitor services here and to the north at the park's Big Oak Flat Entrance. Between Crane Flat and Tuolumne Meadows is a stretch we've labeled "Along Tioga Rd," which covers camping, hiking, and other activities along this section of Hwy 120. North of Tioga Rd lies the park's vast northern wilderness, accessible only by serious backpackers. To the west, a short drive from the Big Oak Flat Entrance, is Hetch Hetchy Reservoir.

Perched 3200ft above Yosemite Valley, Glacier Point is the park's prime viewpoint, reachable during summer via trail from the Valley or by car along Glacier Point Rd. Also on Glacier Point Rd is the Badger Pass Ski Area, open in winter only.

Thirty-six miles south of Yosemite Valley is Wawona, home to a historic hotel and other services for those visiting the giant sequoias of nearby Mariposa Grove. The southeastern corner of the park harbors another large wilderness area.

Entrances

The park has four main gates: Big Oak Flat Entrance (Hwy 120) and Arch Rock Entrance (Hwy 140) from the west, Tioga Pass Entrance (Hwy 120) from the east, and South Entrance (Hwy 41) near Wawona. The only one open year-round is Arch Rock, though Big Oak Flat and Wawona are open when weather permits. Tioga Pass (9945ft) is the highest roadway across the Sierra, usually open between early June and early November, though the dates vary every year.

Major Roads

Hwy 140 runs from the west directly into Yosemite Valley and offers year-round access to the park. Hwy 120 also enters the park from the west, where it becomes Big Oak Flat Rd. Tioga Rd is the only road that crosses the park, running from Crane Flat to Tioga Pass. Hwy 41 enters from the south, passing Wawona and the turnoff for Glacier Point before meeting Hwy 140. Glacier Point Rd runs east from Hwy 41 to Glacier Point.

INFORMATION

The park's two major **visitor centers** are in **Yosemite Valley** (☎ 209-372-0299; open 8am-6pm daily in summer, reduced hours off-season) and **Tuolumne Meadows** (open approximately 9am-6pm daily July-Aug, 9am-5pm in spring and fall). At both, rangers can answer questions and suggest suitable hiking trails, activities and sights. The centers also offer excellent displays on park history and the local environment and a range of maps, hiking and climbing guides, geology and ecology books, and gift items.

In addition, two smaller **information stations** operate at **Big Oak Flat** (☎ 209-379-1899; open 9am-5pm daily Apr-Oct, until 6pm midsummer) and **Wawona** (☎ 209-375-9531; open 8:30am-4:30pm daily late May-early Oct), the latter inside a building labeled Hill's Studio next to the hotel. Less elaborate than the visitor centers, they're both still good places to ask questions, get your bearings, and purchase useful books and maps.

For information on **campground reservation offices**, see the Places to Stay chapter.

Wilderness Centers

Wilderness use permits are required for all overnight backcountry trips – though not for day hikes. These can be obtained in advance or in person on a first-come, first-served basis at one of five locations in the park. Go to the station nearest your trailhead:

Yosemite Valley Wilderness Center (open 7:30am-6pm daily in summer, 8am-5pm daily in fall and spring, closed in winter)

Wawona Information Station (open 8:30am-4:30pm daily June-Sept)

Big Oak Flat Information Station (open 8am-5pm daily June-Sept)

Hetch Hetchy Entrance Station (open during daylight, approximately 7am-8pm daily in summer, 8am-5pm daily in winter)

Tuolumne Meadows Wilderness Center (open 7:30am-6pm daily midsummer, 8am-5pm daily in late spring and early fall, closed usually Oct-May)

At the wilderness centers in Yosemite Valley and Tuolumne Meadows – and to a lesser extent at the stations in Wawona and Big Oak Flat – hikers can buy maps and guidebooks, check current weather and trail conditions, get helpful tips on planning and packing, and rent the all-important bear-proof food canisters ($5). Strongly recommended at all times, the canisters are legally required on the High Sierra Camps loop and at all backcountry sites above 9600ft.

Bookstores

Almost every park store, from the gift shop at Yosemite Lodge to the convenience stores at Wawona and Crane Flat, offers limited stocks of books and park maps. For the best selection of information about the park and Sierra Nevada region, visit the **Yosemite Association Bookstore** (☎ 209-379-2648; W www.yosemitestore.com), inside the Valley visitor center.

The **Ansel Adams Gallery** also carries a great selection of books, including fine art and photography volumes. Peruse the **Happy Isles Nature Center** for nature books. Those seeking hiking maps and guides should head to the **Curry Village Mountain Shop**.

In Tuolumne Meadows, the best places to find books, guides, and maps are the visitor center, the **Tuolumne Meadows Sport Shop** and the **Wilderness Center**.

You'll also find books and maps at the information stations in Wawona and Big Oak Flat. News junkies gravitate to a row of coin-operated **newspaper** boxes outside the store at the Housekeeping Camp in Yosemite Valley.

Policies & Regulations

WILDLIFE

There's one main rule regarding Yosemite's wildlife: Don't feed the bears ... or deer, chipmunks, raccoons, skunks, marmots, and mountain lions. Giving wild animals treats may seem cute, but they learn to associate humans with food. That can lead to trouble, especially for the bears, who are often killed if they become serious nuisances. Do you want that on your conscience? Of course not. Nor do you want a bite from a chipmunk or other small critter, which may not be as polite and cute when it returns for seconds.

FOOD STORAGE

Store *all* food and scented items – cosmetics, toothpaste, soda cans, and any other food-related trash – in the bear-proof storage lockers provided at each campsite and in major parking lots. Don't leave anything in your car – bears have a powerful sense of smell and are adept at breaking into locked vehicles. They also recognize coolers and grocery bags, so even if these are empty and clean, at least cover them with a blanket. Failure to follow these rules can lead to a citation.

When cooking at your campsite, don't leave the locker hanging open and the food spread out. That's an open dinner invitation. Treat the locker like a fridge – pull out only what you need, then shut (and latch) the door.

For backpackers, it's strongly recommended (and in some areas mandatory) that you rent one of the cylindrical bear-resistant containers for food storage ($5 per trip). Available at wilderness centers and stores throughout the park, they weigh just under 3lb each and, when carefully packed, can store three- to five-days' worth of food for one or two people. As with the lockers, keep the canisters closed when cooking.

Fires in Yosemite campgrounds are allowed only within established fire rings or barbecue pits.

CAMPFIRES

Everyone loves a campfire, but take note of a few rules. Fires in Yosemite campgrounds are allowed only within established fire rings or barbecue pits. Wood gathering is illegal in the Valley, so you'll have to buy firewood. To improve air quality, campfires are only allowed between 5pm and 10pm from May 1 through October 15.

Those staying in campgrounds outside the Valley are allowed to gather wood, but it must be downed (on the ground) and dead. It's probably easier to simply buy a bundle ($5-7).

Backcountry campers, take note: Campfires are forbidden in sequoia groves or in the high country above 9600ft.

Make sure fires are *completely* out. Stir the fire and coals with water a half-hour before going to bed or leaving the site, then hold your hand close to check for any lingering hot spots.

Finally, be aware that regulations are stiffened in high winds or extremely dry conditions.

WILDERNESS PERMITS & REGULATIONS

Nearly 95% of Yosemite is officially designated as wilderness, and anyone can enjoy this vast backcountry with a proper wilderness permit. These are required for all overnight backcountry trips, though not for day hikes. As the park issues some 17,000 permits per year, a quota system is in effect for each trailhead. You must spend your first night in the area noted on your permit – from there, you're free to roam. The park service calls this an "unconfined recreational experience."

Permits are available either in advance (between six months and two days ahead) or on a first-come, first-served basis (the day of, or day before, your hike) from the nearest wilderness center. You can make reservations by phone (☎ *209-372-0740*), online (Ⓦ *www.nps.gov/yose/wilderness*), or through the mail *(Wilderness Reservations, PO. Box 545, Yosemite, CA 95389)*. Make checks payable to the Yosemite Association; credit cards are also accepted.

Rangers can offer guidance about starting points and trail conditions, but they aren't travel agents, so don't expect hand-holding. Study your maps, read your guidebooks, and decide where you want to go *before* registering for a permit. Always have a backup plan, as some spots do fill very quickly. Permit reservations are recommended for popular trailheads (Little Yosemite Valley, for example) and are accepted (with a $5 processing fee per person) for hikes between May and September.

For updated trail conditions, call the park information number at ☎ 209-372-0200. For general information on backcountry hiking and camping, peruse the park's excellent website at Ⓦ www.nps.gov/yose/wilderness.

The use of bear-resistant food containers is required at all backcountry campsites above 9600ft and on the High Sierra Camps loop. Campfires are forbidden above 9600ft. Where available, use preexisting campsites to reduce impact, and camp at least 100ft from water sources and trails. Never put soap in the water, even "biodegradable" types. Properly filter all drinking water or boil it for three to five minutes, and don't burn trash. Pack out everything you bring, including toilet paper.

Getting Around

DRIVING

The park speed limit is 45mph, except in Yosemite Valley, where it drops to 35mph. Truth is, you'll likely drive slower than that due to traffic in the Valley and the multitude of RVs and trailers straining to make it up steep grades. For drivers of those behemoths, there are numerous pullouts along major park roads. Be considerate and move over to let faster drivers pass.

Gas & Repairs

You'll find gas stations in Crane Flat, Wawona, and, in summer, Tuolumne Meadows. The stations generally close after dark, but you can gas up anytime by paying at the pump with a credit card. Gas is not available in Yosemite Valley.

For auto repairs, try the **Village Garage** (☎ 209-372-8320) in Yosemite Village across from the Village Store. Towing is available 24 hours.

Parking
Most trailheads have free parking areas where you can leave your vehicle for several days. Make sure to put all food and scented items in a bear box.

In Yosemite Valley, backpackers must park in the hikers' parking area between Curry Village and Happy Isles. Day-use visitors can use the lots either at Curry Village or near Yosemite Village and take the free shuttle bus around the Valley.

You'll find a number of parking areas in Tuolumne Meadows, White Wolf, Crane Flat, Hetch Hetchy, Glacier Point, and Wawona. Overnight parking is not permitted on Tioga or Glacier Point Rds after October 15.

PUBLIC TRANSIT
While public transportation within the park is fairly limited, it is available in certain areas. Note that dates and times vary somewhat each year. Call ☎ 209-372-1240 for an updated schedule or stop by the tour desk in the Yosemite Lodge lobby.

The free **Yosemite Valley Visitor Shuttle** stops year-round at 21 numbered locations, from Happy Isles and Mirror Lake in the east (both inaccessible by car) to Yosemite Lodge in the west, with stops at such popular spots as the Ahwahnee Hotel, Curry Village, Lower Yosemite Fall, and the visitor center. Buses operate 7am to 10pm daily at 10- to 20-minute intervals. This excellent, easy-to-use service is a likely forerunner of future park transportation plans. For a route map, see *Yosemite Today*.

The free **Tuolumne Meadows Shuttle Bus** plies Tioga Rd daily from about mid-June to mid-September (the exact schedule varies annually). The shuttle travels between Tuolumne Meadows Lodge and Olmsted Point, starting at the lodge at 7am and operating at roughly 30-minute intervals until 5:30pm (be sure to check at the visitor center or call ☎ 209-372-1240 for the current sched-

> ✔ **TIP**
>
> Planning a road trip through the park? Pick up a copy of the *Yosemite Road Guide* ($3.50), a booklet published by the Yosemite Association and sold in park bookstores. Descriptions of sights and stops along the park's major roadways correspond to the numbered roadside markers you may have seen and wondered about. For instance, Tioga Pass is at T39, Wawona Campground at W8, and Yosemite Falls at V3. The book also includes lots of great park history.

ule). The last eastbound shuttle usually departs Olmsted Point at 6:30pm. Another shuttle travels between Tuolumne Meadows Lodge and Tioga Pass, departing the lodge at 9am, noon, 3pm, and 5pm.

From spring through fall, a free shuttle runs between the Wawona Hotel and Mariposa Grove. Visitors can use it anytime, but it's mandatory when the small parking lot at the grove is full (park personnel will divert cars).

For information on public transit into and out of the park, see Getting There (p 68).

HIKER & SIGHTSEEING BUSES
From about mid-June to mid-September, buses run from Yosemite Valley to Glacier Point and Tuolumne Meadows, stopping at various points along the way. These are

handy for sightseers as well as hikers, who disembark at elevation and follow any number of trails back down to the Valley.

The **Tuolumne Meadows Tour & Hikers' Bus** (☎ 209-372-1240) travels between the Valley and Tuolumne. The bus departs daily from Curry Village at 8am, from Yosemite Village at 8:05am, and from Yosemite Lodge at 8:20am and stops at Crane Flat, White Wolf, May Lake Junction, Olmsted Point, and Tenaya Lake. It arrives at the Tuolumne Meadows Store about 10:20am and Tuolumne Meadows Lodge at 10:30am. On the return trip, the bus leaves Tuolumne Meadows Lodge at 2:05pm and arrives at Curry Village at 4pm, making all the same stops in between. You can also flag the bus for pickup from any trailhead or ask the driver to drop you at a trailhead along the way.

Reservations are strongly recommended; call up to one week in advance or stop by the tour desk at Yosemite Lodge. Fares vary according to your stop From Yosemite Valley, a round-trip adult ticket to Tuolumne Meadows costs $23; children (ages five to 12) ride for half-price.

To get from the Valley to Tuolumne and other points along Tioga Rd, you can also ride on **YARTS buses**. For schedules and details, see p 69.

YCS runs a four-hour **Glacier Point Sightseeing Tour** (☎ 209-372-1240; round-trip adult/senior/child $30/26/17). If you're hiking back down, fares are half-price. Trips depart from Yosemite Lodge at 8:30am, 10am, and 1:30pm daily from June to October. The eight-hour **Grand Tour** (adult/senior/child $55/48/28) includes both Glacier Point and Mariposa Grove, departing Yosemite Lodge at 8:45am daily from about June to October. YCS also offers a two-hour **Valley Floor Tour** (adult/senior/child $21/19/16) and **Moonlight Tours** on selected evenings; call for schedules and prices. You can also take a one-hour, open-air **Big Trees Tour** (☎ 209-375-1621; adult/senior/child $11/9/6) amid the giant sequoias in Mariposa Grove.

YOSEMITE VALLEY
Map 2

The Valley is what most people come to Yosemite to see. It is undoubtedly the single busiest stretch in the entire Sierra Nevada, with traffic jams, unbearable crowds, and commercial development. But if you find yourself amid the crowds and wonder why you ever bothered, just look around you. Rising some 3000ft from the Valley floor are sheer granite cliffs, vast domes and thundering waterfalls – a truly astounding array of spectacular natural wonders.

Spend a day by car or on foot getting acquainted with the highlights. In addition to landmarks listed below, look on the south side for **Cathedral Rocks** and **Cathedral Spires**, near Bridalveil Fall, and **Sentinel Rock** and **Sentinel Dome**, a little farther east. At the Valley's east end is Half Dome and, immediately south, **Liberty Cap**. Just north of Half Dome, deep and rugged **Tenaya Canyon** runs northeast toward Tuolumne Meadows. On the canyon's west side sit **North Dome** and the **Royal Arches**, while 9926ft **Clouds Rest** rises to the canyon's east. East of Yosemite Falls is **Lost Arrow**, and to the falls' west are the **Three Brothers**, the tallest being 7779ft **Eagle Peak**, reached via the Yosemite Falls Trail. Just west of El Capitan is 1612ft **Ribbon Fall**. Most active in late spring, it's the tallest single-tier, uninterrupted waterfall in the park or, for that matter, North America.

Open year-round, the Valley is most crowded in midsummer and on key holiday weekends. To catch warm weather yet avoid the worst crowds, you're better off visiting in May, June, September, or October. Winters are quiet, with a soft blanket of snow on the cliffs and trees.

ORIENTATION

Meadow-carpeted Yosemite Valley is 7 miles long and a half-mile wide. The Merced River meanders down its middle, within sight of Half Dome on the east end, westward past El Capitan, and out of the park into the Merced River Canyon.

Northside and Southside Drives parallel the valley on either side of the river, each one-way for most of its route. Four bridges span the river, including Sentinel Bridge, which leads to Yosemite Village, the Valley's commercial center.

The Ahwahnee Hotel sits about a half-mile east of the village, while Yosemite Lodge is at the base of Yosemite Falls, less than a mile west the village. Curry Village and the three Pines campgrounds lie south of the river, about a mile east of Sentinel Bridge.

Three highways diverge at the west end of the Valley. Big Oak Flat Rd leads north to Crane Flat (where it meets Hwy 120), Hetch Hetchy, and Tuolumne Meadows; Hwy 140 heads west out of the park to El Portal and Mariposa; and Hwy 41 runs south to Glacier Point Rd, Wawona, and Mariposa Grove.

To catch warm weather yet avoid the worst crowds, you're better off visiting in May, June, September, or October.

GETTING AROUND

Traffic can be heavy in the Valley, especially on summer weekends. **Parking** is free, but finding a convenient spot is not always easy. For day-use, you can park in the lot at Curry Village or the large, centrally located lot within walking distance of Yosemite Village, then hop on a free shuttle bus. Backpackers starting from Yosemite Valley park their vehicles in the hikers' lot south of Curry Village near Upper Pines Campground. Wherever you leave your vehicle, though, be sure to remove *all* food and scented items and place them either in trash cans or bear boxes found at each parking lot.

For emergency road service, call the **Village Garage** (☎ 209-372-8320; open 8am-5pm daily), across the street from the Village Store.

Bicycles are an easy and quite popular means of transport around the Valley, as cyclists can use the shuttle bus roads and 12 miles of paved trails.

For information on the free **Yosemite Valley Visitor Shuttle**, see Public Transit (p 85).

INFORMATION

The Valley boasts the greatest concentration of visitor services – and thus, the most crowded. In addition to accommodations and dining options, you'll find stores, ATMs, a main post office, Internet access, a bookstore, laundry and shower facilities, and medical and dental clinics. Note that all opening and closing seasons, dates, and times are approximate; they change somewhat each year depending on weather, demand, and budgetary constraints.

Yosemite Village houses the park's biggest **visitor center** (☎ *209-372-0299; open 8am-6pm daily in summer, reduced hours off-season)*. Here you'll find helpful staff, a bookstore, a park concessions courtesy phone, and exhibits on Yosemite's natural and cultural history. A free, beautifully photographed 22-minute film, *Spirit of Yosemite*, screens regularly in the center's West Auditorium Theater, which offers air-conditioned respite from the summer heat.

Those seeking to spend a night (or more) in the backcountry must obtain a free permit from the **Wilderness Center** *(open 7:30am-6pm daily in summer, 8am-5pm daily in fall and spring, closed in winter)* in Yosemite Village, two buildings east of the visitor center. The permit office can also supply maps,

YOSEMITE VALLEY PLAN

For well over a century, park employees have struggled to balance preservation of Yosemite's ecosystem with visitors' needs and wants. (To learn more about this effort, pick up Alfred Runte's interesting, well-researched book *Yosemite: The Embattled Wilderness*.)

In 1980 the park service unveiled its General Management Plan (GMP), whose goals included reclaiming the park's natural beauty, enhancing educational efforts, reducing crowding, decreasing traffic congestion, and allowing natural processes to run their course. Over the following decades, the GMP evolved into the Yosemite Valley Plan, which focuses on the Valley's problems and fine-tunes the park's overall goals. The current version has been dubbed the Final Yosemite Valley Plan.

Numerous projects are addressed in the plan, from restoring meadows and the riparian ecosystem along the Merced River to improving visitor access at Lower Yosemite Fall. The plan also reflects recent natural events in the park such as major rockfalls and massive flooding that hit the Valley in 1997. Having wiped out entire campgrounds, the flood certainly heightened awareness of the Merced River floodplain; the campgrounds will not be replaced, while other facilities will be redesigned, including Yosemite Lodge and Housekeeping Camp

The plan also calls for rerouted roads, increased visitor use of shuttle buses (the YARTS buses are a step in this direction, but the NPS want to take it further), and a reduction of parking spaces – and, thus, cars – in Yosemite Valley. This last item has fueled an uproar, as some say it will make the park less accessible to the general populace, especially day-trippers.

For those seeking more details about the plan, the National Park Service website (ⓦ www.nps.gov/yose/planning) lists 'Current Plans & Projects,' as well as full text of the General Management Plan and Yosemite Valley Plan. You can also check the news archives of both the NPS website (ⓦ www.nps.gov/yose/news) and the Yosemite Association (ⓦ www.yosemite.org/newsroom). The Valley Visitor Center offers an exhibit on the plan.

trip-planning guides, checklists of what to bring, and lots of advice about the area.

At the small **Campground Reservation Office** (☎ *209-372-8502; open 8am-5pm daily*) in the day-use parking lot at Curry Village (look for signs along Southside Dr), those without reservations can join a waiting list or seek advice about alternative lodgings.

VISITOR HUBS

Whether you're staying in the Valley or just passing through, the following visitor hubs are good places to find such amenities as food, phones, and film.

Yosemite Village

Regardless of your feelings toward commercial development in one of the world's natural wonders, you'll probably wind up here at one point or another, as the village offers just about every amenity – from pizza pies to wilderness permits.

It was founded in 1899 by David and Jennie Curry as a place where everyday visitors could find "a good bed and a clean napkin at every meal."

Commercial development began in the Valley almost as soon as the public became aware of the park. Quite a few hotels opened around the turn of the 20th century, and by the 1920s a collection of businesses (hotels, photo studios, even a dance pavilion and cinema) had risen just south of the river near Sentinel Bridge. This was the original Yosemite Village. By the 1950s, however, it was downgraded to the "Old Village," as businesses moved north of the river. The site of the Old Village has since reverted to meadow, though the chapel remains (in a slightly different spot). A few buildings were moved to the Pioneer History Center in Wawona, and Best's Studio was moved to the present-day village and eventually renamed the Ansel Adams Gallery.

Though the smell of quick eats and plethora of T-shirts and cheap souvenirs may get on your nerves, some businesses are quite useful, including the **Village Store** for groceries, and the **Sport Shop** (*open 9am-6pm daily, reduced hours in winter*), a good source for last-minute camping supplies.

Other services include a visitor center, post office, ATM, museum, and wilderness permit station. The village is also home to park business offices and employee housing.

Curry Village

Lying directly below Glacier Point, Curry Village is the Valley's second-biggest collection of restaurants, stores, and overnight accommodations. Originally called Camp Curry, it was founded in 1899 by David and Jennie Curry as a place where everyday visitors could find "a good bed and a clean napkin at every meal." Starting with just a handful of tents, the camp quickly grew, thanks in large part to David Curry's entrepreneurial drive and booming personality. One of his biggest promotional schemes was the Firefall, a nightly event and significant tourist draw (see p 245). Curry Village is now owned and run by Yosemite Concession Services (YCS).

More than 100 years later, the Camp Curry sign still hangs over the entrance, but this sprawling complex retains few traces of its turn-of-the-century roots. From the parking lot, a sea of tent cabins fans out toward the base of Glacier Point, radiating from a central cluster of stores and snack bars – not exactly a vision of rustic glory. Still, it's pleasant to settle in for pizza and beer on the patio that faces the amphitheater out back. There's even a small cocktail bar. Or you can head to the charming deck of the old Camp Curry Lounge for a catnap in one of the rocking chairs.

The **Curry Village Mountain Shop** (☎ 209-372-8396) offers the Valley's best selection of camping, mountaineering, and backpacking supplies. Nearby are bicycle and raft rental centers, a tour bus ticket kiosk, and a post office window.

This is a good spot for budget-conscious families who don't want to set up a tent themselves or cook on a propane stove. Hikers appreciate its location, just a short stroll from the popular Happy Isles Trailhead.

Yosemite Lodge

Near the base of Yosemite Falls, the collection of buildings known as Yosemite Lodge includes modern, motel-like accommodations, restaurants, shops, a bar, a bicycle rental stand and other amenities. Unlike the Ahwahnee, it's not a very striking development. Despite efforts to blend it into the natural surroundings, the place feels strangely like a suburban condo development. According to the Yosemite Valley Plan, however, the lodge is earmarked for a makeover.

Though it doesn't appear very old, the lodge dates back to 1915. It underwent extensive redesign and remodeling in 1956 and 1998, leaving little to suggest its history. Behind the lobby lie the commercial concerns, as well as a post office. The amphitheater hosts regular evening programs, and the pool is open to the public.

The Yosemite Valley shuttle bus stops right out front, as do most YARTS and VIA buses. All guided tram tours, ski shuttles, and hiker buses also leave from here; tickets are available from the tour desk in the lobby.

HALF DOME

Rising 8842ft above sea level (and nearly a mile above the Valley floor), Half Dome serves as the park's spiritual centerpiece and stands as one of the most glorious and monumental – not to mention best-known – granite domes on earth.

Its namesake shape is, in fact, an illusion. While from the Valley the dome appears to have been neatly sliced in half, from Glacier or Washburn Points you'll see that it's actually a thin ridge with a back slope nearly as steep as its fabled facade. As you travel through the park, witness Half Dome's many faces. For example, from Mirror Lake it presents a powerful form, while from the Panorama Trail it looks somewhat like a big toe poking out above the rocks and trees.

Half Dome towers above Tenaya Canyon, a classic, glacially carved gorge. Across this canyon rise North Dome and Basket Dome, examples of fully intact domes. In contrast, Half Dome's north face shattered along cracks (joints) as a small glacier undercut the dome's base. The resulting cliff boasts a 93% vertical grade (the sheerest in North America), attracting climbers from around the world. Hikers can reach its summit from the Valley via a long series of trails (p 99). The final 45-degree

THE LEGEND OF HALF DOME

According to Native American legend, one of Yosemite's early inhabitants came down from the mountains to Mono Lake, where he wed a Paiute named Tesaiyac. The journey back to the Valley was difficult, and by the time they reached what was to become Mirror Lake, Tesaiyac decided she wanted to return to her people at Mono Lake. Her husband refused to live on such barren, arid land with no oak trees where he could get acorns. With a heart full of despair, Tesaiyac fled toward Mono Lake, her husband in pursuit. When the spirits heard the couple quarreling, they grew angry and turned the two into stone: He became North Dome, and she became Half Dome. The tears she cried made marks as they ran down her face, forming Mirror Lake.

stretch to the top was first made accessible by George Anderson, a local blacksmith who drilled holes in the granite in 1875 and installed a rope system (later replaced by the steel cables in use today).

YOSEMITE FALLS

This waterfall on the north side of the Valley above Yosemite Lodge is considered the tallest in North America, dropping 2425ft. Some question that claim, however, as Yosemite Falls comprises three distinct tiers: towering 1430ft Upper Yosemite Fall, tumbling 675ft Middle Cascade, and the final 320ft drop of Lower Yosemite Fall. No matter how you measure it, though, Yosemite Falls is a big, beautiful sight, especially during the late-spring thaw.

Interested in a grueling, daylong climb to the top of the falls? See Hiking & Backpacking (p 97). Otherwise, park in the lot just north of Yosemite Lodge and join what may seem like half the park's visitors on an easy quarter-mile stroll to the base of the Lower Fall. Expect to get wet from the spray and watch your step, as rocks are very slippery. On spring nights when the moon is bright, look for a "moonbow." Note that in midsummer, when the snowmelt had dissipated, both the upper and lower falls usually dry up – sometimes to a trickle, other times stopping altogether. In winter check out the inverted ice cone that forms at the base of the falls.

BRIDALVEIL FALL

On the southwest end of the Valley, Bridalveil Fall tumbles 620ft. The Ahwahneechee people call it *Pohono* (Spirit of the Puffing Wind), as gusts often blow the fall from side to side, even lifting water back up into the air. This waterfall usually runs year-round, though it's often reduced to a whisper by midsummer. Expect to get soaked when the fall is heavy.

Park at the large lot where Wawona Rd/Hwy 41 meets Southside Dr. From the lot, it's a quarter-mile walk to the base of the fall. The path is paved, but probably too rough for wheelchairs, and there's a somewhat

EASY SPOTS FOR GREAT SNAPS

Any aspiring Ansel Adams should aim for sunrise at Mirror Lake or Yosemite Falls and sunset from Valley View or Tunnel View. Sentinel Bridge, near Housekeeping Camp, offers an epic perspective of Half Dome.

Free camera walks led by professional photographers leave almost daily during the summer from Yosemite Lodge, the Ansel Adams Gallery, and other locations; check *Yosemite Today* for what's scheduled during your visit.

steep climb at the very end. Avoid climbing on the slippery rocks at its base – no one likes a broken bone.

EL CAPITAN

At nearly 3600ft from base to summit, El Capitan ranks as one of the world's largest granite monoliths. Its sheer face makes it a world-class destination for experienced climbers, one that wasn't "conquered" until 1958. Since then, it's been inundated. Look closely and you'll probably spot climbers reckoning with El Cap's series of cracks and ledges, including the famous "Nose." At night, park along the road and dim your headlights; once your eyes adjust, you'll easily make out the pinpricks of headlamps dotting the rock face. Listen, too, for voices.

The road offers several good spots from which to ogle El Capitan. The Valley View turnout is one. For a wider view, try the pullout along Southside Dr just east of Bridalveil Fall. You can also park on Northside Dr, just below El Capitan, perhaps the best vantage point from which to see climbers.

TUNNEL VIEW

For the best all-around photo op of Yosemite Valley, park in the large, busy parking lot at the east end of Wawona Tunnel, on Hwy 41 just a short drive from the Valley floor. The view encompasses most of the Valley's greatest hits: El Capitan on the left, Bridalveil Fall on the right, the green Valley floor below, and glorious Half Dome front and center.

This viewpoint is often mistakenly called Inspiration Point. That point was on an old park road and is now reachable via a steep hike from the Tunnel View parking lot.

VALLEY VIEW

As you head west out of the Valley along Northside Dr, stop at the Valley View turnout, just past El Capitan Meadow, a nice spot to dip your toes in the Merced River and bid farewell to sights like Bridalveil Fall, Cathedral Rocks, and El Capitan. Look carefully to spot the tip-top of Half Dome in the distance.

YOSEMITE MUSEUM

Next to the Yosemite Valley Visitor Center, the Yosemite Museum (☎ *209-372-0200; admission free; open 9am-4:30pm or*

5pm daily, closed for lunch) features a series of cultural and historical exhibits on the Valley's native Miwok and Paiute people, covering the period from 1850 to today. The museum also displays historic Yosemite photos that illustrate the park's development and offer glimpses from photography's early days. Inside the museum is a **gallery** *(open 10am-4pm daily)* that features paintings and photographs from the museum's permanent collection, including some Ansel Adams prints.

If you're lucky, you'll meet Julia Parker, an expert basket weaver of Kashaya Pomo and Coast Miwok descent. Parker has been a fixture at the park since the early 1960s, demonstrating her craft, teaching workshops, and helping preserve local Native American culture.

Behind the museum, a free, self-guided interpretive trail winds through the **Indian Village of Ahwahnee**, where you can visit full-size, reconstructed Miwok-Paiute buildings. Across the street to the west, the **Yosemite Pioneer Cemetery** lies in a shady, serene spot.

ANSEL ADAMS GALLERY

The Ansel Adams Gallery *(☎ 209-372-4413; W www.ansel adams.com; open 9am-6pm daily in summer, until 5pm otherwise)*, east of the visitor center, is a privately run art gallery housed in a building that was originally Best's Studio, founded in 1902. Owner

NATIVE AMERICAN BASKET WEAVERS

Handwoven baskets were an integral part of Native Americans' daily existence. The exquisitely wrought baskets were so tightly woven, they could be used for drawing and carrying water. They also served as cooking vessels and dinner plates.

Ironically, the survival of the craft owes something to its commercial exploitation by mid-20th-century art collectors. To fetch a higher price from collectors, artists like Lucy Parker Telles, a descendent of Southern Miwok and Mono Lake Paiute, wove larger and more ornate baskets than those of their ancestors. The craft was also given a boost by that era's Yosemite Indian Field Days, when survivors of ancient tribes gathered to demonstrate their crafts.

Though Indian Field Days are no longer held, organizations like the California Indian Basketweavers Association seek to preserve the craft and reaffirm its spiritual significance. One sacred part of that practice is the gathering of traditional materials – sedge, bracken fern, redbud, willow, and waterproofing elements such as pine pitch and soap root. Thus, recent efforts have focused on environmental restoration of traditional gathering sites.

Lucy Parker Telles' daughter-in-law, Julia Parker, is a renowned basket weaver and teacher who makes traditional Kashaya Pomo baskets. Through marriage, she also learned the cultural traditions of her mother-in-law's Yosemite Miwok and Mono Lake Paiute ancestors, passing this knowledge to her daughter, Lucy Parker. Both Julia and Lucy continue to teach their craft and display their baskets and jewelry at Yosemite.

Harry Best was the father of Virginia Best, who married Adams in 1928. The gallery has since moved from its original site south of the river and been extensively remodeled. Today, instead of Best's paintings, it specializes in Adams' photographs and the work of other contemporary artists; it also carries a nice selection of art and ecology books and other gift items. Adams fans should also check out the small, homey display of snapshots, to the left of the fireplace as you walk in.

AHWAHNEE HOTEL

A picture of elegance and rustic grace, the Ahwahnee Hotel (☎ 209-372-1407), about a quarter-mile east of Yosemite Village, has been a popular destination for well-to-do tourists since 1927. If you're not a guest, the building itself is still a sight worth seeing, both inside and out. Built from local granite, pine, and cedar, it is splendidly decorated with leaded glass, sculpted tile, Native American rugs, and Turkish kilims. You'll understand its National Historic Landmark designation once you wander through the Great Lounge and Solarium and peek into the dining room, where diners enjoy fabulous but pricey meals (see the Places to Eat chapter). You don't have to be dressed up to sip a cocktail in the bar or out on the patio, a perfect spot to unwind after a vigorous hike.

LECONTE MEMORIAL LODGE

This rustic, eye-catching, granite and wood lodge (☎ 209-372-4542; W www.sierra club.org/education/leconte; open 10am-4pm Wed-Sun Apr-Sept), on Southside Dr directly across from Housekeeping Camp, was built by the Sierra Club in 1903 to honor Joseph LeConte (1823-1901), a University of California at Berkeley geologist who was a charter member of the Sierra Club.

Sierra Club members staff the lodge, which houses exhibits and information on LeConte, Muir, and Ansel Adams, along with a good library of park-related ecology, geology, and other nature books free for the browsing, not to mention a fun children's corner. Evening activities are posted out front and in *Yosemite Today*.

Designed by Berkeley architect John White, the building was initially erected in Camp Curry, then moved here, stone by stone, in 1919. LeConte Lodge is one of three National Historic Landmarks in Yosemite, along with the Ahwahnee Hotel and the Rangers' Club (a Valley building currently used as employee housing).

HAPPY ISLES NATURE CENTER

Happy Isles lies at the Valley's southeast end, where the Merced River courses around two small islands. The area is a popular spot for picnics, swimming, and short strolls in the woods. It also marks the start of the John Muir Trail and Mist Trail, where hikers begin treks to Vernal Fall, Nevada Fall, and Half Dome.

On the site of a former fish hatchery, the nature center (*admission free; open 10am-noon and 1pm-4pm daily May-Sept*) features great hands-on exhibits that will enthrall kids and adults alike. Displays explain the differences among the park's various pinecones, rocks, animal tracks, and, everyone's favorite subject, scat. Out back, don't miss an exhibit on the 1996 rockfall, when an 80,000-ton rock slab plunged 2000ft to the nearby valley floor, killing a man, felling about 1000 trees, and seriously damaging the nature center.

Happy Isles is about a mile from Curry Village. The road is closed to cars (except those with handicap placards); instead, reach it by either an easy walk or the free shuttle bus. There's a small snack bar at the shuttle stop

ART ACTIVITY CENTER

In summer, the Art Activity Center in Yosemite Village holds free art classes that feature a different artist and medium (watercolor, pastel, acrylic, etc.) each week. Classes usually take place outside, and students must bring their own supplies or purchase them at the center. No experience is necessary. Children older than age 10 can participate, but those under 12 must be accompanied by an adult. Sign up at the center at least a day ahead to ensure a spot.

HIKING & BACKPACKING

The majority of visitors tour Yosemite Valley by car – stopping at pullouts, squinting up at big-name landmarks like El Capitan and Bridalveil Fall, and snapping a few photos. But for a real *feel* for the place, leave the car behind and hit a few trails.

The Valley offers hikes for all levels – you don't have to be a physical dynamo. Those seeking gentle strolls can visit Mirror Lake and wander the Valley Loop as far as they wish. At the other end of the scale is the trek to the summit of Half Dome, perhaps the single most difficult (and popular) day hike in the entire park.

The following are all day hikes. Some of the longer excursions, though – most notably Half Dome and Yosemite Falls – can be extended into overnight excursions. But you must camp 4 miles away from the Valley's populated areas (ie, you can't just pitch your tent halfway up the Nevada Fall Trail because you're plum tuckered). Discuss campsite options with staff at the wilderness permit offices. For information on the John Muir Trail, including the stretch from Yosemite Valley to Tuolumne Meadows, see p 40.

YOSEMITE VALLEY LOOPS
Distance: Varies
Duration: Varies
Challenge: Easy
Elevation Change: 330ft

Among the Valley's secrets are the often uncrowded loop trails, generally flat and easy to follow. While some stretches run alongside the road, most of the time you'll be beneath the trees and – except when you pass a major pullout – on your own.

For the ambitious, a well-marked path leads up and down the entire Valley, more or less following Northside and Southside Drs. However, it's easily broken into segments, making the journey manageable for just about any level of hiker.

A convenient place to begin the 2.6-mile **East Valley Loop** is at Curry Village. From here, the trail heads east to Happy Isles, then continues north to the stables, where you can take a side trip to Mirror Lake if you wish. Head back along the road toward Upper and Lower Pines Campgrounds, cross the bridge, then look for a sign on the right pointing to Curry Village. If you tire of hiking, you're never far from a shuttle bus stop

The 6.5-mile **West Valley Loop** is farther removed from the Valley's central commercial district. It basically follows Northside and Southside Drs between El Capitan and Pohono Bridge, the westernmost bridge over the Merced River, passing Bridalveil Fall along the way. A good starting point is the roadside parking area along Northside Dr, just west of El Capitan Bridge. Begin walking upstream (northeast) a short distance, then cross over north of Northside Dr, where you'll meet the well-worn trail. Head west to Pohono Bridge and cross the river; from here, the trail turns east and leads to Bridalveil Fall. After visiting the fall, continue east and look for a sign pointing to El Capitan. Turn north here, follow the path across the river, and you'll be back where you started.

MIRROR LAKE & TENAYA CANYON LOOP
Distance: 4.5 miles
Duration: 2 hours
Challenge: Easy
Elevation Change: 100ft

At the Valley's east end, a paved trail goes to Mirror Lake and continues into the lower reaches of rugged (and off-limits) Tenaya Canyon. A good part of the year, Mirror Lake is not a lake at all but a meadow – an open, dry patch of grass, gravel, and sand with only a few hints of water. In springtime, water fills the lakebed, and it truly does reflect the surrounding scenery. Ansel Adams took many a photo here, and you can easily see why as you watch early morning and evening light cast the reflection of adjacent Half Dome in the lake's still surface.

Even when the lake's dry, the walk is plenty worthwhile. It's also about as easy as they come. The shuttle bus stops at the Mirror Lake Trailhead, just east of the stables. From here, an old road leads to the lakebed, or you can choose a path through the woods to the right of Tenaya Creek. You can hike just the half-mile to the lake or take the extra 3-mile loop into the canyon and back. Pack a lunch and take your time.

INSPIRATION POINT
Distance: 2.6 miles
Duration: 1.5 to 2.5 hours
Challenge: Moderate-Difficult
Elevation Change: 1000ft

Sure, Tunnel View offers an amazing look into the Valley. But the view is even more impressive along the steep trail to Inspiration Point. Best of all, you'll leave the crowds behind.

Inspiration Point used to be a viewpoint along an old road into Yosemite Valley. The roadbed still exists, but this hike (actually the west end of the Pohono Trail) is now the only way to reach the point. You'll start by climbing a series of switchbacks from the parking lot on the south side of Hwy 41 immediately east of the Wawona Tunnel. Almost immediately the view improves, with fewer trees and no bus tourists to battle for camera position. Short spur trails lead to open viewpoints.

The climb is steep and steady but, thankfully, fairly short and mostly in shade. The view from Inspiration Point itself – a large open area – isn't as spectacular as what you get on the way up, but it's a worthy destination nonetheless, quiet and perfect for a picnic. If you've got the energy, continue up the trail 2.5 miles farther to Stanford Point, another mighty viewpoint.

YOSEMITE FALLS
Distance: 6.8 miles
Duration: 5 to 6 hours
Challenge: Difficult
Elevation Change: 2400ft

This excellent trail (among the park's oldest) leads from the Valley floor to the top of the falls along the north rim. The stiff ascent and equivalent descent make this a strenuous day hike. For those doing the side trip to spectacular **Yosemite Point**, the elevation gain approaches 3000ft. If all that seems a bit much, you can always hike just the first mile (and 1000 vertical feet) to **Columbia Rock**, a justifiably classic viewpoint.

The trailhead is behind Camp 4, at shuttle bus stop 7. From the east side of the campground, head uphill to the northside Valley Floor Trail, then west to the start of the Yosemite Falls Trail.

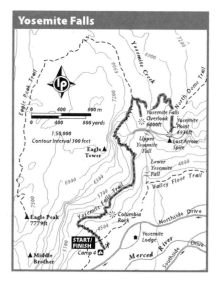

Immediately the trail climbs four dozen short switchbacks up a talus slope through canyon live oaks. After eight-tenths of a mile, the grade eases as the trail follows more switchbacks east to Columbia Rock. This may be enough for many, as the remaining climb is even hotter, steeper, and more exposed.

In another four-tenths of a mile, the trail approaches the top of Lower Yosemite Fall, where breezes may shower you with a fine, cooling mist. Stop to admire the view of Upper Yosemite Fall, then brace yourself for the numerous switchbacks that run steadily up a rocky cleft to the Valley rim. The falls once ran down this cleft.

The trail tops out 3.2 miles from the trailhead and bends east. At the junction, the trail going straight leads to Eagle Peak. Turn right at this junction and follow the trail two-tenths of a mile to the brink of Upper Yosemite Fall at the **Yosemite Falls Overlook** (6400ft). The view of the falls is impressive, but views of El Capitan and Half Dome are obscured. For a wider perspective, go the extra 1.6 miles to Yosemite Point, where you'll see incredible views of Half Dome, North Dome, Clouds Rest, Glacier Point, Cathedral Rocks, and Lost Arrow.

Keep in mind that the falls are often dry by midsummer, so late May and June (after snow has cleared) are the best months to catch the scene in all its frothy glory.

FOUR-MILE TRAIL TO GLACIER POINT
Distance: 9.2 miles
Duration: 4 to 8 hours
Challenge: Difficult
Elevation Change: 3200ft

This fulfilling day hike from Yosemite Valley ascends the Valley's south wall to Glacier Point, the park's most famous viewpoint. Sure, you can easily get there by car or bus, but there's something supremely rewarding about making the journey on foot.

Start from Leidig Meadow along Northside Dr near shuttle stop 7 (Camp 4). A short walk south along a paved footpath leads across the Swinging Bridge to Southside Dr. Walk parallel to the road a short distance west to the Four-Mile Trailhead.

Today the Four-Mile Trail actually spans closer to 4.6 miles, having been rerouted since it was first completed in 1872. It was originally intended as a toll pathway, as at the time it was the quickest route to Glacier Point.

The trail climbs steadily, passing 2000ft Sentinel Fall and Sentinel Rock. At **Union Point**, 3 miles from the trailhead, you'll first catch glimpse of Half Dome. Continue climbing until the trail levels out for the final leg to Glacier Point (and that all-important snack stand).

Return the way you came. Hardy hikers can turn this into an excellent loop trail (and avoid retracing their steps) by continuing on the Panorama Trail to Nevada Fall, then down to Happy Isles.

VERNAL & NEVADA FALLS
Distance: 6.5 miles
Duration: 4 to 7 hours
Challenge: Moderate-Difficult
Elevation Change: 1900ft

The day hike to the top of first Vernal Fall and then Nevada Fall offers more scenic diversity than any other hike in Yosemite Valley – a good choice if you've got time for just one hike. At Nevada Fall, the tallest on the Merced

River, water cascades 594ft over a polished cliff beneath the striking dome of Liberty Cap The whole area is known as the Giant Staircase, a metaphor that becomes clear when viewed from afar at Glacier Point.

The route described here follows the gentle switchbacks of the renowned **John Muir Trail** up to the fall, then down the more spectacular yet steeper **Mist Trail**. Expect to get wet along the latter, as it runs right alongside the tumbling water.

Ride the shuttle bus to stop 16 (Happy Isles). Cross the road bridge over the Merced River, turn right, and follow the riverbank upstream. You'll join a gentle pathway that ascends 400ft over seven-tenths of a mile to the Vernal Fall footbridge – probably the most crowded portion of this hugely popular trail. Shortly beyond the footbridge you'll reach the junction of the John Muir and Mist Trails. Turn right onto the John Muir Trail; the Mist Trail continues straight to the top of Vernal Fall.

Follow gentle switchbacks up the canyon 1.3 miles through Douglas firs and canyon live oaks to **Clark Point** (5480ft). For those who wish to curtail their hike, a spur trail leads north a half-mile to the top of 317ft **Vernal Fall**.

Those bound for Nevada Fall continue on a more level grade one mile to the Panorama Trail junction. Stay on the John Muir Trail for two-tenths of a mile, and you'll reach the footbridge over the Merced atop **Nevada Fall** (5907ft), 3.5 miles from Happy Isles. Picnic or relax on the rocks along the northeast brink of the fall. An oft-overlooked viewpoint lies atop a terrace down a spur trail on the river's north side. Protected by an iron railing, it sits at the very edge of the waterfall.

The shorter but steeper Mist Trail descends 2.8 miles to Happy Isles. From the top of Nevada Fall, walk two-tenths of a mile northeast beyond the footbridge and look for the trail junction near a solar toilet. Turn left onto the Mist Trail beneath Liberty Cap and descend the steep, 500-step rock staircase beside Nevada Fall. Cross another footbridge over the Merced River at the **Silver Apron** and continue along the **Emerald Pool** one-tenth of a mile to Vernal Fall. Below Vernal Fall, descend another short rock staircase and follow the paved pathway from the Vernal Fall footbridge to reach Happy Isles, 1.3 miles from the top of Vernal Fall.

If you prefer a shorter excursion, the hike up the Mist Trail to the top of Vernal Fall is one of Yosemite's most scenic (and popular) day hikes. Vernal is the easiest of Yosemite's waterfalls to "summit," though keep in mind that the trail climbs 1000ft.

HALF DOME
Distance: 17 miles
Duration: 10 to 12 hours
Challenge: Very Difficult
Elevation Change: 4800ft

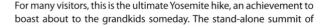

For many visitors, this is the ultimate Yosemite hike, an achievement to boast about to the grandkids someday. The stand-alone summit of this glacier-carved chunk of granite offers awesome 360-degree views, and peering down its sheer 2000ft north face offers a powerful thrill you'll remember the rest of your life.

Ideally, Half Dome is best tackled in two days, allowing you more time to rest up and enjoy the gorgeous surroundings. But since it's so darn popular, you'll have a hard time getting a permit to sleep overnight at the limited legal camping areas on the route (the most popular being Little Yosemite Valley). If you do attempt this hike in a single day (and many, many people do), be ready for some hardcore exertion. Also, get an early start (6am), pack *lots* of water, and bring a flashlight, because you may wind up hiking home in the dark.

Climbing gear is unnecessary. Instead, hikers haul themselves up the final 650ft to the summit between two steel cables. Climbing this stretch is only allowed when the cable route is open, usually late May to mid-October, depending on snow conditions. If you're planning an early-season or late-season trip, confirm in advance that the cables are in place.

Start at Happy Isles and ascend to the top of Nevada Fall on either the John Muir Trail or the Mist Trail (see preceding hike description for details). Continue over a low rise to level Little Yosemite Valley, which boasts views of Half Dome's massive, rounded south side. You'll also find solar composting toilets, bear boxes, and a seasonal ranger station, all welcome features at this well-used campground, one of

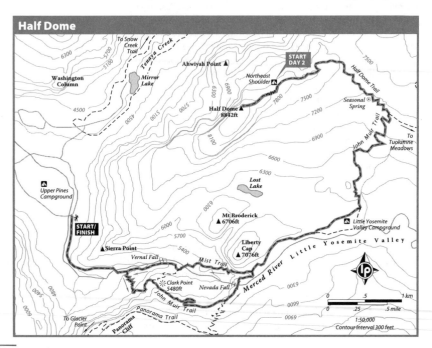

the park's most heavily visited areas.

From the west end of Little Yosemite Valley, the Merced Lake Trail heads east (right) along the river to the Merced Lake High Sierra Camp. Stay on the John Muir Trail, which turns north (left) and climbs steeply through forest 1.3 miles to the Half Dome Trail junction, just 2 miles from the summit.

Take the left fork onto the Half Dome Trail. Ten minutes above the junc-

ALTERNATE HALF DOME ROUTES

As an alternative to the hugely popular route from Happy Isles (which can feel like rucksack rush hour on summer weekends), consider approaching Half Dome from other points in the park. Beginning from higher elevation also saves you the initial climb. Just about anywhere works, depending on how long you want to spend on the trail (overnighting requires a wilderness permit). Good starting points include Tenaya Lake and Glacier Point, the latter leading you along the gorgeous Panorama Trail. From Half Dome, you can descend via the Mist or John Muir Trails.

tion on the left is a somewhat hard-to-spot seasonal spring – the last source of water en route. (Be sure to filter or treat it.) Continue for 30 minutes, first through forest and then up switchbacks to the **northeast shoulder** (7600ft). This is an alternate camping spot, with spectacular views. Those camping here can visit the summit at sunset and sunrise for exquisite solitude. Protect your food at all times from marmots and other varmints.

From here, a rocky 20- to 30-minute trail snakes 650ft up two dozen switchbacks to a notch at the base of the **cables**. The twin steel cables are draped from posts bolted into the granite on the final 600ft ascent up an exposed 45-degree rock face. To protect your hands, grab a pair of gloves from the communal pile at the base. Intermittent wooden cross-boards provide footholds. A trip in light crowds takes only 15 minutes, but on crowded cables (or if you're jittery), expect it to take longer. "Sharing the road" will be your biggest challenge. A word of caution: Don't ascend the cables if there's any chance of a storm. The exposed summit is no place to be when lightning strikes – nor do you want to get stuck halfway up with your hands wrapped around virtual lighting rods.

The top is fairly flat and about 5 acres in size. From here, enjoy amazing views of Yosemite Valley from the overhanging northwest point. Also look for Mt Starr King, Clouds Rest, the Cathedral Range, and the Sierra Crest. Most people spend 30 minutes to an hour on top. As tempting as it is to linger, watch the time carefully to avoid a hazardous descent in darkness.

Camping on the summit is prohibited for three reasons: to reduce human waste; to protect the threatened Mt Lyell salamander, whose habitat was being disturbed as people moved rocks to build wind shelters; and to save the last remaining tree, as six of the seven trees previously growing here were illegally cut for campfires – sad but true. Respect the camping ban and protect this fragile ecosystem.

SUMMER ACTIVITIES
Rock Climbing & Bouldering
Most of the Valley's climbing activity revolves around Camp 4 (aka Sunnyside Walk-in Campground). The **Yosemite Mountaineering School** (☎ 209-372-8344; www.yosemitemountaineering.com), whose main office is at the Curry Village Mountain Shop, offers rock-climbing classes in all expertise levels and private guided climbs for one, two, or three people ($220/310/405). Most classes run from 8:30am to 4pm, and participants must be at least 10 years old. Climbing shoes are available for rent ($8); all other equipment is provided. Beginners are invited to Go Climb a Rock ($70-170 per person), which covers the basics of belaying and rappelling, while the Big Wall Climbing Seminar ($105-200 per person) draws more experienced climbers. Other YMS class offerings include anchoring, leading/multi-pitch climbing, self-rescue/aid, and crack climbing, for which Yosemite is well known.

Bouldering enthusiasts head to the west end of Camp 4, Sentinel Rock, the Four-Mile Trail trailhead, and rocks near Housekeeping Camp and around Mirror Lake.

To watch climbers at work, head to El Capitan meadow and Church Bowl near the Ahwahnee. For an even better view, rent a pair of binoculars from the Village Sports Shop.

Biking
You can rent bikes year-round, weather permitting, from the stand at **Yosemite Lodge** (☎ 209-372-1208) and in summer at **Curry Village** (☎ 209-372-8319). Both charge $5.50/21 per hour/day for basic beach cruisers. Bikes with trailers are available for $11.50/35 per hour/day. The stands are open from 8:30am to 7pm daily.

Horseback Riding
Trips depart from **Yosemite Valley Stables** (☎ 209-372-8348), near North Pines Campground, from early April to mid-October. Guided trail rides cost $40 for two hours, $55 for a half-day, and $80 for a full day. From the Valley, trips wind along Tenaya Creek to Mirror Lake, follow the John Muir Trail, or head to Half Dome. During the popular summer months, you should make a reservation, particularly for the longer rides. If you're traveling with your own horses, there's a **stock camp** (☎ 800-436-7275; $20 per night) at Bridalveil Creek, accessible from Glacier Point Rd; reservations are required and available up to five months in advance.

Rafting
With a consistent current and easy access points, the stretch of the Merced River from Stoneman Meadow to Sentinel Bridge is the designated rafting zone; kayakers can continue on to the Yellow Pine Picnic Area. The waters are gentle enough for children, and **raft rentals** (☎ 209-372-8319; open 10am-4pm daily) for the 3-mile trip are available at Curry Village for $13.50/11.50 adult/child, including all equipment and a return shuttle to the rental kiosk. No permit is required to use your own raft, canoe, or

kayak on the Merced. Shuttles, which operate every 30 minutes, cost $2 for those bringing their own flotation devices.

Availability of raft rentals depends upon water volume and blockages due to fallen trees; technically, the river must measure below 6ft at Sentinel Bridge to allow rafting. There's also talk of limiting the number of floaters to protect the river's ecosystem, but for now you're free to float. Rafting above Yosemite Valley Stables or below Cathedral Beach is forbidden.

Swimming & Soaking
On a hot summer day in the Valley, nothing beats the heat like lounging in the lazy Merced. Swimmers flock to the river at several locations: at Sentinel Beach, just behind Housekeeping Camp, behind Yosemite Lodge, and at the Cathedral Beach/Devil's Elbow area opposite the El Capitan Picnic Area. Basically, you can jump in at any accessible point. Tenaya Creek offers good swimming as well, especially near the bridge leading toward Mirror Lake.

Skin too thin? Curry Village and Yosemite Lodge provide public **outdoor swimming pools** *(adult/child $2/1.50; open mid-June-Sept)*. The price includes towels and showers.

Fishing
Trout frequent the Merced between Vernal and Nevada Falls and above Washburn Lake, although if you catch a rainbow trout, you'll have to throw it back. You're allowed five brown trout per day, and bait is prohibited (use artificial lures instead).

WINTER ACTIVITIES
Some locals believe Yosemite Valley is at its best after a snowfall. A delightful way to spend a winter's afternoon is twirling about on Curry Village's large **outdoor ice-skating rink** *(☎ 209-372-8341; 2.5-hour session $6.50, skate rental $3.25)*. The rink is open from November through March, with daily sessions at 3:30pm and 7pm and additional sessions at 8:30am and noon on weekends. Amenities include a warming hut with lockers, a fire pit, and well-stocked snack stand.

The gorgeous, snow-blanketed Valley is perfect for **snowshoeing** and winter walks past icy monoliths and frozen waterfalls. The John Muir Trail, which begins at Happy Isles, is a popular choice.

GLACIER POINT & BADGER PASS
Map 3

High above the Valley's south side, 7214ft **Glacier Point** offers one of the park's most glorious views. Dare to stand at the railing and peer 3200ft straight down at Curry Village.

The point lies at the far east end of winding Glacier Point Rd, which connects with Hwy 41. The 16-mile road was built in 1936, replacing an old wagon road dating from 1882. Along the road, hiking trails lead to more spectacular viewpoints such as **Dewey Point** and **Sentinel Dome**. The road also passes the **Badger Pass Ski Area** and Bridalveil Creek Campground, adjacent to **Bridalveil Creek**, which runs north and drops into Yosemite Valley as Bridalveil Fall.

ORIENTATION & INFORMATION

From Yosemite Valley, it's 30 miles (about an hour's drive) to Glacier Point. Glacier Point Rd runs east from the Chinquapin junction on Hwy 41, terminating at Glacier Point itself. The road rises from about 6000ft at Chinquapin to 7700ft at the Sentinel Dome parking lot, then down again to 7214ft Glacier Point. Badger Pass Ski Area lies about 5 miles east of Chinquapin; in winter, Glacier Point Rd is closed east of the ski area.

Services are minimal. Near the Glacier Point parking lot, you'll find a **snack bar** *(open 10am-4pm daily)* and adjacent **gift shop** *(open 9am-6pm daily)*, but the closest visitor center is in Yosemite Valley. Wilderness permits are available in Yosemite Valley and Wawona.

The only public transportation to this area is the **Glacier Point Sightseeing Bus** *(☎ 209-372-1240)* from Yosemite Valley, which runs daily from about June to October.

GLACIER POINT

Few viewpoints offer as much scenic payoff for as little physical effort as Glacier Point. A five-minute stroll from the car, you'll find the entire eastern Yosemite Valley spread out before you, from Yosemite Falls to Half Dome, as well as the distant peaks

CALIFORNIA'S FIRST SKI RESORT

Unlikely as it may seem, the California ski industry essentially got its start in Yosemite Valley. Yosemite's All-Year Highway (now Hwy 140) was completed in 1926, and the following year the Ahwahnee Hotel opened its doors. The Valley quickly became a popular winter destination. The Valley floor hosted skating, hockey, ski jumping, and sledding, while the new Western Ski School led ambitious, cross-country jaunts into the high country.

As the 1929 Winter Olympics approached, the newly formed Curry Company and the Yosemite Winter Club put in an impassioned bid to host the games. They lost, and instead the events were held at Lake Placid, New York – where, in a freakish irony, no snow fell that winter. Bales of hay were used in lieu of snow, while the Sierra saw record snowfalls.

When Wawona Tunnel opened in 1933, skiers began congregating at Badger Pass. In 1935 a new lodge opened on Glacier Point Road, and a newfangled contraption called the *upski* was installed at the pass. The crude lift consisted of nothing more than two counterbalanced sleds, but it worked, and Badger Pass became California's first alpine ski resort.

OTTOWAY LAKE Hikers stop to admire Upper Ottoway Lake in the Clark Range. [Photo: Mark & Audrey Gibson]

WAWONA The Pioneer History Center blanketed in snow. [Photo: Lee Foster]

AROUND**YOSEMITE**

CHAPEL Built in 1879 and moved to its present location in 1901, the popular Yosemite Chapel hosts more than 350 weddings each year. [Photo: John Elk III]

CLOUDS REST A hiker ascends Clouds Rest Trail toward the summit (9926ft). [Photo: John Mock]

AROUND**YOSEMITE**

CATHEDRAL PEAK Evening light on Cathedral Peak (10,940ft). [Photo: Greg Gawlowski]

CAMPING A camper reads by lantern at dusk. [Photo: Woods Wheatcroft]

GREETINGS, STARGAZERS

On many summer Saturday nights, the Glacier Point amphitheater hosts various astronomy clubs, which set up telescopes and let the public take a closer-than-usual look at what's deep in the night sky – from the moon's mottled surface to fuzzy, faraway star clusters. These programs are accompanied by "Stars Over Yosemite" discussions, during which rangers point out constellations in the sky above Glacier Point. Bring the kids.

that ring Tuolumne Meadows. Half Dome is practically at eye level – look closely and you may spot hikers on its summit.

To the left of Half Dome lies U-shaped, glacially carved Tenaya Canyon, while to its right you'll see Nevada and Vernal Falls. On the Valley floor, the Merced River snakes through green meadows and groves of trees. The Ahwahnee Hotel is clearly visible, as is the aqua rectangle of the Curry Village swimming pool some 3200ft below – a dizzying perspective.

Almost from the park's inception, Glacier Point has been a popular destination. Getting up here was at first a major undertaking. That changed once the **Four-Mile Trail** opened in 1872. While not exactly an easy climb – neither then nor today – the trail did offer a more direct route to the point. James McCauley financed formation of the trail, for which he charged a toll; he later took over the reigns of the Mountain House hotel, built in 1873 atop Glacier Point. In the 1870s he also conceived the famous Firefall (see the boxed text in the History chapter, p 245), though Curry Village later picked up and heavily promoted the event.

A wagon road to the point was completed in 1882, and the current Glacier Point Rd was built in 1936. As far back as 1929 (and again in the 1970s), there was talk of building an aerial tramway to ferry tourists from Yosemite Valley to Glacier Point. But since the cables would be an eyesore and the system would disturb fragile ecosystems, plans were, thankfully, abandoned.

Following a $3.2 million overhaul in 1997, the park service unveiled a spruced-up viewing area, a new concession building, and a handsome new granite amphitheater on the site of the old Glacier Point Hotel. Built in 1917, the lovely hotel unfortunately burned to the ground in 1969, along with the adjacent McCauley Mountain House.

At the point itself you'll find **Overhanging Rock**, a huge granite slab that sticks out beyond the cliff edge, defying gravity. Through the years, many famous photos have been taken of folks performing wacky stunts on the rock. You'll have to get your kicks from the pictures, as the rock is now off-limits.

To escape the crowds, consider a short hike down the first half-mile or so of the Four-Mile Trail, which drops gently into a quiet forest and – at this point at least – isn't too steep After about 10 or 15 minutes, you'll round a corner to a view of El Capitan and Yosemite Valley's western half. Steep switchbacks start in earnest below this point.

WASHBURN POINT

This viewpoint along Glacier Point Rd is magnificent, though not quite as spectacular as Glacier Point. The point faces east toward the Clark Range and lacks the sweeping view of Yosemite Valley. Still, it's worth seeing and serves as a great warm-up to Glacier Point, less than a mile down the road.

HIKING & BACKPACKING

High-country hikes from Glacier Point Rd lead to spectacular overlooks of Yosemite Valley, including Dewey Point, Taft Point, and Sentinel Dome. The latter offers perhaps the widest, finest view of all, and the hike to its summit takes a mere half-hour.

Trails from the south and east side of Glacier Point Rd wind into some of Yosemite's largest wilderness tracts. Serious backpackers interested in longer hauls can explore such rugged areas as the Merced headwaters or the Clark Range, along the park's southeast border. Check at the Yosemite Valley visitor center for maps and information.

Some of the following hikes link up with other top-notch trails. The hike up the Four-Mile Trail to Glacier Point is described on p 98; the trail from Wawona Tunnel to Inspiration Point (the westernmost leg of the Pohono Trail) is discussed on p 96.

McGURK MEADOW
Distance: 1.6 miles
Duration: 1 hour
Challenge: Easy
Elevation Change: 150ft

Lush, open McGurk Meadow makes a pleasant destination if you're after a short hike and a moment of solitude. Wildflowers add brilliance and color, especially in July. Though the meadows in Yosemite Valley and Tuolumne feature more striking surroundings, the landscape here is plenty pretty, as is the hike itself.

Begin at a pullout along Glacier Point Rd just west of the Bridalveil Creek Campground entrance. The posted trailhead is 100 yards or so west of the parking area. Meander less than a mile through quiet forest till you reach a cabin on your left. The meadow is just ahead, across a small footbridge.

From the meadow, you can continue another 3.2 miles to **Dewey Point** for big, wide views down into the Valley.

SENTINEL DOME

Distance: 2.2 miles
Duration: 1 hour
Challenge: Moderate
Elevation Change: 370ft

The hike to Sentinel's summit (8122ft) is the shortest and easiest trail up one of Yosemite's granite domes. For those unable to visit Half Dome's summit, Sentinel offers an equally outstanding 360-degree perspective of Yosemite's wonders. A visit at sunrise, sunset, or during a full moon adds to the experience.

You can also combine a trip up Sentinel Dome with a walk to Taft Point, an equidistant hike from the same trailhead. The Sentinel Dome/Taft Point parking lot is on the north side of Glacier Point Rd, about 13 miles from Chinquapin. The Glacier Point Hikers' Bus will also drop you at the trailhead.

From the roadside parking lot, take the trail's gently rising right fork. After 20 minutes, it heads northwest across open granite slabs to the dome's base. Skirt the base to an old service road, which leads to the dome's northeast shoulder. From here, head up the granite slope to the top (wear good hiking shoes).

The gnarled, bleached bones of a **Jeffrey pine** crown the dome's summit. The photogenic tree died in a drought in the late 1970s. From the top, the views take in almost the entire park. To the west are Cathedral Rocks and El Capitan, while to the north you'll spot Yosemite Falls and, in the distance, Mt Hoffmann. North Dome, Basket Dome, and Mt Watkins line the valley's northeast side, and Clouds Rest and Half Dome rise dramatically above Tenaya Canyon. In the distance, above Nevada Fall, you'll see the notable peaks of the Cathedral and Ritter Ranges. To the east lie Mt Starr King and the peaks of the Clark Range.

TAFT POINT & THE FISSURES

Distance: 2.2 miles
Duration: 1 hour
Challenge: Easy
Elevation Change: 250ft

Taft Point (7503ft) is a fantastic, hair-raising viewpoint at the edge of a sheer 3000ft cliff, with impressive views of El Capitan and Yosemite Valley. On the same promontory are **The Fissures**, a series of deep, narrow cracks in the granite, some with boulders lodged inside. Choose your steps carefully, especially when accompanying small children.

Park in the same lot as the hike for Sentinel Dome, instead heading west (left) along the trail. After a gentle descent through pleasant forest, you'll emerge on an open, rocky slope. On your right are The

EXPERIENCING YOSEMITE

Fissures, which drop hundreds of feet along the edge of Profile Cliff. Across Yosemite Valley, you'll see the **Three Brothers**, with similar yet longer cracks in the rock.

Ahead is Taft Point, guarded only by a short metal railing. Unless you have a profound fear of heights, approach and peer over the edge – the sheer drop is mind-boggling. Look west through binoculars to spot climbers on the southeast face and nose of El Capitan. After soaking up the views, which include a close-up look at Cathedral Spires, return on a gentle uphill climb to the parking lot.

PANORAMA TRAIL
Distance: 8.5 miles one-way
Duration: 5 hours
Challenge: Moderate-Difficult
Elevation Change: 3200ft descent, 760ft ascent

Connecting Glacier Point and Nevada Fall, this trail is gorgeous, comprising several miles of Yosemite's most picture-perfect scenery. Hikers seeking a full loop from the Valley must first tackle the steep 3200ft ascent on the Four-Mile Trail (see p 98). Those starting from Glacier Point and heading down to the Valley must arrange a car shuttle or reserve a seat on the Glacier Point Hikers' Bus. Or you can simply hike to Nevada Fall and return to Glacier Point the way you came.

At Glacier Point, look for the Panorama Trail signpost near the snack bar. Descend a fire-scarred hillside south toward Illilouette Fall. The route down is largely easy, with magnificent views to your left – including Half Dome, which from here looks like the tip of a giant thumb. If you're lucky, you'll also find blue grouse on the trail, hooting and cooing in gentle, haunting tones. Make sure you bring sunscreen and a hat, as most of the tree cover has burned away.

After about 1.2 miles you'll meet the trail from Mono Meadow. Turn left and take a short series of switchbacks down to Illilouette Creek. The best place to admire 370ft **Illilouette Fall** is a well-worn viewpoint above the creek on the left.

At the two-mile mark, a footbridge crosses **Illilouette Creek**, whose shaded banks invite a picnic. The trail leaves the creek and climbs east to **Panorama Point**, then **Panorama Cliff**. This 760ft climb is the only significant elevation gain on the hike. Vantage points high above the Merced River afford amazing views of the Glacier Point apron, Half Dome, Mt Broderick (6706ft), Liberty Cap, and Mt Starr King (9092ft).

The trail descends to a junction with the John Muir Trail. Turn right and follow the trail two-tenths of a mile to the top of **Nevada Fall**, 3.2 miles from Illilouette Creek.

To reach the Valley, descend the Mist Trail via Vernal Fall or take the slightly longer and gentler John Muir Trail. You'll emerge at Happy Isles on the Valley's east end (see the Vernal & Nevada Falls hike on p 98).

POHONO TRAIL
Distance: 13.8 miles one-way
Duration: 7 to 9 hours
Challenge: Moderate-Difficult
Elevation Change: 2800ft descent

Romantically named Bridalveil Fall was called Pohono by the Ahwahneechee, who thought the fall bewitched. According to Native American legend, an evil spirit who breathed out a fatal wind lived at its base; to sleep near it meant certain death. Some claimed to hear the voices of those who had drowned, warning others to stay away from Pohono.

The Pohono Trail traces 13.8 miles of the Valley's south rim between Glacier Point and the Wawona Tunnel parking area. Highlights include Glacier Point (7214ft), Taft Point, Dewey Point (7385ft), Crocker Point (7090ft), Stanford Point and Inspiration Point. The trail traverses an area high above three waterfalls – Sentinel, Bridalveil, and Silver Strand.

It's best to go from east to west, starting at Glacier Point. (The trail descends more than 2800ft, so hiking the opposite direction would involve a strenuous climb.) Though it's generally downhill, the trail does make some noticeable climbs here and there.

As the trailheads are many miles apart, you'll need either two vehicles or to arrange for pickup following your hike. The Glacier Point Hikers' Bus can take you to Glacier Point from the Valley, but it doesn't stop at the Wawona Tunnel parking area.

Look for the well-marked trailhead near the snack bar at Glacier Point. After about a mile, you'll reach the trail junction for **Sentinel Dome**. You can either climb to the top (see p 107) or keep going, skirting just north of the dome along the Valley rim. After about 2 miles, you'll join the trail to **Taft Point** (see p 107), which leads you across open rock, past The Fissures to the point itself. Peer over the railing before resuming your hike.

The trail continues west along the Valley rim, dipping to cross **Bridalveil Creek**. Past the creek, a trail veers left toward McGurk Meadow. Instead, bear right toward **Dewey Point** and another magnificent view (use extreme caution when peering over the edge). Across the Valley, you'll see 1612ft Ribbon Fall – when flowing, the highest single-tier waterfall in North America.

About a half-mile farther west is **Crocker Point**, again worth a short detour for the view, which takes in Bridalveil Fall. Another short walk brings you to **Stanford Point**, the last cliff-edge viewpoint on this trail. Once you cross Meadow Brook and Artist Creek, you'll begin the steep, 2.5-mile descent to **Inspiration Point**, an overgrown viewpoint along an old roadbed. The final 1.3-mile leg ends at the Wawona Tunnel parking lot.

SUMMER ACTIVITIES

Biking

One of Yosemite's prettiest rides is along peaceful, pine-fringed Glacier Point Rd, which offers smooth pavement, gentle climbs, stunning vistas, and manageable traffic. To ride the full 11.6 miles each way, begin at the pullout near Chinquapin junction – there's ample parking near the phone and restrooms.

For a shorter but equally gorgeous ride, start from the parking area near the Sentinel Dome Trailhead. From here, it's just under 3 miles to the Glacier Point overlook. As you pass Washburn Point and wind around the last curve, Half Dome rises into view in all its magnificent glory.

Hang Gliding

You can actually hang glide from Glacier Point for a mere $5, provided you're an active member of the **USHGA** (☎ 719-632-8300), have an advanced standing or level 4 certification, and you preregister online with the **Yosemite Hang Gliding Association** (YHGA; Ⓦ www.yhga.org). On Saturdays and Sundays from late May to early September, weather permitting, 10 qualified hang gliders can launch from the overlook at 8am, well before any thermal activity rolls in, and float down by 10:30am to Leidig Meadow, just west of Yosemite Lodge. Arrive at the launch pad by 7am and avoid a late landing, or you may face stiff consequences (like a night in jail or hefty fine). The YHGA monitors all jumps, but you must bring your own equipment; no paragliding or tandem flying is allowed.

WINTER ACTIVITIES
Downhill Skiing & Snowboarding

California's oldest ski slope, **Badger Pass Ski Area** (☎ 209-372-1244; Ⓦ www.badgerpass.com; lift ticket adult/child $31/16; open mid-Dec–early Apr) sits at 7300ft on Glacier Point Rd, about 22 miles from the Valley. Known as a family-friendly mountain geared toward beginners and intermediates, it features an 800ft vertical drop, nine runs, five lifts, a full-service lodge, and equipment rental ($20 for a full set of gear). For great money-saving deals, check out the stay-and-ski packages at the Wawona Hotel, Yosemite Lodge, and Ahwahnee Hotel (see the Places to Stay chapter).

The excellent **Yosemite Ski School** (☎ 209-372-8430) is highly regarded for its top-notch instruction, particularly to beginners. Private lessons range from $26-47 and the "Guaranteed Learn to Ski" package costs $40-49. Badger's gentle slopes are well suited for first-time snowboarders, and the school offers a beginner's package for $59, including lessons, equipment rental, and lift ticket; gear rental alone is $30.

A free daily shuttle runs from the Valley to Badger Pass.

Cross-Country Skiing

Twenty miles of groomed track, 90 miles of marked trails, and 23 skating lanes fan out from Badger Pass. From here,

One of Yosemite's prettiest rides is along peaceful, pine-fringed Glacier Point Rd, which offers smooth pavement, gentle climbs, stunning vistas, and manageable traffic.

you can schuss out to the Clark Range Vista and Glacier Point, an invigorating 21-mile round-trip.

The **Yosemite Cross-Country Ski School** *(☎ 209-372-8444)* offers learn-to-ski packages ($40), guided tours (from $40 for a half-day), telemark instruction ($30), private lessons (starting at $28), and equipment rental ($16 for skis, boots, and poles; $14.25 for snowshoes). The school also hosts very popular overnight trips to the **Glacier Point Ski Hut** *(☎ 209-372-8444)*. One-night trips cost $150-180 per person; two nights run $225-270, including meals, wine, accommodation, and guides.

The handcrafted stone **Ostrander Lake Ski Hut** *(☎ 209-372-0740; ⓦ www.ostranderhut.com)*, operated by the Yosemite Association, can accommodate up to 25 skiers in a gorgeous lakeside spot beneath Horse Ridge. Cooking facilities are provided, but you must ski in with all of your supplies. The 10-mile trip requires experience and a high fitness level. Staffed throughout the winter, the hut is open to backcountry skiers and snowshoers for $20 per person per night; a drawing is held for reservations in early November.

Snowshoeing

You can rent snowshoes at Badger Pass ($9.75/14.25 for a half-day/full day), where rangers lead two-hour naturalist treks that are informative, fun, and almost free ($3). Call ☎ 209-372-0299 for details and check the *Yosemite Guide* for the schedule. From February to April, rangers offer "Full Moon Snowshoe Walks," departing at 6:30pm on nights of and leading up to a full moon. Sign up at the Yosemite Lodge Tour Desk.

Snow Camping

The **Yosemite Cross-Country Ski Center** offers an overnight trip at Badger Pass ($150 per person, including meals), with instruction in snow-camping fundamentals and survival skills.

WAWONA
Map 4

Yosemite's historical center, Wawona is home to the park's first headquarters (supervised by Captain AE Wood on the site of the Wawona Campground) and its first tourist facilities. The latter was a simple wayside station run by Galen Clark, who homesteaded in Wawona in 1856. A decade later, Clark was appointed state guardian of the Yosemite Grant, which protected Yosemite Valley and the Mariposa Grove. In 1875 he sold his lodge to the Washburn brothers, who built what's known today as the Wawona Hotel. The Washburns also renamed the area Wawona – thought to be the local Native American word for "big trees."

Completed in 1875, the original Wawona Rd opened the floodgates for tourists curious to see the big trees – as well as wondrous Yosemite Valley to the north. The road was modernized in 1933, following construction of the Wawona Tunnel.

The elegant **Wawona Hotel**, a blend of crisp New England charm and Victorian elegance, stands today as the commercial focal point of the area. The hotel looks out on a large, manicured green lawn and, across Hwy 41, a golf course (built in 1917) and the expansive **Wawona Meadow**, which doubled as the local airport in the early 20th century. To the north is the **Pioneer Yosemite History Center**, which includes some of the park's oldest buildings, relocated from various points including "old Yosemite Village." The center also features a collection of stagecoaches that brought early tourists to Yosemite.

Some 6 miles southeast of Wawona lies the **Mariposa Grove of Giant Sequoias**, the park's largest and most popular sequoia grove. It's home to the 2700-year-old Grizzly Giant and, in the upper grove, the Fallen Wawona Tunnel Tree, which toppled over in 1969. Allow at least an hour to get to the grove from Yosemite Valley.

From 1891 to 1906, the site that's now Wawona Campground was home base for the US cavalry, who were appointed as the first official protectors of the newly formed national park. The cavalry moved its headquarters to Yosemite Valley in 1906. Curiously, considering its significant role in the park's history, Wawona remained private property for decades and wasn't incorporated into the boundaries of Yosemite National Park until 1932. Some parts of the area, in fact, are still in private hands, including the houses that line Chilnualna Rd.

ORIENTATION & INFORMATION

Wawona lies on Hwy 41 (Wawona Rd), 4 miles north of the park's South Entrance, which is about 63 miles north of Fresno. Yosemite Valley is a 27-mile drive north. No public transportation serves Wawona.

The South Fork of the Merced River passes through Wawona, running northwest out of the park. Most visitor services lie just to its south. North of the river is Chilnualna Falls Rd, which runs east into a development of private homes and rental properties.

Between April and October, the free **Mariposa Grove Shuttle Bus** loops between the Wawona Store, the South Entrance, and Mariposa Grove from 9am to 5pm daily. Taking the bus is not only a good idea, it's sometimes your only option for visiting the grove, as the small parking lot there fills up quickly.

The **Wawona Information Station** (☎ *209-375-9531; open 8:30am-4:30pm daily late May–early Oct)* doubles as the area's visitor center and wilderness center, issuing wilderness permits, answering general park questions, and selling some

Wawona Campground was home base for the US cavalry, who were appointed as the first official protectors of the newly formed national park.

maps and books. You can find the station inside **Hill's Studio**, a historic 1886 building (it was the studio of landscape painter Thomas Hill) adjacent to the Wawona Hotel. Small exhibits in the studio include a display of the park's various pinecones.

Backcountry hikers can self-register here for wilderness permits to trailheads at Wawona and those along Glacier Point Rd; for hikes starting in Yosemite Valley, however, you must go to the wilderness center in the Valley.

At the corner of Hwy 41 and Forest Dr, just north of the hotel, are a **general store**, post office, ATM, and gas station.

The stables, the Pioneer Yosemite History Center, and a small **Campground Reservation Office** lie along Chilnualna Falls Rd; cross to the north side of the river and turn right. **Bassett Memorial Library**, which offers free Internet access, and the year-round Pine Tree Market are also on Chilnualna Falls Rd, about a mile east of Hwy 41.

MARIPOSA GROVE

This grove is one of the most popular spots in the park for good reason – massive sequoias pack its 250 acres. You can do as little or as much hiking as you like to take in the approximately 500 mature trees. If you're lucky enough to nab a spot in the grove's tiny parking lot, you won't even have to get out of your car – there are several trees right in the lot. Do get out, though, and take at least the half-mile walk up to the 2700-year-old **Grizzly Giant**, a massive, bloated beast of a tree with branches that are bigger in circumference than most of the pines in this lovely forest.

The **California Tunnel Tree** is a short walk away, and you won't be able to resist walking through it. Incredibly, the tree continues to survive the mutilation that was done to it back in 1895. The more famous **Wawona Tunnel Tree**, however, toppled over in 1969 – its 10ft-high hole gouged from a fire scar in 1881.

Finding solitude in this popular grove is nearly impossible, but if you want to be alone, try visiting after 6pm, when crowds thin out.

Finding solitude in this popular grove is nearly impossible, but if you want to be alone, try visiting after 6pm, when crowds thin out. You'll also probably find a spot in the upper parking lot, which saves you from taking the free shuttle bus from either the park entrance (2 miles away) or the Wawona Store (6 miles).

Give yourself a few hours to explore the grove, as it's quite big, with a lower and upper half; it's well worth taking the time to wander the latter. Between the parking lot and the Wawona Tunnel Tree atop the upper grove, the elevation gain is about 1000ft, but the trail is gentle. The upper grove is also home to the small **Mariposa Grove Museum** *(open 9am-5pm daily May-Sept)*, which explains sequoia ecology.

Three miles from the parking lot, the wide-open overlook at **Wawona Point** (6810ft) takes in the entire area. It's about a mile round-trip from the Wawona Tunnel Tree.

You can also explore the grove on a one-hour guided tour aboard a noisy open-air **tram** (☎ 209-375-1621; adult/child $11/5.50; June-Oct), which leaves from the parking lot.

PIONEER YOSEMITE HISTORY CENTER

Along the South Fork of the Merced River just north of the Wawona Hotel, the Pioneer Yosemite History Center (admission free; always open) is a collection of historic buildings that were relocated here in the early 1960s from various parts of the park, including the original site of Yosemite Village. Mostly furnished, the buildings include a Wells Fargo office, a jail, and the Hodgdon homestead cabin. A covered bridge crosses the river (it dates from 1857 but was modified with walls and a ceiling by Vermont native Henry Washburn in 1875), and a barn south of the river holds a collection of vintage stagecoaches. In summer, the buildings are staffed with folks dressed in period costume who explain their surroundings (though tours of the buildings are self-guided).

A nice spot to spend a little time, the center gives you a sense of what park life was like a century ago. For fun, hop aboard a 10-minute **stagecoach ride** (adult/child $3/2; Wed-Sun June-Sept). On summer weekends, you may even stumble across the occasional **barn dance**; check Yosemite Today.

HIKING & BACKPACKING

Mariposa Grove features quite a few lovely hiking trails, and you could easily spend a half-day or more crisscrossing its 250 acres. A trail connects the grove with Wawona, where an easy loop circles Wawona Meadow and a more difficult trail leads to Chilnualna Fall, one of the park's lesser-known waterfalls. From there, long-distance trails head to such remote areas the Buena Vista Crest and the Clark Range.

WAWONA MEADOW
Distance: 3.5 miles
Duration: 1 to 1.5 hours
Challenge: Easy
Elevation Change: 200ft

Though you won't huff and puff too much on this gentle, shaded loop around pretty Wawona Meadow, you will have to dodge copious amounts of smelly horse manure plopped and squashed along the entire trail. Horseback riders and stagecoaches use the loop, throwing up lots of dust – another unpleasant element, especially on an already hot summer day.

On the other hand, this short, easy trail is a nice way to spend an hour or two beneath the trees beside the meadow. It's especially lovely in spring, when wildflowers are in bloom. If you're lucky, you might even be alone most of the way – aside from the horses.

From the Wawona Hotel, cross Hwy 41 on a small road through the golf course. The trail starts a short distance down on your left and follows an old dirt road around the meadow perimeter. On the return, you'll cross Hwy 41 again and wind up on the hotel's back lawn. Plunk down in an Adirondack chair and soak up the scene.

MARIPOSA GROVE TO WAWONA
Distance: 6.5 miles one-way
Duration: 2 to 3 hours
Challenge: Easy
Elevation Change: 2000ft descent

You can actually do several miles worth of hiking in Mariposa Grove alone, but this trail is a great way to escape the crushing crowds and recover some peace of mind on your way back to Wawona. If you take the free shuttle bus up to the grove, you can enjoy this hike one-way downhill – not a bad way to travel. The trail leaves from the outer loop on the west side of the grove; follow signs from either the museum (if you're in the upper grove) or the parking lot.

CHILNUALNA FALL
Distance: 8.6 miles
Duration: 4 to 5 hours
Challenge: Moderate-Difficult
Elevation Change: 2240ft

Chilnualna Creek tumbles over the north shoulder of forested **Wawona Dome** (6897ft) in an almost continuous series of cascades. The largest and most impressive of these, Chilnualna Fall thunders into a deep, narrow chasm. Unlike its Valley counterparts, this fall is not free-leaping, but its soothing whitewater rush makes it an attractive day hike. Carry lots of water, as the route can be hot. Atop the fall is a nice picnic spot.

Like all Yosemite waterfalls, Chilnualna Fall is best between April and June when streams are at their fullest. July and August are often too hot for an afternoon hike, and by September the fall is limited by low water.

The trailhead is at the east end of Chilnualna Fall Rd. Follow Hwy 41 (Wawona Rd) a quarter-mile north of the Wawona Hotel and store, and take a right just over the bridge on Chilnualna Fall Rd; follow it for 1.7 miles. The parking area is on the right, and the trailhead is marked.

The trail follows the northwest bank of Chilnualna Creek one-tenth of a mile to the first series of tumbling cascades, which in spring shower the trail with a cool mist. Ascend several brief sets of granite steps beside the falls. Above, the stock trail joins the footpath along the Yosemite Wilderness boundary, a short but steep two-tenths of a mile and 600ft above the trailhead.

The trail rises gently yet continually through open, mixed-conifer forest, leveling out as it passes the rushing creek. It then moves away from the creek, taking you on long, sweeping switchbacks. The sheer granite curve of Wawona Dome fills the sky to the east as you rise above forested Wawona Valley. About an hour or an hour and a half from the trailhead, you'll reach an unobstructed viewpoint from a granite overlook (5400ft); it offers the first good view of the fall. To the southwest are the forested Chowchilla Mountains.

The trail climbs several well-graded switchbacks, then a final dynamite-blasted switchback across a granite cliff to the top of Chilnualna Fall (6200ft). While you won't find any better view of the fall, it's worth continuing 15 minutes farther to a nice picnic spot along Chilnualna Creek. If you're on an overnight trip, head for the campsites farther up both Chilnualna and Deer Creeks.

Retrace your steps 4.3 miles to the trailhead in two hours or so, ignoring an inaccurate sign that reads "5.6 miles to Wawona." At a junction two-tenths of a mile from the trailhead, avoid the tempting, broad horse trail (which comes out at a different trailhead) in favor of the footpath that bears left back down along the creek.

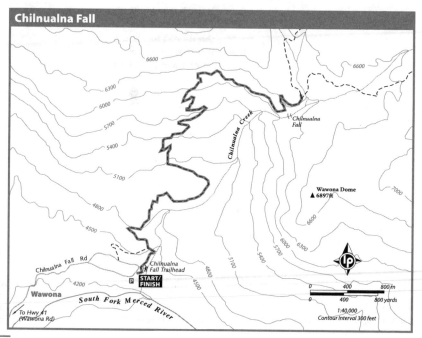

OTHER ACTIVITIES

For good **rafting,** head to the spot where the South Fork of the Merced flows between the campground and Swinging Bridge. You'll find nice swimming holes both near the campground and by Swinging Bridge. The latter is reached via a 2-mile drive east along Forest Dr, which parallels the south bank of the Merced River. Park in a lot beyond private Camp Wawona and walk the short distance to the river.

From early April to mid-October, the Wawona Stables (☎ 209-375-6502) offers guided **horseback riding** behind the Pioneer Center ($40 for two hours), to Chilnualna Fall ($55 for a half-day), and around Deer Canyon Loop ($80 for a full day). There's also a stock camp (☎ 800-436-7275; $20 per night) in Wawona; reservations are required and are available up to five months in advance.

Just outside the park's South Entrance, the **Yosemite Trails Pack Station** (☎ 559-683-7611, 800-635-5807) offers rides to the Mariposa big trees. Or you can rent pack and saddle animals, and the services of a packer, if you want to go it alone. Call ☎ 209-372-8348 for details.

The South Fork of the Merced offers some of the best stream **fishing** in the park.

You'll find good marked **cross-country skiing** trails at Mariposa Grove and just outside the South Entrance in Goat Meadow and along Beasore Rd.

Off-limits in summer, the peaceful and protected Mariposa Grove is open for **snow camping** from December to mid-April. You'll need a wilderness permit, and you must set up your tent uphill from Clothespin Tree. The Wawona Campground also stays open for winter camping on a first-come, first-served basis.

HETCH HETCHY
MAP 5

On Yosemite's west border just north of the Big Oak Flat Entrance lies the Hetch Hetchy Reservoir. This area draws the least amount of traffic, despite the fact that it boasts high waterfalls and steep granite cliffs that rival its more glamorous counterparts in Yosemite Valley.

The chief difference between the two areas is that Hetch Hetchy Valley is now filled with water, following a long political and environmental battle that lasted a dozen years during the early 20th century. Despite the best efforts of John Muir, who led the fight against it, the US Congress approved the 1913 Raker Act, which allowed the city of San Francisco to construct O'Shaughnessy Dam in the Hetch Hetchy Valley. This blocked the Tuolumne River and created Hetch Hetchy Reservoir. Muir's spirit was broken, and he died a year later.

Beneath all that water is a U-shaped, glacially carved region said to be as beautiful as Yosemite Valley. Today, the reservoir and dam supply water and hydroelectric power to much of the Bay Area, including Silicon Valley. When you turn on a tap in San Francisco, out pours Tuolumne River water from the Hetch Hetchy Reservoir. Some politicians and environmentalists (particularly the Sierra Club) still argue for pulling the cork and draining the valley. Who knows? Stranger things have happened in California.

There's one good thing you can say about the dam: By filling in the valley, it has prevented the overdevelopment that plagues Yosemite Valley. Hetch Hetchy remains a lovely, quiet spot – good for a quick day trip or as a jumping-off point for a serious backcountry experience.

Its low elevation makes Hetch Hetchy an especially suitable destination in spring and fall, when much of the high country is still blanketed by ice and snow. In summer, however, it can be very hot and dry – bring a hat, sunscreen, and plenty of water.

ORIENTATION & INFORMATION

The 8-mile-long Hetch Hetchy Reservoir stretches behind O'Shaughnessy Dam, site of the area's trailheads, parking area, and backpackers' campground (available only to those with a valid wilderness permit for backcountry trips in the area).

Hetch Hetchy is a 40-mile drive from Yosemite Valley. From the park's Big Oak Flat Entrance, drive a mile or two west on Hwy 120 and look for the signed turnoff to Hetch Hetchy along Evergreen Rd; turn left (north), drive 8 miles to Camp Mather, and turn right (east) on Hetch Hetchy Rd. The Hetch Hetchy Entrance Station is just a mile beyond the junction; here backpackers can register for a free wilderness permit.

From the entrance, it's about 9 miles to the parking lot beside O'Shaughnessy Dam. About 5.7 miles past the entrance, at roadside marker H3, you'll pass an overlook of the reservoir to the east and lovely Poopenaut Valley some 1200ft below.

The road to Hetch Hetchy is only open during daylight hours – approximately 7am to 9pm in summer, 7am to 7pm in spring and fall, and 8am to 5pm in winter. Hours vary year to year and season to season; they're posted on a sign at the Evergreen Rd turnoff. The gate is locked at night, and the road may close in winter due to heavy snows (carry chains). Vehicles over 25ft are not permitted on the narrow, winding road.

Don't expect any visitor services at Hetch Hetchy. The closest convenience store is in Camp Mather or at the Evergreen Lodge, which also houses a good restaurant and bar.

HIKING

A popular gateway to Yosemite's vast northern wilderness, Hetch Hetchy is also the terminus of the Tuolumne River. Hikers from Tuolumne Meadows can follow the Grand Canyon of the Tuolumne, then continue high above the reservoir's south

There's one good thing you can say about the dam: By filling in the valley, it has prevented the overdevelopment that plagues Yosemite Valley.

shore to Hetch Hetchy Rd. Check with Wilderness Center staff before attempting this hike, as recent burns make the trail difficult to follow.

Day hikers are essentially limited to the Wapama Falls Trail, which traces the reservoir's scenic north shore, a fairly easy hike for just about anyone.

TUEEULALA & WAPAMA FALLS
Distance: 5.4 miles
Duration: 2.5 to 3 hours
Challenge: Easy
Elevation Change: 400ft

Along the north shore of beautiful Hetch Hetchy Reservoir, neighboring falls tumble more than 1000ft over fractured granite walls: the seasonal, free-leaping Tueeulala Falls and the enormous triple cascades of year-round Wapama Falls. You can capture both falls and adjacent Hetch Hetchy Dome (6197ft) in a single spectacular photograph. Nowhere else in the park does a trail bring you so close to the shower and roar of a big waterfall.

The gentle north shore trail is mostly flat, with only a few ups and downs. Plan the hike for mid- to late spring, when temperatures are cooler, butterflies are abundant, and wildflowers are in bloom.

From the parking lot (3813ft), cross O'Shaughnessy Dam and pass through the tunnel on its far side. The broad, oak-shaded trail then heads northeast, above and parallel to the north shore. In just over a mile, after rising gradually past several small seasonal streams, you'll reach a signed trail junction (4050ft). The trail to Lake Vernon, the source of Falls Creek, heads left up a series of switchbacks.

This makes a good stopping point if you're only out for a quick hike. Go in search of a picnic spot on the open granite northeast of the trail junction.

To continue, take the right (east) fork, following the sign reading 1.6 miles to Wapama Falls. The trail descends gently, then bears left onto broad, polished granite slabs. Tueeulala Falls (pronounced **twee**-la-la) springs spectacularly from cliffs more than 1000ft above the trail. Most of its water flows beneath a wooden footbridge, but in spring a small section of the trail fills with runoff. By June, however, the falls are usually dry.

The trail continues 10 minutes down a staircase that switchbacks gently to the base of thundering Wapama Falls (3900ft), where wooden footbridges span **Falls Creek**. In spring, water cascades over the trail beyond the first footbridge and almost covers the second. When the water is high, crossing is dangerous, but at other times the flow is ankle-deep The frothy, gushing torrents create billowing clouds of mist that drench the entire area and make for a cool bath on a warm afternoon.

Southeast across the deep waters of the reservoir, the vertical north face of **Kolana Rock** (5772ft) provides nesting sites for peregrine falcons. Enjoy the sights and sounds of beautiful Wapama Falls and Hetch Hetchy, then return to the trailhead via the same route.

You could continue another 4.7 miles to **Rancheria Falls**, a series of cascades at the reservoir's east end. Visit the falls on a long day hike (14.4 miles round-trip with a 660ft elevation gain) or camp here overnight.

OTHER ACTIVITIES

The road leading to Hetch Hetchy is a great choice for road **biking**. Park at the pullout a mile before the park entrance gate to enjoy the paved and virtually traffic-free 8-mile ride to the reservoir, promising moderate climbs and stellar Sierra views.

Hetch Hetchy is said to house a trove of very large trout; **casting** is permitted from the shore only, though no live bait is allowed.

Those interested in **horseback riding** will find a small **stock camp** (☎ 209-379-1922) just before the reservoir; it's available by reservation during the summer and on a first-come, first-served basis the rest of the year.

BIG OAK FLAT ROAD/CRANE FLAT
MAP 6

Those arriving on Hwy 120 first encounter this section of the park. While not the most spectacular part of Yosemite, it does welcome a steady flow of visitors. While most are just passing through, plenty more bed down in the Hodgdon Meadow and Crane Flat campgrounds.

Big Oak Flat Rd was the second route into the park, completed in 1874, just a month after Coulterville Rd. Both were toll roads. Today, Big Oak Flat Rd follows a modified route into the Valley, though a portion of the old road remains open to cyclists and hikers headed for Tuolumne Grove. In winter the road is popular with cross-country skiers.

ORIENTATION

Sights and services lie along Big Oak Flat Rd (Hwy 120), near either the entrance gate or Crane Flat junction. A gas station and store mark Crane Flat, where Hwy 120 turns east and follows Tioga Rd to Tuolumne Meadows, and Big Oak Flat Rd descends southeast into the Valley. The latter road passes through several tunnels and offers great overlooks of the Merced River Canyon.

INFORMATION

You'll find several useful services just inside the park gate at the Big Oak Flat Entrance. Note that all opening and closing dates are approximate and depend on weather, park budgets, and demand.

The **Big Oak Flat Entrance Station** (☎ 209-379-1899; open 9am-5pm daily Apr-Oct, until 6pm midsummer) serves as a mini-visitor center, with lots of books, maps, and postcards for sale and a few historic photographs on display. You'll find answers to general park questions and may use a courtesy phone to check available lodging. Outside is a **wilderness permit window** *(open 8am-5pm daily June-Sept)*, which issues permits and rents bear-proof canisters ($5).

The staff at the adjacent **Campground Reservation Office** *(open 8am-5pm daily in summer, closed mid-Oct–Apr)* offer advice on camping options and post information on site availability. Spaces at Hodgdon Meadow or Crane Flat sometimes open up

You won't find a store at Big Oak Flat, but there are a few snack and soda vending machines, as well as restrooms and telephones.

At Crane Flat junction, the **Crane Flat Service Station & General Store** *(open 8am-8pm daily in summer, 9am-5pm in winter)* sells limited groceries, firewood, ice, beer, and a few last-minute camping supplies. The gas station stays open year-round, and the pumps operate 24 hours with a credit card.

CRANE FLAT FIRE LOOKOUT

Atop a 1.5-mile spur road, this active fire lookout includes a working heliport and resident fire crew. You can visit the lookout, as long as you follow designated pathways. From the parking area, a short walk leads to the lookout, offering fantastic 360-degree views of the park, including the jagged peaks of the **Clark Range** to the south and (on clear days) the San Joaquin Valley to the west. Look for the turnoff road along Big Oak Flat Rd, less than a mile west of the Crane Flat store. RVs and trailers should not attempt the climb.

HIKING

Both of the area's two main hikes lead to groves of giant sequoias. Though neither grove is as magnificent as Wawona's Mariposa Grove, the crowds are mercifully thinner.

> ### TUOLUMNE GROVE
> **Distance: 2 miles**
> **Duration: 1.5 hours**
> **Challenge: Moderate**
> **Elevation Change: 500ft**

You can reach this moderately-sized grove of sequoias via a short, steep hike down a section of the historic Old Big Oak Flat Rd (now closed to cars). Follow the road and a few switchbacks to the first trees, then meander through the grove and along an interpretive nature trail. The most popular attraction is the Tunnel Tree, (also known as the "Dead Giant"') which was already a stump when a tunnel was cut into it back in 1878. The only bummer about this hike is the steady uphill climb back to the parking area. It's not awful, though, and hikers of any age should be able to handle it given time and patience.

MERCED GROVE
Distance: 3 miles
Duration: 1.5 to 2 hours
Challenge: Easy-Moderate
Elevation Change: 600ft

Though it's the smallest sequoia grove in the park, Merced is also the quietest, thanks in part to its distance from major park sights. If you seek solitude amid the sequoias, this is for you. You'll start from a small parking lot along Big Oak Flat Rd midway between Crane Flat and the Big Oak Flat gate. The trail follows a dirt road (closed to cars), which remains flat for the first half-mile before dipping downhill into the grove. A handful of the trees surround a small log cabin. Reserve your energy for the hike out.

OTHER ACTIVITIES

The steep 2·5-mile out-and-back **biking** route to Tuolumne Grove on Tioga Rd is a short but challenging ride; it starts from the parking area just north of Crane Flat.

You'll find good marked **cross-country skiing** and **snowshoeing** trails in the Crane Flat area, including Old Big Oak Flat Rd, which leads to Tuolumne Grove and Hodgdon Meadow. In winter, Tioga Rd is closed east of here, so that road is another possibility.

ALONG TIOGA ROAD
MAP 7

The only road that bisects the park is Tioga Rd, a 56-mile highway that runs between Crane Flat in the west (at Big Oak Flat Rd junction) and Hwy 395 at Lee Vining, about 12 miles east of Tioga Pass, the park's easternmost gate. Along the way it traverses a superb High Sierra landscape. Be prepared to pull over regularly to gawk at sights such as glorious Tenaya Lake, mighty Clouds Rest, and the backside of Half Dome from Olmsted Point. Bring plenty of film.

Initially called the Great Sierra Wagon Rd, the road was built by the Great Sierra Consolidated Silver Company in 1882-83 to supply a mine at Bennettville near Tioga Pass. Ironically, no significant silver was ever found, and the mine closed soon after the road was completed. Tioga Road was realigned and modernized in 1961. Only a few sections of the original roadbed remain, including the rough, 4.5-mile stretch that leads to Yosemite Creek Campground. Head down this narrow, tortuous road for a glimpse of how much more treacherous park roads used to be – and not even that long ago. You'll return to Tioga Rd with newfound respect for this engineering marvel.

ORIENTATION & INFORMATION

Tioga Rd rises from 6200ft at Crane Flat to 9945ft at Tioga Pass. It's typically closed due to snow from mid-November to mid-May, although in years with heavy snowfall it may not open till late June. In winter the road is used by cross-country skiers and snowshoers.

This section covers the stretch of Tioga Rd between Crane Flat and the vicinity of Tenaya Lake. You'll find few visitor services; for information and supplies, head directly to Tuolumne Meadows, where you'll find an excellent visitor center, a good grocery store, and a post office. Crane Flat, to the west, has a convenience store and gas station, both open year-round. Some 15 miles northeast of Crane Flat is White Wolf, with a small lodge boasting a dining hall, tent cabins, and a very tiny **store** that sells mostly snacks and drinks. White Wolf sits on a short spur road a mile north of Tioga Rd.

During summer the **Tuolumne Meadows Tour & Hikers' Bus** runs once a day each direction along Tioga Rd between Yosemite Valley and Tuolumne Meadows, stopping at trailheads and viewpoints along the way.

SEEING THE SIGHTS

On your way to Tuolumne Meadows, if you pull over at only one viewpoint along Tioga Rd, make it **Olmsted Point**, which offers a stunning view down Tenaya Canyon to the backside of Half Dome. Midway between the May Lake turnoff and Tenaya Lake, the point was named for Frederick Law Olmsted (1822-1903), who was appointed chairman of the first Board of Commissioners to manage the newly established Yosemite Grant in 1864. Olmsted also helped to design Central Park in New York City and did some landscaping for the University of California and Stanford University.

If you pull over at only one viewpoint along Tioga Rd, make it Olmsted Point, which offers a stunning view down Tenaya Canyon to the backside of Half Dome.

Looming over the canyon's east side is 9926ft **Clouds Rest**, a massive mountain comprising the largest exposed chunk of granite in Yosemite. As its name implies, clouds often settle atop the peak. Rising 4500ft above Tenaya Creek, it makes a strenuous but rewarding day hike.

Just east of Olmsted Point, **Tenaya Lake** (8150ft) takes its name from Chief Tenaya, the Ahwahneechee chief who aided white soldiers only to be driven from the land by white militias in the early 1850s. Tenaya allegedly protested use of his name, pointing out that the lake already had a name – *Pywiack*, or "Lake of Shining Rocks," for the polished granite that surrounds it.

Whatever name you choose, you'll certainly call it gorgeous the minute you catch sight of it from Tioga Rd. The lake's shiny blue surface looks absolutely stunning framed by thick stands of pine and a series of smooth granite cliffs and domes. Dominating its north side is **Polly Dome**. The face nearest the lake is known as **Stately Pleasure Dome**, a popular spot with climbers – you may see them working their way up from the road). Sloping up from the lake's south shore are **Tenaya Peak** and **Tresidder Peak**.

HIKING & BACKPACKING

Day hikes and backcountry excursions are plentiful in Yosemite's subalpine wilderness, which stretches north and south from either side of Tioga Rd. Like Tuolumne Meadows farther east, this truly is a hikers' paradise. Several trails from the south side of the road lead to Yosemite Valley, and if you take the hikers' bus up from the Valley, they're more or less downhill all the way – an exquisite and rare treat. Don't worry about your ability or lack thereof: Some of the easiest hikes, such as that to Lukens Lake, are very rewarding.

LUKENS LAKE
Distance: 1.6 miles
Duration: 1 hour
Challenge: Easy
Elevation Change: 200ft

Hike up here early in the morning or late in the afternoon, especially on a weekday, and you just might have the quiet blue lake, green meadow, and surrounding sea of colorful wildflowers all to yourself. (Weekends are a different story.) Revel in the idyllic setting, serene and lovely in the "golden hour" of early evening light. Even beginners can handle the short jaunt from Tioga Rd.

Start from the marked parking area a couple miles east of the White Wolf turnoff. Cross the road (carefully) and begin the trail in the soft woods. Climbing steadily, you'll reach a small ridge, then drop down to the lake. The trail follows the north shore to the far (west) end, where you'll find plenty of shady spots to rest, picnic, or simply sit in quiet contemplation.

An alternate 2.3-mile trail leads to the lake's west side from White Wolf Lodge.

TENAYA LAKE
Distance: 2 miles
Duration: 1 hour
Challenge: Easy
Elevation Change: 50ft

This loop trail is more of a pleasant stroll than a hike. It skirts the south shore of one of the park's biggest natural lakes, the brilliant-blue jewel of Tuolumne's subalpine region.

Begin from the parking lot on the lake's east end, which may be full or close to it, as the adjacent sandy beach is popular (even if the water is rather chilly). Walk south along the beach and look for the trail amid the trees just ahead. As the path traces the shore, small spurs lead down to the water. Though the shoreline is rocky, there are several nice semi-secluded spots for a picnic. When you reach the west end (and the Sunrise Trailhead), you could continue along the lake's north shore beside busy Tioga Rd – not exactly pretty or recommended. Better to either wait for the free shuttle bus back to the parking lot or simply turn around and return the way you came.

MAY LAKE & MT HOFFMANN
Distance: 6 miles
Duration: 4 to 5 hours
Challenge: Moderate
Elevation Change: 2004ft

At the park's geographical center, Mt Hoffmann (10,850ft) commands outstanding views of Yosemite's entire high country. Hiking to its summit takes just a few hours along a good trail that presents no difficulties. The broad summit plateau offers a superb perspective, a vista that drew the first California Geological Survey party in 1863. They named the peak after Charles F Hoffmann, the party's topographer and artist. The first peak climbed in Yosemite, Mt Hoffmann remains one of the park's most frequently visited summits.

Alternatively, hikers can head to **May Lake** (9350ft), on the High Sierra Camps loop, a pristine mountain lake that cries out for a shoreline picnic. It alone is a satisfying destination, with great views of Half Dome, Cathedral Peak, and Mt Clark along the way. The hike takes only about 30 to 40 minutes in each direction.

To turn this into an overnight trip, it's best to stay at the backpackers' campground adjacent to the May Lake High Sierra Camp, although camping on Mt Hoffmann's summit is nothing less than sublime.

Start from the May Lake Trailhead (8846ft), 1.7 miles up a paved section of the old Tioga Rd. The turnoff from Tioga Rd is 2.2 miles west of Olmsted Point and 3.2 miles east of the Porcupine Flat Campground. Be sure to use the bear boxes in the parking lot.

The 1.2-mile stretch to May Lake is fairly easy, although it's a steady 500ft climb. At the lake the trail splits; the right fork leads to May Lake High Sierra Camp, the left to Mt Hoffmann. The Hoffmann trail ascends through a talus field, where it becomes indistinct, although the route is obvious. Follow a small stream, then cross a meadow where the trail turns sharply toward Mt Hoffmann's east summit. Don't be confused by the many paths marked with cairns along this rocky slope – all routes lead to the higher west summit.

Camping is possible on the vast plateau near the east summit, although you must carry water from May Lake or use snowmelt. When ready, retrace your steps to the May Lake trailhead.

CLOUDS REST
Distance: 14.4 miles
Duration: 6 to 7 hours
Challenge: Difficult
Elevation Change: 2205ft

Yosemite's largest granite peak, Clouds Rest (9926ft) rises 4500ft above Tenaya Creek, with spectacular views from the summit and along the trail. More than 1000ft higher than nearby Half Dome, Clouds Rest may well be the park's best panoramic viewpoint. The hike involves a strenuous ascent and equally significant descent, but getting here is definitely worth the effort.

Start from the Sunrise Lakes Trailhead at the west end of Tenaya Lake. Trailhead parking is limited, and the lot fills early. If you're staying in Tuolumne Meadows, a great alternative to driving is the free Tuolumne to Olmsted Point shuttle bus, which stops at the trailhead. The Tuolumne Meadows Tour & Hikers Bus from Yosemite Valley also stops here, but only once a day in each direction.

Follow the trail along Tenaya Creek for your first glimpse of Clouds Rest and Tenaya Canyon's shining granite walls. As the trail climbs steadily up well-constructed switchbacks, the view expands to include prominent Mt Hoffmann (10,850ft) to the northwest and Tuolumne Peak (10,845ft) to the north. After a steady 30-minute ascent, the grade eases atop soft earth amid large red firs. Continue straight past the Sunrise Lakes junction and descend southwest. As Yosemite Valley and Sentinel Dome come into view, the trail reaches the level floor west of **Sunrise Mountain** (9974ft). Paintbrushes, lupines, and wandering daisies bloom here, alongside mats of pink heather and bushes of poisonous white-flowered Labrador tea. Fifteen minutes past a shallow pond you'll reach a creek that's the last water source en route to the summit – so fill up (and filter it).

Twenty minutes later you'll reach the Forsyth Trail junction, although it's not labeled as such on the sign. Bear southwest (right) and ascend the ridgeline that culminates in Clouds Rest. To the southeast are fabulous views of wedge-shaped Mt Clark (11,522ft), the Cascade Cliffs, and Bunnell Point in Merced Canyon. The granite swell of Mt Starr King (9092ft) rises to the southwest. The trail soon passes over a low rise and through a slight but obvious saddle. At a large white pine 20 minutes beyond the saddle, a small unmarked trail forks left; this is recommended for those not willing or able to hike the more exposed summit path.

A sign reading "Clouds Rest Foot Trail" directs you along the granite ridge, which narrows rather thrillingly in one place. Never less than 5ft wide, the narrowest section might look intimidating but takes only five to 10 seconds to cross. The summit itself offers breathtaking views of Half Dome and the Valley. The view stretches from the Sawtooth Ridge and Matterhorn Peak along the park's north border to Mt Ritter and Banner Peak, standing dark and prominent to the southeast. Mts Conness and Dana on the Sierra Crest and the closer Cathedral Range are all outstanding. This is one of the Sierra Nevada's most inspiring viewpoints – savor the sights before retracing your steps to the trailhead.

You can extend your hike by continuing down to Yosemite Valley (see the Tenaya Lake to Yosemite Valley hike on p 128).

NORTH DOME
Distance: 8.5 miles
Duration: 4.5 to 5 hours
Challenge: Moderate
Elevation Change: 1000ft descent, 422ft ascent

Though North Dome (7542ft) sees relatively few hikers, it's perhaps the best vantage point along the Valley rim, with a view of Half Dome, Quarter Domes, and Clouds Rest rising on the far side of granite-walled Tenaya Canyon.

The trail descends 1000ft and rises 422ft on the way there, so be ready for a climb on the return trip, though the gradient is rarely steep A side trip to the natural arch on Indian Ridge adds another 240ft climb. Keep in mind that it's mostly downhill on the way out to North Dome and uphill on the way back, although the gradient is rarely steep.

From Tioga Rd, start at the Porcupine Creek Trailhead (8120ft), 1.3 miles east of Porcupine Flat Campground. To reach the trailhead from the campground, walk to the south side of the highway from the camp entrance and follow the footpath that parallels the road.

An abandoned road leads beneath red firs until the pavement ends and the trail crosses Porcupine Creek via a log. After an easy 30-minute ascent into the forest, you'll reach a sign for the Snow Creek Trail to the Valley. Continue straight another 50ft to a second trail junction and take the left fork toward North Dome.

The trail climbs gently up Indian Ridge for 10 minutes to an inviting view across the Valley to Sentinel Dome and Taft Point. The trail soon turns sharply and ascends steadily for another 10 minutes, leading to the marked Indian Rock trail junction.

A worthwhile but optional 30-minute side trip leads to Yosemite's only visible **natural arch**. Follow the short, steep spur trail to the arch (8360ft), which affords good views of Clouds Rest, the Clark Range, Mt Starr King, and Sentinel Dome. Clamber onto the rock for a view of Half Dome framed by the arch.

At the Indian Rock trail junction, the main trail continues south, leading to a spectacular **viewpoint** at the end of the ridge: front and center is Half Dome, and across the Valley is hard-to-see Illilouette Fall. North Dome lies directly below to the south, and Basket Dome's rounded peak (7612ft) lies to the southeast. This is a fantastic spot to camp; if you do decide to spend the night here (or on North Dome), you'll need to bring water, as none is available nearby.

DOWN FROM
THE MOUNTAIN

Instead of driving between Tioga Rd and Yosemite Valley, why not consider hiking? There are numerous ways to do it, including those mentioned in the North Dome hike. The Tenaya Lake to Yosemite Valley hike is one of the classics, allowing you an up close look at the major landscape changes. If you take the hikers' bus up from the Valley and start from the trailheads along Tioga Rd, your journey will be mostly downhill.

The trail drops south (left) off the ridgeline in the direction of Half Dome and descends on switchbacks across open granite. Cairns lead to the marked North Dome Trail junction. Turn east (left) for the final half-mile stretch. The rough trail descends steeply before a short final ascent to the summit. West are the Sentinels, Cathedrals, El Capitan, the Three Brothers and Yosemite Point (Yosemite Falls lie hidden). To the northeast are Basket Dome, Mt Watkins, and the distant peaks of the Cathedral Range. Horse Ridge rims the horizon to the south, while dominating the scene is the sheer north face of Half Dome – surely one of Yosemite's most impressive sights.

It will take about two hours to retrace your steps along Indian Ridge and return to the trailhead.

You can extend the hike by descending to the Valley on either the Snow Creek Trail (which heads down to Tenaya Canyon and Mirror Lake) or on the trail west to Yosemite Point and Yosemite Falls Overlook. From the latter, take the Yosemite Falls Trail down to Camp 4.

Use the hikers' bus from the Valley to reach the North Dome Trailhead in the morning. You can also start hiking from the Valley and visit North Dome on a very demanding round-trip of eight to 10 hours. For an especially vigorous day hike, traverse the Valley's north rim via North Dome by ascending the Snow Creek Trail's 100-plus switchbacks and returning via the Yosemite Falls Trail.

TENAYA LAKE TO YOSEMITE VALLEY
Distance: 17.2 miles
Duration: 2 days
Challenge: Difficult
Elevation Change: 2205ft ascent, 6321ft descent

The most spectacular trail from Tioga Rd to Yosemite Valley traverses the summit of **Clouds Rest** (9926ft), arguably Yosemite's finest panoramic viewpoint. An easier variation bypasses Clouds Rest completely and follows Sunrise Creek. Both hikes descend through Little Yosemite Valley and past world-renowned Nevada and Vernal Falls to Happy Isles. Hearty hikers can also include a side trip to the top of Half Dome. On stormy days, steer clear of both Half Dome and Clouds Rest.

The trailheads are almost 50 miles apart by road. Unless you plan to shuttle two vehicles, instead use YARTS or the Tuolumne Meadows Tour & Hikers Bus for the uphill leg.

On **Day 1**, start from the well-marked Sunrise Lakes Trailhead, at the west end of Tenaya Lake off Tioga Rd. Trailhead parking is limited, and the lot fills early. Those leaving from Tuolumne Meadows can instead use the free Tuolumne to Olmsted Point shuttle bus, which stops at the trailhead.

See the Clouds Rest hike (p 126) for a description of the 7.2-mile trail to the summit. From the summit, head down granite steps off the south side to the forested ridge below. In six-tenths of a mile you'll reach a signed junction with a bypass trail for horses. Continue straight, down through scattered ponderosa pines, chinquapins and manzanitas. Twenty minutes beyond the horse trail junction, you'll pass beneath granite domes and continue the descent on switchbacks for another hour. Near the bottom of the knee-pounding 2726ft descent, the trail enters refreshingly shady forest.

Two hours (3.8 miles) from the summit of Clouds Rest, you'll reach the marked junction with the John Muir Trail (7200ft). Nearby Sunrise Creek offers several forested campsites and provides the first water since well before Clouds Rest. Turn west (right) onto the John Muir Trail and descend a half-mile to the signed junction with the heavily traveled Half Dome Trail. Go south (left) and head down the trail 1.3 miles to the established and busy campsites in **Little Yosemite Valley** (6100ft) along the Merced River. Beware: Both Sunrise Creek and Little Yosemite Valley experience chronic problems with bears.

Day 2 follows either the Mist Trail or the John Muir Trail some 1065ft down to Happy Isles in Yosemite Valley.

Those not inclined to visit the Clouds Rest summit can follow an easier, forested **alternative trail** along Sunrise Creek, which

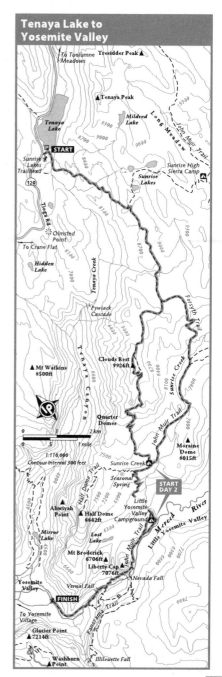

eventually meets the trail from Clouds Rest and descends to Little Yosemite Valley.

To begin, follow the Day 1 description above for 2.5 hours (4.7 miles) to the signed junction (9100ft) with the Clouds Rest and Forsyth Trails. Bear southeast (left) and follow the Forsyth Trail across a meadow into the pine and granite landscape. The trail leads down a slope of red firs, offering good views of the Clark Range, Merced Canyon, and Mt Starr King. Follow **Sunrise Creek** until a slight ascent takes you to the marked junction (8000ft) with the John Muir Trail, also known here as the Sunrise Trail. Go southwest (right) on the John Muir Trail one-tenth of a mile to another junction, where a trail to Merced Lake heads east (left). Stay on the John Muir Trail, heading west (right) along Sunrise Creek, then descend switchbacks to the junction (7200ft) with the Clouds Rest Trail. Continue a half-mile to the busy Half Dome Trail, then turn south and descend the John Muir Trail to Little Yosemite Valley.

OTHER ACTIVITIES
Rock Climbing & Bouldering
You'll find plenty of great climbing around Tenaya Lake, most notably on Polly Dome. Stately Pleasure Dome, the side of Polly adjacent to the lake, is the most popular spot, offering a good mix of easy and moderate routes. The granite rocks in this part of the park are well suited for slab and friction climbing, both well represented on Stately Pleasure.

For more difficult climbing, try the backside of Pywiack and Medlicott Domes, both just northeast of the lake toward Tuolumne Meadows. The beach at the east end of Tenaya Lake is an ideal spot for watching climbers.

For good bouldering, head to The Knobs, just over a mile north of Tenaya Lake on the west side of the road. Beginners will find excellent climbing on nearby Low-Profile Dome, particularly along the Golfer's Route.

For advice, classes, and books, stop by **Yosemite Mountaineering School** (YMS; ☎ 209-372-8344), with a summer base at the Tuolumne Meadows gas station. After Labor Day, YMS continues to offer private

HALF DOME DETOUR

Some hikers on the Tenaya Lake to Yosemite Valley Trail camp near the junction of the John Muir and Clouds Rest Trails along **Sunrise Creek** (7200ft), breaking up the 3826ft descent between Clouds Rest and Little Yosemite Valley into two days. Campsites on the far side of the creek are more desirable than those near the trail junction. Camping along Sunrise Creek also puts you just a half-mile from the Half Dome Trail junction, a good spot to be if you want to include the side trip to the summit of Half Dome. It's also possible to push beyond Sunrise Creek and camp along Half Dome's northeast shoulder.

climbing sessions around Tenaya Lake from its main office at Curry Village – of course, as long as the weather holds and Tioga Rd remains open.

Biking

Many people bicycle along formidable Tioga Rd. If you succumb to the temptation, keep in mind that this winding, climbing route has many blind spots and often fields a lot of traffic. It's a tough, relentless grind, so start riding early in the morning and keep well hydrated. From Crane Flat, it's just under 100 miles to Tioga Pass and back.

Boating

Motorless boats of any kind can use beautiful and easy-to-access Tenaya Lake – hands down the best place to boat in the park. Lounging at the foot of John Muir's beloved Mt Hoffmann is tranquil May Lake, a lovely place to paddle an inflatable – that is, unless you want to hoof anything heavier for the 1.2 miles from the trailhead along Tioga Rd.

Swimming

If you can handle cold water, Tenaya Lake offers some of the most enjoyable swimming in the park. It's hard to resist this glistening lake that beckons with sapphire waters. A sandy half-moon beach wraps around the east end. Sunbathers and picnickers are also drawn to the many rocks that rim its north and west sides.

TUOLUMNE MEADOWS
MAP 8

Arriving at Tuolumne (pronounced **twol**-uh-me) Meadows after the drive up from the Valley is like stepping into another world, even though the two areas are only about 55 miles apart. Instead of being surrounded by waterfalls and sheer granite walls, you emerge in a subalpine wonderland marked by jagged peaks, smooth granite domes, brilliant blue lakes, and the meadows' lush grasses and wildflowers.

Flowing from the Sierra Crest, the Lyell and Dana Forks of the Tuolumne River – not to mention creeks such as Budd, Unicorn and Delaney – all converge at Tuolumne Meadows (8600ft elevation). At 2.5 miles long, the main flat cradles the Sierra's largest subalpine meadow, a great spot for picnicking, fishing, kite flying, or just lounging in the sun with a good book. The surrounding peaks and domes make Tuolumne a paradise for climbers and hikers, with trails stretching in all directions.

Lying deep in the high country of the Sierra, the region enjoys a brief, glorious summer. The meadows' blossoms peak in July, after the snowmelt but before the first frosts set in, usually by September.

Areas like this are often quite remote and hard to reach. But at Tuolumne you can simply peer out your car window for a close look at one of the world's best-known and most beautiful mountain ranges. In summer, anyone who visits Yosemite for more than just a day should absolutely make the trek up here for a taste of the high country.

Tuolumne is far quieter than the Valley, though the area around the store, campground (the park's largest), and visitor center can get crowded, especially on midsummer weekends. Many hiking trails, such as Dog Lake, are also well traveled. With only a little effort, however, you'll quickly find solitude in the Sierra.

Temperatures in Tuolumne Meadows and the surrounding high country are 15°F to 20°F cooler than in Yosemite Valley, a benefit for hikers and anyone else who has a hard time in the heat. At the same time, nights are much chillier up here, so be sure to pack warm clothes. And remember, snow can fall here in any month of the year, though typically no later than June and no earlier than September.

Anyone who visits Yosemite for more than just a day should absolutely make the trek up here for a taste of the high country.

ORIENTATION & INFORMATION

Tuolumne Meadows sits along Tioga Rd (Hwy 120) west of the park's Tioga Pass Entrance. The main meadow is about 2.5 miles long and lies on the north side of Tioga Rd between Lembert Dome to the east and Pothole Dome to the west. The visitor services face the meadow from the road's south side. Limited parking is available for hikers and meadow meanderers in pullouts along Tioga Rd (or you can take the shuttle bus). You'll find larger parking lots near Lembert Dome, the visitor center, and the wilderness center.

Facilities and trails in Tuolumne Meadows are open only when Tioga Rd is clear, usually between late May or June and October. Most facilities open one to two weeks after the road opens and are closed by September. Note that specific opening hours vary each year depending not only on the weather (sometimes Tioga Rd stays closed until July), but also on available budget and staff.

The free **Tuolumne Meadows Shuttle Bus** travels along Tioga Rd between Olmsted Point and Tioga Pass daily. The **Tuolumne Meadows Tour & Hikers' Bus** makes a daily journey from Yosemite Valley to Tuolumne Meadows and back from mid-June to mid-September. For schedules and more information on both services, see Public Transit (p 85).

At the **Tuolumne Meadows Visitor Center** *(☎ 209-372-0263; open approximately 9am-5pm daily, until 6pm July-Aug)*, about a mile west of the campground, rangers answer questions on what to do and see, sell books and hiking maps, and have helpful handouts describing local trails. A few good displays clearly explain common glacial features.

The **Wilderness Center** *(open 7:30am-6pm daily in midsummer, 8am-5pm in late spring and early fall)* is the place to go for wilderness permits and trail information. Since Tuolumne's mountains, lakes, and trails are such a draw for backpackers, it's often a busy spot. You can buy books and maps here, and hikers can check trail conditions. The center sits on the south side of Tioga Rd just east of Lembert Dome, on the spur road leading to Tuolumne Meadows Lodge. The lodge offers public **showers** *(open to nonguests noon-3pm; $2)* and hot meals.

The **Tuolumne Meadows Store** *(☎ 209-372-8428; open 8am-8pm daily July-Aug, reduced hours otherwise)* is well stocked with groceries for campers and backpackers alike; the same complex includes the **Tuolumne Meadows Grill** and a small **post office**, where tourists can buy stamps and long-distance hikers can pick up food drops.

The **Tuolumne Meadows Sport Shop** *(open 8:30am-6pm daily July-Aug, reduced hours otherwise)*, next door at the **gas station**, sells a variety of backpacking gear, including maps, dehydrated food, and bear-resistant food containers. It's also serves as summer home to the **Yosemite Mountaineering School and Guide Service** *(☎ 209-372-8435)*.

In a small, attractive old building at the entrance to Tuolumne Meadows Campground, the **Campground Reservation Office** offers information on available campsites every morning.

MAIN MEADOW

The **main meadow** itself is a beautiful sight to behold, especially during sunset, when golden light ripples across the green grass and lashes up the sides of distant peaks into the still blue sky. Grab a fishing pole and dip into the gently rolling river as the

JOHN MUIR'S "HIGH PLEASURE-GROUND"

Spend any time here and you'll see why Tuolumne Meadows was one of John Muir's favorite spots in the Sierra, an area he called in his book *My First Summer in the Sierra* a "spacious and delightful high pleasure-ground." The meadows caught his eye on his very first visit to the park, when he tended sheep up here one summer in 1868. Smitten, he returned repeatedly. One of his milestone camping trips occurred in 1889, when he came here with Robert Underwood Johnson, editor of then-popular *Century* magazine. It was during that trip the pair famously plotted to save the meadow from development and overgrazing by making it part of the soon-to-be Yosemite National Park. Muir wrote two articles for *Century* in favor of extending the park's proposed boundaries to include the meadows. By the end of the following year, Yosemite was named America's second national park – Tuolumne Meadows included.

LIBRARY OF CONGRESS PHOTO

sunlight drifts away, or just find a quiet spot to sit and stare at the landscape as the mood shifts and the colors shimmer.

The meadow is a perfect place for quiet contemplation, but there's actually a lot of activity going on here. Given such a short growing season, plants and animals take full advantage of the summer sun. Walk the interpretive trail from the stables to Soda Springs for a look at what's really happening beneath the meadow's deceptively still surface.

SODA SPRINGS & PARSONS LODGE

Soda Springs is a muddy area at the north end of the main meadow where carbonated water bubbles up in red-tinted pools. People used to drink the stuff, though the park service now discourages the practice due to possible surface contamination – no big deal, as it's not exactly an appealing method for quenching your thirst anyway.

Nearby is Parsons Memorial Lodge, a simple but beautifully rugged cabin built in 1915 from local granite. It initially served as a Sierra Club meeting room and was named for Edward Taylor Parsons (1861-1914), an active Sierra Club member who helped found the club's outings program. The park service bought the lodge in 1973. Inside you'll find a big fireplace, historical displays, and, a few times each week, ranger talks and other programs (see *Yosemite Today* for the current schedule).

Not far away sits the old McCauley Cabin, now closed to the public. Gone, however, is one of the meadows' earliest structures, a cabin built by Jean-Baptiste Lembert, a shepherd who homesteaded here in the late 1800s. Lembert Dome bears his name.

The springs and lodge are a short, pleasant walk across the flat middle of the meadow – probably the gentlest hike in the entire park. There are two approaches, both about a half-mile. The first starts opposite the visitor center on Tioga Rd; signs will direct you to the wide, gentle trail. The other begins in the Lembert Dome parking area. Take the gravel road past the stables, then follow an auto-free portion of the historic old Tioga Rd to the springs. Along the way, interpretive signs explain the meadow's history and ecosystem.

From Soda Springs, a trail leads northwest toward Glen Aulin High Sierra Camp and the Grand Canyon of the Tuolumne.

POTHOLE DOME

This dome marks the west end of Tuolumne Meadows. It's small by Yosemite standards, but the short, 200ft climb to the top offers great views of the meadows and surrounding peaks – especially, of course, at sunset. Park along Tioga Rd, then follow the trail around the dome's west side and up to its modest summit. It's a fairly quick trip and well worth the effort.

Walk the interpretive trail from the stables to Soda Springs for a look at what's really happening beneath the meadow's deceptively still surface.

PEAKS & DOMES

During the Tioga glacial period just 20,000 years ago, the massive Tuolumne Glacier, a 2000ft-thick river of ice, coursed from the Sierra Crest through Tuolumne Meadows and completely filled Hetch Hetchy Valley. The contrasting shapes of peaks around Tuolumne are a record of this period – the smooth dome-like peaks were worn down beneath the glacier, while the sharp, jagged summits of the Cathedral Range and Sierra Crest remained above the ice that quarried their slopes.

CATHEDRAL RANGE

The Cathedral Range runs northwest from the Sierra Crest, between the Tuolumne and Merced Rivers. Its granite pinnacles are immediately striking, in particular **Cathedral Peak** (10,911ft), visible from numerous spots in the region, including along Tioga Rd. At certain angles, its summit appears to be a near-perfect pinpoint, though in reality it's a craggy, double-pronged affair. Other mountains in the range include Tresidder Peak, Echo Peaks, the Matthes Crest, and **Unicorn Peak** (10,823ft), another standout with a horn-shaped protuberance, just east of Cathedral Peak.

TIOGA PASS

East of Tuolumne Meadows, Tioga Rd (Hwy 120) climbs steadily toward **Tioga Pass**, which at 9945ft is the highest auto route over the Sierra. The short ride by car or free shuttle bus from Tuolumne Meadows takes you across dramatic, wide open spaces – a stretch of stark, windswept countryside near the timberline. You'll notice a temperature drop and, most likely, widespread patches of snow.

The road parallels the Dana Fork of the Tuolumne River, then turns north, where it borders the beautiful **Dana Meadows** all the way to Tioga Pass. To the east you'll see great views of Mt Gibbs and 13,053ft Mt Dana, the park's second-highest peak after Mt Lyell (13,114ft).

For even more amazing views, drive over Tioga Pass and begin the more than 3000ft descent into **Lee Vining Canyon**, a fantastically rugged and dry landscape. At the bottom is **Mono Lake** (see p 202), a stunning jewel at the edge of the Great Basin Desert, only a half-hour drive from Tioga Pass.

HIKING & BACKPACKING

The vast wilderness surrounding Tuolumne Meadows is a hikers' mecca. The reasons become glaringly obvious the minute you set out on one of the region's stunning trails. You'll find an

The **High Sierra Camps** (Map 9) are a more relaxing way to experience the backcountry, as you don't have to carry a tent or cooking gear – hearty meals and accommodations are provided. There are five camps in the high country surrounding Tuolumne Meadows. For information on making reservations at one of the camps, see p 170.

assortment of pristine alpine lakes, vast glacial cirques, broad green meadows, brilliant wildflowers, and breathtaking overlooks. Many would argue that the park's best hiking is found around Tuolumne Meadows.

Most of the hikes that follow are easily completed in a day. Others are best enjoyed over one or more nights in the backcountry – an experience well worth the necessary planning and preparation. No cross-country hikes are listed; all follow marked (and often well-worn) trails.

Except in the highest of the high country, the hiking season generally begins in June and runs into September or early October, depending on the weather, of course. Summer skies are frequently clear, though afternoon thundershowers are common in August. Be sure to watch the skies, and never attempt to summit a high dome or peak if a storm threatens.

For a hiking overview, stop at the visitor center, where you can pick up a free day-hike handout and rangers can suggest trails best suited to your ability and schedule. As for picking a favorite, however, they have no easy answers. "You can't go wrong," veteran Tuolumne Meadows rangers will boast, because, frankly, the trails are all pretty much fantastic.

Backcountry hikes take more advance planning. Make sure you have a good map, and check with the wilderness center not only for proper permits, but also for an update on trail conditions. For peace of mind while you sleep beneath the stars, be sure to rent a bear canister. They're only $5 per trip, and you won't have to bother hanging your food from trees (a stopgap solution at best).

In addition to the multiday hikes listed below, several of the day hikes can be extended into overnight excursions, including Cathedral Lakes, Mt Dana, and Glen Aulin.

LEMBERT DOME
Distance: 2.8 miles
Duration: 2 hours
Challenge: Moderate
Elevation Change: 850ft

Named for 19th-century shepherd Jean-Baptiste Lembert, who homesteaded in Tuolumne Meadows, prominent Lembert Dome (9450ft) rises from the meadows' east end opposite the campground. The view from the summit overlooks the meadows and surrounding peaks. It's a more strenuous climb than Pothole Dome, but it's still a manageable journey for just about any level of hiker. You can easily combine this with the hike to Dog Lake.

Two similarly named trails lead to Lembert Dome. The one from the parking lot at the very base of the dome is a steep, borderline un-

HANG GLIDING Hang gliding from Glacier Point promises an unbeatable view. [Photo: Mickey Pfleger]

AROUND**YOSEMITE**

VERNAL FALL Gazing at Vernal Fall from the Mist Trail. [Photo: Rob Blakers]

HETCH HETCHY RESERVOIR This controversial reservoir flooded the once-spectacular Hetch Hetchy Valley, but the area still offers solitude, excellent hiking, and a gateway to the vast northern wilderness. [Photo: Mark & Audrey Gibson]

MONO LAKE Tufa towers on the shores of Mono Lake. [Photo: Eddie Brady]

BEYOND**YOSEMITE**

MAMMOTH LAKES Horseback riding around Duck Lake. [Photo: Lee Foster]

BODIE A 1927 Dodge pickup parked for keeps at Bodie State Historic Park, a genuine California ghost town. [Photo: Eddie Brady]

KINGS CANYON NATIONAL PARK A hiker crosses a wooden suspension bridge over Woods Creek. [Photo: John Mock]

pleasant trail that's been damaged by storms. To reach the preferred Dog Lake Trail, drive east from the campground, cross the bridge, and turn south onto the road leading to Tuolumne Meadows Lodge. Park in the Dog Lake parking lot, about a half-mile up the road; this is also shuttle bus stop 2.

From the trailhead, follow the Young Lakes Trail to the Dog Lake Trail, which crosses to the north side of Tioga Rd. Continue up a series of well-graded switchbacks amid lodgepole pines till the path levels out. At a signed junction, the trail to Lembert Dome forks northwest (left). Continue six to eight minutes to a forested saddle between Lembert Dome and the smaller Dog Dome, where a sign points west to "Lembert Dome Parking" and east to "Dog Lake Parking."

The one-way route to the top of Lembert Dome (three-tenths of a mile) leaves the trail here. Turn southwest and walk up the gentle granite slope 10 minutes to the summit. The Sierra Crest from Mt Conness to the Kuna Crest stretches to the east. Look south to find the Cathedral Range and west to take in the broad expanse of Tuolumne Meadows. Relax and enjoy the view and perhaps a picnic lunch before retracing your steps. Follow the signs back to the Dog Lake parking lot.

For an alternative route back, turn west at the forested saddle and descend the steep, eroded trail to the Lembert Dome parking lot, shuttle bus stop 4. A level trail crosses Tioga Rd and joins the John Muir Trail. Head east for a half-mile along this trail, which parallels the road and passes the wilderness center before reaching the Dog Lake parking lot. Allow two hours total for this hike.

DOG LAKE
Distance: 2.8 miles
Duration: 2 hours
Challenge: Moderate
Elevation Change: 600ft

Beautiful, scenic Dog Lake (9170ft) is accessible via the same trail that accesses Lembert Dome. Be prepared, though, to share this subalpine gem with fellow hikers; on weekends, it may resemble your local reservoir, as people lug abundant picnic supplies and even inflatable rafts up to the lake's forested shores. Be sure to bring water and an extra shirt, as the lake is often breezy; if you don't wear it, you can use it as a pillow – the lakeshore is ideal for a quick afternoon nap

Like the trip to Lembert Dome, there are two trailheads for Dog Lake. The best one leaves from the appropriately named Dog Lake parking lot, near Tuolumne Meadows Lodge. Follow this trail to the base of Lembert Dome (described above). When you reach the turnoff for the summit, continue straight. A half-mile or so up the fairly flat trail is another junction; turn right toward Dog Lake (left is a steep downhill to the Lembert Dome parking lot). It's about another half-mile to the lake. A pathway meanders around the lake itself.

ELIZABETH LAKE
Distance: 4.8 miles
Duration: 3 to 4 hours
Challenge: Moderate
Elevation Change: 900ft

This small mountain lake is a beauty in itself, and its near flawless location, tucked beneath spiky Unicorn Peak, adds to the stunning scene. Getting here involves a short but fairly steep climb. All the panting and sweating up the hill is worth the effort.

The trail is easy to access if you're camping at Tuolumne Meadows, as it leaves from inside the campground. Look for the marked trailhead just behind the group camp restroom on the B loop (ask for a campground map at the entrance kiosk). The trail pulls no punches, the hardest climb coming in the first half of the hike. On hot summer days, you'll be glad for the plentiful shade. The trail levels out somewhat about a mile from the lake. Once there, find a nice big rock and sit for a spell, soaking up the view (and enjoying the picnic lunch you hopefully remembered to bring).

CATHEDRAL LAKES
Distance: 7.6 miles
Duration: 4 to 6 hours
Challenge: Moderate
Elevation Change: 1000ft

The neighboring Cathedral Lakes lie beneath the white granite flanks of the Cathedral Range. These sister pools are among the prettiest in the region. In addition to near-perfect scenery, the lakes promise fine – if chilly – swimming. Camping is possible with a wilderness permit. It takes some effort to get here, including a couple of steady uphill climbs, but the views of the north mountains and double-pronged spire of Cathedral Peak should keep you going.

The hike starts from a parking area south of Tioga Rd, 1.7 miles west of the visitor center. Since it's a popular hike, and pullouts are often full, consider parking at the visitor center and taking the free shuttle bus, which stops at the trailhead. The journey follows a section of the John Muir Trail most of the way. Expect to dodge plenty of manure on the trail, as it's used by pack trains supplying Sunrise High Sierra Camp, south of Cathedral Lakes.

From Tioga Rd, the trail rises steadily beneath tree cover for the first half-mile, then levels off with views of surrounding peaks. The massive mountain before you is Cathedral Peak.

Take a rest, then push up the second major ascent, about as long, steep, and steady as the first. When the view opens up along this stretch, it's a knockout. The trail flattens out again, passing through woods and wildflowers, then dips slightly to a junction.

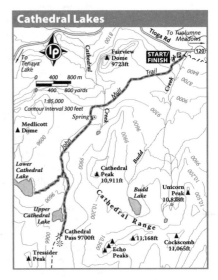

Turn right and walk another half-mile to reach **Lower Cathedral Lake** (9288ft), the best choice if you only have time to see one lake. You'll emerge in a gorgeous granite bowl, or glacial cirque, with the pointed, photogenic spire of Cathedral Peak at your back and the lake spread out before you. Find a spot on the rocks and soak up this classic Sierra subalpine scene. Bring a jacket, too, as winds here keep temperatures a bit cool.

Back at the junction, the John Muir Trail continues south about another half-mile to **Upper Cathedral Lake** (9585ft), the smaller of the two. It's somewhat quieter here, too, though the far shore is popular with backpackers. The view east toward craggy Echo Peaks is quite impressive. If you've come this far, top off the day by hiking another half-mile to **Cathedral Pass** (9700ft), which offers stunning views of the Cathedral Range, including Tresidder Peak, Echo Peaks, and the Matthes Crest. To the south, a spacious green meadow full of wildflowers beckons. When you can finally tear yourself away, retrace your steps.

GLEN AULIN
Distance: 11 miles
Duration: 6 to 8 hours
Challenge: Moderate
Elevation Change: 600ft

This hike is the first leg of a multiday excursion along the **Grand Canyon of the Tuolumne**; it's also on the High Sierra Camp circuit (see p 170). But it's a great day hike, too, following the Tuolumne River as it winds toward Waterwheel Falls and Hetch Hetchy Reservoir. Most of the elevation change is gradual; the only major dip comes in the final stretch. Since it's downhill on the way in, save energy for the return climb.

To reach the trailhead, head east on Tioga Rd from the Tuolumne Meadows Campground, cross the Tuolumne River bridge, and turn left into the Lembert Dome parking area north of the road. At the end of the short road (which also leads to the stables) is a gate at the signed Glen Aulin Trailhead. Park along the road, either at the Lembert Dome parking lot (day-use only) or at the stables. You'll find bear-proof lockers halfway along the road – store all coolers and food boxes here. Shuttle bus stop 4 is a quick walk from the trailhead.

From the gate, follow the trail a half-mile to Soda Springs, watching for Glen Aulin Trail signs to the right of Parsons Lodge. This is a section of the lengthy Pacific Crest National Scenic Trail (PCT), one well worn by not only through-hikers but also pack trains supplying the High Sierra Camp (you'll find plenty of aromatic evidence along the way).

The trail leads through open lodgepole pine forest, crosses shallow Delaney Creek, then continues to a signed junction with the Young Lakes Trail, 1.3 miles from Soda Springs. Take the left fork, heading northwest through lodgepole pines. You'll emerge on riverside meadows with inspiring views of Fairview Dome, Cathedral Peak, and Unicorn Peak. Make sure to bring lots of film – you'll need it here. Thirty minutes farther, the level, cairn-dotted trail crosses a vast, glacially polished granite slab over which the Tuolumne River flows. The river's roar signals the end of Tuolumne Meadows and the start of a series of cascades that tumble toward the Grand Canyon of the Tuolumne.

The trail climbs briefly over a granite rib, affording distant views of Matterhorn Peak (12,264ft) and Virginia Peak (12,001ft) on Yosemite's north border and a first view of the huge, orange-tinged granite cliff above Glen Aulin. Descend through forest to a two-part wooden footbridge spanning the river, 2.3 miles from the Young Lakes Trail junction.

The trail descends steadily, alternating between forest and riverside before reaching **Tuolumne Falls**. Continue along the plunging river to a signed junction with the May Lake Trail and then a steel girder footbridge spanning the river. Cross it and you'll reach two trail junctions in close succession. To the right is the Glen Aulin High Sierra Camp. At the second junction, the PCT continues north (straight) to a backpackers' campground and on to Cold and Virginia Canyons.

You can hang out here, or turn west (toward Waterwheel Falls) and continue a short distance into Glen Aulin itself – a long, level forested valley where the river flows green and tranquil beneath a massive water-stained granite wall.

To extend this into an overnight excursion, see the following description for the hike to Waterwheel Falls.

GAYLOR LAKES
Distance: 3 miles
Duration: 2 to 3 hours
Challenge: Moderate
Elevation Change: 560ft

This trail climbs up amid the Gaylor Lakes, set in pristine alpine territory just inside the park boundary near Tioga Pass. The short, steep path is a popular one – don't think you'll be entirely alone. It's also a high-altitude hike, so prior acclimatization (spending a day bumming around Soda Springs, for instance) is a good idea. Also expect to find snow. No camping is allowed, so leave the tent in the car.

Park in the small parking lot immediately west of the Tioga Pass Entrance Station. You can also take the free Tuolumne to Tioga Pass shuttle, which departs from Tuolumne Meadows Lodge. The trail begins from the parking lot and wastes no time in starting its steep ascent. At the crest, **Lower Gaylor Lake** (10,334ft) lies in a basin below you, with great views everywhere you turn. The trail skirts the lower lake and then climbs to **Upper Gaylor Lake** (10,510ft).

For an extra bonus, head past the lake and climb again to the site of the old **Great Sierra Mine**, where the views are even wider and more stunning. All told, the alpine countryside here is knockout beautiful, so budget some time for poking around.

MONO PASS
Distance: 7.4 miles
Duration: 4 hours
Challenge: Moderate
Elevation Change: 915ft

A saddle on the Sierra Crest between the rounded summits of Mts Gibbs (12,764ft) and Lewis (12,296ft), Mono Pass was the highest point on an ancient Native American trade route that linked the Mono Lake area with Tuolumne and continued to Yosemite Valley via Cathedral Pass. Remnants of late-19th-century log buildings remain along the trail and on the historic pass, alongside subalpine meadows and lakes with great views of the Tuolumne high country.

The day hike from Dana Meadows follows the well-marked historic trail past meadows and through open forest to the expanse of the lake-crowned pass. To make this an overnight trip, camp at Upper Sardine Lake east of Mono Pass, just outside the park in the Ansel Adams Wilderness.

The well-signed Mono Pass Trailhead (9689ft) is on Tioga Rd at road marker T37, 1.4 miles south of Tioga Pass and 5.6 miles east of Tuolumne Meadows Campground. The free Tuolumne to Tioga Pass shuttle bus stops at the trailhead four times daily – a smart option, since the lot often fills up and you can't just park along the road.

The trail heads southeast through open forest within the shadow of 13,053ft Mt Dana to the northeast. After an easy half-mile hike alongside **Dana Meadows**, the trail crosses the Dana Fork of the Tuolumne River, then crosses two small ridges before passing beneath stately lodgepole pines beside several small, buttercup-filled meadows. Emerging from the pines, the trail makes a gentle ascent along Parker Pass Creek, with

✔ TIP

"Alpine" refers to the high-elevation biogeographic zone that lies above tree line, such as in the European Alps. "Subalpine" is the term for the mountainous terrain just *below* the tree line.

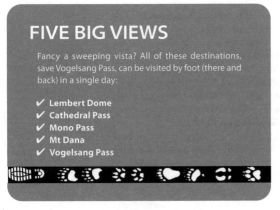

FIVE BIG VIEWS

Fancy a sweeping vista? All of these destinations, save Vogelsang Pass, can be visited by foot (there and back) in a single day:

✔ **Lembert Dome**
✔ **Cathedral Pass**
✔ **Mono Pass**
✔ **Mt Dana**
✔ **Vogelsang Pass**

the reddish bulk of Mt Gibbs above and to the east.

When you reach the signed Spillway Lake trail junction, follow the left fork toward Mono and Parker Passes. Small whitebark pines mix in amid the lodgepole pines – watch for resident chipmunks. The trail passes the remains of a log cabin and opens on a large meadow beside a small creek, with impressive views of Kuna Crest and Mammoth Peak (12,117ft). Thirty minutes (1.4 miles) past the Spillway Lake junction, a small trail marked only by a rock arrow branches right toward Parker Pass. Keep going straight, however, past wind-twisted whitebark pines and two small lakes to Mono Pass (10,604ft).

Tiny Summit Lake lies to the west, while east of the pass are Upper and Lower Sardine Lakes. Farther down, Walker Lake lies in an area known as Bloody Canyon. Tree frogs chirp from the banks of **Summit Lake** in early summer. Flourishing in meadows along its north side are scrub willows, Sierra onions, and yellow potentillas. At the south end of the pass sit three historic log cabins.

Retrace your steps to the trailhead, enjoying the expansive views of the Kuna Crest and Dana Meadows as you descend.

MT DANA
Distance: 5.8 miles
Duration: 6 to 7 hours
Challenge: Very Difficult
Elevation Change: 3108ft

Yosemite's second-highest peak, Mt Dana (13,053ft) takes its name from American geologist James Dwight Dana. This strenuous day hike, with a vertical rise of more than 3100ft above Tioga Pass (9945ft), offers unrivaled views of Mono Lake, the Grand Canyon of the Tuolumne, and the rest of the Yosemite high country. Remember, though, that this is a steep, high-altitude hike – you're *starting* at nearly 10,000ft. Prior acclimatization will ease your struggle.

The hiking season runs from July to mid-September, though snow may block the trail in early summer. Don't even start the hike if a storm threatens.

The unsigned trailhead is just east of the park boundary at the Tioga Pass Entrance. You'll find parking areas on either side of the entrance. You can also get here via the free eastbound Tuolumne to Tioga Pass shuttle, which departs four times daily from Tuolumne Meadows Lodge. From

Tioga Pass, the trail heads east, passing between two broad, shallow pools, then begins to climb. The trail passes through flower-filled meadows on the 1700ft climb to a west-descending ridge, marked by a large, loose cairn, 1.8 miles from Tioga Pass.

From this cairn, several indistinct paths head up the rocky west slope to the summit. Shun the leftmost path through difficult talus blocks in favor of paths to the right, which offer easier footing. The views from Mt Dana's summit are so outstanding that some hikers spend the night on top in the shelter of two small rock windbreaks. From the summit, retrace your steps downhill to the trailhead.

LYELL CANYON (MAP 9)
Distance: 17.6 miles
Duration: 2 days
Challenge: Moderate
Elevation Change: 200ft

For those who loathe uphill climbs, this hike in gorgeous Lyell Canyon is a great choice, as it's surely the most level stretch of trail anywhere in the Sierra Nevada, gaining only 200ft over 8 miles. It follows a section of the John Muir Trail along the Lyell Fork of the Tuolumne River, passing through quintessential subalpine meadows and forest to the base of 13,114ft Mt Lyell, the park's tallest peak. The hike described here is a two-day affair, though you can, of course, spend even more time trekking in the area – exploring nearby Ireland Lake, taking the John Muir Trail south over 11,000ft Donohue Pass into the Ansel Adams Wilderness, or turning the trip into a loop by jaunting west past Evelyn Lake to Vogelsang. Any way you approach it, you'll find yourself on an unforgettably scenic journey, strolling the lovely forested meadows along the winding Lyell Fork beneath the Sierra Crest.

A popular place to park is the lot adjacent to the wilderness center (shuttle bus stop 3); look for a hidden trail sign reading "Tuolumne Lodge, John Muir Trail" and walk southeast, paralleling the road. A foot-bridge crosses the Dana Fork near the lodge, then the trail heads south to meet the John Muir Trail. Alternately, if you're coming from the campground, walk to a trail in Loop A opposite site A88 and follow it along the river. The trailhead sign here reads "To Pacific Crest, John Muir." This path joins the John Muir Trail and in about 30 minutes meets the trail from the lodge.

The trail soon crosses Rafferty Creek and turns southeast into Lyell Canyon, along the river's meadow-lined south bank. Bypassing the turnoff to Ireland and Evelyn Lakes, the trail crosses Ireland Creek, passes beneath Potter Point, and continues to **Lyell Base Camp**, a busy climbers' camp below Donohue Pass.

✔ TIP

For those unable to stay overnight in Lyell Canyon, it's easy to treat this as a day hike. Since there is no real "destination," simply hike in as far as you like, then turn around and head back out.

You can take a daylong side trip to the summit of Mt Lyell, but only experienced climbers should attempt it. The ascent alone gains over 4000ft, and the difficult route traverses a glacier, involves steep and complex climbs, and requires safety ropes. Best to admire the view from below.

If you're up to it, though, you can continue another few miles up the John Muir Trial to Donohue Pass (a 2000ft climb), admiring the impressive peaks and glaciers along the way.

On your second day, the task is simple: Follow the John Muir Trail along the Lyell Fork back to the trailhead.

VOGELSANG
Distance: 27 miles
Duration: 3 days
Challenge: Moderate-Difficult
Elevation Change: 3852ft

Crossing Tuolumne and Vogelsang Passes through Yosemite's **Cathedral Range**, you'll make a remarkable circuit through what John Muir called the "Range of Light." The smooth curve of polished pale granite walls, domes, and ridges crowned by upthrust summit blocks tells the story of once-vast glaciers where beautiful lakes now fill the cirques. The sloping subalpine meadows and streams on either side of gentle Tuolumne Pass (9992ft) provide a scenic backdrop for some of the Sierra Nevada's most delightful hiking. The trail also takes in multiple cascades and sweeping views of distant peaks in several mountain ranges, including the hard-to-see Clark Range.

The peak, lake, pass, and High Sierra Camp all take their name from the Vogelsang brothers, who headed the California Fish and Game Board from 1896 to 1910. The name itself translates aptly from German as "a meadow where birds sing."

Camping at **Vogelsang Lake** and crossing the alpine **Vogelsang Pass** (10,660ft) rank among the highlights of this journey around Vogelsang Peak. A three-day affair, this hike takes you past the Vogelsang High Sierra Camp to Vogelsang Lake the first night, then on a loop south toward Merced Lake and back north to Emeric Lake before returning north to Tuolumne Meadows.

On **Day 1**, the hike strikes out on the same trail (and using the same trailheads) as the Lyell Canyon hike. Once you meet up with the John Muir Trail, head southeast into lodgepole forest beyond the riverside meadow. Twenty minutes (eight-tenths of a mile) ahead at Rafferty Creek, turn south (right), leaving the John Muir Trail. The 2.5-hour-long, 4.9-mile ascent along Rafferty Creek begins with a rugged uphill climb. Gouged out by the steel-shod hooves of packhorses and mules that supply the Vogelsang High Sierra Camp, the trail clambers over granite steps and cobblestones through forest for some 20 to 30 minutes before it eases and nears Rafferty Creek's left bank. To the north you'll see Mt Conness and White Mountain, while the Lyell Fork Meadows spread out

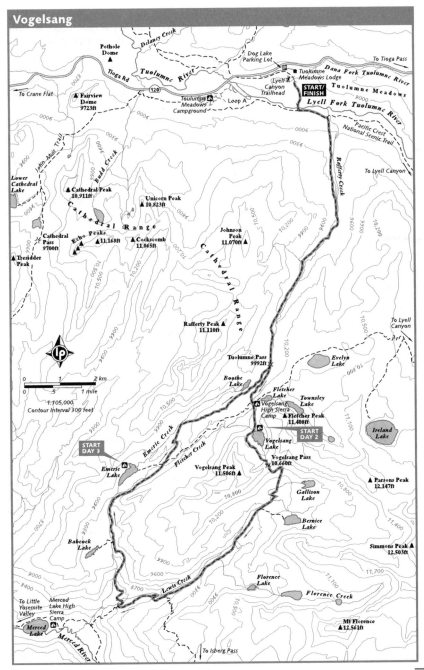

Vogelsang

Pothole Dome ▲

Delaney Creek

Tioga Rd

Tuolumne River

Dog Lake Parking Lot

To Tioga Pass

Dana Fork Tuolumne River

Tuolumne Meadows Lodge

Lyell Canyon Trailhead

START/FINISH

Tuolumne Meadows

To Crane Flat

120

Fairview Dome 9723ft ▲

Toulumne Meadows Campground

Loop A

Lyell Fork Tuolumne River

Pacific Crest National Scenic Trail

John Muir Trail

Budd Creek

Lower Cathedral Lake

Cathedral Peak 10,911ft ▲

Unicorn Peak ▲ 10,823ft

C a t h e d r a l R a n g e

Cathedral Pass 9700ft

Echo Peaks ▲ 11,168ft

Cockscomb 11,065ft ▲

Johnson Peak 11,070ft ▲

▲ Tresidder Peak

C a t h e d r a l R a n g e

Rafferty Peak 11,110ft ▲

Rafferty Creek

To Lyell Canyon

To Lyell Canyon

Tuolumne Pass 9992ft ✕

Evelyn Lake

Boothe Lake

Fletcher Lake

Townsley Lake

Vogelsang High Sierra Camp

Fletcher Peak ▲ 11,408ft

START DAY 2

Ireland Lake

START DAY 3

Emeric Creek

Fletcher Creek

Vogelsang Lake

Vogelsang Pass 10,660ft ✕

▲ Parsons Peak 12,147ft

Emeric Lake

Vogelsang Peak 11,506ft ▲

Gallison Lake

Bernice Lake

Simmons Peak ▲ 12,503ft

Babcock Lake

To Little Yosemite Valley

Merced Lake High Sierra Camp

Lewis Creek

Florence Lake

Florence Creek

Mt Florence ▲ 12,561ft

Merced Lake

Merced River

To Isberg Pass

LP

0   .5   1   2 km
0   .5   1 mile
1:105,000
Contour Interval 300 feet

some 500ft below to the east. As you ascend, you'll enjoy expansive views of the **Kuna Crest, Sierra Crest,** Mt Conness, and Mt Dana.

The steepest part of the trail now behind, you'll gradually ascend an attractive little valley, following the west bank of Rafferty Creek. The forested trail gently climbs another 30 to 40 minutes, then enters a small open meadow. Passing beneath lodgepole pines and across several smaller branch streams, the well-worn trail finally emerges into a lovely meadow along Rafferty Creek.

Fletcher Peak's bulky mass and Vogelsang Peak's pointed granite summit rise above the open horizon ahead. To the immediate right is a blocky granite ridge that includes Johnson Peak (11,070ft) and Rafferty Peak. Finally, 6.1 miles from the trailhead, you'll arrive at gentle **Tuolumne Pass** (9992ft).

At the signed Tuolumne Pass junction, take the left fork and head southeast. The trail offers enticing views of Boothe Lake and the granite ridge above it as it travels eight-tenths of a mile to **Vogelsang High Sierra Camp** (10,130ft). At a signed junction, a backpackers' campground lies to the left (east), while the trail to the right (west) descends to Merced Lake High Sierra Camp Instead, continue straight (south) to Vogelsang Pass.

In the distance to the west, you can see Clouds Rest, the top of Half Dome, and the white spot of Sentinel Dome. A half-mile beyond the High Sierra Camp you'll reach large **Vogelsang Lake** (10,341ft), set in a picture-perfect cirque beneath Fletcher and Vogelsang Peaks. Above the northeast shore are campsites set among whitebark pines.

Day 2 is a 10.2-mile journey with Emeric Lake as your destination. Expect it to take about six hours. To begin, the trail ascends above the southwest end of Vogelsang Lake, eventually crossing a large, cold stream just below its spring-fed source. The view of the lake below and Cathedral Range beyond is sublime. Five minutes farther you'll reach the pass, in the serrated granite ridge that descends from Vogelsang Peak (11,506ft).

From here the trail rises a bit and provides a long view of the upper Lewis Creek Basin. Lovely **Gallison Lake**, surrounded by meadow, issues forth a cascading stream. Large **Bernice Lake** spreads out at the base of a massive granite ridge beneath Mt Florence (12,561ft). Half a dozen more lakes lie hidden in a chain above Gallison Lake, fed by permanent snow from the slopes of Simmons Peak (12,503ft) at the valley's head. To the southwest is the more distant Clark Range, sweeping from the west to the southeast: Mt Clark (11,522ft), Gray

A half-mile beyond the High Sierra Camp you'll reach large Vogelsang Lake, set in a picture-perfect cirque beneath Fletcher and Vogelsang Peaks.

Peak (11,573ft), Red Peak (11,699ft), Merced Peak (11,726ft), and Triple Divide Peak (11,611ft).

Descend a series of switchbacks that follow the course of a small stream. At the base, enter a forest along the level valley floor. Braided streams course across the lush meadow, involving a few crossings. Continue straight past the Bernice Lake junction, heading downstream along Lewis Creek as the descent grows steeper.

Three miles from the Bernice Lake trail junction, you'll pass the Isberg Pass trail junction. Continue a mile down the trail through a dramatic canyon for a view of distant Half Dome before passing large junipers to the signed Merced Lake trail junction (8160ft). It's only 1.8 miles (45 minutes) from this junction to **Merced Lake**, but camping is not allowed at the lake itself (backpackers must camp away from the lake in a dense forest behind the Merced Lake High Sierra Camp). For a nice view of Merced Lake, more than 1000ft below, you need only walk a short distance down this trail. The lake hardly justifies the full dusty descent and subsequent ascent the next morning.

Instead, turn north (right) at the junction and follow the trail up Fletcher Creek. After crossing a footbridge, the trail climbs beside the creek, which cascades along the base of an enormous granite dome in the middle of the valley. Crossing several side streams, the trail stays mostly in the shade, climbing high above the left bank of this beautiful stretch of Fletcher Creek. The trail levels out about one hour past the footbridge, offering a fabulous vista over Merced Canyon and the Clark Range.

Leaving the views behind, head beneath lodgepole pines past the signed Babcock Lake trail junction. You'll climb at first gently and then more steeply beside the creek. After 25 minutes, the trail emerges in a lovely meadow. Admire the views of Vogelsang and Fletcher Peaks as you stroll through the charming granite-lined field to a four-way trail junction. Turn northwest (left) and head four-tenths of a mile to the large **Emeric Lake** (9338ft). Cross its inlet to reach good campsites above the northwest shore.

On **Day 3**, retrace your steps to the four-way junction. The trail to the northeast (right) leads 2.2 miles back to the Vogelsang High Sierra Camp, but its relatively heavy use makes it dusty. Instead, take the north (left) trail, a less-traveled route to Boothe Lake. Both trails eventually lead to Tuolumne Pass, but the trail via Boothe Lake gets you there with 150ft less ascent and one-tenth of a mile less distance; it's altogether more pleasant.

Large and lovely **Boothe Lake**, 2.5 miles (one hour) from the junction, was the original site of the High Sierra Camp before the

Admire the views of Vogelsang and Fletcher Peaks as you stroll through the charming granite-lined field.

camp was moved and renamed Vogelsang. The trail stays well above the lake, where camping is prohibited. Arrive once again at **Tuolumne Pass**, four-tenths of a mile and 15 minutes beyond Boothe Lake. From here, you can retrace your steps easily in less than three hours: 4.9 miles (2.5 hours) down Rafferty Creek to the John Muir Trail and 1.2 miles (30 minutes) to the Lyell Canyon Trailhead. Either fork of the Tuolumne River beckons you for a refreshing dip to wash off the trail dust.

WATERWHEEL FALLS
Distance: 18 miles
Duration: 2 days
Challenge: Difficult
Elevation Change: 2260ft

The **Grand Canyon of the Tuolumne River** stretches 15 miles between Tuolumne Meadows and Hetch Hetchy Reservoir. Waterwheel Falls is the last and most impressive in a series of six cascades before the Tuolumne River plunges even farther into the canyon. Within the canyon lies forested **Glen Aulin**, a peaceful interlude between the otherwise continuous cascades. If you're in good shape, you could do this hike in a single monumental day, but you would scarcely have time to savor the remarkable falls, canyon, and forested glen without taking time for an overnight.

The hiking season lasts from mid-June to October, but the falls are at their best before August.

For the first several miles of the hike on **Day 1**, follow the trail to Glen Aulin (p 139). At the junction for the Glen Aulin High Sierra Camp, keep straight on the trail; at the very next junction, the Pacific Crest Trail heads north, but you'll turn west instead and head toward Waterwheel Falls, 3.3 miles downstream.

From the junction, the trail crosses a low granite rib and descends an orange-stained granite slope into Glen Aulin. Pass through a ghost forest of dead lodgepole pines, their drooping white branches delicately brittle. The trail meanders between the forest and the river's edge, inviting a dip in the placid waters, then crosses an area made marshy by a stream that descends from Cold Mountain to the north.

After a 40-minute stroll, you'll reach the far end of the peaceful glen, where the river flows briskly to the brink of the first in a series of near continual cascades. The trail, too, plunges along the river, dropping over gorgeous orange-tinted granite. Ahead, the Grand Canyon of the Tuolumne stretches as far as the eye can see. The trail continues between the sheer, polished granite walls of Wildcat Point (9455ft) to the north and the 8000ft granite wall of Falls Ridge on the opposite bank. **California Falls** and **LeConte Falls** are the most prominent cascades in this section; most are unnamed. If you have to ask yourself, "Is this Waterwheel Falls?" keep going – you'll know it when you see it.

An hour after leaving the glen, you'll reach a small unsigned junction where a hard-to-see spur trail branches southwest (left) to a viewpoint of Waterwheel Falls. The obvious roar tells you this is the spot, although the falls remain hidden from view. From the main trail, walk two minutes to the edge of the massive falls, named for the distinctive 15ft- to 20ft-high plumes of water that curl into the air like a wheel midway down the more than 600ft-long falls.

If you have to ask yourself, "Is this Waterwheel Falls?" keep going – you'll know it when you see it.

After you admire the cascade, return to the main trail, turn west (left), and descend another 10 minutes. As you approach the scattered junipers beside an obvious dark granite rib perpendicular to the trail, turn south (left) and head down a sandy slope through manzanitas, following a trail that parallels the rocky rib. It leads to a large, forested **campsite** (6440ft) that's partly visible from the main trail above. Camp beneath big ponderosa pines and incense cedars, about three-tenths of a mile below Waterwheel Falls, with the green and tranquil Tuolumne River about 200ft away.

On **Day 2**, retrace your steps 9 miles to the trailhead. The initial and steepest ascent takes you back to Glen Aulin. Once across the steel bridge over the Tuolumne River, track the trail carefully as it crosses open granite, being careful not to wander off the path. Small stones mark the way. The final stretch through forest along Tuolumne Meadows to Soda Springs seems long, but frequent and spectacular vistas of the Cathedral Range break the monotony. When you reach Soda Springs, take a few minutes to explore and (if it's open) peek inside Parsons Lodge.

OTHER ACTIVITIES
Rock Climbing & Bouldering
Come summer, the climbing base camp relocates from Camp 4 (Sunnyside) in Yosemite Valley to the cooler and quieter Tuolumne Meadows campground. Check the bulletin board at the campground entrance for climbing-related notices, as well as announcements for the casual climbing coffee gatherings hosted by the rangers on Sunday mornings.

From late June through early September, the **Yosemite Mountaineering School** (☎ 209-372-8344, Ⓦ *www.yosemite mountaineering.com*), usually found in Yosemite Valley's Curry Village, operates a second staging area in the sport shop at the Tuolumne Meadows gas station. The friendly and knowledgeable staff enthusiastically offer suggestions based on your skill level and objectives. For information on different classes and prices, see the Yosemite Valley section of this chapter.

Swimming

The Tuolumne River is an excellent choice for high-country swimming, with many easy-to-reach sandy-bottomed pools and slightly warmer temperatures than other High Sierra rivers. From the pullout at the west end of Tuolumne Meadows, follow the trail along Pothole Dome and the river for about a mile to a gorgeous waterfall and hidden swimming spot. Just east of the Tioga Pass Entrance, Saddlebag Lake (see p 201) is chilly but pristine.

Fishing

The Lyell and Dana Forks of the Tuolumne River, particularly behind the campground and along the trail to Glen Aulin, both make good fishing spots. The best time is right at dusk. The season runs from the end of April until mid-November; you must have a valid California fishing license.

Horseback Riding

Some of the park's most scenic riding trips leave from the **Tuolumne Meadows Stables** (☎ 209-372-8427) from May to September. Shorter rides ($40 for two hours) circle the meadow, while longer adventures follow the river out to Waterwheel Falls ($55/80 for half-day/full day). There's also a nearby **stock camp** (☎ 800-436-7275; $20 per night); reservations are required and are available up to five months in advance.

The **Yosemite High Sierra Camps Saddle Trips** (☎ 559-253-5674; $664 and up per person, meals and tent-cabin lodging included) are far and away the most popular way to tour the park by horse, with mules schlepping all the supplies. These four- to six-day trips depart from Tuolumne Stables for the lovely High Sierra Camps circuit and fill up months in advance.

Essentials

GROCERIES

The biggest and best grocery store in the park is the **Village Store** (open 8am-10pm daily in summer, reduced hours in winter) in Yosemite Village. The **Tuolumne Meadows Store** (open 8am-8pm daily in summer) has a surprisingly good selection. Small stores operate in Curry Village, Wawona, and White Wolf, but if you really want to stock up, supermarkets outside the park offer better prices and selection. See the Places to Eat chapter for details.

CAMPING SUPPLIES & GEAR

The park's best source for camping supplies and backpacking and climbing gear is the **Curry Village Mountain Shop** (☎ 209-372-8396; open 8am-8pm daily, reduced hours in winter) in Yosemite Valley, with a good selection and not bad prices. The shop also rents a limited amount of gear.

In Yosemite Village, the **Sport Shop** (open 9am-6pm daily, reduced hours in winter) is another decent place to browse. Open in summer, the **Tuolumne Meadows Sport Shop** (open 9am-5pm daily mid-June–mid-Sept) offers a good selection for campers, hikers, and climbers.

Minor supplies such as batteries, propane canisters, and cooking utensils are sometimes available at the park's generic gift and grocery stores, such as those in Crane Flat and Wawona.

MONEY

There are no banks in the park, but there are ATMs at several locations in Yosemite Valley, including the Village Store and the Art Activity Center in Yosemite Village, in the Yosemite Lodge lobby, and at the grocery/gift store at Curry Village. There's also an ATM at the store in Wawona.

YCS runs a check-cashing service at the Art Activity Center.

TELEPHONES

You'll find pay phones at every developed location in the park, including Yosemite Village, Curry Village, Tuolumne Meadows, Wawona and most campgrounds. Cellular phones generally do not work in Yosemite Valley, though some may pick up a signal at higher elevation, such as at Glacier Point or Tuolumne Meadows. They may also work in Wawona.

Cellular phones generally do not work in Yosemite Valley.

POSTAL SERVICES

The park's main post office in Yosemite Village accepts general delivery mail; the zip code is 95389. There are five **post office** branches in the park:

Yosemite Village *(open 8:30am-5pm Mon-Fri, 10am-noon Sat)*

Yosemite Lodge *(open 11:30am-2:45pm Mon-Thur, 11:30am-4:30pm Fri)*

Curry Village *(open 11:30am-2:30pm Mon-Fri, closed approximately mid-Sept–mid-June)*

Wawona *(open 9am-5pm Mon-Fri, 9am-1pm Sat)*

Tuolumne Meadows *(open 9am-4pm Mon-Fri, 9am-noon Sat, closed approximately mid-Sept–mid-June)*

INTERNET ACCESS

For free Internet access in Yosemite Valley, head to the **public library** *(☎ 209-372-4552; open Mon-Thur)* in the Girls' Club Building next door to the Valley visitor center. Sessions are limited to 30 minutes and access is sporadic, so call ahead for details. Reserve a terminal in advance to beat the lines.

Free Internet access is also available in Wawona at the **Bassett Memorial Library** *(☎ 209-375-6510; 7971 Chilnualna Rd; open 1pm-5pm Mon-Fri, 10am-2pm Sat in summer, reduced hours in winter)*. Sessions are also limited to 30 minutes, but it's less crowded.

MEDICAL SERVICES & EMERGENCIES

For emergencies, call ☎ 911. The **Yosemite Medical Clinic** *(☎ 209-372-4637)* and **Dental Clinic** *(☎ 209-372-4200)* are in Yosemite Valley, on the Ahwahnee Hotel road near Yosemite Village. Hours vary, but emergency care is available around the clock.

Wheelchairs are available for rent from the medical clinic or the Yosemite Lodge bike stand.

RELIGIOUS SERVICES

Built in 1879, the **Yosemite Valley Chapel** *(☎ 209-372-4831)* is the oldest park structure still in use. In 1901 it was moved about a mile to its present site. Sunday morning services are nondenominational.

SHOWERS & LAUNDRY

Campgrounds do not have showers. For a mere $2, though, travelers can get clean at public showers in Curry Village, Housekeeping Camp, and Tuolumne Meadows Lodge.

Public, coin-operated laundry facilities are available in Housekeeping Camp (open 7am-10pm daily, closed in winter).

TRASH & RECYCLING

Properly disposing of trash is a vital issue in and around Yosemite. Bear-proof trash cans are everywhere, and you should use them. Some are sidewalk-sized cans; others (especially in campgrounds) are dumpsters with small latched doors. Whatever you do, don't leave trash in your car or, for heaven's sake, your tent. The bears *will* find it.

The NPS maintains recycling bins for glass, plastic, and aluminum cans in most public areas, as well in all campgrounds.

LOST & FOUND

There are two numbers to call if you lose or find an item. For anything left or recovered in restaurants, hotels, or on buses, call YCS at ☎ 209-372-4357. For items astray elsewhere, call the NPS at ☎ 209-379-1001.

YOSEMITE MAP SECTION

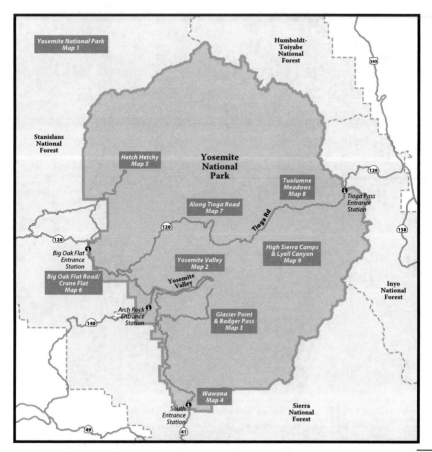

Map 1 **Yosemite National Park**

Parker Pass

Helen Lake

▲ Koip Peak 12,962ft

▲ Donohue Peak 12,023ft

Donohue Pass 11,056ft

North Fork San Joaquin River

Twin Island Lakes

Marie Lakes

Ansel Adams Wilderness

Pacific Crest National Scenic Trail

John Muir Trail

▲ Mt Ansel Adams 11,760ft

East Fork Granite Creek

▲ Johnson Peak 11,070ft

Tuolumne Pass

Evelyn Lake

Parsons Peak 12,147ft

Simmons Peak 12,503ft

▲ Mt Maclure 12,880ft

▲ Mt Lyell 13,114ft

Lyell Glacier

▲ Mt Florence 12,561ft

▲ Forester Peak 12,058ft

Sadler Lake

▲ Echo Peaks

▲ Rafferty Peak 11,110ft

Fletcher Peak 11,408ft

Vogelsang Peak 11,506ft

Florence Lake

Cathedral Range

see Map 9

Emeric Lake

Merced Lake

Washburn Lake

Clark Range

▲ Merced Peak 11,726ft

Joe Crane Lake

Chain Lakes

Ansel Adams Wilderness

Sierra National Forest

▲ Tenaya Peak

Tenaya Lake

Sunrise Lakes

John Muir Trail

Echo Creek

▲ Mt Clark 11,522ft

120

Pywiack Cascade

Tenaya Canyon

Clouds Rest 9926ft

Moraine Dome 8015ft

Little Yosemite Valley

Merced River

▲ Mt Starr King 9092ft

Illilouette Creek

Royal Arch Lake

Johnson Lake

South Fork Merced River

see Map 7

Tioga Rd

Indian Ridge

Indian Rock 8522ft

North Dome 7542ft

Half Dome 8842ft

Upper Yosemite Fall

Yosemite Valley

Vernal Fall

Nevada Fall

Glacier Point 7214ft

Glacier Point

Buena Vista Creek

Buena Vista Lake

Buena Vista Peak 9709ft

Ostrander Lake

Crescent Lake

Yosemite Creek

Lower Yosemite Fall

see Map 2

El Capitan 7569ft

Yosemite Valley

Bridalveil Fall

Taft Point 7503ft

Glacier Point Rd

Badger Pass

see Map 3

Bridalveil Creek

Chilnualua Creek

Mariposa Grove of Giant Sequoias

To Fish Camp & Oakhurst

Wawona Point

Wawona Dome 6897ft

Wawona

Cascade Creek

Wawona Tunnel

Inspiration Point

Badger Pass

Chinquapin

Chilnualua Fall

Alder Creek

Wawona Rd

South Entrance Station

see Map 4

41

120

140

Arch Rock Entrance Station

Yosemite West

South Fork Merced River

To Buck Meadows, Groveland & Manteca

Rd

South Fork Tuolumne River

Crane Tioga Rd

Tuolumne Grove

Big Oak Flat Rd

Merced Grove

see Map 6

Crane Flat

Big Oak Flat Entrance Station

120

Stanislaus National Forest

El Portal

140

Merced River

To Midpines, Mariposa & Merced

Sierra National Forest

8 km
4 mile

4

2

0

0

------- Hiking Trail

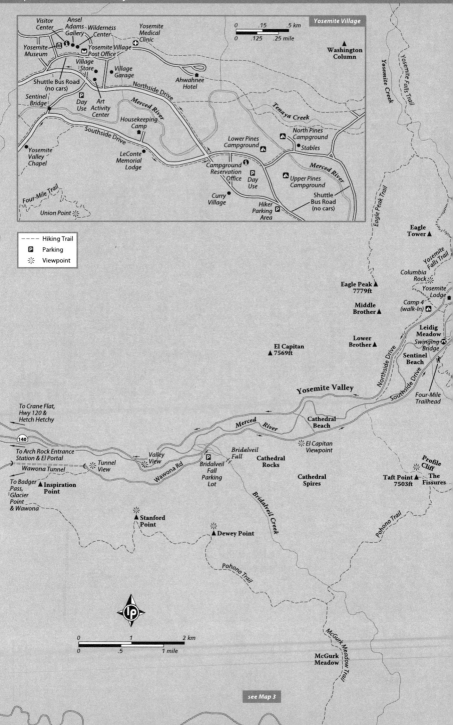

Map 2 Yosemite Valley

Yosemite Village

Visitor Center
Ansel Adams Gallery
Wilderness Center
Yosemite Medical Clinic
Yosemite Museum
Yosemite Village Post Office
Village Store
Village Garage
Shuttle Bus Road (no cars)
Ahwahnee Hotel
Sentinel Bridge
Northside Drive
Day Use
Art Activity Center
Merced River
Housekeeping Camp
Southside Drive
Yosemite Valley Chapel
LeConte Memorial Lodge
Tenaya Creek
North Pines Campground
Stables
Lower Pines Campground
Merced River
Upper Pines Campground
Campground Reservation Office
Day Use
Shuttle Bus Road (no cars)
Four-Mile Trail
Curry Village
Union Point
Hiker Parking Area

0   .15   .5 km
0   .125   .25 mile

Washington Column ▲

Yosemite Creek
Yosemite Falls Trail

---- Hiking Trail
P Parking
☼ Viewpoint

Eagle Tower ▲

Yosemite Falls Trail

Columbia Rock ☼
Yosemite Lodge

Eagle Peak ▲ 7779ft

Middle Brother ▲

Camp 4 (walk-In) ▲

Lower Brother ▲

Leidig Meadow
Swinging Bridge
Sentinel Beach

El Capitan ▲ 7569ft

Northside Drive
Southside Drive

Yosemite Valley

Four-Mile Trailhead

To Crane Flat, Hwy 120 & Hetch Hetchy

Merced River

Cathedral Beach

☼ El Capitan Viewpoint

140

To Arch Rock Entrance Station & El Portal
Wawona Tunnel

☼ Tunnel View
☼ Valley View

Wawona Rd

P Bridalveil Fall Parking Lot

Bridalveil Fall

Cathedral Rocks

Cathedral Spires

Profile Cliff
The Fissures

Taft Point ▲ 7503ft

To Badger Pass, Glacier Point & Wawona
▲ Inspiration Point

Bridalveil Creek

Pohono Trail

☼ Stanford Point

☼ Dewey Point ▲

Pohono Trail

McGurk Meadow Trail

McGurk Meadow

0   1   2 km
0   .5   1 mile

see Map 3

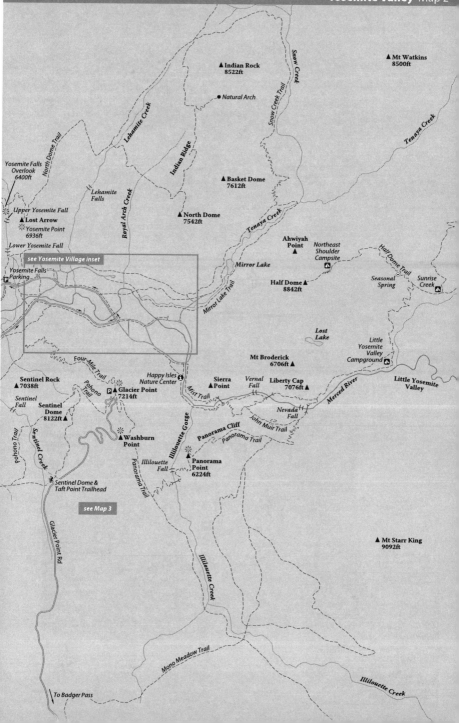

▲ Indian Rock
8522ft

• Natural Arch

▲ Mt Watkins
8500ft

Snow Creek

Lehamite Creek

Snow Creek Trail

Tenaya Creek

North Dome Trail

Indian Ridge

▲ Basket Dome
7612ft

Yosemite Falls
Overlook
6400ft

Lehamite
Falls

Royal Arch Creek

Tenaya Creek

Upper Yosemite Fall
▲ Lost Arrow
☀ Yosemite Point
6936ft
Lower Yosemite Fall

▲ North Dome
7542ft

Ahwiyah
Point
▲

Northeast
Shoulder
Campsite

Half Dome Trail

Sunrise
Creek

see Yosemite Village inset

Mirror Lake

Yosemite Falls
Parking
P

Mirror Lake Trail

Half Dome ▲
8842ft

Seasonal
Spring

Sunrise
Creek

Lost
Lake

Little
Yosemite
Valley
Campground

Four-Mile Trail

Mt Broderick
6706ft ▲

Happy Isles
Nature Center

Sierra
▲ Point

Vernal
Fall

Liberty Cap
7076ft ▲

Little Yosemite
Valley

Sentinel Rock
▲ 7038ft

Pohono
Trail

Mist Trail

Merced River

Sentinel
Fall

P ▲ Glacier Point
☀ 7214ft

Illilouette Gorge

John Muir Trail

Nevada
Fall

Sentinel
Dome
8122ft ▲

Pohono Trail

Sentinel Creek

☀ Washburn
Point

Panorama Cliff

Panorama Trail

▲ Illilouette
Fall

▲ Panorama
Point
6224ft

☀ Sentinel Dome &
Taft Point Trailhead

Panorama Trail

see Map 3

Glacier Point Rd

▲ Mt Starr King
9092ft

Illilouette Creek

Mono Meadow Trail

↖ To Badger Pass

Illilouette Creek

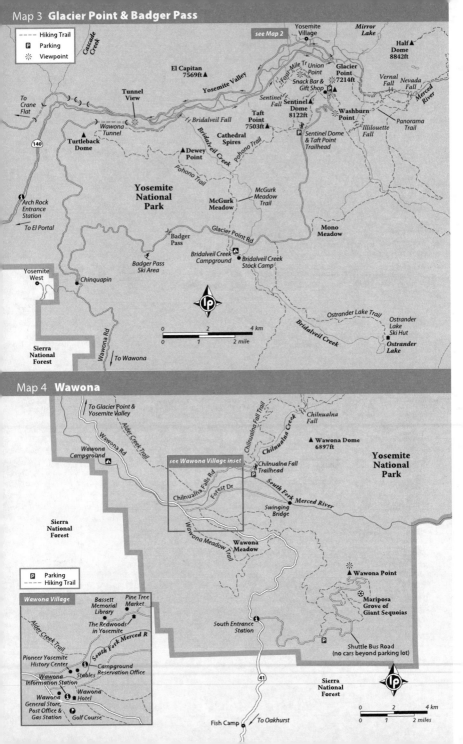

Map 3 **Glacier Point & Badger Pass**

- - - - Hiking Trail
🅿 Parking
☀ Viewpoint

Cascade Creek

see Map 2

Yosemite Village

Mirror Lake

Half △ Dome 8842ft

To Crane Flat

El Capitan 7569ft △

Yosemite Valley

Four Mile Tr

Union Point

Snack Bar & Gift Shop 🅿

Glacier Point 7214ft

Vernal Fall

Nevada Fall

Merced River

Tunnel View

Sentinel Fall

Sentinel Dome 8122ft △

Washburn Point

Bridalveil Fall

Taft Point 7503ft △

Pohono Trail

Panorama Trail

Illilouette Fall

Wawona Tunnel

140

Turtleback Dome △

△ Dewey Point

Cathedral Spires

Bridalveil Creek

Sentinel Dome & Taft Point Trailhead 🅿

Arch Rock Entrance Station

To El Portal

Yosemite National Park

Pohono Trail

McGurk Meadow

McGurk Meadow Trail

Mono Meadow

Glacier Point Rd

Badger Pass

Bridalveil Creek Campground

Bridalveil Creek Stock Camp

Ostrander Lake Trail

Ostrander Lake Ski Hut

Yosemite West

Chinquapin

Badger Pass Ski Area

Bridalveil Creek

Ostrander Lake

Wawona Rd

To Wawona

0   2   4 km
0   1   2 mile

Sierra National Forest

Map 4 **Wawona**

To Glacier Point & Yosemite Valley

Chilnualna Fall Trail

Chilnualna Creek

Chilnualna Fall

Wawona Rd

Alder Creek Trail

Wawona Dome 6897ft △

Yosemite National Park

Wawona Campground

see Wawona Village inset

Chilnualna Fall Trailhead 🅿

Chilnualna Falls Rd

Forest Dr

South Fork

Merced River

Swinging Bridge

Sierra National Forest

Wawona Meadow Trail

Wawona Meadow

Wawona Point △

☸ Mariposa Grove of Giant Sequoias

🅿 Parking
- - - - Hiking Trail

Wawona Village

Bassett Memorial Library

Pine Tree Market

The Redwoods in Yosemite

South Fork Merced R

Alder Creek Trail

Pioneer Yosemite History Center

Campground Reservation Office

Wawona Information Station

Stables

Wawona Hotel

Wawona General Store, Post Office & Gas Station

Golf Course

South Entrance Station

Shuttle Bus Road (no cars beyond parking lot)

41

Sierra National Forest

Fish Camp

To Oakhurst

0   2   4 km
0   1   2 miles

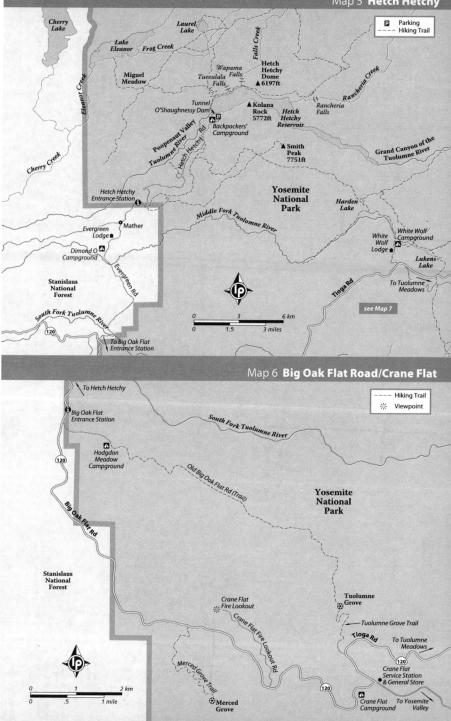

Map 5 Hetch Hetchy

Map 6 Big Oak Flat Road/Crane Flat

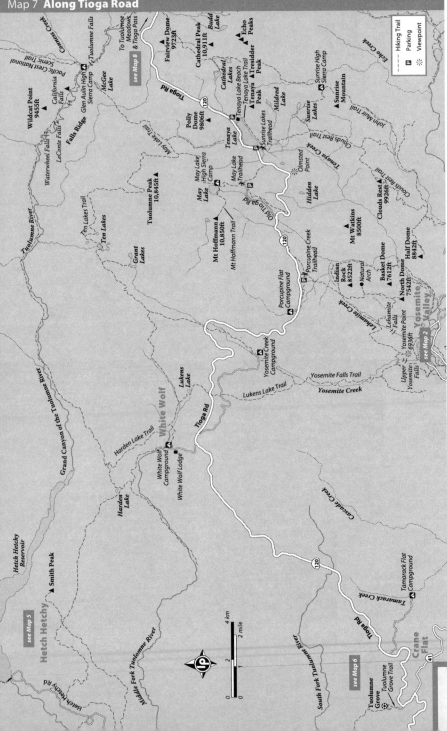

Map 7 **Along Tioga Road**

Canness Creek

Pacific Crest National Scenic Trail

To Tuolumne Meadows & Tioga Pass

Fairview Dome 9731ft

Cathedral Peak 10,911ft

Budd Lake

Echo Peaks

Glen Aulin High Sierra Camp

Tuolumne Falls

California Falls

McGee Lake

Cathedral Lakes

Tenaya Lake Trail

Tresidder Peak

Sunrise High Sierra Camp

Wildcat Point 9455ft

LeConte Falls

Falls Ridge

Tioga Rd

120

Tenaya Lake Beach

Tenaya Peak

Mildred Lake

Sunrise Mountain

Waterwheel Falls

Polly Dome 9806ft

Tenaya Lake

Sunrise Lakes Trailhead

Sunrise Creek

Sunrise Lakes

John Muir Trail

Moy Lake Trail

Olmsted Point

Clouds Rest Trail

Tenaya Creek

Tuolumne River

May Lake High Sierra Camp

May Lake Trailhead

Hidden Lake

Clouds Rest 9926ft

Clouds Rest Trail

Tuolumne Peak 10,845ft

May Lake

Ten Lakes Trail

Mt Hoffmann 10,850ft

Old Tioga Rd

Mt Watkins 8500ft

Half Dome 8842ft

Ten Lakes

Mt Hoffmann Trail

120

Basket Dome 7612ft

Grant Lakes

Porcupine Creek Trailhead

Indian Rock 8522ft

Natural Arch

North Dome 7542ft

Porcupine Flat Campground

Lehamite Creek

Yosemite Valley

Grand Canyon of the Tuolumne River

Lehamite Falls

Yosemite Point 6936ft

see Map 2

Yosemite Creek Campground

Upper Yosemite Falls

Lukens Lake

Yosemite Falls Trail

Lukens Lake Trail

Yosemite Creek

White Wolf

Tioga Rd

Harden Lake Trail

White Wolf Campground

White Wolf Lodge

Cascade Creek

Harden Lake

Hetch Hetchy Reservoir

Smith Peak

120

Tamarack Creek

Tamarack Flat Campground

see Map 5

Hetch Hetchy

Hetch Hetchy Rd

Middle Fork Tuolumne River

4 km

2 mile

2

1

0

0

South Fork Tuolumne River

Tioga Rd

Crane Flat

see Map 6

Tuolumne Grove

Tuolumne Grove Trail

Legend:
- - - - Hiking Trail
Parking
Viewpoint

see Map 8

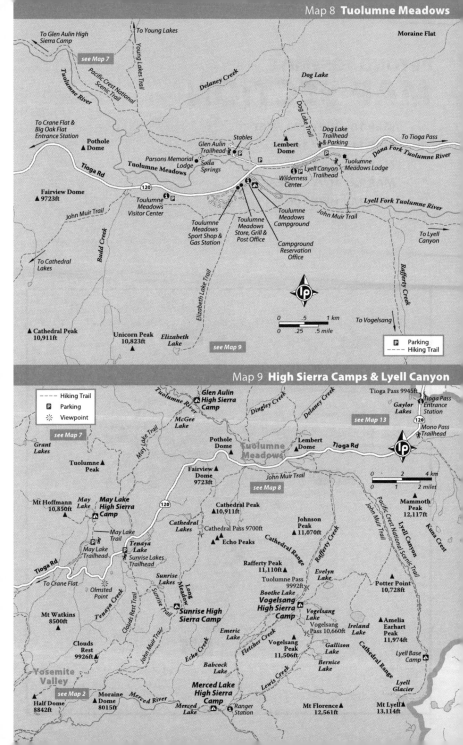

Map 8 Tuolumne Meadows

To Glen Aulin High Sierra Camp
To Young Lakes
Moraine Flat
see Map 7
Pacific Crest National Scenic Trail
Young Lakes Trail
Delaney Creek
Dog Lake
Dog Lake Trail
Dog Lake Trailhead & Parking
To Tioga Pass
Dana Fork Tuolumne River
Tuolumne River
To Crane Flat & Big Oak Flat Entrance Station
Pothole Dome
Stables
Glen Aulin Trailhead
Lembert Dome
Tuolumne Meadows Lodge
Tioga Rd
Parsons Memorial Lodge
Tuolumne Meadows
Soda Springs
Wilderness Center
Lyell Canyon Trailhead
120
Fairview Dome ▲ 9723ft
Tuolumne Meadows Visitor Center
John Muir Trail
Lyell Fork Tuolumne River
John Muir Trail
Budd Creek
Toulumne Meadows Sport Shop & Gas Station
Tuolumne Meadows Store, Grill & Post Office
Toulumne Meadows Campground
To Lyell Canyon
Rafferty Creek
To Cathedral Lakes
Campground Reservation Office
Elizabeth Lake Trail
To Vogelsang
▲ Cathedral Peak 10,911ft
Unicorn Peak 10,823ft
Elizabeth Lake
see Map 9
0   .5   1 km
0   .25   .5 mile
P Parking
Hiking Trail

Map 9 High Sierra Camps & Lyell Canyon

- - - Hiking Trail
P Parking
☼ Viewpoint
see Map 7
Tuolumne River
Glen Aulin High Sierra Camp
Dingley Creek
Delaney Creek
Tioga Pass 9945ft
Tioga Pass Entrance Station
Gaylor Lakes
120
Mono Pass Trailhead
McGee Lake
May Lake Trail
see Map 13
Grant Lakes
Tuolumne ▲ Peak
Pothole Dome
Suolumne Meadows
Lembert Dome
Tioga Rd
Fairview ▲ Dome 9723ft
John Muir Trail
Mt Hoffmann 10,850ft
May Lake
May Lake High Sierra Camp
120
see Map 8
Cathedral Peak ▲10,911ft
Johnson Peak ▲ 11,070ft
Pacific Crest National Scenic Trail
Lyell Canyon
Kuna Crest
Mammoth Peak 12,117ft
May Lake Trailhead
Cathedral Lakes
Cathedral Pass 9700ft
Echo Peaks
Cathedral Range
Rafferty Creek
John Muir Trail
Tenaya Lake
Sunrise Lakes Trailhead
Sunrise Lakes
Long Meadow
Rafferty Peak 11,110ft ▲
Evelyn Lake
Potter Point 10,728ft
Tioga Rd
To Crane Flat
Olmsted Point
Cloud's Rest Trail
Tenaya Creek
Sunrise Trail
John Muir Trail
Tuolumne Pass 9992ft
Boothe Lake
Vogelsang High Sierra Camp
Vogelsang Lake
Vogelsang Pass 10,660ft
Ireland Lake
▲ Amelia Earhart Peak 11,974ft
Mt Watkins 8500ft
Clouds Rest 9926ft
Emeric Lake
Echo Creek
Vogelsang Peak 11,506ft
Fletcher Creek
Gallison Lake
Bernice Lake
Cathedral Range
Lyell Base Camp
Babcock Lake
Lewis Creek
Lyell Glacier
Yosemite Valley
see Map 2
Half Dome 8842ft
Moraine ▲ Dome 8015ft
Merced River
Merced Lake High Sierra Camp
Merced Lake
Ranger Station
Mt Florence ▲ 12,561ft
Mt Lyell 13,114ft
0   2   4 km
0   1   2 miles

MAP SECTION

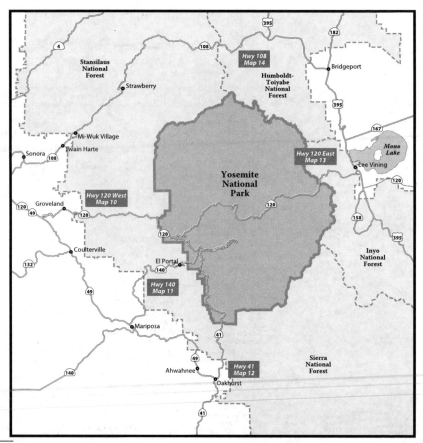

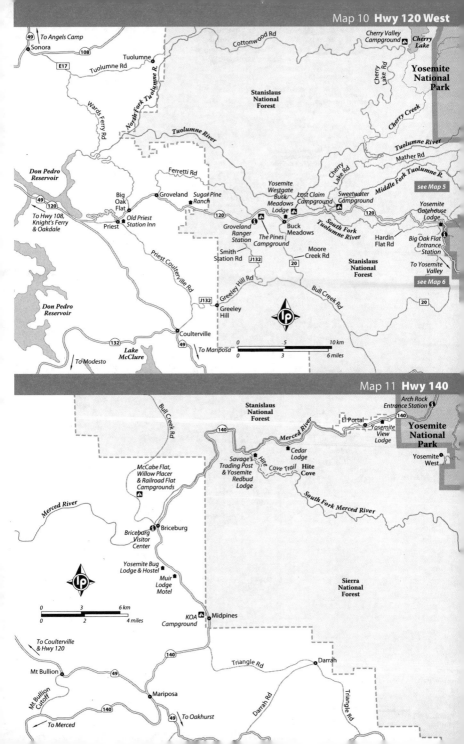

Map 12 **Hwy 41**

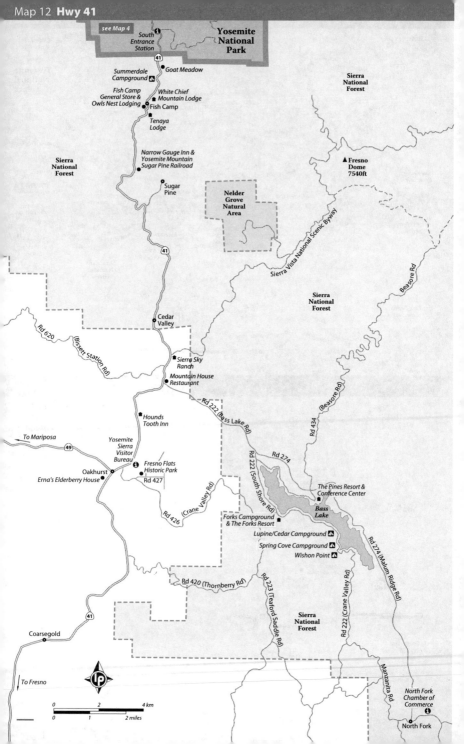

see Map 4

South Entrance Station

Yosemite National Park

Sierra National Forest

41

Goat Meadow

Summerdale Campground

White Chief Mountain Lodge

Fish Camp General Store & Owls Nest Lodging

Fish Camp

Tenaya Lodge

▲ Fresno Dome 7540ft

Narrow Gauge Inn & Yosemite Mountain Sugar Pine Railroad

Sierra National Forest

Sugar Pine

Nelder Grove Natural Area

41

Sierra Vista National Scenic Byway

Sierra National Forest

Beasore Rd

Rd 620

Bissett Station Rd

Cedar Valley

Sierra Sky Ranch

Mountain House Restaurant

Rd 222 (Bass Lake Rd)

Rd 434

(Beasore Rd)

Rd 274

Hounds Tooth Inn

To Mariposa

49

Yosemite Sierra Visitor Bureau

Rd 222 (South Shore Rd)

The Pines Resort & Conference Center

Bass Lake

Fresno Flats Historic Park

Oakhurst

Rd 427

Erna's Elderberry House

Rd 426

(Crane Valley Rd)

Forks Campground & The Forks Resort

Lupine/Cedar Campground

Spring Cove Campground

Wishon Point

Rd 274 (Malum Ridge Rd)

Rd 420 (Thornberry Rd)

Rd 223 (Teaford Saddle Rd)

Rd 222 (Crane Valley Rd)

Sierra National Forest

41

Coarsegold

To Fresno

Manzanita Rd

North Fork Chamber of Commerce

North Fork

0   2   4 km
0   1   2 miles

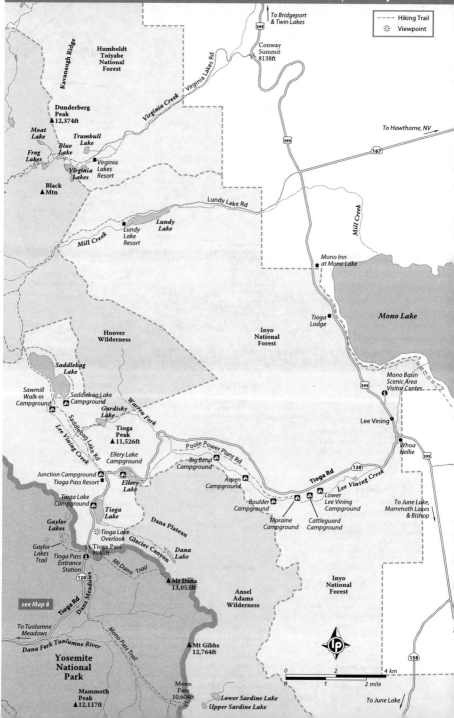

Map 14 **Hwy 108**

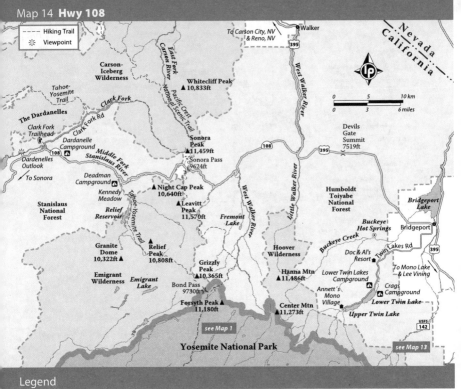

Legend

ROUTES

................Freeway
................Primary Road
................Secondary Road
................Tertiary Road
- - - - ....Dirt Road
→)——(←....Tunnel
- - - - ....Trail

ROUTE SHIELDS

- 🛡80 Interstate Freeway
- 🛡101 US Highway
- 🛡95 State Highway
- 🛡G4 County Road

HYDROGRAPHY

................River; Creek
................Canal
................Lake
⊙ ....Spring; Rapids
................Waterfalls
................Dry; Salt Lake
................Swamp; Mangrove

AREAS

................National Park
................Wilderness Area
................National Forest

BOUNDARIES

— ·· — ·· —....State Boundary

POPULATION SYMBOLS

- ◉ **STATE CAPITAL** ....State Capital
- ◐ **Large City** ....Large City
- ● **Medium City** ....Medium City
- ● **Small City** ....Small City
- ○ Town; Village ....Town; Village

MAP SYMBOLS

- ★ ....Place to Stay
- ▼ ....Place to Eat
- ● ....Point of Interest
- ✈ ....Airfield
- ✈ ....Airport
- ....Archaeological Site; Ruin
- ....Bank
- ....Baseball Diamond
- ....Battlefield
- ....Bike Trail
- ....Bus Station; Terminal
- ....Cable Car; Chairlift
- ....Campground
- ....Cave
- ....Church
- ....Cinema
- ....Footbridge
- ....Gas Station
- ....Hospital
- ....Information
- ....Lookout
- ....Mine
- ....Monument
- ▲ ....Mountain
- ....Museum
- ....Park
- P ....Parking Area
- ....Pass
- ....Picnic Area
- ....Police Station
- ....Pool
- ....Post Office
- ....Pub; Bar
- ....RV Park
- ....Shopping Mall
- ....Skiing - Cross-Country
- ....Skiing - Downhill
- ....Telephone
- ....Toilet - Public
- ....Trailhead
- ....Tram Stop
- ....Transportation
- ....Volcano

Note: Not all symbols displayed above appear in this book.

NOTES

NPS PHOTOGRAPHS

One of the biggest questions facing Yosemite visitors is where to spend the night. During the height of the summer tourist season, accommodations fill up faster than you can say "bear box." Newcomers with visions of sleeping soundly under the stars often find that rooms and campsites are full, having been reserved weeks and even months in advance.

YOSEMITE PLACES TO STAY

If that reservationless person is you, keep in mind that your overnight options don't stop at the park borders. Of course, it's most convenient – and in many cases most fun – to stay inside the park. But outside the park boundaries there are plenty of good, attractive campgrounds, not to mention motels and lodges. Many of these are no farther from Yosemite Valley than some of the park's own facilities.

Most lodges and campgrounds both inside and outside the park open and close at slightly different times each year, depending on weather. One year the snow might clear early enough to allow Tioga Pass to open before Memorial Day; the following year it might stay closed until July, keeping Tuolumne Meadows out of reach. Check before you go. Also keep in mind that rates change with the seasons. Rates within Yosemite are usually set in advance; outside the park, room prices can fluctuate on a monthly, weekly, or even daily basis.

Inside the Park

Finding a place to sleep in Yosemite can be a battle – or as easy as a single phone call. All that really separates the two is a little advance planning.

Reservations are *strongly* recommended. Simply showing up at the park gate with your fingers crossed is a bad idea – especially if you arrive late in the day on a summer weekend. Nearly four million people visit Yosemite each year, some as day visitors but many vying for one of the 1505 campsites or 1517 rooms and tent cabins available in the park.

To keep headaches to a minimum, Yosemite has two centralized reservation systems, one for campsites and one for all other park lodging.

CAMPING

During the height of summer, when all facilities are open, more than 9000 people may be packed into Yosemite's campgrounds on any given night. Those hoping to get in touch with nature may find they're more in touch with their neighbors, who are often clanging pans, slurping beer by the fire or snoring in their tents just 10- or 20ft away. It gets especially crowded in Yosemite Valley, where 464 sites sleep up to 2736 people, most of them crammed into three large campgrounds. Overnighters looking for a quieter, more rugged experience are better off in spots like Bridalveil Creek, Yosemite Creek, and Porcupine Flat.

Types of Campgrounds

Campgrounds in Yosemite range from primitive backpacker camps to developed sites that can accommodate large RVs. Most have flush toilets and potable water. The exceptions are the park's three primitive sites (Tamarack Flat, Yosemite Creek, and Porcupine Flat), which have vault (pit) toilets and require you to bring your own water or a means of purifying water from nearby streams.

All park campsites include a picnic table, a fire pit with a barbecue grill, and a bear-proof food storage locker. Bears have nothing against your personally, but they do want your food, so use that food locker at *all* times.

None of the campgrounds have showers. If you need to cleanse yourself, head to Curry Village or Housekeeping Camp or, during summer, the Tuolumne Meadows Lodge; all three have public **showers** for $2. If you didn't bring enough underwear and socks, Housekeeping Camp also offers public **laundry facilities**.

Campground elevations are important to consider. For instance, the campgrounds along Tioga Rd and in Tuolumne Meadows, some of which sit above 8000ft, may boast warm weather during the day, but come nightfall, you'll be wishing you'd packed that wool sweater.

Yosemite has four campgrounds open all year: Upper Pines, Camp 4, Wawona and Hodgdon Meadow. The rest are open seasonally.

Backpackers' Campgrounds To accommodate backpackers heading into or coming out of the wilderness, the park has set up three walk-in backpackers' campgrounds at popular trailheads. If you hold a valid wilderness permit, you may spend the night before and the night after your trip in one of these campgrounds. They're found in the center of the Tuolumne Meadows Campground, just before the dam overlook at Hetch Hetchy, and behind the North Pines Campground in Yosemite Valley. The cost is $5 per person, and reservations are not necessary. For information on wilderness permits, see p 84.

Making Reservations

The best way to ensure you have a campsite is to make an advance reservation. Campgrounds requiring reservations include North Pines, Upper Pines, and Lower Pines in Yosemite Valley; Wawona and Hodgdon Meadow (between May and September only); Crane Flat; and half of the sites in Tuolumne Meadows. The rest of the park's campgrounds (and Hodgdon Meadow and Wawona during the off-season) are available on a first-come, first-served basis.

Reservations for all park campgrounds are handled by the **National Park Reservation Service** *(NPRS;* ☎ *301-722-1257, 800-436-7275;* W *http://reservations.nps.gov; open 7am-7pm daily PST).* You can also mail in your reservation request to: NPRS, PO Box 1600, Cumberland, MD 21502. Requests received more than two weeks before the desired camping dates go on sale will be returned. Include desired location, whether you're staying in a tent or RV, the number of people and pets in the party, and the method of payment.

HIGH SIERRA CAMPS

In the backcountry near Tuolumne Meadows, the enormously popular High Sierra Camps (Map 9) provide accommodations and meals for hikers who'd rather not carry a tent. The camps are at Glen Aulin, May Lake, Sunrise, Merced Lake, and Vogelsang, each within a leisurely day's hike of one another (less than 10 miles). The Tuolumne Meadows Lodge completes the circuit, although the lodge is also open to the public. Some hikers do the whole circuit, a weeklong loop on established trails. Others visit just one or two camps.

The camps consist of dormitory-style canvas tent cabins with beds, wool blankets or comforters, plus showers and a central dining tent. Breakfast and dinner are included in the $109/ per person per night fee. Guests bring their own sheets and towels. The accommodations are hardly luxurious, but the knockout settings – not to mention the convenience of not having to carry a tent and food – make the High Sierra Camps appealing.

The seasons are so short (roughly June to September) and the camps so popular that reservations are doled out by lottery. Applications for the lottery, which is held in mid-December, are accepted only between October 15 and November 30. To obtain an application, contact Yosemite Concession Services (☎ 559-253-5674; W www.yosemitepark.com/html/accom_hi sierra.html). You can also call at the last minute to check if there are any cancellations.

While the High Sierra Camps are only for reserved guests, each has an adjacent backpackers' campsite available to anyone with a wilderness permit. The backpackers' campsites come complete with bear boxes, toilets, and potable water taps. It's also possible to reserve meals only at a High Sierra Camp, which can ease the burden of carrying your own food; call a day or two in advance.

Campsites can be reserved between four and five months in advance. Reservations become available on the 15th of every month in one-month blocks. Thus, if you want to camp between July 15 and August 14 of any given year, the first date you can make that reservation is March 15. Be sure to act quickly, as most dates in summer fill up the first day reservations become available.

Confused? Call the park's **campground office** (☎ 209-372-8502) or check the website (W www.nps.gov/yose/trip/camping.htm) for guidance.

If you have a reservation, proceed directly to the campground gate to check in. If you're going to be more than 24 hours late, call the campground office; otherwise you may lose your reservation.

Trying Your Luck

If you arrived without reservations, you still have a couple of options. You can put yourself on a waiting list for one of the reserved sites or try your luck at a first-come, first-served campground.

A number of previously reserved sites open up due to cancellations and people leaving early. It doesn't happen every day, but most days there are a few available. To nab one of these, put your name on a waiting list at one of the four **Campground Reservation Offices**. The reservation office in **Yosemite Valley** (☎ 209-372-8502) is open year-round, generally 8am-5pm daily. You'll find additional offices in **Wawona** near the Pioneer Yosemite History Center and at the **Big Oak Flat Entrance**, both closed from about mid-October to April. The office at **Tuolumne Meadows**, near the campground entrance, is open from about mid-June to mid-September.

CAMP NAME	LOCATION	# OF SITES	ELEVATION (FT)	OPEN (APPROX)	RESERVATIONS REQUIRED?	DAILY FEE	FEATURES	DESCRIPTION	PAGE
Bridalveil Creek	Glacier Point Rd	110	7200	July–Sept	No	$12		Near Glacier Point; some attractive sites; removed from Valley crowds	175
Camp 4	Yosemite Valley	35	4000	Year-round	No	$5		Walk-in campground, popular with climbers; price is per person; campers share sites; tents only	174
Crane Flat	Crane Flat	166	6191	June–Sept	Yes	$18		Large family campground spread across five loops, varied sites; easy drive to Yosemite Valley	176
Hodgdon Meadow	Big Oak Flat Rd	105	4872	Year-round	May–Sept only	$18 May–Sept, $12 Oct–Apr		Close to park entrance, utilitarian, can be crowded and noisy; easy drive to Yosemite Valley	176
Lower Pines	Yosemite Valley	60	4000	Mar–Oct	Yes	$18		Smaller Valley campground; again, don't expect much privacy	173
North Pines	Yosemite Valley	81	4000	Apr–Sept	Yes	$18		Smaller Valley campground, slightly removed from commercial development; close to Mirror Lake, adjacent to stables	173
Porcupine Flat	Tioga Rd	52	8100	July–Sept	No	$8		Primitive, close to road but relatively quiet; RV access from half only	177
Tamarack Flat	Tioga Rd	52	6315	June–Sept	No	$8		Quiet, secluded, primitive; accessed via a rough 3-mile road; RVs not recommended	177
Tuolumne Meadows	Tuolumne Meadows	304	8600	July–Sept	Half reserved	$18		Park's biggest campground, many sites well dispersed over large area	178
Upper Pines	Yosemite Valley	238	4000	Year-round	Yes	$18		Largest Valley campground, expect little privacy, especially in summer, close to Happy Isles	173
Wawona	Wawona	93	4000	May–Sept only	No	$18 May–Sept ($12 otherwise)		Located along river; nicer sites in back section (open summer only); short drive to store	175
White Wolf	Tioga Rd	74	8000	April–Oct	No	$12		Attractive setting but sites very close together.	177
Yosemite Creek	Tioga Rd	75	7659	July–Sept	No	$8		Park's most secluded, quiet, primitive campground; accessed via rough 4.5-mile road; RVs not recommended	177

All campgrounds have: bear boxes, parking, picnic tables, fire pits, trash receptacles, public phones

Dogs allowed (on leash)

Flush toilets

Drinking water

Ranger/information station nearby

Summertime campfire programs

Great for families

Restaurant nearby

Grocery store nearby

Wheelchair accessible

RV dump station

Get there early to sign up, then return at the prescribed time (usually 3pm) to find out if you've gotten one. It's not a great way to get settled, however; even if you're lucky enough to land a site, it's only for one night. If you want to stay longer, you'll have to go through the entire process again the following day.

A more hassle-free method is to try one of the first-come, first-served campgrounds. The Campground Reservation Offices can give you information on these sites, including charts that list which campgrounds have filled up so far that day. Campgrounds also post signs along the main road when they're full.

Even in the heat of summer, getting a first-come, first-served campsite isn't that difficult if you arrive early enough. The park recommends 9am, but on weekdays you'll probably be fine before noon.

The method is simple: Drive or walk around the campground loops until you see an unoccupied site – that means no tents, equipment, or hired bodyguards there to hold it, and no receipt hanging from the site's little signpost. If it's free, take it, because if you're too picky, it might be gone the next time you drive by. Remember that checkout time is not until noon at most campgrounds, so late risers may not clear out until close to lunchtime. Take a look at the check-out date printed on the campsite receipt for some guidance. And be patient.

Once you have claimed a site, head back to the campground entrance and follow instructions listed there for paying and properly displaying your receipt. Pay for as many days as you expect to stay; and if you extend your stay, just pay again in the morning before check-out time.

LODGING

The word "lodge" usually connotes an eye-catching, stately structure with stone fireplaces, beamed ceilings, and rustic but well-kept rooms. In Yosemite, however, "lodge" can mean anything from standard motel-like rooms to a group of canvas tents with nothing but cots and candles inside.

✔ TIP

RV ROAD RULES

Most roads and campgrounds in Yosemite are accessible to the majority of RVs. Here are a few rules and tips to keep in mind:

✔ The maximum length for RVs in the Valley is 40ft.
✔ RVs over 24ft are not recommended for the Porcupine Flat, White Wolf, Tamarack Flat, or Yosemite Creek Campgrounds.
✔ RVs are not permitted at walk-in or group campsites.
✔ There are no electrical hookups at any Yosemite campgrounds.
✔ Generators can be used in campgrounds between 7am and 7pm, but only sparingly.
✔ The park's only year-round dump station is in Yosemite Valley near the Upper Pines Campground. In summer, there are also stations in Wawona and Tuolumne Meadows.
✔ If you're stuck for a place to park and bed down, you can park for one night at the Tioga Lake Overlook, on Hwy 120 just east of Tioga Pass.

Of the Yosemite lodging options, **tent cabins** are the most basic. Curry Village, White Wolf Lodge, and Yosemite Lodge feature motel-like **standard rooms** with showers and bathrooms. Top of the heap are rooms at the park's two **historic hotels**, the lovely Wawona and the *über*-deluxe Ahwahnee.

Making Reservations

Yosemite Concession Services *(YCS; ☎ 559-252-4848, fax 559-456-0542;* W *www.yosemitepark.com/html/accommodation.html; open 7am-7pm Mon-Fri, 8am-5pm Sat-Sun)* manages nearly all the lodging in the park, from tent cabins to hotels (exceptions are the homes and cabins in Yosemite West and the Redwoods in Yosemite). YCS is a division of the corporation Delaware North, which took over the park's concessions in 1993.

Reservations are available 366 days in advance of your arrival date. Places get snapped up early for summer months, especially on weekends and holidays, but if you're flexible, there's often some space available on short notice, especially midweek.

Room prices listed in this chapter apply during high season, approximately May to September. For the places that remain open all year, prices often drop during the winter months (holidays excluded). Bargain hunters can also check the YCS website for various seasonal specials.

YOSEMITE VALLEY
(MAP 2)

Most visitors spend nearly all their time in this small area of the park – which means that everyone wants to sleep here, too. If that includes you, make sure you reserve well in advance for campgrounds as well as tent cabins and hotels. All campgrounds and lodging areas in the Valley are accessible via the free shuttle bus service.

Camping

While Yosemite Valley campgrounds are convenient to many of the park's major sights and activities, they're also very crowded, often noisy, and definitely lacking in privacy. Don't camp here expecting to get away from it all – for solitude, you're better off in less-visited areas of the park.

Yosemite Valley's three Pines campgrounds (North Pines, Upper Pines, and Lower Pines) can be booked through the reservation system; they each charge $18 per night. They're all located east of Yosemite Village at the far end of the Valley and are open to both RVs and tent campers. Those with reservations can proceed directly to the campground, where the attendant at the entry gate will assign a site. If you arrive without a reservation, stop by the **Campground Reservation Office** *(open 8am-5pm daily)* in the day-use parking lot near Camp Curry. If nothing's available, put your name on a waiting list or try the Valley's fourth campground, the walk-in Camp 4.

The largest Valley campground (and one of the park's biggest) is **Upper Pines** *(open year-round)*, which sits along the bus and pedestrian road to the Happy Isles Nature Center and trailhead, only a short walk away from Curry Village. With 238 sites spread under a forest of pine, it's pretty but not exactly serene.

Directly west is the smaller but very similar **Lower Pines** *(open Mar-Oct)*, set amid the trees on the south shore of the Merced River. Damaged during the 1997 flood, this campground has been reduced to only 60 sites.

Across the Merced River from Lower Pines is **North Pines** *(open Apr-Oct)*, which has 81 sites. Though similar to its sisters, it's probably the quietest of the bunch, being the farthest from Curry Village and most auto traffic. It's directly adjacent to the stables, though, so if you can't stand the smell of horse puckey, bed down elsewhere. There's also a small backpackers' walk-in campground here.

The only first-come, first-served campground in the Valley is **Camp 4** *(tent sites $5 per person; open year-round)*, formerly known as Sunnyside, located just north of Yosemite Lodge. Popular with climbers, it often fills to capacity by 9am from May to September. Camp 4 charges per person, and each site holds six people. Unless that's the size of your group, additional campers may be assigned to your site. It's a cheap, friendly, and low-key place to stay, but it's more utilitarian than attractive. Camp 4 is a walk-in area; cars must be left in an adjacent parking lot, and sites are for tent campers only.

Lodging

If you don't want to camp, the Valley offers the greatest range and number of room options, from simple tent cabins to standard motel units to luxurious accommodations at the historic Ahwahnee. All cabins and rooms are reserved through Yosemite Concession Services (see Making Reservations). If you arrive without a reservation, the visitor center has a white courtesy phone you can use to inquire about room availability throughout the park.

South of the Merced River and not far from Yosemite Village is **Housekeeping Camp** *(up to four people $58, additional person $4; open Apr-Oct)*, with 266 tent cabins grouped tightly together, plus a store, showers ($2), and laundry facilities (open 8am-10pm). Cabins have concrete walls and a canvas roof; each sleeps up to six people and comes with a covered outdoor sitting area, fire pit, bear-proof food locker, and electrical outlet. These are the only lodging facilities that allow cooking. Bring your own linens or rent bedding from the front desk for an additional $2.50 per person.

The vast and crowded **Curry Village** *(tent cabin for one or two people $59, cabin with/without bath $92/77, standard room $112; open year-round)*, at the east end of Yosemite Valley directly below Glacier Point, has operated since 1899, growing from a handful of tents to include several levels of accommodation – not to mention a mini-mall's worth of stores and restaurants. There's also a pool with showers ($2), an amphitheater, a bike rental office, and, in winter, an ice rink.

The 427 canvas tent cabins each sleep up to five people but are very close together, making the place feel like a labor camp; they include linens but no heating, electrical outlets, or fire pits. Some tents have propane heaters and are open during winter. The wooden cabins are a bit nicer: 80 share a central bath and have propane heaters but are still crowded together; another 102 boast private baths, electric heat and outlets, plus more spacious and cozy quarters. Curry Village also contains 19 standard motel-style rooms but with no TVs or phones.

Yosemite Lodge *(standard/lodge rooms $112/143, children under 12 free; open year-round)* is a collection of motel units, shops, and restaurants spread among several condo-like buildings near the base of Yosemite Falls. The 19 standard rooms are about as exciting as those in your average motel; the 229 lodge rooms are larger and feature a private patio or balcony. All have a telephone but no TV. The lobby serves as the lodge's focal point, and the complex also includes an amphitheater, pool, bar, post office, tour desk, and bike rental office.

Overnighters get the royal treatment at the gorgeous **Ahwahnee Hotel** *(front desk ☎ 209-372-1407; rooms and cottages from $359)*, a National Historic Landmark in operation since 1927 and by far the most luxurious place in the park. Tucked away in its own quiet, secluded corner of the Valley, this impressive hotel is worth a visit even if you're not staying overnight. The 99 rooms, all tastefully decorated with Native American touches, boast

CAMPING RULES

Some rules to remember from the National Park Service:

✔ Camping is allowed in designated sites only.
✔ A maximum of six people (including children) and two cars are allowed at each campsite.
✔ There's a 30-day limit on camping within Yosemite during each calendar year. From May 1 to September 15, however, the limit is 7 days in the Valley and Wawona, 14 days elsewhere.
✔ Check-out time is 10am in Yosemite Valley, noon in the rest of the park.
✔ Store all food, toiletries, and scented items in a bear-safe locker – not in your car.
✔ Camp wastewater must be disposed of in designated utility drains.
✔ Pets are permitted in all campgrounds except Camp 4, Tamarack Flat, Porcupine Flat, and all group campsites. Pets must be on a leash and not left unattended.
✔ Quiet hours last from 10pm to 6am.

great views and supremely comfortable beds. Other options include 24 cottages out back and a handful of suites. The hotel also features an upscale restaurant, friendly bar, pool, tennis courts, occasional evening programs, and an amazing series of public common rooms. A night here is worth the splurge, especially in winter, when prices often drop.

GLACIER POINT
(MAP 3)

Until 1969, the historic Glacier Point Hotel and adjacent Mountain House were perched cliffside at Glacier Point, where the stone amphitheater now sits. Unfortunately, the stately structures burned down that year. Today, the only overnight option (aside from wilderness camping) in this part of the park is the **Bridalveil Creek Campground** *(sites $12; open July-early Sept)*, 8 miles up Glacier Point Rd from Hwy 41. It's a good alternative to camping in the Valley, though it requires a 40-minute drive. The 110 sites are first-come, first-served, and most are spread out nicely among the pines. The campground includes drinking water and flush toilets and a horse camp at the back.

The private development known as **Yosemite West** *(☎ 559-642-2211;* W *www .yosemitewest.com; studios from about $100)* rents contemporary homes, cabins, rooms, and apartments in a community just west of Hwy 41. Although it's outside the park proper, Yosemite West is only accessible from inside the park. Look for the turnoff a half-mile south of the intersection with Glacier Point Rd. Drive about a mile and you'll reach a sign, where there are maps and phone numbers of the local establishments. Rates are for double occupancy, but larger units are available; prices rise with the size of the group.

There are also a few B&Bs here, including **Yosemite Peregrine** *(☎ 209-372-8517; 7509 Henness Circle; rooms $150-200)* and **High Sierra** *(☎ 209-372-4808; 7460 Henness Ridge Rd; rooms $130-190).*

WAWONA
(MAP 4)

The south fork of the Merced River cuts through this southernmost section of Yosemite, and the **Wawona Campground** *(sites in summer $18, off-season $12)* includes some sites situated right alongside its banks. It's a pleasant place to set up your tent or RV, though some of the nicer spots are in the back section, which is only open during summer (approximately May to September), when the whole campground goes on the reservation system. The rest of the year it's first-come, first-served.

The **Wawona Hotel** *(front desk ☎ 209-375-6556; rooms with/without bath $168/113)*, a National Historic Landmark dating from 1879, is a collection of eight graceful, New England-style buildings, each painted white and lined with wide porches. The 104 rooms come with Victorian furniture and other period items, and most open up onto a veranda. About half the rooms share bathrooms; those with private facilities are a bit larger. None have TVs or phones. The grounds are lovely, and the spacious lawn is dotted with numerous Adirondack chairs. There's an excellent restaurant in the main building, as well as bar service nightly in the relaxing lobby lounge or out on the porch.

The Redwoods in Yosemite *(☎ 559-375-6666; ⓦ www.redwoodsinyosemite.com; Chilnualna Falls Rd; homes $104-611 per night)* is a private, non-YCS outfit that rents some 125 fully furnished vacation homes of various sizes and levels of comfort. There's a three-night minimum stay in summer, two nights otherwise. The main office is 2 miles east of Hwy 41 on Chilnualna Falls Rd; look for the junction just north of the Wawona Store.

HETCH HETCHY
(MAP 5)

The only place to stay in this area is at a backpackers' campground – and that's reserved for those with wilderness permits in the Hetch Hetchy area only. For the closest camping and lodging options, see the entry for Mather (p 178).

BIG OAK FLAT ROAD/CRANE FLAT
(MAP 6)

Two large campgrounds sit along this section of Big Oak Flat Rd (Hwy 120), between the park's Big Oak Flat Entrance and Crane Flat, the intersection where Hwy 120 turns east to follow Tioga Rd. Both campgrounds offer flush toilets and potable water. Look for the **Campground Reservation Office** *(open 8am-5pm daily, Apr-Oct)* in a small complex of buildings just as you enter the park.

Just east of the Big Oak Flat Entrance, **Hodgdon Meadow** *(sites summer $18, winter $12; open year-round)* is a popular campground with 105 decent sites; a few of the nicer ones are walk-ins, though you won't have to go more than 20 yards. All campsites here must be reserved during summer (May-Sept) but are first-come, first-served the rest of the year.

About 8 miles east is an even bigger campground, **Crane Flat** *(sites $18; open June-Sept)*, which sits near the Crane Flat store and the junction with Tioga Rd. Sites lie along five different loops, most in the trees and some very nicely dispersed. The central location is great for those wanting to split their time between Tuolumne Meadows and Yosemite Valley.

ALONG TIOGA ROAD
(MAP 7)

You'll find a number of lodging options along Tioga Rd (Hwy 120) as it heads east from Crane Flat to Tuolumne Meadows. Note that due to snow and high elevation, the road (and everything along it) is only open during summer, usually mid-June to mid-September. Exact dates are impossible to predetermine, so always call ahead.

The four campgrounds along this stretch of the road include two of the most rugged, quiet, and beautiful in the park. All four operate on a first-come, first-served basis. White Wolf offers flush toilets, while the other three are primitive, with only vault toilets (aka outhouses, albeit relatively clean ones) and no safe drinking water; be sure to bring your own, or be prepared to purify water from local streams.

One of the most serene and spacious places in the park to set up your tent is **Tamarack Flat** *(sites $8)*, 3 miles down a rough, barely paved road that's as steep and narrow as it is woodsy and beautiful. Expect about a 15-minute drive off Tioga Rd each way, and don't attempt the journey with an RV or big trailer. The 52 sites are well dispersed among trees, some near a creek – which lends the campground a very open feel, with lots of sun and sky. The parts of the park accessible by road are rarely this quiet.

Located north of Tioga Rd on a mile-long spur road, the 74-site **White Wolf Campground** *(sites $12)*, adjacent to the White Wolf Lodge, enjoys a pleasant setting among pine trees and granite boulders. While it's an attractive and convenient alternative to Valley camping, White Wolf is unfortunately a claustrophobic campground, with most sites packed too tightly together.

Drive 4½ miles (about 20 minutes) down a stretch of the old Tioga Rd – a narrow, winding, and very chopped-up piece of roadway that's no good for RVs or trailers – and you find yourself in **Yosemite Creek** *(sites $8)*, the most secluded, spacious, and serene car-accessible campground in the park. The sites are surprisingly well dispersed, some in the trees, others in the open. A trail from here leads to the top of Yosemite Falls. The back half of the campground has been closed for a while due to a downed bridge.

If you like your camping primitive but want closer access to Tioga Rd, try 52-site **Porcupine Flat** *(sites $8)*, which sits about halfway between Crane Flat and Tuolumne Meadows, the latter only a 20-minute drive away. The sites up front can handle RVs and campers, but the quieter and more rustic back half is for tents only.

White Wolf Lodge *(tent cabins $59, cabins with bath $93; open summer only)* enjoys its own little world a mile up a spur road, away from the hubbub and traffic of Hwy 120 and the Valley. It also features nice hiking trails to Lukens and Harden Lakes. The complex includes 24 tent cabins and other small buildings, plus a dining room and tiny store. Most accommodations are in the spartan tent cabins, which come with beds, linens, candles, and wood stoves with wood but no electricity; they share central bathrooms. A step up are the four hard-walled cabins, housed in two duplex buildings right off the parking lot. Each has a private bathroom, two double beds, a porch, and all the ambience of a standard motel room.

TUOLUMNE MEADOWS
(MAP 8)

In the centerpiece of Yosemite's high country, you'll find a campground, lodge, fast-food grill, grocery store, gas station,

Find yourself in Yosemite Creek, the most secluded, spacious, and serene car-accessible campground in the park.

visitor center, and wilderness permit office all within a few miles of each other along Tioga Rd (Hwy 120).

Tuolumne Meadows *(sites $18; open July-Sept)* is the largest campground in the park, with 304 sites for tents or RVs. Amazingly, many of the sites are well dispersed and tucked beneath the trees, making the place feel far less crowded than other park campgrounds. Evening programs take place in a central campfire circle. The premises also include a horse camp, group camp, and walk-in backpackers' camp for those with wilderness permits.

Half the sites here are on the reservation system, while the other half are kept first-come, first-served. The **Campground Reservation Office** is right at the entrance; show up by 10am and you'll probably snatch a site. If this campground is full, you can backtrack about a half-hour west to those along Tioga Rd.

Tuolumne Meadows Lodge *(tent cabins $63; open June-mid-Sept)* is a collection of 69 wood-framed, canvas-covered tent cabins. Set on a platform, each tent contains four beds (linens included), a wood stove, and candles (no electricity). Bathrooms and showers are shared. The lodge complex – which is part of the original High Sierra Camp loop – also includes a dining hall serving breakfast, box lunches, and dinner.

Outside the Park

The small towns on Yosemite's western fringe are mostly old mining settlements that now thrive on the park's overflow. These are good places to stay if you arrive without a tent or room reservation, though don't expect cheap motels to actually *be* cheap.

Numerous **campgrounds** line each of the highways leading into the park, a few of them private but most run by the US Forest Service (USFS). You'll also find plenty of **motel** options along each of the main corridors, but keep in mind that the closer you get to the park, the higher the rates. The prices quoted are average summer rates; prices generally drop a bit during the week, and you can often find bargains during the winter.

B&Bs are scattered throughout the hills to the west and south of the park, most small establishments with only two or three rooms. These and the various **inns** and **lodges** are usually the priciest accommodations, though they offer homey touches and, in some cases, good breakfast spreads. The local chambers of commerce and visitor centers can guide you to some area B&Bs.

The towns are listed according to their distance from Yosemite, starting with those closest to the park.

HIGHWAY 120 WEST
(MAP 10)

The most popular route for those heading to Yosemite from the San Francisco Bay Area, Hwy 120 W offers several options for overflow accommodations.

Mather
(Map 5)

The **Dimond O Campground** *(☎ 877-444-6777; sites $13; open Apr-Oct)*, along the Middle Fork of the Tuolumne River, contains 38 fairly nice campsites with bear boxes and grills. Some can be reserved; others are first-come, first-served. The campground lies 6 miles north of Hwy 120 W on Evergreen Rd, in the Stanislaus National Forest.

About a mile south of the small, woodsy settlement of Mather is the inviting **Evergreen Lodge** *(☎ 209-379-2606; W www.evergreenlodge.com; 33160 Evergreen Rd;*

cabins from $89; open Apr-Oct). Here you can relax in the lovely dining room and bar or stay overnight in a rustic cabin set among the trees.

Buck Meadows

The **Yosemite Gatehouse Lodge** *(☎ 209-379-2260;* **W** *www.yosemitecabins.com/gate house; 34001 Hwy 120; rooms from $86, cabins from $106; open Apr-Nov)* offers cabins and rooms set among the trees, just 1 mile west of the Big Oak Flat Entrance,

About 10 miles west of the park boundary, **Sweetwater** *(☎ 209-962-7825; sites $12; open Apr-Oct)* is a safe but unexciting Stanislaus National Forest campground that'll do in a pinch.

Much nicer and more secluded is the primitive **Lost Claim** *(☎ 209-962-7825; sites $10; open May-Sept),* 12 miles west of the park and a half-mile east of Buck Meadows; keep watch for the small campground symbol along the road. The sites, set among pine and oak, might feel a bit spooky if you come in at night, but you'll awaken to a genuinely lovely spot.

A large property, **Yosemite Westgate Buck Meadows Lodge** *(☎ 209-962-5281, 800-253-9673; fax 209-962-5285; 7633 Hwy 120; rooms $99-129)* is just 12 miles from the park entrance. The older building features remodeled rooms with modern amenities; newer rooms overlook the pool and cost slightly more.

Groveland

Groveland is an adorable town filled with restored gold rush–era buildings along both sides of Hwy 120 (here called Main St). You'll find several B&Bs in the area, plus some historic hotels. It makes a convenient place to spend the night, just 22 miles from the Big Oak Flat Entrance.

The Stanislaus National Forest includes a few campgrounds scattered along Hwy 120 in the vicinity of Groveland. **The Pines** *(☎ 209-962-7825; sites $10; open year-round)* offers a handful of sites in an open meadow about one mile east of the Groveland Ranger Station.

The **Hotel Charlotte** *(☎ 209-962-7872, 800-961-7799;* **W** *www.hotelcharlotte.com; rooms $81, suites $146),* in the middle of town, was first opened in 1918 by Italian immigrant Charlotte DeFerrari. Rates in the vintage rooms include breakfast, and the suites sleep up to four people.

Across the street is the stately **Groveland Hotel** *(☎ 209-962-4000, 800-273-3314;* **W** *www.groveland.com; 18767 Main St; rooms $135-210),* a historic property that dates back to 1850 and now houses a nice old saloon, an upscale restaurant, and 17 quaint, lovingly decorated rooms.

Sugar Pine Ranch *(☎ 209-962-7823;* **W** *www.bizware.com/sugarpine; 21250 Hwy 120; rooms $110-150)* offers B&B accommodations on a 60-acre ranch 4 miles east of Groveland.

HIGHWAY 140
(MAP 11)

The YARTS bus system travels along Hwy 140, the only all-year highway into the park, making this route the easiest option for travelers without cars.

El Portal

Immediately west of the park's Arch Rock Entrance, El Portal makes a convenient Yosemite base.

Less than 2 miles from the park entrance, the **Yosemite View Lodge** (☎ *209-379-2681, 800-321-5261, fax 209-379-2704; 11136 Hwy 140; most rooms $125-155)*, is a big, modern complex with pools, hot tubs, and restaurants. Among the 278 rooms, the nicest feature kitchenettes, fireplaces, and views of the Merced River.

Cedar Lodge (☎ *209-379-2612, 888-742-4371, fax 209-379-2712; 9966 Hwy 140; rooms from $95)*, approximately 9 miles west of the Arch Rock Entrance, is a sprawling establishment with more than 200 adequate rooms, a pool, and a couple of restaurants. It's owned by the same company as the Yosemite View Lodge, but it's not nearly as nice.

On the west end of El Portal, where the south and main forks of the Merced River meet, is the **Yosemite Redbud Lodge** (☎ *209-379-2301; rooms $80-128)*. Each of the eight individually decorated rooms features artwork, nice furniture, and matching linens. Terrace rooms boast deck views, kitchen facilities, and fireplaces; all rooms have BBQs, and rates include coffee, fruit, and bagels in the morning.

Briceburg

Some 20 miles from Yosemite's Arch Rock Entrance, where Hwy 140 meets the Merced River, is the BLM's Briceburg Visitor Center (☎ 209-379-9414; open summers only). Turn north on the small dirt road adjacent to the center, travel a few miles, and you'll find three primitive campgrounds along the river, **McCabe Flat**, **Willow Placer** and **Railroad Flat** *(sites $10)*. Long trailers and large RVs are not recommended.

Midpines

The highlight of this almost nonexistent town is the **Yosemite Bug Lodge & Hostel** (☎ *209-966-6666, fax 209-966-6667;* ⓦ *www.yosemitebug.com; 6979 Hwy 140)*, tucked away on a forested hillside about 25 miles from the park. Removed from the busy highway, it's more of a convivial mountain retreat than a typical hostel. At night, friendly folks of all ages from around the globe share stories, music, and inexpensive, delicious meals at the café. Choices include standard dorm beds ($13-16), campsites ($17), tent cabins ($30-50), private rooms with shared facilities ($40-70), and uniquely decorated cabins with private bath ($55-115). Dorm dwellers have access to a kitchen. The Bug rents mountain bikes ($12-15) and snowshoes ($8) and features laundry facilities, a small retail shop, and Internet access. If you don't have a car, you can often catch a ride into Yosemite with another visitor; otherwise, the Bug sells discounted roundtrip tickets for the YARTS bus.

If you're determined to camp, and the few sites at the Bug are full, try the nearby year-round **KOA Campground** (☎ *209-966-2201, 800-562-9391; tents $21-27, RVs $31-38, cabins $50-60)*.

Removed from the busy highway, it's more of a convivial mountain retreat than a typical hostel.

If you're after a motel room, the affordable and basic **Muir Lodge Motel** (☎ 209-966-2468; 6833 Hwy 140) rents rooms for $30 and up.

Mariposa

This cute town is just under an hour's drive from the park (around 34 miles). Filled with moderately priced motels, it makes for a pleasant stopover on your way to or from Yosemite.

The **Sierra View Motel** (☎ 209-966-5793, 800-627-8439; 4993 7th St; rooms from $58) claims to be the oldest motel in town, constructed in 1941. A block removed from Hwy 140 on a quiet side street, it features an attractive, small courtyard and pleasantly groomed grounds. Rooms have TVs but no phones.

Close to downtown, the **Mother Lode Lodge** (☎ 209-966-2521, 800-398-9770; W www.mariposamotel.com; 5051 Hwy 140; rooms from $68) offers simple rooms set back from the road, plus a pool. Rooms come with TVs but no phones.

Directly across the street is the simple, well-kept **Mariposa Lodge** (☎ 209-966-3607, 800-966-8819; W www.mariposalodge.com; rooms from $79), which boasts clean, quiet rooms (with TVs and phones) and a pleasant staff.

Right in the center of town along Hwy 140 is the historic **Mariposa Hotel-Inn** (☎ 209-966-4676, 800-317-3244; W www.yosemitehotel.com; 5029 Hwy 140; rooms $90-125), a Victorian-flavored hotel with a half-dozen quaintly decorated rooms housed upstairs in a restored building full of antiques.

Merced

This town along Hwy 99 in the San Joaquin Valley is about two hours' drive from Yosemite, too far to work well as a home base while visiting the park. Still, if you're traveling through – by bus, train or car – it makes an easy overnight stop.

The **Merced Home Hostel** (☎ 209-725-0407; dorm beds for HI members/nonmembers $15/18, couples room $34-39; closed 8am-5:30pm daily) is a family-style hostel in the home of longtime Merced residents who know tons about Yosemite; they even offer a travel talk nightly at 9pm. The hosts will pick up and drop off travelers at points in town, including the bus and train stations. They also rent sleeping bags ($3) and tents ($5) for travelers on the way to the park.

HIGHWAY 41
(MAP 12)

Hwy 41 runs from the South Entrance of Yosemite down to Fresno. Several good B&Bs and comfortable inns are scattered along the road and around the small town of Fish Camp, while the bigger town of Oakhurst contains quite a few motels.

The Sierra National Forest's **Summerdale Campground** (☎ 877-444-6777; sites $16; open May-Sept) is very convenient to the park and often a popular choice when the Wawona Campground in Yosemite is full. It's a pleasant spot along Big Creek, too, with sites fairly well dispersed in an area of grassy meadow and trees.

Fish Camp

The cheapest option in town is the **White Chief Mountain Lodge** (☎ 559-683-5444; W www.sierratel.com/whitechiefmtnlodge; 7776 White Chief Mountain Rd; singles/doubles from $70/75), a 1950s-era motel with simple, standard rooms and a restaurant on the grounds. It's located a few hundred yards east of Hwy 41; watch for the sign.

If you're staying for a few days, the **Owls Nest Lodging** (☎ 559-683-3484; 1237 Hwy 41; rates for two people $85-125; closed Jan-Mar) offers four spacious rentals that are a great value. Two are private cabins that sleep up to six, each with a kitchen, VCR, and a nice deck. The two large guest rooms include private baths and VCRs. A three-night minimum stay is required in summer, two-night minimum in spring and fall.

Tenaya Lodge (☎ 559-683-6555, 888-514-2167; W www.tenayalodge.com; 1122 Hwy 41; standard rooms from $249) is a hulking, modern hotel and conference center just 2 miles from Yosemite's South Entrance. The 244-room resort was formerly a Marriott, which explains why it looks and feels like a convention hotel. Despite the location outside the park, it's actually owned by Yosemite Concession Services.

Adjacent to the popular Sugar Pine Railroad is the **Narrow Gauge Inn** (☎ 559-683-7720, 888-644-9050; 48571 Hwy 41; W www.narrowgaugeinn.com; rooms in low/high season from $79/129; open year-round), a beautiful, friendly, and supremely comfortable inn with a pool, hot tub, small bar, and one of the finest restaurants around. Each tastefully appointed room (with TV and phone) features unique decor and a pleasant deck facing the trees and mountains.

Bass Lake

The closest campgrounds lie along the lake's south shore, accessed via Rd 222, including (from west to east) **Forks**, **Lupine/Cedar**, **Spring Cove**, and **Wishon Point** (sites $18; open approximately May-Sept).

The Forks Resort (☎ 559-642-3737; W www.theforksresort.com; 39150 Rd 222; cabins from $85 per night, $600 per week) has rooms and cabins near the lake, some sleeping up to eight people.

The Pines Resort & Conference Center (☎ 559-642-3121, 800-350-7463; W www.basslake.com; chalets from $159, suites from $219) is a massive modern hotel and restaurant complex. Nearby North Shore Rd is packed with side-by-side vacation homes.

Oakhurst

At the junction of Hwys 41 and 49, about 15 miles south of the park entrance, Oakhurst is a bustling if uninspiring town filled with supermarkets, gas stations, and chain motels.

The 60-unit **Oakhurst Lodge** (☎ 559-683-4417, 800-655-6343; W www.oklodge.com; 40302 Hwy 41; rooms from $60), right in the center of town, presents a perfectly fine budget option, with quiet, clean, newly remodeled rooms and a pool.

A few miles north of Oakhurst is the **Hounds Tooth Inn** (☎ 559-642-6600; W www.houndstoothinn.com; 42071 Hwy 41; rooms $95-175), a pleasant, Victorianesque hotel with a dozen rooms, some with spas and fireplaces.

Two miles farther north is the intersection with Rd 632, which leads to Nelder Grove. Turn east and you'll immediately find **Sierra Sky Ranch** (☎ 559-683-8040; W www.sierratel.com/skyranch; 50552 Rd 632; rooms from $89; closed Jan and Feb), a former ranch dating back to 1875. The rustic rooms have no TVs or phones, but the beautiful old lodge and grounds do feature a restaurant, saloon, pool, and numerous outdoor activities on 14 attractive acres.

HIGHWAY 120 EAST
(MAP 13)

The short stretch of Hwy 120 E between Yosemite and Lee Vining is lined with steep cliffs and incredible views. Campgrounds here are popular overflow areas for park visitors, and RVs can park free overnight at the Tioga Lake Overlook, a half-mile east of the Tioga Pass Entrance (one night limit, no tents or fires).

Nine campgrounds line steep and rocky Tioga Rd as it winds its way down rugged Lee Vining Canyon. They're run by either the Inyo National Forest (☎ 760-647-3041) or the Mono County Department of Public Works (☎ 760-932-5252). All the campgrounds operate on a first-come, first-served basis, and they're open only when Tioga Pass is cleared of snow, usually sometime in June to approximately mid-October. Note that in this area camping is allowed in designated (and open) campgrounds only.

The campgrounds closest to Tioga Pass include **Tioga Lake** (*sites $15*), with bland, exposed sites right on the lake; **Junction** (*sites $9*), an attractive, primitive campground along a stream at the turnoff to Saddlebag Lake; and **Ellery Lake** (*sites $15*), with sites tucked out of sight of the road. All are run by the USFS and lie within a few miles of the park entrance.

Once you drop out of the canyon and get closer to Lee Vining, you'll find six more campgrounds along Lee Vining Creek to the south of the highway. Except for Big Bend, these are managed by Mono County.

About 10 miles east of Tioga Pass is the turnoff for Poole Power Plant Rd; turn south here and follow the signs to reach **Moraine**, **Boulder** and **Aspen**, all with $8 sites set among pine, aspen, and desert sage alongside Lee Vining Creek. Farthest up Poole Rd is **Big Bend** (*sites $15*), a USFS campground in a beautifully thick stand of aspen and pine, though sites are a bit close together. Less than a mile farther east on Hwy 120 are two more campgrounds: **Cattleguard** (*sites $8*) is the first you come to and the nicer of the pair; **Lower Lee Vining Campground** (*sites $8*) is next. All are first-come, first served.

Founded in 1914, **Tioga Pass Resort** (☎ 209-372-4471; W *www.tiogapassresort.com; rooms from $80, cabins per week from $840*) is a complex of 10 cabins, a store, a café, and a dining room on a hillside just 2 miles east of Tioga Pass. It attracts a loyal clientele, and no wonder; the location's lovely and convenient. Each cabin comes with a kitchen, porch, bathroom, and linens. Summer season usually runs from late May to mid-October, depending on snow; winter season (you must ski in) is February to April. Reserve well in advance.

Lee Vining

On the shore of beautiful Mono Lake, Lee Vining is only 12 miles (about a 30-minute drive) from Yosemite's east entrance, where Hwy 120 (Tioga Rd) meets Hwy 395.

Right in town, **El Mono Motel** (☎ 760-647-6310; *rooms with shared/private bath $49/67; open Easter-Halloween*) is the closest thing Lee Vining has to a hostel, in business since 1927. The atmosphere is casual and friendly, though the rooms are tiny and rather basic, with TV but no phone. Rates drop in spring and fall.

Murphey's Motel (☎ 760-647-6316, 800-334-6316; W *www.murpheysyosemite.com; singles/doubles from $83/88*) is a large, modern property on the north end of town.

Yosemite Gateway Motel (☎ 760-647-6467, 800-282-3929; W *www.yosemitegate waymotel.com; 51340 Hwy 395; rooms $99*), the only motel in town on the east side of the highway, rents rooms that look out directly onto Mono Lake.

Whether you're looking for a sit-down meal or just a quick sandwich for the road, the listings below will guide you to just about every option available in Yosemite, plus many of the better restaurants outside the park's borders. This chapter also includes grocery store information for those planning on camping or backpacking, as well as some of the more intriguing bars and saloons both inside and outside the park. Many local restaurants are associated with hotels and lodges; for accommodations information, check the Places to Stay chapter.

YOSEMITE PLACES TO EAT

Inside the Park

Depending on how much time and energy you have, bringing a supply of your favorite foods for simple picnic lunches or full-on campground feasts may result in the finest eating you'll do in the park. Even with a single-burner camp stove, you might surprise yourself with how well you can cook outside your home kitchen. It doesn't have to be elaborate; there's something about dining by a fire and under the stars that makes the simplest food taste heavenly.

Do keep in mind, though, that whether you're at your campsite, inside your hotel, or out for a day hike, you need to remove every scrap of food from your car (or backpack or bicycle) and store it in a bear-proof locker or bear canister. This is true whether you're taking a multi-day backpacking trip or just spending a few hours meandering through the museum. It may seem like a hassle to put your picnic lunch in a locker, but if you come back to a ransacked car with broken windows and torn-up upholstery, who's going to be whining then?

If storing your food properly (or pulling out the camp stove on a cold, dark night) sounds like too much trouble, there are plenty of sandwiches, quick meals, and even fancy sit-down dinners available in Yosemite Valley and a few other spots in the park. The upscale establishments, though pricey, serve delicious meals; as for the rest of the options, don't get your hopes up beyond a mediocre cafeteria meal, an overpriced deli sandwich, or a greasy cheeseburger.

A few places are open year-round, though in most cases hours are reduced during winter. Other restaurants are only open from spring through fall, and businesses in the higher elevations only operate in summer. Specific opening and closing dates vary year to year – especially in the high country – and may be different than those listed. It's a good idea to call ahead.

All Yosemite restaurants (and most lodging facilities) are run by **Yosemite Concession Services**. If a specific phone number does not appear in a listing, call the central YCS number (☎ *209-372-1000*) or check the website (Ⓦ *www.yosemitepark.com /html/dining/html*). You can also find hours for YCS businesses listed inside the brochure *Yosemite Today*, free at each entry station.

YOSEMITE VALLEY
(MAP 2)
For quick bites, try Yosemite Village or Curry Village, though Yosemite Lodge offers some options, too. For more elegant dining, head to Yosemite Lodge or, at the top of the heap, the Ahwahnee Hotel. No matter where you choose to eat, remember to take a moment and appreciate the scenery. The view of Half Dome reflected in the golden light of early evening will add pizzazz to even the crummiest hamburger.

Yosemite Village
The biggest and best grocery store in the park is the **Village Store** *(open 8am-10pm daily in summer, reduced hours in winter)*, found smack in the center of Yosemite Village. It comes in handy whether you're after last-minute items or full-on dinners. The store carries decent produce, fresh meat and fish, and even some surprising items like tofu dogs, hummus, udon noodles, and polenta. You'll also find a small section of camping supplies along with plenty of T-shirts and other gift items (as in just about every Yosemite retail outlet).

The restaurant choices in Yosemite Village are, frankly, not going to get any gourmets salivating. The best of the bunch is probably **Degnan's Deli** *(lunch from about $6; open year-round)*, an easy and acceptable lunch stop offering fresh sandwiches, soups, and lots of snacks and beverages. Next door sits **Degnan's Cafe** *(open mid-Apr-Oct)*, where you can indulge in espresso drinks, smoothies, and pastries. Upstairs is a pizza parlor, **Degnan's Loft** *(personal pizza from $4.50, large pizza from $14; open mid-Apr-Oct)*, in a spacious room with an A-frame ceiling and a bland ski-lodge feel.

A few buildings south, the **Village Grill** *(cheeseburger from $4; open mid-Apr-Oct)* is a standard fast-food counter with patio seating.

Curry Village
Curry Village opened in 1899, but its facilities now belong to YCS, as do all the other stores and restaurants in the valley. The dining choices here are hardly exciting, but they're convenient if you're staying in one of the Curry tent cabins or returning hungry from a grueling hike via the nearby Happy Isles trailhead.

GOOD GROCERY STORES

The best stores for groceries and supplies lie on your way into the park, but two inside Yosemite actually offer decent selections.

✔ **Richland Market** (Oakdale)
✔ **Raley's** (Oakhurst)
✔ **Pioneer Market** (Mariposa)
✔ **Tuolumne Meadows Store** (Yosemite National Park)
✔ **Yosemite Village Store** (Yosemite National Park)

The **Curry Village Store** is more about snacks, sodas, gifts, and beer than vital dining supplies.

The tiny **Taco Stand** *(lunch under $5; open mid-Apr-Oct)*, facing the parking lot and next to the Mountain Shop, serves burritos, taco salads, and other Mexican dishes.

Around the corner is **Pizza Patio** *(personal pizza from $5, large pizza from $12; open mid-Apr-mid-Oct)*, a walk-up window with outdoor seating. Expect a crowd on summer evenings.

The **Curry Dining Pavilion** *(breakfast adult/child $8/5, dinner adult/child $12/6; open mid-Apr-Oct)*, a spacious indoor cafeteria, serves mediocre all-you-can-eat breakfasts and dinners in the grand tradition of Las Vegas buffets. Also inside is the small **Coffee Corner** *(open year-round)*, where you can pick up pastries, ice-cream treats, and espresso drinks.

Next to the pizza window is the tiny **Terrace Bar**, serving a couple of decent microbrews on tap and a full range of cocktails.

Yosemite Lodge

Near the base of Yosemite Falls, this "lodge" is not a single rustic building but rather a cluster of contemporary condo-type hotel units, gift shops, and restaurants.

For meals, the cheapest option is the self-service **Food Court** *(breakfast and lunch $4-7, dinner $6-10; open daily year-round)*, just behind the lodge's main lobby. There's

COCKTAILS WITH CHARACTER

These spirited joints are the best places for martinis, highballs, and brews in and near the park.

✔ A top-shelf spot is the **Ahwahnee Hotel**, one of the West's most stunning hotels. Cocktails are professional creations here. Sip a martini in the friendly bar or out on the patio with Half Dome looming overhead.

✔ The 1879 **Wawona Hotel** serves sophisticated cocktails in its piano-lounge lobby or outside facing the spacious green lawn.

✔ When it comes to a good value and a homey atmosphere, you can't beat the **Yosemite Bug Lodge & Hostel,** tucked away on a quiet hillside in Midpines. There's wine by the glass, a couple of hearty beers on tap (including Guinness), and lots of travelers spinning yarns day and night.

✔ The **Iron Door Grill & Saloon** in Groveland claims to be the oldest watering hole in the state. It's got a honky-tonk appeal, but it also draws lots of tourists, who dig the memorabilia-covered walls.

✔ In Oakdale, the simple neon sign of the **H-B Saloon** is a welcoming beacon. The place boasts plenty of honest Western character, including a well-worn bar that's a favorite with cowboys and other thirsty locals.

✔ **Hondo's Steakhouse** in Oakhurst is not extraordinarily charming, but the bar is an easy, comfortable spot to grab one of several decent microbrews on tap.

✔ At the **Inn at Mono Lake** it's tough to choose between the deck with perfect views and the huge stone fireplace with comfy chairs.

indoor seating, and dinner choices range from basic burgers to hot pasta plates.

At the far pricier **Mountain Room Restaurant** *(dinner entrées $16-25; open year-round)*, you can enjoy your dinner in an airy, contemporary room with picture-window views of Yosemite Falls. The menu is loaded with beef but also includes fish and a vegetarian stew.

Across the courtyard is the **Mountain Room Lounge**, a full-service bar with a spacious interior and more big windows.

Ahwahnee Hotel

Taking a meal in the supremely impressive **Ahwahnee Dining Room** *(☎ 559-372-1489; breakfast and lunch $10-15, dinner entrées $24-36; open year-round)* is certainly worth the splurge, if only to sit by candlelight under the 34ft-high beamed ceiling and lose yourself in the incredible scenery, viewed through massive picture windows. The food is generally excellent, though compared with the surroundings, it may come in second as a draw here. There's a dress code at dinner, but you can wear shorts and sneakers at breakfast and lunch. Expect a lovely spread for Sunday brunch (served 7am to 3pm).

If your pockets aren't deep enough for the dining room (even breakfast is a serious setback) but you still want to partake of the hotel's charms, stop by the **Ahwahnee Bar** for a cocktail. Drinks aren't exactly cheap – a "classic martini" runs a whopping $13 – but you can get a pint of Bridalveil Ale for $5. In any case, it's a small price to pay for the classy, relaxed atmosphere, whether you're inside or out on the patio soaking up that warm evening glow.

WAWONA
(MAP 4)

You'll find two small stores in this enclave near the South Entrance to the park, both open all year. The **Wawona General Store**, a short walk from the Wawona Hotel, offers a few picnic and camping items but focuses more on snacks and gifts. Slightly better is the tiny **Pine Tree Market**, a mile east of Hwy 41 amid The Redwoods in Yosemite, a collection of vacation rental homes; turn east of Chilnualna Falls Rd, which is just north of the Pioneer History Center.

The **Wawona Hotel Dining Room** *(☎ 209-375-1425; breakfast $4-6, lunch $7-9, dinner $17-27; open daily Easter-Oct, weekends Nov-Mar)* is another Yosemite treasure – a beautiful dining room with Victorian touches and upscale cuisine inside the historic 1879 Wawona Hotel. Come for a good deal at breakfast, or a barbecue on the lawn every Saturday during summer. "Tasteful, casual attire"

> ✔ **TIP**
>
> While dinner at the classy **Wawona Hotel** is pricey, breakfast is a surprisingly good value. Delicious breakfast entrées average around $6 – a bargain considering the lovely setting. Hungry visitors will love the $10 buffet.

is the rule to remember at dinner. Seating is first-come, first-served, though reservations are required for parties of eight or more. The restaurant is also open during the Thanksgiving and Christmas seasons.

The Wawona's wide, white porch makes a snazzy destination for evening cocktails, served from 5pm to 10pm. In the hotel's lobby – which doubles as its lounge – listen for pianist Tom Bopp, who's been running through his repertoire of Yosemite chestnuts since 1983.

ALONG TIOGA ROAD
(MAP 7)

Like Tuolumne Meadows, the small enclave of White Wolf is only open during the summer.

A mile north of Tioga Rd, the White Wolf Lodge area includes a campground and tent cabins, an almost miniscule **store** with snacks, coffee, and very basic sandwiches that could use some adornment (a piece of lettuce, at least?), plus a small, rustic **dining room** (☎ 209-372-8416; breakfast $5-6, dinner $6-16) with cozy seating inside or on the screened-in porch. Reservations are highly advised for dinner; note that during busy weeks, the restaurant only feeds lodge guests.

TUOLUMNE MEADOWS
(MAP 8)

Located along Tioga Rd (Hwy 120) at 8500ft, this region of the park is only open during summer, from approximately June to mid-September. Exact dates vary each year, depending on snowfall.

The **Tuolumne Meadows Store** (open 8am-8pm daily in summer) offers a surprisingly decent selection of food. The store's not very big, but its stock rivals that of the larger Yosemite Village Store and the mediocre markets in most nearby towns. Vegans will be happy to find a couple of shelves devoted to tofu dogs and other meatless delights; you can also buy limited produce, a few camping supplies, firewood, books, maps, liquor, and decent brands of packaged food. The main drawback is that prices are noticeably steep

Next door is the small **Tuolumne Meadows Grill** (breakfast and lunch from around $5), a standard, greasy fast-food counter serving eggs, burgers, and snacks.

For a hearty sit-down breakfast or dinner, make a reservation at the **Tuolumne Meadows Lodge** (☎ 209-372-8413; breakfast $5-10, dinner $10-20), where you dine in a rustic canvas structure along the Tuolumne River. The restaurant mainly serves lodge guests, but others can call to see if seating is available. Meals are served family style.

✔ TIP

Be on the lookout for the special **Rangers' Coffee**, offered summer Sunday mornings at 9am in Tuolumne Meadows and at other times of the year in Camp 4. Bring a mug and join rangers, climbers, and fellow campers for coffee, conversation, and inside information.

Outside the Park

After a few days of deli sandwiches and mediocre pasta dishes, you might crave a little variety. If you don't mind driving, you'll find more restaurant options outside the park. Some towns involve a substantial drive, so you're more likely to try them on your way to or from Yosemite. Others, such as Oakhurst and Lee Vining, are close enough for a dinner visit, especially if you're staying in a nearby corner of the park. Gateway towns are also a great place to stock up on groceries.

HIGHWAY 120 WEST
(MAP 10)
Mather
(Map 5)

In summer, this small woodsy settlement 8 miles north of Hwy 120 on Evergreen Rd (the road to Hetch Hetchy) operates as a family summer camp for lucky San Franciscans. About a mile before you reach Mather is **Evergreen Lodge** (☎ 209-379-2606; W *www.evergreenlodge.com; 33160 Evergreen Rd; dinner $12-20; open Apr-Oct)*, where you can enjoy salmon, steak, or pasta suppers in the dining room, grab a sandwich in the deli ($5), or sip cocktails in the lively bar.

Groveland

Old West charm survives in Groveland, a cute gold-rush town with historic buildings along Main St (Hwy 120). About 25 miles from Yosemite's Big Oak Flat Entrance, it's also a convenient place to grab a meal on your way into or out of the park.

Need to make a grocery run? Your best bet is **Ken's Market** *(Hwy 120 at Ferretti Rd; open 8am-8pm Sun-Thurs, 8am-9pm Fri-Sat)*, on the east end of town just north of the highway and directly behind PJ's Cafe and Pizzeria. The place isn't huge and the selection isn't stellar, but you'll still find plenty here to cobble together a few meals.

Several eateries and hotels line Hwy 120 at the town's historic center, including the **Iron Door Grill & Saloon** *(W www. iron-door-saloon.com; 18761 Main St; lunch $5-8, dinner $12-20)*, which claims to be the oldest watering hole in the state. The bar makes an excellent cocktail destination – with live music every weekend – while the adjacent dinner house serves burgers, steaks, and pasta dishes. Kids can get a treat at the soda fountain, and road-weary souls can grab a quick espresso at **Coffee Time**, across the street.

The most elegant meal option in town is the Victorian dining room at the historic **Groveland Hotel** *(☎ 209-962-4000; W www.groveland.com; 18767 Main St; dinner entrées $10-20)*. The menu changes regularly and often includes baby-back ribs, beef, and salmon. Reservations are recommended, especially on weekends and holidays. The hotel also has a nice bar.

Old West charm survives in Groveland, a cute gold-rush town with historic buildings along Main Street.

Big Oak Flat

At the very top of steep Old Priest Grade Rd, overlooking the San Joaquin Valley, **Old Priest Station Inn** *(☎ 209-962-4181; Ⓦ www.oldprieststation.com; lunch $6-12, dinner $10-18; open year-round)* was originally established in 1853 as a stagecoach stop. This motel and restaurant now sits in its place and makes a great place to grab a beer and watch the sun set over the hazy, dusty farmland far below or to tuck into a meal of steak, burgers, or pasta. The deck offers unbeatable views.

Knights Ferry

This tiny, historic town lies just to the north of Hwy 108/120 along the Stanislaus River. At its center is the **Knights Ferry Creamery** *(snacks and lunch less than $5)*, serving excellent milkshakes along with sandwiches and espresso drinks.

A block up the street is the secluded, comfortable **Knights Ferry Resort** *(☎ 209-881-3349; brunch $10-16, lunch $7-15, dinner $9-25; open for lunch and dinner Wed-Sun, brunch Sat-Sun)*, where you can get meals in a rustic dining room or outside on a deck overlooking the river. There's also a cozy, full-service bar area. The restaurant is open all year, but weekends only in winter.

Loaded with Western-style character, the place includes an old bar that's perfect for knocking back a brew with the local cowboys.

Oakdale

This utilitarian town some 70 miles west of Yosemite offers numerous places to eat and grab groceries. You'd be hard-pressed to find a better food store in this part of the state than the **Richland Market** *(Maag Ave at Hwy 108/120)*, a large, modern supermarket about a mile east of downtown Oakdale. The extensive produce section includes some organic items.

Oakdale Brewing Company *(☎ 209-845-2739; 160 N Third Ave; lunch $6-10, dinner $7-20)* serves hot meals and cold house-brewed beers in a spacious room that used to be a Dodge dealership.

If you stop for dinner at the **H-B Saloon** *(☎ 209-847-2985; 401 E F St; dinners $15-19, sandwiches from $8)*, you won't leave hungry, as the gut-busting, family-style meals include soup, salad, beans, stew, french fries, and wine. Lunch is served Monday through Friday, dinner Wednesday through Saturday, both under the name Bachi's Family Style Dinners. Loaded with Western-style character, the place includes an old bar that's perfect for knocking back a brew with the local cowboys.

HIGHWAY 140
(MAP 11)
El Portal

This hamlet sits only about 2 miles west of the Arch Rock Entrance to Yosemite. The tiny **El Portal Market** *(open 8am-8pm summer, 9am-7pm winter)* marks the center of town, but if you're looking for a meal, your best options are at the nearby motel restaurants.

Yosemite View Lodge (☎ *209-379-2681*), located east of the El Portal Market and quite near the park entrance, houses the casual **Little Bear's Pizza** *(large pizza from $15, sandwiches from $6)* and the pricier **Yosemite View Restaurant** *(dinner $10-26)*, offering pasta and stir-fry dishes along with a range of meaty entrées.

To the west of central El Portal is **Cedar Lodge** (☎ *209-379-2316; 9966 Hwy 40)*, where you can get Mexican food in the **Diner** *(meals from $6)* and steaks, pasta, and chicken in the **Cedar Lodge Restaurant** *(dinner $10-20)*. The adjacent **lounge** whips up cocktails in a room that looks like an overeager cross between a sports bar and a 1950s diner.

Midpines

There isn't much to Midpines, but if you're hungry, the most satisfying meals you'll find this side of Yosemite are available at the relaxing, friendly **Yosemite Bug Lodge & Hostel** (☎ *209-966-6666;* Ⓦ *www.yosemitebug.com; breakfast $4-6, box lunch $5.50, dinner $7-12)*, about 25 miles west of Yosemite's Arch Rock Entrance. The complex sits on a quiet, secluded hillside out of sight of Hwy 140. The main building features a lovely, low-key café serving breakfast, lunch, and dinner daily; the latter boasts tasty meals such as smoked pork, trout, or pasta. You won't pay a whole lot, and you'll walk away full and happy. There's wine by the glass and even Guinness on tap And no, you don't have to be an overnight guest (see p 180) to partake of the Bug's bounty.

> *You won't pay a whole lot, and you'll walk away full and happy.*

CHEAP EATS

Unless you're cooking your own, meals aren't exactly easy on the budget inside Yosemite. There are, however, a few affordable eateries not far from the park's boundaries where the food's as decent as the price.

✔ **Yosemite Bug Lodge & Hostel** (Midpines): Considering the humane prices, creative, tasty dishes, and woodsy surroundings, a meal at this low-key café is a true treat for road-weary souls.

✔ **High Country Café** (Mariposa): Next to the High Country Health Food Store, this is your best lunchtime bet for healthy salads and vegan sandwiches (don't fret, they make some with meat, too).

✔ **Knights Ferry Creamery** (Knights Ferry): At the center of this tiny riverside town is this small sandwich and snack stop, which churns out some of the best milkshakes around.

✔ **Pete's Place** (Oakhurst): Order at the counter inside this nothing-fancy joint, then await one of the hearty burgers, full breakfasts, or reasonably priced dinner plates. It's quick but a long way from fast food.

Mariposa

This sizable town lies some 34 miles east of Yosemite's Arch Rock Entrance Station and makes good place to stock up on groceries. The **Pioneer Market** (☎ 209-742-6100) is a medium-sized supermarket with a decent selection. It's about a mile east of downtown on Hwy 140; turn left (north) on Coakley Circle, just past the Burger King.

For coffee, the best bet in town is the small **Pony Espresso** (☎ 209-966-5053; 5053 Hwy 140), with acceptable espresso drinks, smoothies, bagels, and muffins.

If you've got the time and you're nuts about beans, it's worth making the detour to the **Mariposa Coffee Company** (☎ 209-742-7339; 2945 Hwy 49 S; open daily), tucked amid the trees on the west side of Hwy 49, about a 15- or 20-minute drive south of Mariposa. The coffee's roasted fresh each day, and you can buy it by the pound or the cup. Owner Gerry Caputo is also putting in a pick-your-own berry patch and revamping an old stagecoach stop to keep visitors entertained as well as caffeinated.

The cheapest meals in Mariposa are probably at **Happy Burger** (☎ 209-966-2719; Hwy 140 at 12th St; sandwiches $3-6), an acceptable roadside joint offering breakfast items, burgers, and sandwiches.

If you're after healthier fare, the **High Country Café** (☎ 209-966-5111; Hwy 140 at Hwy 49; sandwiches from $5; closed Sun) serves salads, soups, and both vegan and meat-filled sandwiches at lunchtime.

Red Fox (☎ 209-966-7900; Hwy 140 at 12th St; breakfast and sandwiches from $5, dinner from $10), a nice sit-down restaurant across the street from Happy Burger, features grandmotherly decor and good, affordable food. The steaks are nicely grilled and the dinner salads surprisingly fresh and tasty.

A rung higher on the food ladder is **Charles Street Dinner House** (☎ 209-966-2366; 5043 Hwy 140; dinners $13-20), a fairly traditional steakhouse with a dark, moody interior.

HIGHWAY 41
(MAP 12)
Fish Camp

The small **Fish Camp General Store**, which pretty much defines the "center of town," sells sandwiches ($4.50) and box lunches ($7.95), along with a limited amount of groceries and supplies year-round.

Excellent food coupled with knockout views make the dining experience at the **Narrow Gauge Inn** (☎ 559-683-7720; W www.narrowgaugeinn.com; dinner entrées $12-25; open Apr-Oct) one of the finest in the Yosemite region. It's a little expensive, but the dinners are creatively prepared, the lodge-like atmosphere is casual but elegant, and windows look out on lush mountain vistas. Reservations are recommended. Cozy up to the

Excellent food coupled with knockout views make the dining experience at the Narrow Gauge Inn one of the finest in the Yosemite region.

fireplace on colder evenings or warm yourself up at the small **Buffalo Bar**, perfect for a cocktail or glass of Chardonnay. The inn sits along Hwy 41 a couple miles south of the Fish Camp Store and about 5 miles from Yosemite's South Entrance.

Bass Lake

About 13 miles south of Yosemite is the **Mountain House Restaurant** (☎ 559-683-5191; 42525 Hwy 41; dinner $12-18), at the corner of Rd 222, which leads to Bass Lake. It serves standard pastas, sandwiches, salads and steak and chicken dinners.

From the Mountain House, turn east on Rd 222 to reach Bass Lake, where you can dine facing the water at **Ducey's on the Lake** (☎ 559-642-3131; Ⓦ www.basslake.com; 39255 Marina Dr; dinner entrées $18-26), located behind The Pines Resort & Conference Center. Near the lobby of the resort is **The Pines Bar**, a loud, party-friendly place with pool tables and more lakeside views. (John Candy and Dan Aykroyd were filmed drinking at the bar in the 1988 comedy *The Great Outdoors*). To reach The Pines and Ducey's, follow Bass Lake Rd (Rd 222) for a few miles until it forks; bear left onto Malum Ridge Rd (Rd 274). A couple miles farther, turn right on Beasore Rd (Rd 434).

Oakhurst

The widest range of meals this side of the park are found in this unexciting town, which sits at the confluence of Hwys 41 and 49, about 17 miles south of Yosemite.

For groceries, you have a few good supermarket choices, including the massive and modern **Raley's** (☎ 559-683-8300; open 6am-11pm daily), in a shopping complex at the traffic-clogged intersection of Hwys 41 and 49.

Yosemite Coffee Roasting Company (☎ 559-683-8815; 40879 Hwy 41), about a mile north of town, sells coffee, espresso drinks, pastries, and sandwiches.

At **Pete's Place** (☎ 559-683-0772; 40093 Hwy 41; breakfast and lunch about $5, dinner $6-10) you order at the counter and eat at plastic tables and chairs. But it's not your average fast-food place; servers bring your order and come around with coffee refills. And Pete serves more than just burgers, try his hearty

WHERE TO SPLURGE

Tired of peanut butter crackers, cheese sandwiches, and reheated spaghetti? Try one of these expensive but oh-so-worth-it dining options.

- ✔ **Ahwahnee Hotel** (Yosemite National Park)
- ✔ **Erna's Elderberry House** (Oakhurst)
- ✔ **Groveland Hotel** (Groveland)
- ✔ **Mono Inn at Mono Lake** (Mono Lake)
- ✔ **Narrow Gauge Inn** (Fish Camp)
- ✔ **Wawona Hotel** (Yosemite National Park)

breakfasts and reasonably priced dinner plates full of pork chops, steaks, and fish.

Next door, **Hondo's Steakhouse** (☎ *559-683-7427; 40083 Hwy 41; dinner $12-20)* boasts a dark atmosphere, red vinyl booths, and lots of wood trim in typical steakhouse style. The menu focuses on beef but also includes salmon and other meats. Head to the comfortable bar if all you want is a nice microbrew on tap (try the strong and smooth Bridalveil Ale).

Got extra cash or an expense account to burn up? Then definitely make a reservation at **Erna's Elderberry House** (☎ *559-683-6800;* W *www.chateaudusureau.com/house.htm; prix-fixe dinner $82).* Erna's offers a renowned California-French dining experience in humble Oakhurst, on the same property as the super-luxurious Château du Sureau hotel. Look for it about a mile south of town on the west side of Hwy 41.

HIGHWAY 120 EAST
(MAP 13)
Tioga Pass

Just 2 miles east of Yosemite's Tioga Pass Entrance is the historic **Tioga Pass Resort** (☎ *209-372-4471;* W *www.tiogapassresort.com; breakfast $5-9, lunch $7-10, dinner $10-25; dining room open mid-June–mid-Sept),* which includes cabins for rent, a small store, a cozy indoor diner, and a new dining room housed under a tent on the porch. The latter serves lunches and dinners that feature steaks, sandwiches, and veggie options; you can also order espresso drinks from a separate counter up front. The diner has only a small counter and two tables but plenty of rustic character; it's open daily in summer (7am-9pm) and for the resort's ski-in patrons in winter.

Lee Vining

This small town sits along the shore of brilliant Mono Lake, near the intersection of Hwys 395 and 120 (Tioga Rd) and only about 12 miles east of Yosemite's Tioga Pass Entrance. There are a fair number of places to eat here, some mediocre and predictable, others surprisingly delicious.

The **Mono Market** (*open 7am-10pm daily in summer, reduced hours in winter)* is a decent grocery store with quality meats, a few camping supplies, and even some organic produce.

For morning fare, the tiny **Latte Da Coffee Cafe** (☎ *760-647-6310; Hwy 395 at Third St; open 7am-9pm daily Easter-Halloween)* sells organic coffee, espresso drinks, and muffins from a shop inside the lobby of the El Mono Motel.

Nestled in a Mobil station near the intersection of Hwys 120 and 395, the wildly popular **Whoa Nellie** (☎ *760-647-1088; breakfast $5-10, lunch from $6, dinner $9-17)* draws folk from near and far to dine on phenomenally tasty and creative treats like lobster taquitos

TOP SPOTS FOR LIVE MUSIC

Birdsongs and babbling brooks not meeting all your entertainment needs? The park doesn't offer a lot of music beyond what nature can supply, especially when it comes to live honky-tonk, blues, and rock and roll, but music lovers do have a few nearby options. Groveland's **Iron Door Saloon** hosts rock and country bands on Friday and Saturday nights. In Bass Lake, **The Pines Bar**, adjacent to the lobby of the fancy Pines Resort, is a loud, party joint with pool tables, a deck, and live bands on weekends. The resort also occasionally holds bigger concerts down by the pool at **Ducey's on the Lake**.

and buffalo meatloaf. This spot also offers margaritas, wine, and craft-brewed beer from the Mammoth Brewing Company.

About 2½ miles north of Lee Vining along Hwy 395 is **Tioga Lodge**, a great old roadside complex with a small, Victorian-flavored dining room called **Me & Manuel** (☎ *760-647-6423; breakfast $5-$9, dinner $9-$18*). The excellent food includes smoked trout and pecan-crusted pork chops.

Some 5 miles north of Lee Vining you'll find the **Mono Inn at Mono Lake** (☎ *760-647-6581;* W *www.monoinn.com; 55620 Hwy 395; entrées $19-26; open Wed-Mon May-Oct, Thurs-Sun Nov-Apr, closed Jan and Feb)*, a recently restored 1922 lodge and dining room that's now a restaurant run by Sarah Adams, granddaughter of photographer Ansel Adams. The decor is rustic yet elegant, the views superb, and the menu inventive and fabulous, featuring locally grown produce, top-notch wines, and such dishes as roasted venison, fresh salmon, and duck. Reservations are recommended.

Yosemite is surrounded by stunning alpine scenery, much of it preserved as official wilderness areas under the jurisdiction of the United States Forest Service (USFS). Long-distance hikers may need to cross some of these areas – if so, be sure to obtain proper wilderness permits when planning an overnight backcountry trip. But these wilderness areas are not just a playground for high-endurance hikers; daytrippers, too, can easily access such spots as 20 Lakes Basin and Virginia Lakes.

BEYOND YOSEMITE

Hiking isn't the only pastime around these parts. There are lots of things to see and do, from rafting the wild waters of Cherry Creek to driving the Sierra Vista Scenic Byway, marveling at massive sequoias in secluded Nelder Grove, or pondering the otherworldly tufa formations at Mono Lake.

You'll find more camping options here than within the park itself, both USFS campgrounds and dispersed camping, which is allowed in most national forests. Dispersed camping is a great way to go if you crave solitude (no nearby campers) and affordability (it's free) – but remember, you're entirely on your own, which means no toilets or potable water (bring your own or come with a means to filter or purify stream water). If you're going to build a fire, you'll also need a free fire permit, which you can pick up at one of the local USFS ranger stations. Ranger stations also sell detailed USFS maps, helpful for navigating the maze of dirt roads. Finally, note that some areas (along Tioga Rd east of the park, for instance) don't allow dispersed camping; watch for signs.

North & West of Yosemite

The vast **Stanislaus National Forest** dominates this area, covering more than 250,000 acres of open terrain and 800 miles of rivers and streams. Along Yosemite's western border, you can take your pick of outdoor activities, particularly rafting, fishing, and swimming. To the north, the forest wreathes all of Emigrant Wilderness and portions of the Carson-Iceberg and Mokelumne Wilderness areas, which you can access via Hwys 108, 4, and 120. The neighboring wilderness areas attract lots of hikers and backpackers; pick up a free overnight permit at the ranger station. Mountain biking is also permitted on many trails within the forest, with a range of terrain suitable for all skill levels.

A PARK BY ANY OTHER NAME ...

NATIONAL PARKS & MONUMENTS

A division of the Department of the Interior, the National Park Service was created in 1916 to preserve the land, its history, and its wildlife and to allow people to enjoy the parks. Since then, debates continue to rage between preservationists and those lobbying for greater public services.

National parks include famous spots like the Grand Canyon, Yellowstone and, of course, Yosemite. However, the NPS also oversees other types of parks, including national monuments, national historic sites, and countless more national seashores, cemeteries, rivers, preserves, and recreation areas. Each designation offers a slightly different level of protection (national preserves allow hunting and oil exploration, for instance), with national park status topping the heap.

National monuments can be created by a presidential signature, while national parks involve approval by Congress.

NATIONAL FORESTS

The US Forest Service (USFS), under the jurisdiction of the Department of Agriculture, administers national forests. Less protected than national parks, their "multiple use" designation allows logging and mining. This is why you might see logging roads and grazing cattle on allegedly "protected" lands. National forests are also open to public recreation and rarely charge a fee for anything but developed campgrounds.

NATIONAL WILDLIFE REFUGES

Brought together under the National Wildlife Refuge System Administration Act in 1966, these refuges protect wildlife habitats. In California this often means wetlands for migrating birds. A curious irony is that these "refuges" are not always safe havens, as many allow hunting.

WILDERNESS

The Wilderness Act of 1964 afforded federal lands an additional layer of protection from development. Wilderness areas truly are nature preserves – no roads, buildings, cattle grazing, or even campgrounds are allowed. Wilderness areas are managed by different agencies; the NPS is in charge of the acreage within Yosemite, while nearby Hoover and Ansel Adams wildernesses are managed by the US Forest Service. Backpackers must obtain free wilderness permits.

BUREAU OF LAND MANAGEMENT

The BLM manages public use of federal lands, from cattle ranges to 4WD vehicle roads. Very few activities are restricted on BLM lands – a laissez-faire approach that means you can pretty much do as you please. Camping is free, although the BLM does maintain some fee-based campgrounds.

STATE PARKS

The rules and regulations at the nation's state parks vary from state to state. California's state park system began in the early 1900s with the acquisition of redwoods at Big Basin near Santa Cruz. Individual park units now number in the hundreds. Each park generally charges a day-use fee; camping is often available. An annual pass ($35) covers the daily entrance fee at all California state parks.

If you plan to explore any part of the forest, be sure to stop by the **Groveland Ranger Station** (☎ 209-962-7825; 24545 Hwy 120) for friendly advice, maps, and detailed trail descriptions. You can also consult the extremely helpful and well-organized website Ⓦ www.r5.fs.fed.us/stanislaus.

SCENIC SONORA PASS
(MAP 14)

Northeast of Sonora (see p 208), Hwy 108 winds through dense forest and aspen-filled meadows before cresting out at Sonora Pass (9624ft). From here, the road corkscrews, with a 26% grade in stretches, before leveling out and joining Hwy 395. Not for the road weary, the absolutely stunning drive sometimes feels more like a roller-coaster than a highway. It zigzags past pristine roadside Sierra scenery, including several good places to **hike** or simply take in the sights.

From the Vista Trail at the Dardanelles Outlook on Hwy 108, about 1¼ hours east of Sonora, you can enjoy an unobstructed view north of the namesake volcanic cones and the sprawling Carson-Iceberg Wilderness. The nearby Clark Fork Trailhead, accessed via Forest Rd 6N06, is a good starting point for hikes into both the Carson-Iceberg and Emigrant Wilderness areas. The 4-mile hike to Boulder Lake is a popular choice, as is the 7-mile Dardanelles Loop, a challenging day hike.

Some of the best wilderness access is from Kennedy Meadow, along the Stanislaus River on Hwy 108, about 6 miles east of Dardanelle. The 12½-mile Emigrant Meadows Trail is a major pathway into the Emigrant Wilderness, while the 3-mile Relief Reservoir Trail is popular for both camping and fishing. From the trailhead atop Sonora Pass (about 5 miles east of Kennedy Meadow), you can access a segment of the Pacific Crest Trail.

There are literally a dozen or so very nice campgrounds along the stretch of road from Dardanelle to Sonora, and even in the thick of summer you stand a very good chance of finding a sweet spot. With good fishing nearby, **Dardanelle Campground** offers 28 sites with tables, stoves, and vault toilets; closer to Sonora Pass, **Deadman Campground** has 17 pretty sites with the same conveniences. You can find information on the different campgrounds online at Ⓦ www.r5.fs.fed.us/stanislaus/visitor/camping.htm.

CHERRY LAKE
(MAP 10)

Cherry Lake, the largest within Stanislaus National Forest, lies along Yosemite's border just west of Hetch Hetchy. Getting there, however, involves some meandering. Exit the park at the Big Oak Flat Entrance, then make a quick right onto Evergreen Rd, following that road to its intersection with Rd 12; turn left (west). Rd 12 runs into Rd 17, also called Cherry Lake Rd; turn right and follow the road to the lake. You can also access Cherry Lake Rd directly from Hwy 120, about 9 miles west of the Big Oak Flat Entrance.

If motorboats don't bother you, Cherry Lake is a nice place to swim, paddle, and fish. Spectacular vistas of Tuolumne River Canyon abound.

You'll find several hikes off Cherry Lake Rd, including the 4½-mile Preston Flat Trail, an easy, scenic option. Stop on the right just past the bridge and follow the trail along the north side of the Tuolumne River. You'll pass several swimming holes and big rocks that are ideal for lounging about or having a picnic.

Farther downstream you'll find more fishing and swimming holes where the Middle Fork of the Tuolumne crosses Evergreen Rd en route to Hetch Hetchy. But be wary of venturing upstream – rumor has it marijuana farmers have booby-trapped the area, currently under ranger surveillance.

The **Cherry Valley Campground** *(sites $12; open Apr-Oct)* features 46 first-come, first-served sites.

ACTIVITIES

The Stanislaus National Forest offers plenty of hiking, biking, and other land-based activities, but for a real rush, leave the trail behind and run for the river.

Whitewater Rafting

Rafting is a thrill within the Stanislaus, with lots of fast white water and a trove of Class III to IV+ rapids that really pick up once the runoff starts, usually sometime in April. The **Tuolumne River** runs well into October, while the **Merced River** usually wraps up by mid-July; both are well-suited for beginning to intermediate rafters. Several outfitters offer one- to three-day excursions, with prices that vary by season and day of the week. Rafters must be at least 12 years old. You can run the river with any number of outfitters or solo, provided you have a permit (see W www.r5.fs.fed.us/stanislaus/groveland/tcover.htm for details).

Arta River Trips *(☎ 209-962-7873, 800-323-2782;* W *www .arta.org)* runs single- and multi-day Tuolumne trips ($179-469 per person) between March and early September, departing from Groveland, as well as day trips on the Merced that leave from El Portal ($99-129) from mid-April to mid-July. **Ahwahnee Whitewater** *(☎ 209-533-1401, 800-359-9790;* W *www.ahwah nee.com)* offers comparable trips and prices.

For white-knuckle rafting, try rollicking Cherry Creek, on the upper Tuolumne near Buck Meadows, 15 miles west of Hetch Hetchy. Not for the timid or aquaphobes, this 9-mile stretch is a virtually continuous run of Class V and V+ rapids, marked by narrow shoots, huge boulders, sheer drops, precarious ledges, and vertical

For white-knuckle rafting, try rollicking Cherry Creek, marked by narrow shoots, huge boulders, sheer drops, precarious ledges, and vertical holes.

HOOVER WILDERNESS

Hoover is a sliver of backcountry that hugs Yosemite's northeast shoulder. No more than 4 miles wide, it comprises almost 50,000 acres along the eastern Sierra crest. A mini alpine wonderland, Hoover is full of tarns and lakes, jagged 12,000ft peaks and small glaciers, promising excellent hiking, fishing, horseback riding and lake-hopping. Hikers can access the area from trailheads at Saddlebag Lake, Virginia Lakes, Lundy Lake, or Twin Lakes. For more information, visit W www.fs.fed.us/htnf/hoover.htm.

holes. The 15 named rapids have a gradient average of 100ft per mile (as opposed to 40ft per mile elsewhere on the Tuolumne). Rafters must be at least 18 years old with plenty of experience. **OARS** (☎ 800-346-6277; W www.oars.com) runs a one-day trip on Cherry Creek for $225 per person, and **All-Outdoors Whitewater Rafting** (☎ 800-247-2387, 925-932-8993; W www.aorafting.com) takes rafters out on a 1½-day trip for $349 per person.

A bit farther afield, the North Fork of the Stanislaus is another great rafting option, particularly the 5-mile stretch from Dorrington to Calaveras Big Trees State Park. For more information and outfitters, check out W www.stanislaus-river.com.

Hiking & Biking

Off Evergreen Rd, which runs north from Hwy 120 toward Hetch Hetchy, you'll find several good hikes, such as the 1½-mile trail leading to beautiful **Carlon Falls**, a cluster of deep green pools and small falls that cascade down a mossy wall. The trailhead is about a mile north of Hwy 120.

Wildflower fanatics gravitate toward **Hite Cove** each spring, when blooms are at their peak. The 9-mile round trip begins beside Savage's Trading Post, at the confluence of the South and Middle Forks of the Merced River, and follows the South Fork upstream. Park along Hwy 140 opposite the store and lodge, about 8 miles west of Yosemite's Arch Rock Entrance. Technically, the hike lies within the Sierra National Forest (see South of Yosemite), as the river marks the south border of the Stanislaus. Note that the trail is often only open in spring.

In Midpines, about 25 miles west of Yosemite, the Yosemite Bug Lodge & Hostel (see p 180) offers a wealth of information and maps for bike rides in both the Sierra and Stanislaus National Forests, as well as the Merced River Canyon area. You can also rent a mountain bike for $15 per day (guests $13).

East of Yosemite

East of the park lie several pretty lakes, from the hidden anglers' paradise of Lundy Lake to the distinctive volcanic bowl of Mono Lake. You'll find plenty of places to explore along Hwys 120 and 395. Several, like Saddlebag Lake and the 20 Lakes Basin, are only a few miles outside the park entrance. Others are about an hour's drive from the park, but well worth a visit. The wilderness areas offer vigorous day hikes and secluded backcountry camping, and the lakes are great for boating, fishing, swimming, or just a leisurely picnic by the water.

Portions of Hwy 120 are closed from November to as late as May, depending on snowfall. Call ahead to check.

SADDLEBAG LAKE
(MAP 13)
About 2 miles east of the Tioga Pass Entrance is Saddlebag Lake Rd, which leads north for another 2½ miles to Saddlebag Lake, home to a **campground** and small **store**. The dam was built in 1919 to help power Lee Vining before the water was diverted to Los Angeles. The store, which dates from 1947, includes a lunch counter and rents boats *(two hours $25, eight hours $60)* for fishing or just plain cruising. Tours of the lake are $5, as is the boat-launch fee for those who tow their own. One word of warning: The store's posted hours (7am-7pm) aren't to be trusted.

Hiking & Backpacking
From Junction Campground (at the turnoff to Saddlebag Lake from Hwy 120), a mile-long trail leads to the former site of **Bennettville**, a onetime mining town.

About a mile north on Saddlebag Lake Rd you'll find a trailhead for **Gardisky Lake**, an oft-overlooked gem tucked beneath 11,526ft Tioga Peak. The hike is short but steep, with an elevation gain of almost 800ft in about a mile. It's not horrible, but be prepared to sweat. The reward? Lovely timberline scenery and stunning views of Mts Conness (12,590ft) and Dana (13,057ft). Also watch for bighorn sheep

Perhaps the finest trails in this region, though, lie in **20 Lakes Basin**, an easy day hike or overnight trip from Saddlebag Lake. The scenery rivals any in Yosemite and makes the short trek out of the park well worth the trouble. Be forewarned, though, the basin is no secret, so expect fellow hikers, especially during summer weekends. The Saddlebag Lake store sells maps of the area ($1).

The trail to 20 Lakes Basin starts in the day-use parking area beside Saddlebag Lake; after crossing the dam, hikers skirt the west side of the lake. You might consider the **boat taxi** *(roundtrip tickets adult/child $8/5)*, which will ferry you to the far end of the lake, saving you 1½ miles each way. Buy tickets at the store.

From the lake's north end, the trail leads into the south end of Hoover Wilderness, meandering over a couple of alpine passes and passing numerous small, brilliant lakes such as Greenstone, Steelhead, and Shamrock. A hike from the Saddlebag Lake parking area to

BACKCOUNTRY SKI TOURING

Tioga Pass Resort *(☎ 209-372-4471;* W *www.tiogapassresort.com)* sits at 9600ft just 2 miles from Yosemite's east gate, near the junction with Saddlebag Lake Rd. In winter this rustic but refined compound serves as a base camp for forays into the backcountry bowls and chutes of the Ansel Adams Wilderness, Saddlebag Lake basin, and the peaks encircling Mt Dana. The cozy resort attracts a loyal clientele during its open season, from the Saturday before Christmas until late April. Don't expect to drive here, though – the road is closed during winter. Visitors approach from Lee Vining and park their cars along Hwy 120. From there, they ski more than 6 miles to the resort.

If you're looking for a customized backcountry trip, the well-regarded **Sierra Guides Alliance** *(☎ 209-379-2231;* W *www.yosemiteguides.com)* offers exceptional snowshoeing, skiing and snowboarding excursions around Tioga Pass and elsewhere east of Yosemite. Prices vary based on type of trip and number of participants; all trips include expert guides, equipment, meals, and lodging, as well as avalanche awareness and other backcountry training.

Shamrock Lake and back is approximately 6 miles. Explore as much or as little of the area as you like, then return the way you came.

Want to see more? Consider overnight backcountry camping. Free wilderness permits are available from either the small **information kiosk** *(open 6:30am-3pm Thur-Mon)* in Saddlebag Lake Campground or the Mono Lake Visitor Center in Lee Vining.

Inyo National Forest (☎ 760-647-3041) also runs two campgrounds in this area. **Sawmill** *(sites $9)* requires a short walk (approximately a half-mile) from a parking lot along Saddlebag Lake Rd (about midway between the lake and Hwy 120), but the payoff is stunning scenery and relative seclusion. At the end of Saddlebag Lake Rd is **Saddlebag Lake Campground** *(sites $15)*, perched atop a hill overlooking the lake.

Fishing

Local anglers are quite fond of the lakes and creeks along Tioga Road (Hwy 120) east of Yosemite. Each summer the fish and game department stocks Saddlebag, Tioga, and Ellery Lakes with trout. The main waterway running east toward Mono Lake is **Lee Vining Creek**, and several campgrounds lie right along its banks, allowing you to yank in a fat rainbow and slap it straight into the pan, all without leaving your campsite.

MONO LAKE
(MAP 13)

North America's second-oldest lake, this glistening expanse of alkaline water spreads lazily across the chalky white desert. Though the basin and lake are Ice Age remnants,

RESTORE MONO LAKE

In 1941 the City of Los Angeles Department of Water and Power (DWP) bought most of Mono Basin and diverted four of the five streams that feed Mono Lake to the California Aqueduct to provide water to Los Angeles. Over time, the lake dropped 40ft and doubled in salinity. In 1976, environmental activist David Gaines began to study the effects of the diversion and projected that the lake would dry up within about 20 years. Because Mono Lake serves as a major breeding ground for California gulls and provides habitat for eared grebes and red-necked phalaropes, its potential demise posed a major ecological threat. Gaines formed the Mono Lake Committee in 1979 and, through numerous campaigns and court battles, managed to win water back from Los Angeles.

A fluke of nature aided the struggle. In 1989 heavy snows caused dams to overflow into previously dry spillways, rejuvenating streams that had not seen water for 10 years. When fish were found in the streams, the courts ruled that although the DWP technically owned the water rights, the department could not allow the fish to die and, thus, was obliged to maintain the streams at life-sustaining levels. In 1994 the courts required that the lake level return to 6377ft above sea level (estimated to take 15 years) before the DWP can take water from the lake or its tributaries. Bumper stickers and T-shirts bearing the "Save Mono Lake" slogan changed to read "Restore Mono Lake." Mono is indeed rebounding, and faster than expected, having gained back 19ft of its lost water within just eight years. But development of a *full* restoration plan for the basin's stream and wetlands is still underway.

formed more than 700,000 years ago, the area's most interesting features spring from more recent volcanic activity. Rising like weathered sand castles on or near the lakeshore, Mono's tufa (pronounced **too**-fah) towers are composed of calcium carbonate that bubbles up from freshwater springs beneath the surface. Also look for Paoha, a white island, and Negit, a black island, formed when magma pushed sediment above the surface between 300 and 1700 years ago. It's possible to boat to both, though the islands are closed from early April through August to protect nesting gulls.

Mono Lake is very close to Yosemite – just a few miles north of Lee Vining, east of the Tioga Pass entrance. The **Mono Basin Scenic Area Visitor Center** (☎ 760-647-3044; open 9am-4:30pm daily late June–early Sept), about 2 miles north of Lee Vining (see the Gateway Corridors chapter), features a stunning view of the lake, good interpretive displays, a well-stocked bookstore, and bear canister rentals ($3).

Also worth a stop is the **Mono Lake Committee Visitor Center** (☎ 760-647-6595; W www.monolake.org; open 9am-5pm daily late June-mid-Sept) in Lee Vining on the west side of Hwy 395. Here you'll find Internet access, maps, a great selection of books, and a free 30-minute video about the history and geology of the Mono Lake area – as well as people who are passionate about preserving the lake. The center offers interpretive talks, hikes, and photo excursions, plus one-hour canoe tours (adult/child $17/7), which begin at 8am, 9:30am and 11am every Saturday and Sunday from mid-June to early September. Reservations are required.

Tufa spires ring the lake. You'll find the biggest grouping at the **South Tufa Reserve** (adult/child $3/free), on the south rim, where a mile-long interpretive trail winds along the lakeshore. From mid-May to Labor Day, take advantage of daily naturalist-led tours; check the visitor center for times. The best spot for swimming and canoeing is **Navy Beach**, just east of the reserve, though there are no showers and the lake water can leave a thick, salty residue.

Away from the lakeshore, on a dirt road between the South Tufa Reserve and Hwy 120, you'll find **Panum Crater**, the youngest (about 640 years old), smallest, and most accessible of the craters that run south toward Mammoth Mountain. A panoramic trail circles the crater rim (about 40 minutes), and a short but steep "plug trail" puts you at the crater's core.

On the north shore are the **Black Point Fissures**, narrow crags that formed when Black Point's lava mass cooled and contracted about 13,000 years ago. To reach the fissures requires an often hot and dry 5-mile round-trip hike – a substantial but worthwhile trek. Check in at one of the visitor centers before heading out. You can access Black Point from three places: east of Mono Lake County Park, from the west shore off Hwy 395, or south of Hwy 167.

Also on the north shore, free guided bird walks depart from Mono Lake County Park near Danburg Lake at 8am on Friday and Saturday from mid-June to early September.

You'll find plenty of reasonably priced places to eat and stay in Lee Vining (see the Places to Stay and Places to Eat chapters). At the north end of the lake, **Mono Inn at Mono Lake** (p 195) is a popular stop for dinner or drinks. It features a big stone fireplace, handcrafted furniture, and a large terrace with views of the lake, islands, Bodie Hills, and White Mountains. There's also an adjacent **Ansel Adams Gallery** in case you the missed the one in Yosemite.

The historic **Tioga Lodge** (☎ 760-647-6423; cabins $55-105; open Apr-Oct), on Hwy 395 just 2½ miles north of Hwy 120, offers nice cabins and a good restaurant in the main building – a big white house with a large porch. Some of the surrounding cabins were relocated from Bodie around the turn of the century.

LUNDY LAKE
(MAP 13)

About 7 miles north of Lee Vining, Lundy Lake Rd leads 5 miles west to its shimmering namesake. A gorgeous spot, especially when wildflowers are abloom or fall foliage lights up the canyon, it's nonetheless often overlooked and, thus, uncrowded and well worth the short detour. The lake is long and narrow, with steep canyons feeding its west end.

The low-key **Lundy Lake Resort** (☎ 626-309-0415; Lundy Lake Rd; tent/RV sites $11/15, cabins $55-100; open late Apr-Oct) draws fishers and hikers. At the first-come, first-served campsites, you'll find flush toilets and hot showers. The facilities also include a laundry, boat rentals, and a store. Before you reach the lake, the road passes a decent **county campground** (sites $7) with pit toilets and running water.

On a flat dirt road a few miles past Lundy Lake Resort is trailhead parking for the Hoover Wilderness, with self-service wilderness permits. From here it's a lovely hike over Lundy Pass to the 20 Lakes Basin and Saddlebag Lake.

VIRGINIA LAKES
(MAP 13)

A bit farther north on Hwy 395, Virginia Lakes Rd climbs west for 6 miles along Virginia Creek to a series of lakes flanked by Dunderberg Peak (12,374ft) and Black Mountain (11,797ft).

From a trailhead at the end of the lakes, it's an easy hike into Hoover Wilderness and onto the Pacific Crest Trail, which follows Cold Canyon down into Yosemite. On Yosemite's border, Summit Lake (5 miles each way) makes a nice day hike. About 4 miles northwest of the trailhead is another group of lakes, rumored to offer fantastic fishing.

You can sleep and rent fishing tackle at **Virginia Lakes Resort** (☎ 760-647-6484; Virginia Lakes Rd; from $462 per week; open mid-May-mid-Oct). The snug cabins sleep up to six and rent by the week in summer; before June 15 and after Labor Day there's a three-night minimum. The nearby **Virginia Lakes Pack Station** (☎ 760-937-0326) offers backcountry horseback excursions.

TWIN LAKES
(MAP 14)

Just north of Bridgeport, these lakes are shadowed by the jagged Sawtooth Ridge, which includes 12,279ft Matterhorn Peak. Primarily a fishing resort revered for its trout and Kokanee salmon, Twin Lakes is another good access point into Hoover and Yosemite's lake-riddled eastern reaches. Several trails fan out from the west end of Barney Lake.

The road to Twin Lakes intersects Hwy 395 at Bridgeport and crosses rolling pastures and foothills, passing five good campgrounds on Robinson Creek. The route has little traffic, a smooth surface, and few serious hills, making it an excellent, 12-mile scenic biking excursion.

Just before reaching the lower lake, S Twin Rd heads south to the USFS **Lower Twin Lakes Campground** (☎ 760-932-7070, 888-444-7275; sites $13; open May–mid-Oct), with sites on the quiet east shore. Nearby **Crags Campground** (sites $13; open May–mid-Oct) is sunnier and more spread out.

For a step up, try **Doc & Al's Resort** (☎ 760-932-7051; tent/RV sites $13/17, cabins $42-98, trailers $47-60), on Robinson Creek (reached via the road to Twin Lakes). Newer cabins ($67-98) sleep four to 10 people and feature showers and kitchens; rustic cabins ($42) share showers and toilets.

At the far end of the upper lake, the road ends at **Annett's Mono Village** (☎ 760-932-7071, fax 760-932-7468; W www.monovillage.com; tent/RV sites $11/18, rooms $50-60, cabins $65-125; open late Apr-Oct). This sprawling affair offers cheap but fairly cramped lodging, plus boat rental and launch facilities and a greasy spoon restaurant. The campground offers 300 first-come, first-served spaces.

Buckeye Hot Springs
On the way to Twin Lakes, the road also passes these hot springs, which can be a little tricky to find. The springs surface atop a steep embankment above Buckeye Creek and trickle down into rock-ringed pools. The largest pool, right beside the creek, is cold when the creek is high. A smaller one, next to a solitary tree atop the embankment, commands a great view of the surrounding forest. Clothing is optional.

If approaching from the west on Twin Lakes Rd, look for Doc & Al's Resort, then turn north onto a graded dirt road. After about 3 miles, cross Buckeye Creek, then turn right onto Buckeye Hot Springs Rd. Unmarked parking will be on your right.

South of Yosemite

The Sierra National Forest stretches south from Yosemite some 100 miles to King's Canyon National Park. Oakhurst, the region's biggest town, offers plenty of motels, grocery stores, and restaurants; see the Gateway Corridors chapter for more information. Less than 10 miles east of town is Bass Lake, a popular resort area.

SIERRA NATIONAL FOREST
(MAP 12)
The Sierra National Forest blankets the area between the Merced and Kings Rivers and brushes Yosemite from the south. You'll find lots of camping, much of it rather rustic, as well as excellent fishing, hiking, and swimming.

More than 60 developed campgrounds dot the forest; for reservations, call ☎ 877-444-6777 or check the Internet at w www.reserveusa.com. Dispersed camping is also allowed. The Sierra National Forest map is a big help in navigation, and developed campgrounds are clearly marked. If camping isn't your bag, the nearby towns of Fish Camp and Oakhurst provide motel rooms, or you can stay in the resort town of Bass Lake. See the Places to Stay chapter for more information.

North Fork, a small community about 18 miles south of Oakhurst, is the main service and information center for points in the Sierra National Forest. You'll find the **North Fork Super Market**, an ATM, and a post office at the intersection of Rds 225 and 222 (pick up a local map, as it's easy to get turned around). From the intersection, a driveway leads to the USFS **Minarets Ranger Station** (☎ 559-877-2218; open 8am-4:30pm

STUCK IN THE MIDDLE
Probably the oddest "attraction" around North Fork is the geographic center of California – little more than a simple cement monument on a scrappy, dry hillside, marking the state's very center. Hey, at least it's a nice drive. From North Fork, follow Rd 225 east for 3.7 miles, then turn right onto one-lane Italian Bar Rd. After 3 miles, you'll see a small pullout; the monument is on the left.

Mon-Fri), which offers information on campgrounds, hikes, and sights in the forest. The office issues free fire permits, necessary if you want to build a campfire (you may be fined without one). You can also obtain wilderness permits here for overnight trips in the nearby Ansel Adams Wilderness.

About a mile east of town is the **North Fork Chamber of Commerce**, where you can pick up information on local sights, including the Sierra Vista Scenic Byway.

Ansel Adams Wilderness

The former Minarets Wilderness was renamed in 1984 to honor California's most famous photographer, who spent lots of time in this part of the Sierra. The wilderness hugs Yosemite's southeast border. Access is from the west, as well as from the east via Mammoth Lakes and the June Lake Loop (see the Excursions chapter). Visitors enjoy backpacking amid the region's rugged scenery.

For those entering from the west, the Minarets Ranger Station in North Fork issues permits for overnight excursions. Permits are free if obtained in person; you can also call ☎ 559-877-2218 to make a reservation in advance ($5).

Sierra Vista National Scenic Byway

Not every beautiful California mountain highway runs through Yosemite or even makes it across the Sierra Nevada. Set entirely within Sierra National Forest, this scenic byway follows USFS roads in a loop that takes you from 3000ft near Oakhurst and North Fork up to nearly 7000ft. Along the way are dramatic vistas, excellent fishing, and camping almost anywhere you like (dispersed camping is allowed in most areas). It's a great way for car campers – and curious day trippers – to lose themselves within the mountains.

Along the way are dramatic vistas, excellent fishing, and camping almost anywhere you like

Begin your drive in North Fork, where you can pick up a map from the chamber of commerce (☎ *559-877-2410).* The route takes a half-day to complete, emerging on Hwy 41 a few miles north of Oakhurst. Open from June to November, the road is paved most of the way, but narrow and laced with curves.

The byway accesses trails into the Ansel Adams Wilderness, most notably Clover Meadow, where a small ranger station opens each summer. It also passes Mile-High Vista, with views as sweeping as the name promises; Mammoth Pool Reservoir, a popular fishing, camping, and swimming spot; Fresno Dome, well worth a hike to the top; and the Nelder Grove of giant sequoias.

Numerous campgrounds line the byway, including **Fish Creek** *(sites $13; open May-Sept)*, a small, woodsy, creekside campground that's the first you encounter after driving the 19 miles from North Fork. You'll find other popular campgrounds near Mammoth Pool Reservoir and Clover Meadow.

Nelder Grove

It's for good reason that crowds pack Yosemite's Mariposa Grove most days of the year. But if all you want is to walk in solitude among majestic giant sequoias – with nary a chattering tourist in sight – head to this small but lovely grove in the Sierra National Forest instead. The trees aren't as plentiful as in Mariposa, but the scenery is moody and mystifying and the atmosphere impressively quiet (you just might be the only visitor, even in summer).

To reach the grove from Yosemite's South Entrance, follow Hwy 41 south 10 miles to Rd 632 (Sky Ranch Rd). Turn left, then follow the winding road (part of the Sierra Vista National Scenic Byway) about 7 miles to a turnoff for the grove. Signs mark the way. After another mile, head left toward the Shadow of the Giants Trail, with pit toilets at the trailhead. The easy one-mile stroll beneath the trees takes just 30 minutes.

The scenery is moody and mystifying and the atmosphere impressively quiet.

BASS LAKE
(MAP 12)

In commercialized contrast to the serenity of Nelder Grove, this hugely popular resort area is just a short drive from Oakhurst and Hwy 41. Surrounded by thick forest, Bass Lake makes a beautiful stop, but don't expect to have it to yourself. Boaters, anglers, swimmers, and car campers pack the place all summer long

Most development lies on the northeast shore, where you'll find **The Pines Village**, which includes galleries, gift shops, a grocery store, a post office and **The Pines Resort & Conference Center** (☎ *559-642-3121, 800-350-7463;* W *www.bass lake.com)*, a massive modern hotel and restaurant complex.

If you've got plenty of time on your hands, or you're traveling to and from Yosemite by car, you'll find lots of nearby parks, towns and attractions worth exploring. Some areas are perfect for a scenic drive; others boast great hiking, biking, or skiing. The Sierras are also chock-full of cute Gold Country towns and scenery as magnificent as that found anywhere in the state. From sparkling Lake Tahoe to the ancient, giant trees of Sequoia National Park, Yosemite is surrounded by landscapes of astonishing variety and startling beauty.

YOSEMITE EXCURSIONS

Sonora

About two hours from Yosemite's West Entrance on Hwy 108 lies historic Sonora. Settled in 1848 by miners from Sonora, Mexico, this town once thrived as a cosmopolitan center with Spanish plazas, elaborate saloons, and the Southern Mines' largest concentration of gamblers, drunkards, and gold. The Big Bonanza Mine, at the north end of Washington St where Sonora High School now stands, yielded 12 tons of gold in two years (including a 28lb nugget). Still bustling as the Tuolumne County seat, Sonora boasts a well-preserved downtown, some good cultural offerings, and several noteworthy sites. Although it's not the quaintest of Gold Country towns, it's a good base for whitewater rafting. Novice rafters head to the nearby Stanislaus River, while the Tuolumne River, with its Class IV rapids, is better for intermediates. **Sierra Mac River Trips** (☎ 209-532-1327, 800-457-2580) has a good reputation and offers a wide variety of trip lengths and destinations. Day trips cost $180, and two-day trips are $375. The trips leave from Groveland (a 45-minute drive toward Yosemite), but with advance notice the guides can usually arrange transportation from Sonora.

The **Tuolumne County Visitors Center** (☎ 209-533-4420; Ⓦ *www.thegreat unfenced.com; 542 Stockton St; open 9am-7pm Mon-Thur, 9am-8pm Fri, 10am-6pm Sat, 10am-5pm Sun in summer; 10am-6pm Mon-Sat in winter*) provides lots of information on recreation, road conditions, and lodging.

Sonora Days Inn (☎ 209-532-2400; *160 S Washington St; motel rooms from $73, hotel rooms $80-105*) occupies one of Sonora's oldest and most central hotel structures, though there's a modern motel addition behind the original hotel. Guests enjoy the rooftop pool.

In the charming **Gunn House Hotel** (☎ 209-532-3421; *286 S Washington St; rooms $55-85*), charcoal-gray with white trim, rooms are a tad weathered but still nice, with

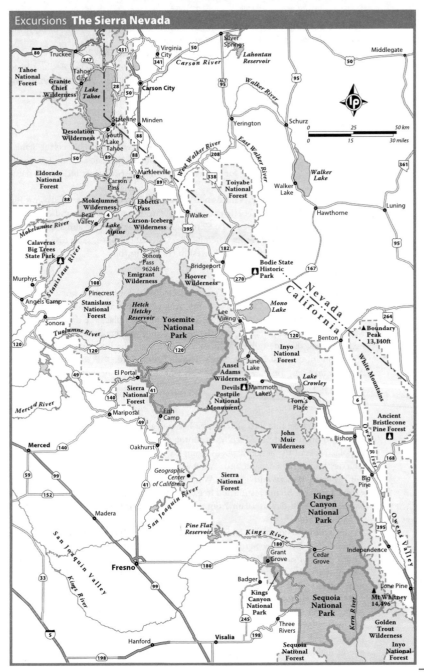

wrought-iron beds and quilts, and the new owners are redoing the bathrooms. There's also a small pool out back and a cozy bar upstairs.

For local color and comfort food, check out **Wilma's** (☎ *209-532-3116; 275 S Washington St; barbecue dinners $7-11; open 6am-9pm)*. The pies and huge breakfasts are famous in these parts. The adjacent nightclub **Wilma's Flying Pig Saloon** *(☎ 209-532-3116)* features live music on weekend nights.

Highway 4

Stretching along an illustrious gold-rush mining route, scenic Hwy 4 bisects the Stanislaus National Forest, skirts three wilderness areas, and jogs through a handful of quaint Gold Country towns, making for a drive that's both historically significant and naturally beautiful.

From Angels Camp, Hwy 4 heads northeast to Murphys, then passes Calaveras Big Trees State Park, crosses Ebbetts Pass and descends to meet Hwy 89 and eventually Hwy 395, on the eastern side of the Sierra. It's a breathtaking drive and a worthwhile and convenient excursion. From Yosemite's Big Oak Flat Entrance, it's an easy two-hour drive to Angels Camp. Take Hwy 120 west to Hwy 49 north.

ANGELS CAMP

Famous as the place where Mark Twain collected notes for his short story "The Celebrated Jumping Frog of Calaveras County," Angels Camp makes the most of this historic tie. The International Frog Jump Competition takes place the third weekend in May; Mark Twain Days happen over the Fourth of July weekend; and bronze frogs, embedded along the sidewalk of Main St, commemorate the International Frog Jump champions of the past 50 years. **Sue's Angels Creek Café** *(☎ 209-736-2941; 1246 S Main St; breakfast and lunch around $6)* is where locals go for pancakes, eggs, hamburgers, and hot sandwiches.

MURPHYS

With a main street that looks like a cross between a Norman Rockwell painting and a Randolph Scott Western, Murphys is thoroughly charming and, consequently, very popular. Most of the action happens along leafy Main St, dotted with antique stores, galleries, boutiques, a day spa, and several wine-tasting rooms, including Zucca Mountain, Milliaire Winery, and Stevenot Winery (all free and most open 11am-5pm daily except Tuesday). An interesting and free one-hour walking tour of historical Murphys leaves every Saturday at 10am from outside the **Murphy's Old Timers Museum** *(☎ 209-728-1160)*.

One mile from downtown on Sheep Ranch Rd are the **Mercer Caverns** *(☎ 209-728-2101; adult/child $10/6; open 10am-4:30pm Sun-Thur, 10am-6pm Fri-Sat Oct-May; extended hours in summer)*. A 45-minute guided tour takes you 161 vertical feet down well-lit stairs, closely passing enormous stalactites, stalagmites, and vaulted chambers with names such as Chinese Meat Market and Organ Loft.

Murphys Historic Hotel & Lodge *(☎ 209-728-3444, 800-532-7684; 457 Main St; rooms $75/85 weekdays/weekends)*, commanding a center-of-town locale, exemplifies old-time Murphys. It's also the best value around, particularly the nine historical rooms. Check out the hotel register, which lists the names and signatures of illustrious guests, including Mark Twain. The restaurant serves salads, burgers, steaks, and fish

($12-18), and the spacious street-front bar features live music on weekends, plus plenty of local color and a nice selection of Calaveras County wines by the glass.

For upscale picnic fixings, fancy sandwiches ($7), or a glass of wine and light meal, head to **Alchemy Market & Wine Bar** (☎ 209-728-0700; 191 Main St; open 7am-7pm Sun-Tue, 7am-10pm Thur-Sat).

Grounds (☎ 209-728-8663; 402 Main St; breakfast and lunch daily $6-10, dinner Wed-Sun only around $14) is an excellent, stylish place for a sophisticated meal featuring fresh ingredients and California cuisine; it also makes a good place to hang out with coffee and a book. The pastas are particularly good.

CALAVERAS BIG TREES STATE PARK

This park, at about 5000ft, is a great place to hike, camp, and tree-gaze among giant sequoias. Though small and undeveloped, it is easily accessible (4 miles northeast of Arnold on Hwy 4) and not too crowded.

The park encompasses two giant sequoia groves, 6000 acres of pine forest, and the Stanislaus River and Beaver Creek, which offer good trout fishing and great swimming. During the winter, the North Grove stays open for snow camping and cross-country skiing.

At the park entrance, you'll find the visitor center (open 11am-4pm weekends in winter, daily in summer), the **ranger station** (☎ 209-795-2334), the main parking lots, and the **North Grove Campground**. Less crowded is the **Oak Hollow Campground**,

WINE TASTING IN CALAVERAS COUNTY

Wine making has long been associated with Gold Country, which during the 1870s boasted more than 100 wineries in Calaveras County alone. But as the gold-rush boom years ended, so did the call for wine, and the makers who did hang on were later hit hard by Prohibition. After that, grape growing and wine producing virtually disappeared, except for a few families who continued to bottle their own. But the 1960s ushered in a newfound passion for California wines. Blessed with dry mountain air, warm temps, and lots of golden sun, the Sierra foothills drew a fresh generation of wine makers desiring to restore old vineyards, plant new varietals, and produce quality handcrafted wines.

These days, Calaveras County houses a trove of small-production vineyards, with old-time Murphys the unofficial hub of the more than 600 acres devoted to grape growing. Specialty varietals seem to thrive in the rolling hills and nutrient-rich soils. And a perfect collection of microclimates and varied elevations also help produce niche-style grapes that ordinarily hail from sun-splashed regions of Europe, like Nebbiola, Barbera, Sangiovese, Tempranillo, Cabernet Frank, and a handful of Portuguese varietals used for making port in Sonora.

Wine touring through the foothills can be an enjoyable and intimate experience, with crowd-free tasting rooms, complimentary tasting flights, and some exceptional wines. And if you really want to check out the goods up close, head to the Calaveras Grape Stomp, held the first weekend of October in Murphys. Check out W www.calaveraswines.org for information.

9 miles farther on the park's main road. Tent sites ($12) at both can be reserved through Reserve America (☎ 800-444-7275).

The North Grove Big Trees Trail, a 1-mile self-guided loop, begins next to the visitor center and winds along the forest floor past the Big Stump and a tree named Mother of the Forest. A 4-mile trail that branches off from the self-guided loop climbs out of the North Grove, crosses a ridge, and descends 1500ft to the Stanislaus River.

Not accessible by car and devoid of any picnic areas or campgrounds, the **South Grove** is a designated nature preserve in the park's most remote and pristine reaches. Far fewer people visit this part of the park, though it's only a mile walk from the Beaver Creek Bridge to the grove. From the Beaver Creek picnic area (a half-mile from the visitor center), follow the South Grove Trail; hardy types can go the full 9 miles on the trail, though you don't have to hike the whole thing to have a memorable experience.

For more information about the park, see Ⓦ www.sierra.parks.state.ca.us/cbt/cbt.htm. Admission is $2 per car, and the park is open year-round, sunrise to sunset.

BEAR VALLEY

Hwy 4 becomes more densely forested as it winds up to tiny Bear Valley (elevation 7073ft), a snug and beautifully situated enclave with a population of 150. It's also home to a popular winter resort, the **Bear Valley Ski Area** (☎ 209-753-2301; lift tickets $38), which boasts 2000ft of vertical rise, 11 lifts, and a **cross-country ski center** (☎ 209-753-2834; trail fees and rentals $32). The resort's somewhat off-the-beaten-track location gives it a friendly, local feel; definitely a place to have fun in the snow rather than to see and be seen. In summer Bear Valley hosts a music festival (☎ 209-753-2574), draws mountain bikers to its network of fine single-track trails, and attracts hikers as an excellent jumping-off point for treks into the Stanislaus, Carson-Iceberg and Mokelumne Wildernesses, with many trailheads dotting Hwy 4. **Bear Valley Adventure Company** (☎ 209-753-2834), on the left as you arrive in town from the west, is the one-stop shop for outdoor activity information.

The gorgeous Lake Alpine, 3 miles west of town, offers good swimming, fishing, boating, and several trailheads. You'll find good **rock climbing** in Box Canyon, with 70ft to 100ft crack and face climbs, all less than a mile east of Bear Valley. Or seek out excellent **bouldering** at Hells Kitchen and Tamarack Boulders. For a short but rewarding **hiking** experience, try Inspiration Point (1.4 miles), accessible from Lake Alpine. The uphill scramble rewards you with spectacular

The resort's somewhat off-the-beaten-track location gives it a friendly, local feel.

views of Spicer Reservoir and the Dardanelles. For maps and directions to these sites, stop in at the **ranger station** (☎ 209-795-1381), just before town.

Several campgrounds (sites $15) dot the area, including the first-come, first-served **Silvertip**, with 23 Aspen-fringed spaces and flush toilets, and **Lake Alpine**, with 25 shady sites and easy access to the lake. Look for signs to both on Hwy 4.

Tamarack Pines Inn & Lodge (☎ 209-753-2080; *rooms from $45, cabins from $95*), 2 miles west of town on Hwy 4, is a quiet, pretty spot with a variety of rooms, a few cabins, and cross-country ski trails from the backyard.

Accommodations at **BaseCamp Lodge, Pub & Restaurant** (☎ 209-753-2344; *148 Bear Valley Rd*), right off Hwy 4, range from bunks to private rooms ($15-55), most with shared baths. The restaurant serves delicious and hearty fare (entrées $10-15), and after dinner locals toss darts, play pool, and discuss the day's adventures.

The lovely **Lake Alpine Lodge** (☎ 209-753-6358; *open May 1-Oct 15; cabins $35-110*) looks over its namesake lake with a handful of fully equipped and cozy one- and two-bedroom cabins, as well as tent cabins. The **restaurant** (*entrées $15-24; lunch and dinner daily, breakfast on weekends*) serves pasta, meats, and seafood and features a long deck with views of the lake, a great spot for a post-hike pint. Rowboat, kayak, and canoe rentals start at $15 for two hours; and motorboats $30. Mountain bikes cost $15 per day. The lodge is right on Hwy 4, which winds past the lake a couple miles east of Bear Valley.

Headwaters Coffee House (☎ 209-753-2708; *3 Bear Valley Rd; open 7am-2:30pm daily, closed in Oct*) serves home-baked items and good coffee, with gourmet pizzas, salads, and a nice selection of beer and wine at lunch. High-speed Internet access costs $1 for five minutes. You'll also find a friendly and laid-back scene next-door at the **Bear Valley Pizza Company** (☎ 209-753-2872; *open 5pm-9pm Thur-Mon*), with creekside outdoor tables and a welcoming bar. Monday nights are all-you-can-eat. In winter you can get delivery service via snowmobile.

EBBETTS PASS

From Lake Alpine, Hwy 4 continues east past picturesque Mosquito Lake before slaloming through Hermit Valley, entering the Toiyabe National Forest, and winding up and over the summit of Ebbetts Pass (8730ft), once viewed as a potential route for the transcontinental railway. This is another easy access point to the Pacific Crest Trail. Although Ebbetts is closed after the first major snowfall, the road is usually plowed from the west up to Bear Valley.

MARKLEEVILLE

A worthy 8-mile detour north on Route 89 at the end of Hwy 4 leads to historic Markleeville. Blink and you'll miss this tiny town, host of the annual **Death Ride** (☎ 530-694-1766), a Tour of the California Alps for cyclists hell-bent on climbing 16,000ft over five passes and 129 miles; it happens each July.

The 700-acre **Grover Hot Springs State Park** (☎ 530-694-2248; *tub admission $2*), 4 miles west of the town's center on County Rd 016 (Grover Hot Springs Rd), includes a kiwi-green hot pool and baby-blue cool pool, both adorned with views of sweeping meadows and peaks. Nearby are hiking trails, a fishing creek, and 76 campsites (☎ 800-444-7275; *open May–early Oct*). For a list of primo fishing holes, pick up a map from the **Markleeville General Store** (☎ 530-694-2448) or **Carson River Resort** (☎ 530-694-2229; *cabins $50-100*), just south of town.

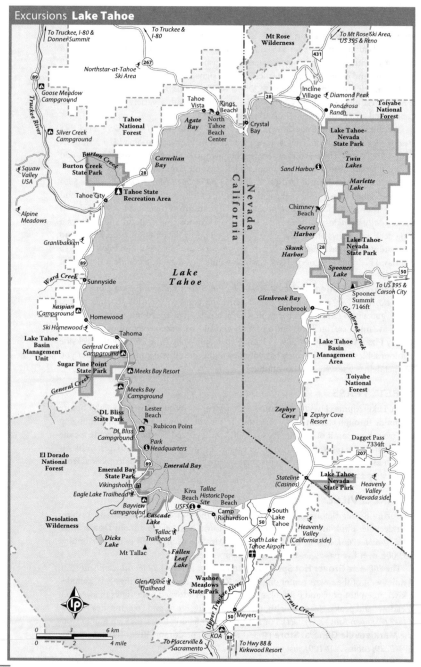

To Truckee, I-80 &
Donner Summit

To Truckee &
I-80

Mt Rose
Wilderness

To Mt Rose Ski Area,
US 395 & Reno

431

267

Northstar-at-Tahoe
Ski Area

89

Goose Meadow
Campground

Incline
Village

Diamond Peak

Ponderosa
Ranch

Toiyabe
National
Forest

Tahoe
Vista

Kings
Beach

28

Silver Creek
Campground

Tahoe
National
Forest

Agate
Bay

North
Tahoe
Beach
Center

Crystal
Bay

Lake Tahoe-
Nevada
State Park

Burton Creek

Carnelian
Bay

Sand Harbor

Twin
Lakes

Squaw
Valley
USA

Burton Creek
State Park

Marlette
Lake

28

Tahoe City

Tahoe State
Recreation Area

Chimney
Beach

Alpine
Meadows

Secret
Harbor

Lake Tahoe-
Nevada
State Park

Granlibakken

89

Skunk
Harbor

28

Ward Creek

Sunnyside

Lake
Tahoe

Spooner
Lake

50

Spooner
Summit
7146ft

To US 395 &
Carson City

Kaspian
Campground

Homewood

Glenbrook Bay

Glenbrook

Ski Homewood

Tahoma

Lake Tahoe
Basin
Management
Unit

General Creek
Campground

Lake Tahoe
Basin
Management
Area

Sugar Pine Point
State Park

Meeks Bay Resort

Glenbrook Creek

California

Nevada

Toiyabe
National
Forest

General Creek

Meeks Bay
Campground

DL Bliss
State Park

Lester
Beach

Zephyr
Cove

Zephyr Cove
Resort

Rubicon Point

DL Bliss
Campground

Park
Headquarters

Dagget Pass
7334ft

El Dorado
National
Forest

207

Emerald Bay
State Park

89

Emerald Bay

Stateline
(Casinos)

Lake Tahoe-
Nevada
State Park

Vikingsholm

Kiva
Beach

Tallac
Historic
Site

Heavenly
Valley
(Nevada side)

Eagle Lake Trailhead

Pope
Beach

Bayview
Campground

USFS

Camp
Richardson

South
Lake
Tahoe

Desolation
Wilderness

Cascade
Lake

Heavenly
Valley
(California side)

Dicks
Lake

Tallac
Trailhead

South Lake
Tahoe Airport

Mt Tallac

Fallen
Leaf
Lake

Glen Alpine
Trailhead

Washoe
Meadows
State Park

Upper Truckee River

Trout Creek

89

50

Meyers

0   3   6 km
0   2   4 mile

89

KOA

To Placerville &
Sacramento

To Hwy 88 &
Kirkwood Resort

The friendly owners of **Bed, Bike and Bagel** (☎ 530-694-2781), located on Hot Springs Rd, rent out a terrific two-bedroom creekside cottage with funky decor, decks galore, a sauna, and a wood-burning stove. Prices start at $130 for two people, including wood, bicycles, and a morning bagel and cappuccino next door at their pretty and bedecked **M's Coffee House**. And just 2 miles down the road is **Villa Gigli** (☎ 530-694-2248; 145 Hot Springs Rd; dinner $15; open Fri-Sat Feb-Nov), perhaps the best reason of all for a detour to Markleeville. A kind and artistic Italian couple operates this trattoria, cantina, and gallery out of their warm home, serving delicious handmade pastas and antipasti.

Lake Tahoe

The California-Nevada state border cuts lengthwise through brilliantly blue Lake Tahoe, a striking natural wonder nestled among the Sierra's rugged peaks. Parks abound everywhere, though along the highway much of the land is developed, with towering casinos flashing from the Nevada side, especially along the grotesquely *über*-developed south shore. Besides the big, modern casinos (in Stateline, Nevada), you'll find (in adjacent South Lake Tahoe) countless shopping malls and cheap (but not always inexpensive) motels. Heavenly Valley is nearby, but most of the area's ski resorts lie closer to the lake's north shore.

Simply driving all the way around Lake Tahoe isn't the best strategy for exploring – it's better to pick a spot and settle in for hiking, picnicking, or simply taking in the view.

NORTH & EAST SHORES

Tahoe City is the north shore's largest town. For lodging, dining, hiking, and skiing information, visit the **North Lake Tahoe Chamber of Commerce** (☎ 530-581-6900; 245 N Lake Blvd; open 9am-5pm Mon-Fri), near the junction of Hwys 89 and 28. A popular activity right in town, especially with kids, involves crowding onto Fanny Bridge and watching the fish swim by underneath.

As you head northeast on Hwy 28, you'll pass Tahoe Vista and Kings Beach, with attractive motels and some well-preserved 1950s charm.

Crystal Bay is an aging casino town, while affluent **Incline Village** is home to the tacky theme park **Ponderosa Ranch** (☎ 775-831-0691; W www.ponderosaranch.com; adult/child $9.50/5.50; open Apr-Oct), where the TV Western *Bonanza* was filmed.

On Tahoe's northeastern shore, **Lake Tahoe-Nevada State Park** (☎ 775-831-0494) features cross-country skiing at Spooner Lake in winter, mountain bike trails in summer, and a nice (albeit often crowded) beach at Sand Harbor (parking $6).

On I-80 northwest of Tahoe, the former mining and railroad town **Truckee** contains restaurants, shops, and hotels; in winter it caters heavily to skiers. Nearby **Donner Lake** is surrounded by small, woodsy resorts. At the east end of Donner Lake, the **Emigrant Trail Museum** (☎ 530-582-7892; admission $1) chronicles the Donner Party's fateful 1846 journey, when a combination of winter storms and poor planning wiped out half of the 87 travelers; in one of the West's best-known tales, survivors had to eat human flesh to avoid starvation. The museum is inside **Donner Memorial State Park** (cars $2).

WEST & SOUTH SHORES

If you only have one day here, **DL Bliss State Park** (☎ 530-525-7232; day-use $5) is a good place to spend it. Expect clear turquoise water, white sand, and access to unspoiled hiking trails. The park is on the west shore of Lake Tahoe, along Hwy 89, about 17 miles south of Tahoe City

Narrow **Emerald Bay** is one of Tahoe's major attractions, containing the lake's only island and waters that truly justify its name. Here, too, is **Vikingsholm Castle** (☎ 530-525-7277), off Hwy 89 at the lake's edge and reached by a steep 1-mile descent. Tours ($1) of this dowdy Scandinavian mansion, built in 1928, take place daily from June to September.

At the **Tallac Historic Site**, about 3 miles north of the intersection of Hwys 89 and 50, sit three century-old luxury estates, with grounds that make for pleasant wandering and an interesting **museum** (☎ 530-541-5227; open 11am-4pm daily June-Sept) displaying historic photos of the area.

Few people, even locals, have good things to say about **South Lake Tahoe** and its faceless motels and shopping malls. It does, however, offer the area's most affordable accommodations, along with the helpful **South Lake Tahoe Chamber of Commerce** (☎ 530-541-5255; 3066 Lake Tahoe Blvd; open 9am-5pm Mon-Sat). Immediately across the Nevada border is **Stateline**, where you can gamble away your future at Harvey's, Harrah's, or Caesar's Tahoe.

ACTIVITIES

A popular day hike is the 5-mile climb up 9735ft Mt Tallac in the Desolation Wilderness, directly southwest of the lake. Pick up maps and permits at the **USFS Lake Tahoe Visitor Center** (☎ 530-573-2674; open 8am-4:30pm daily mid-June–late Sept, weekends only in May and Oct), near the Tallac Historic Site.

The lake is surrounded by ski resorts, including the following:

Alpine Meadows (☎ 530-581-8375; W www.skialpine.com; $54) – off Hwy 89 near Tahoe City

Heavenly Valley (☎ 775-586-7000; W www.skiheavenly.com; $57) – off Hwy 50 near Stateline

Kirkwood (☎ 209-258-6000; W www.kirkwood.com; $52) – off Hwy 88

Squaw Valley USA (☎ 530-583-6985; W www.squaw.com; $56) – off Hwy 89 near Tahoe City

You'll find marked cross-country and snowshoe trails at **Camp Richardson** (☎ 530-542-6584; adult $15), on Hwy 89 a couple miles north of South Lake Tahoe, and at **Tahoe Cross Country Ski Area** (☎ 530-583-5475; adult $17.50) in Tahoe City.

PLACES TO STAY & EAT

Sugar Pine Point State Park (☎ 530-525-7232; sites $12; open year-round), on the west shore, has campsites among the trees. The park is 10 miles south of Tahoe City along Hwy 89.

In South Lake Tahoe, **Doug's Mellow Mountain Retreat** (☎ 530-544-8065; 3787 Forest Ave; beds $15) is an independent hostel in a nondescript suburban house.

Motel prices around Lake Tahoe can vary widely depending on the season, demand, and day of the week. Summer weekends cost the most, with rates at even modest motels sometimes climbing over $100. Some motels and casinos offer package deals combining rooms and lift tickets; check casino or ski resort websites and visitor center pamphlets.

Dozens of budget motels line Hwy 50, from Stateline west to the junction with Hwy 89, an area still commercial but removed from the casino madness. A typical spot is the **Tahoe Sundowner** (☎ 530-541-2282; 1211 Emerald Bay Rd; rooms from $35), just south of the Hwy 50/89 split.

Near Tahoe City is **River Ranch Lodge** (☎ 530-583-4264, 800-535-9900; Ⓦ *www.riverranchlodge.com; Hwy 89 at Alpine Meadows Rd; rooms $85-160)*, where rooms sport classy lodgepole pine furniture, TV, data ports, and river views.

For a worthwhile splurge, try dinner at **Wolfdale's** (☎ 530-583-5700; 640 N Lake Blvd; entrées from $20), facing the lake in Tahoe City.

GETTING THERE & AROUND

Lake Tahoe sits between Hwy 50 and I-80. Two main routes head to the lake from Yosemite; neither is terribly direct (three to four hours' drive), but both are definitely scenic.

From the west side of the park, head west on Hwy 120 to Hwy 49; turn north and follow that road through California's Gold Country to Hwy 50 in Placerville. Turn east on Hwy 50 and follow it to South Lake Tahoe. From Tioga Pass, head east down the canyon and turn north on Hwy 395. Just before Carson City, Nevada, turn left (west) on Hwy 50 and climb up to South Lake Tahoe.

A third option is to follow Scenic Hwy 4 to Markleeville, then continue on Hwy 89 to South Lake Tahoe.

In winter, Hwy 89 (Emerald Bay Rd), which meanders along the lake's west shore, is usually closed, and tire chains are often required on I-80 and Hwy 50. For road conditions, call ☎ 800-427-7623.

South Lake Tahoe Ground Express (STAGE; ☎ 530-542-6077; ride $1.25) buses make frequent stops along Hwy 50 between Zephyr Cove and the intersection with Hwy 89.

Tahoe Area Rapid Transit (TART; ☎ 530-550-1212, 800-736-6365; ride $1.25) buses connect Tahoe City, Truckee, Tahoe Vista, and Incline Village.

The main casinos operate free shuttles that run until 2am and will stop at any south shore motel. During ski season, selected resorts also provide free shuttle service daily from numerous hotels and designated roadside stops.

Bodie State Historic Park

The combination of its remote location and unrestored buildings makes Bodie *(adult/child $2/free; open 9am-7pm daily late May–Sept, to 4pm rest of year)* one of California's most authentic and well-preserved ghost towns. Gold was discovered along Bodie Creek in 1859, and within 20 years the place grew from a rough mining camp to an even rougher mining town, with a population of 10,000 and a reputation for lawlessness sustained by gambling halls, cigar stores, brothels, and no fewer than 65 saloons. Robberies, street fights, and stagecoach holdups occurred almost daily, and the "bad men from Bodie" were known far and wide.

All tallied, more than $100 million worth of ore came from the 30 mines in the surrounding hills, but when the supply petered out, people moved on (mostly to the Comstock Lode in Nevada) and left Bodie's buildings to the elements and a devastating fire in 1932. About 5% of them still remain, maintained and lived in by the State Park Service but untainted by restoration. You can still see traces of elegant wallpaper in some of the homes. An excellent **museum and visitor center** (☎ 760-647-6445; open 10am-5pm daily late May-Sept) offers historical maps, exhibits, and free daily guided tours.

Easily accessible from Yosemite's Tioga Pass Entrance Station, Bodie is about a 45-minute drive from the junction of Hwys 120 and 395. Take the latter road north, then turn east onto Hwy 270 and follow it for 13 miles. Note that Hwy 270 is unpaved for the last 3 miles and often closed in winter.

June Lake Loop

Just 15 miles from Yosemite's Tioga Pass Entrance Station, Hwy 158 makes a 16-mile loop west off of Hwy 395. This scenic route passes Grant, Silver, Gull, and June Lakes, flanked by massive Carson Peak to the west and Reversed Peak to the east. The mountains to the near west are part of the Ansel Adams Wilderness, which runs smack into Yosemite, easily reached by trail (see the Beyond Yosemite chapter).

All four lakes have excellent trout fishing, and Grant and Silver Lakes both offer free public boat launches. You'll find a colorful commercial hub in June Lake Village and a sandy beach at the south end of the lake. The route also makes for a very enjoyable bike ride. You can park your car near the information kiosk at the loop's southern entrance and do an out-and-back if you don't want to brave Hwy 395 on the return.

Much smaller and less crowded than nearby Mammoth, **June Mountain Ski Area** (☎ 760-648-7733, 888-586-3686; lift tickets adult/teen/senior and child $45/35/25) is a friendly kind of place. And, at 10,135ft, it's no mole hill. There's nary a line at the eight lifts, including two high-speed quads, which serve 500 acres of trails along 2600 vertical feet. The area also includes two terrain parks and a superpipe.

At Silver Lake, the **Frontier Pack Train** (☎ 760-648-7701 in summer, ☎ 760-873-7971 in winter) offers guided horseback rides ($25/55/85 for one hour/half-day/full day) and multiday trips into the Sierra backcountry (from $500), including a five-day trip over Donohue Pass into Yosemite and Tuolumne Meadows.

In summer, **fishing** is hugely popular, and numerous boat and tackle rental places operate along the loop. Most also sell fishing licenses. Get some friendly advice at **Ernie's Tackle & Ski Shop** (☎ 760-648-7756) in downtown June Lake. **Gull Lake Marina** (☎ 760-648-7539) rents paddleboats and canoes for $10-15 per hour.

Between the resort and pack station, the Rush Creek Trailhead is a departure point for wilderness trips; here you'll find a day-use parking lot, posted maps, and self-registration permits. Gem and Agnew Lakes make spectacular day hikes, while Thousand Island and Emerald Lake (both on the Pacific Crest/John Muir Trail) are good overnight destinations in the Ansel Adams Wilderness (see p 206). For more information on day hikes, visit the Mono Lake or Mammoth Lakes ranger stations.

PLACES TO STAY & EAT

There are six USFS campgrounds with $13 sites along the full loop, including **June Lake Campground**, small and shady but crowded, and **Oh Ridge Campground**, on an arid ridge above the lake's south end, with nice views and beach access but not much shade. Both have running water and are open from mid-April to late September; call ☎ 800-444-7275 for reservations.

For a little more comfort, try the private **Pine Cliff Resort Campground** (☎ 760-648-7558; tent sites $11, sites with hookups $16-20), next to Oh Ridge. It includes a store and public hot showers ($1) and offers trailer rental by the week ($160-400).

The Haven (☎ 619-648-7524; cottages $55-95), a block off June Lake's main drag on Knoll Ave, is a homey and comfortable abode, with a long wooden deck, whirlpool, tasteful furnishings, and two-story cottages and studios, some with fireplaces or woodstoves.

Double Eagle Resort & Spa (☎ 760-648-7004, 877-648-7004, fax 760-648-7016; cabins $216-298) is a swanky spot for these parts. Sleek cedar cabins come complete with VCRs and outside decks. The posh spa boasts a full menu of indulgences, including 11 types of massage, and a fancy fitness center. Spa-weary folk can rent bikes ($9/35 per hour/day), sign up for a guided fishing outing ($30 and up), or hook a trout right on the grounds. The woodsy and elegant **restaurant** (☎ 760-648-7897; breakfast and lunch $6-11, dinner $6.50-20) features a high ceiling, cozy booths, a huge fireplace, and a warm saloon with timber barstools and a flagstone floor.

Local art adorns the walls at **Trout Town Joe** (☎ 760-648-7170), which serves delicious salads and homemade wraps ($4-7). **The Tiger** (☎ 760-648-7551; 2620 Hwy 158; dishes $4-15), a town hallmark since 1932, is *the* place to visit in the evening for burgers, burritos, fish, and beer, though you can also get good breakfasts and lunches.

Mammoth Lakes

Mammoth Lakes is the eastern Sierra's commercial hub and a four-season resort, backed by a ridgeline of jutting peaks, ringed by clusters of crystalline alpine lakes, and enshrouded by the dense Inyo National Forest. Ski bums flock to 11,053ft Mammoth Mountain from December to early May, while the rest of the year hikers, mountain bikers, backpackers, anglers, and all types of outdoor enthusiasts are drawn to the stunning, and surprisingly crowd-free, wilderness areas. About an hour's drive south on Hwy 395 from its junction with Hwy 120, Mammoth makes an easy trip from Yosemite's east entrance.

Mammoth's humble origin as a ski resort began in the 1930s, when just a few adventurous souls made use of a few simple rope tows; the first chairlift went up in 1955. Long before that, Mammoth was a mining and lumber town with stamp mills, sawmills, flumes, waterwheels, and a rough-and-tumble main street of tent cabins and saloons. Most of the original town, on the west end of Old Mammoth Rd, burned to cinders, but a 14ft flywheel and some other old structures remain.

Mammoth, as most people refer to it, is laid-back, friendly, and decidedly unpretentious. People come more to see and play in the stellar surroundings than to be seen in Prada. But outdoor frolicking rules the place to such an extent that the locals have perhaps paid too little attention to the aesthetic consequences of burgeoning commercial growth. Alas, downtown Mammoth has turned into a string of low-rise shopping centers and clusters of lackluster condominiums. That said, a major facelift to the tune of $1 billion is well underway, which will no doubt transform the town's character.

ORIENTATION & INFORMATION

At the Mammoth Lakes turnoff from Hwy 395, Rte 203 heads west for 3 miles to town. After the first traffic light, Rte 203 becomes Main St, which continues as Lake Mary Rd past the second traffic light. (In winter Lake Mary Rd is closed

Mammoth's humble origin as a ski resort began in the 1930s, when just a few adventurous souls made use of a few simple rope tows.

past Twin Lakes.) North from the same intersection, Minaret Rd leads past the new Village at Mammoth to the Mammoth Mountain Ski Area; in summer the road continues south to the Reds Meadow/Devils Postpile area.

The **Mammoth Lakes Visitors Bureau** (☎ 760-934-2712, 888-466-2666; fax 760-934-7066; W www.visitmammoth.com; open 8am-5pm daily) shares space with the **Mammoth Lakes Ranger Station** (☎ 760-924-5500) in a building on the north side of Hwy 203, just before the first traffic light. This one-stop information center issues wilderness permits and offers accommodations and campground listings, road and trail condition updates, and details on local attractions.

SKIING & SNOWBOARDING

Mammoth Mountain Ski Area (☎ 760-934-0745, 800-626-6684; W www.mammoth mountain.com) is a true skiers' and snowboarders' resort, where playing hard and having fun are more important than what kind of car you drove to the mountain. An inactive volcanic peak, Mammoth offers a fantastic combination of tree-line and open-bowl skiing, and the 3100 vertical promise some long runs; at the top are some nearly vertical chutes. The resort includes 28 chairlifts, two gondolas, and enough terrain to keep any type of snow hound busy for a week – about 30% of the runs are geared toward beginners, 40% toward intermediates, and 30% toward advanced skiers.

Lift tickets for adults cost $56/45 per full day/afternoon, $42/34 for ages 13 to 17 and $28/22 for seniors over 65 and children ages seven to 12. Multiday tickets are cheaper. With all the expansion underway, expect prices to go up a few dollars every year. Slopes are open 8:30am to 4pm daily; night skiing until 9pm is offered weekends and holidays.

Five hubs line the base of the mountain: Main Lodge, Canyon Lodge, Little Eagle, Outpost Chair 14, and The Mill Cafe – each with parking and ticket sales. At Main Lodge and Canyon Lodge, ski schools and state-of-the-art rentals are available. You'll usually find slightly better prices at outfitters in town, including **Footloose** (☎ 760-934-2400; 3043 Main St) and **Mammoth Sporting Goods** (☎ 760-934-3239).

A new gondola connecting the new Village at Mammoth is slated to open in early 2003. Parking lots tend to fill quickly, so until the gondola opens, it's best to use the free shuttle buses that connect the ski mountain with the town.

CROSS-COUNTRY SKIING

You can do free cross-country skiing along the Blue Diamond Trails System behind New Shady Rest Campground, along Sawmill Rd about a half mile north of Hwy 203. Maintained by the USFS, trails are mostly ungroomed.

A better, if more costly, option is the **Tamarack Cross Country Ski Center** (☎ 760-934-5293; Lake Mary Rd; adult $18/13/10 per full day/afternoon/twilight, senior and child $13/10/8; open first snowfall to mid-Apr). Right at Twin Lakes on Lake Mary Rd, Tamarack features 45km of groomed track, skating lanes, marked backcountry trails, guided nature tours, rentals, and lessons. It's also a good spot for snowshoeing. Rentals for skis and snowshoes cost $17/13 per full day/afternoon, and lessons start at $30.

For backcountry skiing, try the popular network of beautiful trails from Agnew Meadows; the route to Reds Meadow is a favorite.

MOUNTAIN BIKING

Over the years, Mammoth has quietly developed into a hotbed for mountain bikers. Come summer, Mammoth Mountain becomes a massive **Mountain Bike Park**

Excursions **Mammoth Lakes**

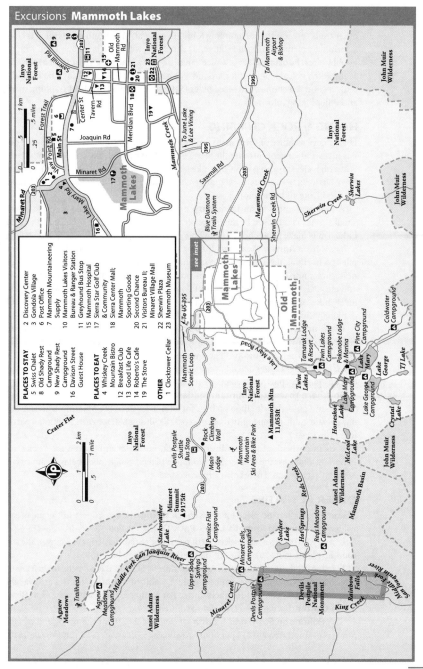

PLACES TO STAY
5 Swiss Chalet
8 Old Shady Rest Campground
9 New Shady Rest Campground
16 Davison Street Guest House

PLACES TO EAT
4 Whiskey Creek Mountain Bistro
12 Breakfast Club
13 Good Life Cafe
14 Roberto's Cafe
19 The Stove

OTHER
1 Clocktower Cellar
2 Discovery Center
3 Gondola Village
6 Post Office
7 Mammoth Mountaineering Supply
10 Mammoth Lakes Visitors Bureau & Ranger Station
11 Greyhound Bus Stop
15 Mammoth Hospital
17 Sierra Star Golf Club & Community
18 Sierra Center Mall; Mammoth
20 Second Chance Sporting Goods
21 Visitors Bureau II; Minaret Village Mall
22 Sherwin Plaza
23 Mammoth Museum

(☎ 760-934-0706), with more than 80 miles of well-tended single-track trails. Several other trails traverse the surrounding forest. In general, Mammoth-style riding is characterized by plenty of hills and soft, sandy shoulders, which are best conquered with big knobby tires. **Footloose** rents a nice range of spiffy bikes just right to float through Mammoth's volcanic terrain for around $10 per hour or $32-48 all day; the shop also rents a good selection of kid-sized bikes ($10/24) and offers excellent trail tips, maps, and other biking information.

HIKING & ROCK CLIMBING

Hikers have a choice of three main trailheads, all with parking lots and access to good day hikes and longer trails over the Sierra Crest. **Horseshoe Lake**, in Mammoth Basin, is at a high elevation, so you needn't hike far to reach the gorgeous alpine scenery of the Inyo National Forest; its good trails venture down into Reds Meadow and up to McLeod Lake and Mammoth Pass.

Also in Mammoth Basin, **Lake Mary**, on Lake Mary Rd, offers easy access to several small alpine lakes backed by the impressive Mammoth Crest; the **TJ Lake** and **Crystal Lake** Trails make good choices from here.

Trails from **Agnew Meadows** (just past the ski resort, on the road to Devils Postpile) go north along the Pacific Crest/John Muir Trail into the Ansel Adams Wilderness, surrounded by the Minarets, some of the Sierra's most stunning sawtooth peaks, and cirque lakes. **Shadow Lake**, about 7 miles round-trip from Agnes Meadows, is a lovely hike. Also from here, the High Trail (6 miles round-trip) traverses a high shoulder along the San Joaquin River leading to lakes at the base of the Ritter Range.

Mammoth Mountaineering Supply (☎ 760-934-4194; Ⓦ www.mammoth gear.colm; 3198 Main St) offers friendly advice, topo maps, equipment rentals, and guided wilderness excursions. The owners also run **Second Chance** (☎ 760-934-8464; in the Vons Center on Old Mammoth Rd), which sells outdoor gear and clothing on consignment, plus last season's merchandise from the flagship store.

Southern Yosemite Mountain Guides (☎ 760-415-9596; Ⓦ www.symg.com) leads year-round guided rock-climbing trips for all skill levels in the Mammoth area. A full-day private guide for one or two people costs $330; add $80 for each additional participant (up to six).

Kids in particular like the **Climbing Rock**, on the lawn between the Yodler and Panorama Stations (the lifts used by mountain bikers). Single, staff-belayed climbs cost $8; a day pass is $28. There's also a ropes course.

OTHER ACTIVITIES

Mammoth is a terrific place for **horseback riding**, thanks in part to the area's easy wilderness access. **Mammoth Lakes Pack Outfit** (☎ 760-934-2434, 888-475-8747; Lake Mary Rd) offers a wide selection of one-hour to half-day trips to many of the surrounding lakes ($30-70) and a full-day outing to Barney Lake ($95).

Starting on the last Saturday in April, the dozens of lakes that give the town its name lure in fly and trout fishers from near and far. California **fishing** licenses are available at sporting goods stores throughout town. For equipment and advice, head to **Rick's Sport Center** (☎ 760-934-3416; Main St at Center St).

The **Pokonobe Store and Marina** (☎ 760-934-2437), on the north end of Lake Mary, rents motor boats ($14 per hour), rowboats ($8), canoes ($12), and kayaks ($10).

Caldera Kayaks (☎ 760-935-4942) has single ($30 for a half-day) and double kayaks ($40) for use on Crowley Lake.

PLACES TO STAY & EAT

Most of the 20 or so USFS campgrounds in and around Mammoth Lakes are open from about mid-June to mid-September. You'll find some of the nicest campsites on the shores of **Twin Lakes, Lake Mary,** and **Lake George.** Sites are available on a first-come, first-served basis and cost $13-16. Head to the Visitors Bureau for a full campground list, specific opening dates, information about space availability, and public showers.

Davison Street Guest House (☎ *760-924-2188, 619-544-9093 for reservations; 19 Davison St; dorm beds $18-27)* is a friendly, hostel-like A-frame with five rooms, a communal kitchen, a lounge, and a sundeck ringed with mountain views.

Mammoth abounds with holiday condominiums, which can be an excellent and affordable option, especially for groups of four or more. Contact **Mammoth Reservation Bureau** (☎ *760-934-2528, 800-462-5571, fax 760-934-2317; Ⓦ www.mammoth vacations.com)* or **Central Reservations of Mammoth** (☎ *760-934-8816, 800-321-3261, fax 760-934-1703; Ⓦ www.mammothlakes.com).*

Swiss Chalet (☎ *760-934-2403, 800-937-9477; Ⓦ www.mammoth-swisschalet.com; 3776 Viewpoint Rd; rooms $60-75/80-120 in summer/winter)* is a charming two-story lodge with friendly owners and nicely decorated rooms that contain comfy beds, TVs, and telephones. After a day on the trails or slopes, wind down in the hot tub or sauna, both with superb mountain views.

Kind people run the classic and charming **Tamarack Lodge & Resort** (☎ *760-934-2442, fax 760-934-2281; Ⓦ www.tamaracklodge.com; cabins $120-350, lodge rooms $82-230),* on the shore of Lower Twin Lake. The cozy lodge includes a fireplace, bar, excellent restaurant, and three upstairs rooms. Cabins sleep up to nine people and come with full kitchen, telephone, private bath, porch, and wood-burning stove.

Mammoth has no shortage of places to get that morning coffee jolt and fuel up on carbs for the day's activities, including the **Breakfast Club** (☎ *760-934-6944; 2987 Main St)* and **The Stove** (☎ *760-934-2821; 644 Old Mammoth Rd),* both local favorites.

Good Life Cafe (☎ *760-934-1734; Mammoth Mall on Old Mammoth Rd; breakfast and lunch $4.50-9.50)* has some selections for the health-conscious, including generously filled wraps and sandwiches and big bowls of salad.

Roberto's Café (☎ *760-934-3667, 271 Old Mammoth Rd; dishes $8-10)* serves Mammoth's hands-down best Mexican food and a selection of more than 30 tequilas. Locals pack the outdoor deck to look out on a beautiful wildflower garden.

Whiskey Creek Mountain Bistro (☎ *760-934-2555; Lake Mary Rd; entrées $12-16),* a popular and noisy hangout, offers salads, pastas, steaks, seafood, and an excellent selection of signature vegetable sides. Upstairs is **Mammoth Brewing Company** (☎ *760-934-2555),* with daily brews and pub eats.

For a splurge, try **The Lakefront Restaurant** (☎ *760-934-3534; dishes $6-27),* at Tamarack Lodge. The chef, who hails from Alsace, crafts specialties like elk medallions *au poivre* and heirloom tomatoes with Basque cheese. The romantic dining room overlooks Twin Lakes.

For now, the best nightlife spot is the **Clocktower Cellar** (☎ *760-934-2725; Minaret Rd),* located in the basement of the Alpenhof Lodge. Locals frequent this warm and welcoming den of a bar, which features pool, foosball, and 30 beers on draft.

Devils Postpile National Monument

The 60ft, multisided columns of blue-gray basalt at this monument are the most conspicuous and interesting evidence of the area's volcanic activity. The accordion-like columns first took shape about 10,000 years ago, when lava, which flowed through Mammoth Pass, cooled and fractured vertically. A glacier came through later, giving them their cracked, shiny surface and causing several to snap off, forming the pile of broken posts at the base. Don't miss the view from above, where the distinct hexagonal honeycomb design is particularly visible.

The road to the monument, 10 miles west past the ski area, is open from June to September weather permitting, and you can drive there (road use fee $5) if you go before 7am or after 7pm, both glorious times to visit the site, or if you have campground reservations. Otherwise, you can only get there on foot or aboard a free shuttle bus, which departs every 30 minutes between 7am and 7pm daily from the Gondola Building outside the ski area's Main Lodge. The shuttle bus stops at campgrounds, viewpoints, and the **Devils Postpile Ranger Station** (☎ *760-934-2289; open 9am-4pm daily*). From here, expect to hike about 1.5 miles to the columns or 2.5 miles through fire-ravaged forest to the spectacular Rainbow Falls, a 101ft sheet cascade. Daily ranger-guided walks to the columns leave from the station at 11am. The shuttle's last stop is at

EASTERN SIERRA HOT SPRINGS

Thanks to its volcanic past and wealth of underground mountain-fed springs, the eastern Sierra is prime hot springs country, and the stretch of Hwy 395 from just north of Bridgeport south to Lone Pine is sprinkled with secluded spots for soaking. Over the years, first shepherds, then locals, have crafted actual drainable tubs, with rubber hosing used to divert the springs. Many are well-known and thus can get crowded on weekends, so if you're after seclusion, it's best to spring-hop in midweek or off-season. At a few of the more public places, like Hot Creek, posted signs list an alarming number of warnings and potential dangers, such as fatally hot or arsenic-laced springs, all worth noting. Other spots have taken on a party scene atmosphere and can be littered with broken glass and empty bottles. But a few remain lovely and worth at least a look if hot springing is your kind of thing. For a full list and detailed directions and maps, pick up a copy of Matt Bischoff's *Touring California and Nevada Hot Springs*.

About 9 miles south of Mammoth, Benton Crossing Rd juts east off of Hwy 395, accessing a trove of hot springs. Locals call this "Green Church Rd," on account of the juncture's unmistakable marker. About 1 mile down Benton, Forest Rd 2507 cuts north, eventually connecting with Hot Creek Rd, and more springs. All told, there are no fewer then 10 different hot springs along this loop. **The Hot Tub** is easy-to-find, well maintained and one of the best. Head east on Benton Crossing Rd for 1.2 miles (passing the Whittmore Hot Springs Public Pool on the right) and turn left on Forest Road 2507. After 1.1 miles, turn right onto a faint but distinct dirt road; the tub is ahead about 100yd. Here you'll find a nice patio area and sweeping vistas of the Sierra Nevada. The tub, which has a well-designed drain for emptying after use, can fit four comfortably.

the **Reds Meadow Resort** (☎ 760-934-2345, 800-292-7758), with a café, general store, pack station, and campground. The entire one-way trip takes about 45 minutes.

If you drive yourself, though, particularly in the evening, you'll have plenty of time to linger over the spectacular view from the **Minarets Vista**, about 5 miles from the ski area and just off to the right past the ranger station. Here you'll find one of the best views around, looking over the San Joaquin River valley and out toward Banner Peak, Mt. Ritter, and the picturesque Minarets, named for their resemblance to the spires of Moslem temples. At sunset, these lacy granite spires seem to come alive in the rosy alpenglow.

Bishop

Bishop is the largest town south of Mammoth Lakes, less than an hour's drive southeast on Hwy 395, or about two hours from Yosemite's east gate. The old part of town features classic Western Americana, with covered sidewalks, classic 1950s neon signs, and hunting and fishing stores aplenty. Its unpretentious appearance stands in stark contrast to the wonderland of nature surrounding it. A major recreation hub, Bishop offers access to excellent fishing in nearby lakes, climbing in the Buttermilks just west of town, and hiking in the John Muir Wilderness via Bishop Creek Canyon and the Rock Creek drainage. It's a nice place to visit year-round, but unless you like crowds, you may want to skip Memorial Day weekend, when some 40,000 people descend on the town to celebrate Mule Days (☎ 760-872-4263; W www.muledays.org), featuring mule parades, mule races, and a mule rodeo.

Bishop also serves as the northernmost gateway to the **Owens Valley**, a once fertile agricultural region reduced to a desertlike wasteland. Since the early 20th century, water from the Owens River has been siphoned off by the Los Angeles Aqueduct. Some environmental restoration is now underway, but the area is still in recovery mode.

The earliest inhabitants of the Owens Valley were Paiute and Shoshone Native Americans who today live on four reservations; the largest is the Bishop Indian Reservation. The **Paiute Shoshone Cultural Center** (☎ 760-873-4478; 2300 W Line St; adult/child $4/1; open 10am-5pm daily) acts as tribal headquarters and gathering place. A museum showcases extensive collections of baskets, arrowheads, tools, clothing, and dwellings, including a sweat lodge and a cooking shelter. There's a gift shop, too. Plans are underway to hold an annual film festival at the center each fall.

The Owens River Gorge, 9 miles north of town on the east side of Hwy 395, offers excellent **rock climbing**, as do the Buttermilk Hills, west of town on either side of Hwy 168; the latter are terrific for **bouldering**, as are the aptly named Happy Boulders nearby.

Some of the friendly staff at **Wilson's Eastside Sports** (☎ 760-873-7520; 224 N Main St) are experienced climbers with good route suggestions; the shop rents equipment and sells maps and guidebooks. The folks at **Sierra Mountain Center** (☎/fax 760-873-8526; W www.sierramountaincenter.com; 175 W Line St) consider themselves Sierra backcountry experts and offer year-round instruction and guided ascents in the eastern Sierra ($140-360 per day for up to four people). They also book a wide range of climbing, hiking, mountaineering, backcountry skiing, and other activity-specific trips.

A short drive west via Hwy 168 takes you to **Bishop Creek Canyon Recreation Area**, a High Sierra alpine playground with pine forests, lakes, and streams. Farther west the road forks, the south fork ending at pretty **South Lake**, surrounded by jagged peaks.

Many trails depart from the lake's trailhead, heading up to Bishop Pass and countless lakes in the John Muir Wilderness. There are several campgrounds in the area.

The north fork ends at sparkling **Lake Sabrina**, encircled by craggy peaks of the Sierra Crest. Sabrina is gorgeous, especially in fall when the trees turn golden. A ribbon of a trail winds along the north shore, leading to a small waterfall (about 2 miles away) and passing several good spots to swim, if you can stomach the cold. Nearby is the much smaller North Lake. Both lakes make excellent stops for fishing. **Lake Sabrina Boat Landing** (☎ 619-873-7425) rents boats with or without motors for $20-35 per half-day, and there's a little café with a sun-splashed deck for a post-activity cold beer.

PLACES TO STAY & EAT

For a scenic night, stretch out your sleeping bag beneath the stars. Ten nice USFS campgrounds lie along Bishop Creek, 9 miles west of town via Hwy 168, all of them surrounded by trees and close to fishing and hiking. Most sites cost $11, and all are first-come, first-served. Closer to civilization, **Brown's Town** (☎ 760-873-8522; sites $14-19), on the south edge of town off Hwy 395, is a nicely shaded campground with grassy sites, hot showers, laundry, and other amenities.

THE LEGACY OF GALEN ROWELL

Long before he became known as one of the world's preeminent outdoor adventure photographers, Galen Rowell was an accomplished rock climber and avid outdoors lover, having grown up taking Sierra Club hiking trips; he first climbed in Yosemite at age 16. During the 1960s and '70s, he tallied more than 100 first ascents in the High Sierra, including 30 in Yosemite. No doubt his elite skill level, combined with his passion for the natural world, enabled him to capture a photographic perspective others could not – the raw beauty of mountains as seen by someone who had explored them intimately.

An impassioned environmentalist, Rowell shot for a long list of top magazines, and his talent for capturing alpine areas worldwide is legendary. In 1984, he received the Sierra Club's Ansel Adams Award for Conservation Photography, which was followed by numerous other grants and adulation. Over the years, he produced dozens of large-format books documenting his more than 35 expeditions all over the world.

A Berkeley, California, native, Galen and his wife, Barbara (also an accomplished photographer and his constant comrade), moved to Bishop in 2000, relocating the gallery and workshop headquarters they'd opened in 1983. They bought the old bank on Main St, converting it into the museum-quality **Mountain Light Gallery** (☎ 760-873-7700; Main St at Line St; W www.mountainlight.com), which showcased their images and acted as base camp for popular and inspirational workshops.

Tragically, Galen and Barbara were killed on August 11, 2002, when their chartered plane crashed just shy of the Bishop airstrip, a stone's throw from home, where they were returning after teaching a workshop in Alaska. They deeply loved the Sierra, served as board members of the Yosemite Fund, and supported numerous other park programs. In 2001 the Yosemite Association published a paperback edition of John Muir's The Yosemite, which included more than 100 of Rowell's gorgeous photos of the park.

Matlock House *(☎ 760-873-3133; 1313 Rowan Lane; rooms $75-85),* tucked behind an auto parts store just before the bend in Hwy 395, is a B&B with decor that harks back to the good old days.

Joseph House Inn Bed & Breakfast *(☎ 760-872-3389; 376 W Yaney St; rooms $130-165),* a newly restored ranch-style home, includes gardens, a patio, and five nicely furnished rooms, some with fireplaces, all with TV and VCR. Guests enjoy a complimentary gourmet breakfast and afternoon wine and cheese.

Erick Schat's Bakkery *(☎ 760-873-7156; 763 N Main St; sandwiches $6-7),* a much-hyped spot, has been making shepherd bread and other baked goodies since 1938. The bakery also features a popular sandwich bar and espresso drinks.

Los Palmas Taqueria *(☎ 760-873-4337; 136 E Line St; dishes $3-10)* boasts a festive feel, red leather banquets, and plenty of local customers who keep coming back for the vegetarian "buffalo burritos" and salsa bar.

An old-fashioned, self-service eatery, **Bar-B-Q Bill's** *(☎ 760-872-5535; 187 S Main St; meals under $10)* slow-cooks smoked meat in delicious barbecue sauce. Non-carnivores will welcome the well-stocked salad bar.

Whiskey Creek *(☎ 760-873-7174; 524 N Main St; dishes $10-18),* in a gabled country inn, serves appetizers and simple dishes in a woodsy bar with a nice patio; you can feast on more-elaborate meals in the slightly stuffy dining room.

Kava Coffeehouse *(206 N Main St)* makes great coffee, smoothies, and ice-lemon slush in a space with upbeat ambience and Internet service. Hikers and climbers gather here to fuel up on breakfast, baked goods, and sandwiches.

Ancient Bristlecone Pine Forest

For amazing views, take the hour-long drive to the Ancient Bristlecone Pine Forest *(☎ 760-873-2500).* Perched above 10,000ft in the White Mountains, these gnarled, picturesque trees are the planet's oldest living things, some dating back 4000 years. To get there from Bishop, drive 15 miles south to Big Pine, then head east on Hwy 168 another 13 miles to the marked turnoff. The road, usually open from late May to October, is paved to the top, where you'll find hikes of varying lengths, a nice primitive campground (free), and a visitor center.

Kings Canyon & Sequoia National Parks

These two national parks, which sit side by side in the central Sierra, encompass some of the most incredible alpine scenery in the state, from rugged canyons to the world's largest living thing (the General Sherman Tree, a giant sequoia). The crowds here feel almost sparse compared with those at Yosemite, a bonus for those who don't like people getting in the way of their nature experience. There is also much less commercial development.

Sequoia was designated a national park in 1890 (the second in the USA after Yellowstone). That same year, the Grant Grove of giant sequoias became General Grant National Park. Decades later, that tiny parcel was absorbed into the new Kings Canyon National Park, established in 1940. In 2000, to further convey protection for sequoia groves, the US government designated more than 327,000 acres of land in the Sequoia National Forest as the Giant Sequoia National Monument.

Kings Canyon and Sequoia lie about 100 miles south of Yosemite, though it takes two to three hours to make the drive. From Wawona, follow Hwy 41 south to Fresno, then head east on Hwy 180. Note that traffic often gets snarled around Fresno.

Part of the reason Kings Canyon and Sequoia aren't heavily visited is their limited accessibility. No highway crosses the Sierra here, unlike in Yosemite, and just two roads enter the parks: Hwy 180 (arriving in Grant Grove) and Hwy 198 (Ash Mountain), the latter a series of steep, narrow switchbacks. Inside the parks, the main north-south road is the 48-mile Generals Highway, which occasionally closes due to snow.

Both park entrances are open year-round, though some facilities are seasonal.

The two parks, though distinct, operate as one unit, with a single admission of $10 per car, $5 for anyone on a bicycle or on foot. Admission is valid for seven days.

INFORMATION

For 24-hour recorded information, including winter road conditions, call ☎ 559-565-3341; the parks' comprehensive website is W www.nps.gov/seki.

The biggest service hub in Kings Canyon, **Grant Grove Village** stays open year-round and contains a market, restaurant, ATM, showers ($3), and post office. The **visitor center** (☎ 559-565-4307; 8am-6pm daily in summer, shorter hours otherwise) offers a good history exhibit and a slide show.

Cedar Grove Village, at the bottom of Kings Canyon (31 miles northeast of Grant Grove Village), consists of a market, restaurant, lodge, showers ($3), laundry, and small **visitor center** (☎ 559-565-3793; open 9am-5pm daily late May-Sept). The road is usually open from late April to October or November, but most services don't start until late May. You'll find a wilderness permit station 6 miles east of the village at Roads End.

The main hub in Sequoia National Park is **Lodgepole Village**, with a market, deli, post office, coin-operated showers, laundry facilities, and **visitor center** (☎ 559-565-3782; open 9am-6pm daily in summer, shorter hours otherwise).

The **Foothills Visitor Center** (☎ 559-565-3135; open 8am-5pm daily June-Sept, 8am-4:40pm daily otherwise), at Sequoia's southern Ash Mountain Entrance, displays exhibits on the local ecosystem. There's also a small **ranger station** (☎ 559-565-3768; open 7am-4:30pm daily late May-early Sept) in **Mineral King**, a rugged onetime mining area.

Gas is not available in either park, but it is sold at Kings Canyon Lodge and Hume Lake, both private facilities on USFS land north of Grant Grove.

KINGS CANYON NATIONAL PARK

Kings Canyon National Park is divided into two areas: Grant Grove and Cedar Grove, linked by Hwy 180, which makes a dramatic descent into Kings Canyon along the South Fork of the Kings River. The canyon itself, plunging 8200ft, is the deepest in the contiguous 48 states.

General Grant Grove includes the General Grant Tree and several other impressive giants. North of Grant Grove, Kings Canyon Hwy drops 2000ft to Cedar Grove. The 36-mile drive takes about an hour and ranks among the most magnificent in any national park, including Yosemite. Views from the road into the valley are spectacular, with roaring rivers, rugged peaks, and steep granite cliffs in view. Six miles beyond Cedar Grove, **Roads End** is just that, with trailheads, overnight parking, and a ranger kiosk that issues wilderness permits.

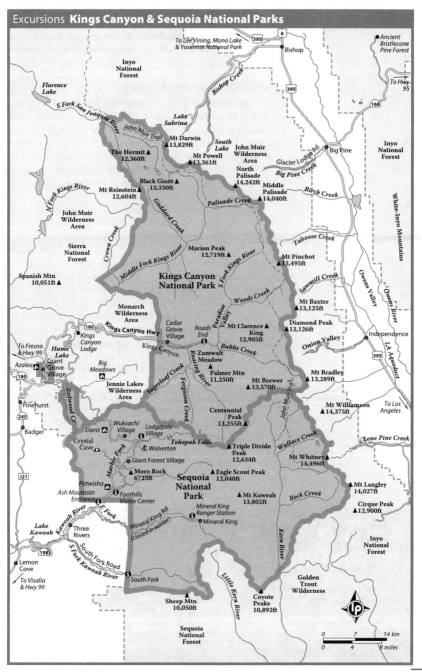

To Lee Vining, Mono Lake & Yosemite National Park

To Hwy 95

Ancient Bristlecone Pine Forest

Bishop

Inyo National Forest

Florence Lake

S Fork San Joaquin River

Bishop Creek

John Muir Trail

Lake Sabrina

Mt Darwin ▲13,829ft

South Lake

John Muir Wilderness Area

North Palisade ▲14,242ft

Big Pine

Inyo National Forest

The Hermit ▲12,360ft

Mt Powell ▲13,361ft

Glacier Lodge Rd

Big Pine Creek

Black Giant ▲13,330ft

Mt Reinstein ▲12,604ft

Goddard Creek

Middle Palisade ▲14,040ft

Birch Creek

Palisade Creek

White-Inyo Mountains

N Fork Kings River

John Muir Wilderness Area

Crown Creek

Sierra National Forest

Middle Fork Kings River

Marion Peak ▲12,719ft

Taboose Creek

Mt Pinchot ▲13,495ft

Owens Valley

Owens River

Spanish Mtn 10,051ft ▲

Kings Canyon National Park

S Fork Kings River

Sawmill Creek

Woods Creek

Mt Baxter ▲13,125ft

Monarch Wilderness Area

Kings Canyon Hwy

Cedar Grove Village

Roads End

Paradise Valley

Mt Clarence King ▲12,905ft

Diamond Peak ▲13,126ft

Onion Valley

Independence

To Fresno & Hwy 99

Kings Canyon Lodge

Hume Lake

Big Meadows

Kings Canyon

Bubbs Creek

Zumwalt Meadow

Roaring River

LA Aqueduct

Azalea

Grant Grove Village

Jennie Lakes Wilderness Area

Palmer Mtn ▲11,250ft

Mt Brewer ▲13,570ft

Pinehurst

Redwood Cr

Sugarloaf Creek

Ferguson Creek

Mt Bradley ▲13,289ft

Mt Williamson ▲14,375ft

To Los Angeles

Badger

Centennial Peak 13,255ft ▲

John Muir Trail

Wuksachi Village

Lodgepole Village

Dorst

Wallace Creek

Lone Pine Creek

Crystal Cave

Wolverton

Tokopah Falls

Triple Divide Peak ▲12,634ft

Mt Whitney ▲14,496ft

Giant Forest Village

Moro Rock 6725ft

Eagle Scout Peak ▲12,040ft

Sequoia National Park

Mt Langley ▲14,027ft

Potwisha

Marble Fork

E Fork

Ash Mountain Entrance

Foothills Visitor Center

Mt Kaweah ▲13,802ft

Rock Creek

Cirque Peak ▲12,900ft

Mineral King Ranger Station

Mineral King Rd (closed in winter)

Mineral King

Kern River

Lake Kaweah

Three Rivers

Kaweah River

South Fork Road

Little Kern River

Inyo National Forest

Lemon Cove

To Visalia & Hwy 99

S Fork Kaweah River

South Fork

Sheep Mtn 10,050ft

Coyote Peaks 10,892ft

Golden Trout Wilderness

Sequoia National Forest

0   7   14 km
0   4   8 miles

The stunning backcountry makes the canyon a favorite place among serious hikers and climbers. For casual visitors, however, beautiful **Zumwalt Meadow** is an easy and worthwhile destination. From the Roads End parking lot, it's about a half-hour walk each way.

SEQUOIA NATIONAL PARK

The top destination for first-time visitors and those with limited time is **Giant Forest**, home to the massive General Sherman Tree, the world's largest by volume. From the parking lot, you can access the Congress Trail, a worthwhile 2-mile paved pathway passing General Sherman and other impressive trees.

The nearby **Giant Forest Museum** (☎ 559-565-4480; open 9am-4:30pm daily) contains exhibits about sequoia ecology and history, plus a bookstore.

For mind-boggling views of the Great Western Divide, climb the steep quarter-mile staircase up **Moro Rock**. The trailhead is 2 miles up a steep, winding road from the Giant Forest.

Discovered in 1918 by two fishermen, **Crystal Cave** extends some 3 miles into the earth and features formations estimated to be 10,000 years old. The 50-minute cave tour (adult/child $8/4) covers a half-mile of chambers; a two-hour, small-group tour ($15) is also available in summer. The cave lies at the end of a twisty 7-mile paved road leading west from the General's Highway just a couple miles south of the Giant Forest. From the parking lot it's a half-mile hike to the cave entrance. Buy tickets at the Lodgepole and Foothills visitor centers, not at the cave.

A scenic, subalpine valley at 7500ft, **Mineral King** – site of much silver mining in the late 1800s – has become Sequoia's backpacking mecca and is a good place to find solitude. Proposals to develop the area into a massive ski resort were thwarted when Congress affixed it to the national park in 1978. Access the area via Mineral King Rd, which heads east from Hwy 198 between the town of Three Rivers and the Ash Mountain Entrance. Open in summer only, it's a twisting, steep, and narrow 25-mile road that manages to weed out all but those with a mission.

MT WHITNEY

Mt Whitney (14,496 feet), the tallest point in the continental US and the southern terminus of the John Muir Trail, sits smack on the eastern border of Sequoia National Park. The main summit trail leaves from Whitney Portal in the eastern Sierra, about 13 miles west of Lone Pine, and climbs some 6000ft over 11 miles. The biggest obstacle to reaching the top, however, is obtaining a required wilderness permit ($15), distributed via a lottery. Contact the **Wilderness Permit Office** (☎ 760-873-2483, fax 760-873-2484; w www.r5.fs.fed.us/inyo) for details.

ACTIVITIES

With 800 miles of marked trails, the parks are a **backpacking** heaven. Cedar Grove and Mineral King offer the best backcountry access, while the Jenny Lakes Wilderness Area (accessible from the Big Meadows Trailhead near Big Meadows Campground) boasts pristine meadows and lakes at lower elevations. Trails usually open by mid-May. Bear-proof food canisters, sometimes mandatory, can be rented at the parks' visitor centers and markets.

Wilderness permits are required for all overnight trips and are available free of charge at visitor centers and ranger stations. If you want to reserve ahead, though, there's a $10 fee, which must be received three weeks in advance. Fax or mail your request to **Wilderness Permit Reservations** (☎ 559-565-3708, fax 559-565-4239; HCR 89, Box 60, Three Rivers, CA 93271).

In winter, **cross-country skiing** revolves around Grant Grove Village and the **Sequoia Ski Touring Center** (☎ 559-565-3435) in Wolverton, 2.5 miles south of Lodgepole. Both regions provide rental equipment and marked trails.

PLACES TO STAY & EAT

Accommodations in Kings Canyon are managed by **Kings Canyon Park Service** (KCPS; ☎ 559-335-5500, 866-522-6966; W www.sequoia-kingscanyon.com), while **Delaware North Parks Service** (DNPS; ☎ 559-784-1500, 888-252-5757; W www.visitsequoia.com) is in charge of Sequoia.

Free dispersed **camping** is possible in Sequoia National Forest and Giant Sequoia National Monument; pick up details and a fire permit from a visitor center or ranger station.

NPS campgrounds are first-come, first-served, with the exception of Lodgepole and Dorst Creek (☎ 800-365-2267 for reservations). Sites come with bear-proof boxes, tables, and fire pits; most have flush toilets. Campgrounds start opening around May and close in October. Camping fees range from $8 for primitive sites to $16 for reservable campsites with running water and flush toilets. **Lodgepole Campground** and **Azalea Campground** stay open year-round; the rest, including the four inside Kings Canyon, are usually open May to October. Call ☎ 559-565-3341 for updates. The biggest cluster of campgrounds is around the Grant Grove area.

Most lodges close from early October to May, except Grant Grove and Wuksachi. **Grant Grove Lodge** rents tent cabins ranging from rustic ($45) to deluxe ($112), with private bathrooms and electricity. **Grant Grove Restaurant**, open year-round, is an above-average coffee shop with meals under $10.

Cedar Grove Lodge (rooms from $99) offers motel-style accommodations. Halfway between Grant Grove and Cedar Grove, the privately run **Kings Canyon Lodge** (☎ 559-335-2405; rooms and cabins from $79) is a better value. Its cozy, rustic café-bar, built in the 1930s, serves meals and cocktails daily. Even the gas pumps are antiques.

Once a pristine wilderness and sacred home to a small Native American population, Yosemite has become one of the nation's premier tourist attractions, rivaled only by Lake Tahoe as a popular California mountain retreat. Even before Western explorers first beheld Yosemite Valley, people regarded its secluded granite monuments and leaping cascades as unique treasures worthy of special regard – indeed, from Yosemite sprang the very concept of a publicly held and protected wilderness park. Renowned artists, writers, environmentalists, adventurers, politicians, and preachers have all made pilgrimage here. Many return again and

Theodore Roosevelt and John Muir
on Glacier Point, 1906

LIBRARY OF CONGRESS

again. These people are a part of Yosemite's evolving story, just as the rocks, plants, and wildlife are a part of its soul.

YOSEMITE HISTORY

Living off the Land

Less than 150 years have passed since tourists first came to Yosemite Valley. Historians, poets, artists, and photographers offer a rich portrayal of this recent history, but the story of Yosemite's earlier human inhabitants emerges only through interpretation of Native American myths and of the stone artifacts found in scattered archeological sites.

Although much of the archeological evidence dates to within the last 3000 years, artifacts at a few sites go as far back as 12,000 years ago. Most historians agree that the ancestors of these earliest Americans came to the continent from eastern Asia, crossing to Alaska over an Ice Age land bridge that spanned the Bering Strait.

Artifacts found in the Sierra Nevada suggest that the Native Americans' way of life here did not change dramatically over the millennia. Most Sierra native groups migrated with the seasons, both to enjoy the best weather and to make use of natural resources. Many of the archeological sites in the higher elevations appear to be warm weather hunting camps, often identified by the presence of lithic scatter (chips of rock left over when obsidian is made into knives or arrowheads). The prehistoric hunters set up camp near sources of good drinking water and in locations with good vantage points for watching game animals.

In the lower, thickly forested regions, the sites tend to be found along ecotones – areas near clearings where different plant and animal communities intermingle, providing a great variety of resources. Heavy snow cover on the western slopes discouraged year-round habitation above 5000 feet, but the hospitable oak forests of the lower western foothills, and the piñon-juniper forests on the eastern escarpments show abundant evidence of long-term and year-round use, including house pits, rock art, and milling stations – large, flat rocks pocked with deep depressions where acorns, a dietary staple for most California Indians, were ground into flour.

While most natives traveled only when migrating or when hunting and gathering, trading parties did regularly cross the Sierra on foot to exchange goods. Obsidian and pine nuts from the eastern Sierra were in great demand by western slope and coastal peoples, who traded them for acorns and seashells. Early Euro-American explorers making their way over the Sierra often found themselves on these ancient trade routes. Use of some of these trails continues to this day, although for largely different purposes.

YOSEMITE'S NATIVE CULTURES

Some descendents of these ancient residents still live within their traditional territories, and recently many groups have made strides in the revival of their cultural traditions. Some of the native peoples of the Sierra Nevada continue to speak their own distinct languages.

Yosemite is Sierra Miwok country, although today most of the Sierra Miwok live in reservations called *rancherías* located in the foothills. Miwok lore maintains that a subgroup called the *Ahwahneechee* (translated as "people who live in the valley of the gaping mouth") originated in the Valley and that at some point the subtribe dispersed after a fatal illness decimated their numbers. The survivors of this plague joined other tribes. Some time before 1851, Teneiya, an Ahwahneechee chief who was born and raised with the Mono Lake Paiute, gathered other Ahwaneechee descendants and reestablished his people's home in Yosemite Valley. To read about the tragic demise of the Ahwahneechee, see the Mariposa Battalion section, later in this history.

The Yosemite General Management Plan of 1980 calls for the creation of a Native American cultural center at the site of the last occupied native village in Yosemite Valley. Conceived through a cooperative agreement between the National Park Service and the American Indian Council of Mariposa County (Southern Sierra Miwok), the center will serve as a place for traditional ceremonies and for educational programs meant to give modern tourists insight into the ancient cultures. The Miwok, who consider much of Yosemite Valley to be sacred ground, continue to weigh in on many decisions having to do with implementation of the Yosemite Plan.

Native American woman and child, Yosemite Valley.

T I M E L I N E

4000 BC	Ahwahneechee (Miwok) people settle in Yosemite Valley.
1833	The Joseph Reddeford Walker party sees Yosemite Valley.
1848	Mexico cedes California to the US; gold is discovered at Sutter's Mill, starting the gold rush.
1851	Members of the Mariposa Battalion become the first white men to enter Yosemite Valley.
1853	Chief Teneiya is killed, and the Ahwahneechee (Miwok) disperse.
1855	First tourists (total of 42 people) visit Yosemite Valley.
1864	President Lincoln signs the Yosemite Grant, establishing Yosemite Valley and Mariposa Grove as a state park.
1868	John Muir makes his first visit to Yosemite.
1878	The Valley's first public campground opens.
1890	Congress passes the Yosemite Act of 1890, establishing Yosemite National Park.
1892	The Sierra Club is chartered, with John Muir as its first president.
1899	The Currys establish their camp at the base of Glacier Point.
1906	The State of California cedes Yosemite Valley and Mariposa Grove to Yosemite National Park.
1908	Hetch Hetchy water rights are granted to the City of San Francisco.
1913	Automobiles are officially allowed in Yosemite National Park. Total annual visitation reaches 12,255.
1916	The National Park Service is founded; Tioga Rd and the John Muir Trail open.
1922	Park visitation surpasses 100,000 per year.
1923	O'Shaughnessy Dam is built across the Tuolumne River in Hetch Hetchy Valley.
1927	The luxurious Ahwahnee Hotel opens.
1943-45	The Ahwahnee Hotel goes into service as a naval hospital during WWII.
1954	Annual visitation surpasses 1,000,000.
1980	As visitation reaches 2,500,000 per year, the park creates its first General Management Plan.
1984	The park becomes a UNESCO World Heritage Site.
1997	Floods on the Merced wash out sections of road, and the park closes for several months.
2000	The Yosemite Valley Plan is adopted.

Exploring California

In 1542, when Spain had established its empire in Mexico, the incessant quest for gold and spices turned northward, and explorers set sail along the Pacific coast in search of the proverbial northwest passage. Looking in on the territory then known as *Alta California*, the Spaniards could see snow-capped mountains, and so the first maps of the territory show *sierras nevadas*, snow-covered, sawtooth ranges. But the lofty realm that would become known as the Sierra Nevada remained essentially unknown until the inland excursions of the 1770s, when Spanish missionaries sought to make Catholics out of the Native Americans living in the *tulares* (tule marshes) of the Central Valley. From several inland vantage points, the missionaries could see the dense forests, rushing rivers, and high, snowy peaks of the great range. But it would be another 60 years before any Europeans set foot in the Yosemite region.

A party led by Jedediah Smith finally crossed the Sierra Nevada in 1827, traveling west to east. Six years later, an able frontiersman named Joseph Reddeford Walker led the first party across the range from east to west. Autumn snow in the high country made the journey arduous, so the Walker party was too exhausted to appreciate the extraordinary sight of Yosemite Valley as they looked down on it from its north rim. Nor were the travelers inclined to linger in the grove of giant sequoias they found as they fled mounting snows. Fortunately, a young member of the party, a clerk named Zenas Leonard, recorded these events; Leonard's descriptions of streams shooting off precipices have helped convince historians that Walker's party traveled through Yosemite.

The next decade saw a remarkable shift in the patterns of westward expansion, as rumors of rich farmlands in Alta California (at that time held by Mexico) reached emigrants on the Oregon Trail. Several groups (including the notorious cannibalistic Donner Party) made the difficult trans-Sierra trek. The emigrants' destination was inevitably Sutter's Fort,

Fallen monarch, September 15, 1911, Mariposa Big Tree Grove

LIBRARY OF CONGRESS

a nascent community on the Sacramento River created in a utopian vision by an expatriate Swiss named John Sutter.

As Sutter saw his community growing, he decided to build a flour mill. With little wood for construction available near the fort, Sutter sent his foreman, James Marshall, up into the conifer forests to build a sawmill. Marshall chose a site on the South Fork of the American River. The rushing river would provide power, and the wood could be floated down the river to the fort. But Marshall's labors were destined to have an outcome quite different from what he and John Sutter had envisioned.

Gold Rush Upheaval

In February 1848, as Marshall constructed the sawmill, he found flecks of gold in the water. Contrary to what is widely believed, this was not the first time gold had been discovered in the Sierra Nevada. The Native Americans knew of the yellow ore but saw no value in it, and Mexicans working their vast land grants in the southern Sierra foothills had taken gold from the ground but believed the deposits to be small. No one then knew the huge extent of the gold-bearing veins. Even the easily mined placer gold in the Sierra riverbeds remained a secret until Marshall's discovery leaked out in March 1848.

The news set off a stunning reconfiguration of the landscape and an utter change in the demographics of the region. While more and more travelers turned their wagons toward the Sierra, others booked passage on ships leaving from Atlantic ports to sail to San Francisco Bay.

Those taking up the rugged life in the primitive Sierran mining camps were primarily men. A number came from northern Europe or from the eastern US, but in the early years of the gold rush, many of the miners were Chinese, South American, and Mexican. In a bitterly ironic coincidence, the Treaty of Guadalupe Hidalgo was signed in February 1848, ending the Mexican War and ceding the entire Southwest, including Alta California, to the US. The Mexican-Californians, some of whom could trace their lineage to the conquistadors, became foreigners in US territory. Along with the Chinese and South Americans, they were systematically divested of their rights to a share of the gold through a series of legislative acts passed in the 1850s.

The Native Americans of the Sierra faced an even grimmer fate during the gold rush, when they found themselves overrun by the thousands staking claims to gold, lumber, water, game, and the fertile cropland of the lower elevations. The genocide that began with diseases introduced in the earlier, missionary period progressed through enslavement and internment to outright slaughter. The native inhabitants of California were not a warring bunch – Hollywood portrayals notwithstanding – but eventually self-defense did prompt them to rise up against the gold rush incursion.

At first, the State of California attempted to make treaties that called for the Native Americans to cede their gold-rich lands and move onto reservations in the Central Valley. Many bands of resisters fled east into more remote parts of the range and then carried out raids on the mining camps. As these raids increased, the state sanctioned the creation of militias, and soon guns settled most land rights issues.

THE MARIPOSA BATTALION

It was in this climate that the prospector James D Savage began mining on the Merced River in an area known since the Spanish explorations as Mariposa. He set up a trading post and took several Miwok and Yokut "wives" whose relatives were working the local placer mines in exchange (they hoped) for the firearms they needed to defend themselves. As the miners' relations with the tribes broke down, a series of clashes culminated in the burning of Savage's store.

Savage formed a militia called the Mariposa Battalion. When Savage learned that the raiding Indians might belong to a holdout group of Sierra Miwok from a valley farther up the Merced, the militia hastened upriver to root them out. On the way, the vigilantes encountered Chief Teneiya, who was returning with some of his people from the Central Valley reservation where they'd been relocated back to the tribe's original home in Yosemite Valley. Teneiya might have believed that he could save his people by complying with the white men, so he agreed to lead the little band back to the reservation. Savage's men continued on to the Valley, where the chief said they would find the home of the rest of the Ahwahneechee.

The Mariposa Battalion entered Yosemite Valley on March 27, 1851. Among them was a young recruit named Lafayette Bunnell, who was especially taken by the scenery and proceeded to name many features, giving the valley the name Yosemity – as he thought that was the name Teneiya had used for it. In all likelihood, Teneiya had spoken of a grizzly bear – *uzumate* in the Miwok language.

The Mariposa Battalion made several forays into the Yosemite region that spring in continuation of their gruesome pursuit, sometimes with Chief Teneiya as a reluctant guide. Bunnell tried to honor the chief by giving his name to a lake, but Teneiya did not understand the convention of naming natural features after famous people. Musical and evocative names like Hetch Hetchy, Kolana, Pohono, Pywiack, Tueeulala, Wapama, and Wawona are all that remain of the Miwok language in Yosemite.

At one point, the militia captured five young braves and held them as hostages. As the captives tried to escape, one was shot – Teneiya's son.

The following winter, Teneiya and some of his people were finally released from the reservation. They returned to Yosemite, and some moved back to live again with the Mono Lake Paiute. But hostilities continued in the following years, and in circumstances that are still a matter of debate, Teneiya was killed in Yosemite Valley, perhaps by Mono Lake Paiute angered over the theft of some horses, perhaps by the Mariposa Battalion.

Early Visitors

Tales of cascading waterfalls and towering stone columns followed the Mariposa Battalion out of Yosemite and soon spread into the public awareness. In 1855 an entrepreneurial Englishman named James M Hutchings made the journey to Yosemite Valley to see if the rumors of stunning natural beauty were true. He brought with him a party of pleasure seekers that included an artist, Thomas A Ayers, who created illustrations for Hutchings' paeans to Yosemite (first published in *Hutchings' Illustrated California Magazine* the following year). The party's enthusiastic reports spurred three other groups to visit in the summer of 1855 – the proto-park received a grand total of 42 visitors that first summer. Among them were several individuals who would help shape the tourist experience for years to come.

Two brothers, Milton and Houston Mann, immediately began building the Wawona Rd, hoping that they'd make a big profit from the tolls they'd collect. However, their monopoly crashed when a Coulterville resident carved out a good (and free) footpath from Coulterville the following summer.

Another summer of '55 visitor, Galen Clark, came back in 1856 to establish a homestead on the Wawona Rd not far from the Mariposa Grove of giant sequoias. At age 42,

Clark suffered from health problems and imagined spending his waning years at Wawona. But the environment seemed to agree with him, and he lived on in the park until his death at the age of 95. From the start, Clark's camp served as a lodge and artists' camp. Clark himself took on the role of Yosemite guardian, a title that became official when the park became public land in 1864; he continued on as guardian until 1896.

Lafayette Bunnell of the Mariposa Battalion came back in 1856 with an entrepreneurial-minded group that put in the valley's first hotel, opened in 1857. Hutchings returned with a similar intention and eventually became a dominant hostelier in the valley while continuing to promote tourism through his publications. Hutchings' target audience was San Francisco's burgeoning upper class, but he also attracted sophisticated world travelers from the East Coast.

As entrepreneurs and homesteaders began to divvy up the real estate of Yosemite Valley, they created a ramshackle assemblage of roads, structures, fences, and trash heaps. They cut down the native forests for building materials and firewood and planted the meadows with gardens and orchards. They brought in horses, cows, and chickens, and started running sheep into the high mountain meadows where the trampling hooves destroyed wildflowers and delicate grasses.

Meanwhile, gold fever was still raging in the foothills, and although the gold-bearing quartz veins of the Mother Lode ran substantially west of Yosemite, a vast amount of lumber and waterpower fed the mining activities. The very people who were profiting from Yosemite's natural beauty were among those developing schemes to sell off the region's natural resources.

Establishing Yosemite

As if by divine intervention, the Reverend Thomas Starr King, a Unitarian minister, arrived to help rescue Yosemite from runaway commercialism. After a visit to Yosemite Valley and the Mariposa Grove in 1860, King wrote a series of letters to the *Boston Evening Transcript* describing his trip. The gifted orator and nature writer was well known to East Coast readers (even more so than Henry Thoreau), and he found a

TERRIBLE TREE-TMENT

Even before tourists discovered Yosemite Valley in 1855, they were flocking to the Calaveras Grove of giant sequoias, northwest of Yosemite along the Stanislaus River. A series of businessmen had the idea that the trees should go on tour, and in 1853 a tree was cut down and shipped to New York City and London. The following year, another giant tree was stripped of its bark, and the bark was sent off with the same itinerary.

Back at the grove, one stump was polished up to serve as a dance floor for the wealthy city folk who were looking for novel entertainment. The revellers could dance into the wee hours and then tumble off to bed in a hotel built on the stump of another downed giant.

Entrepreneurs also bored through living trunks so tourists could tell the folks back home that they had driven their carriage through one of the colossal trees. And just because it was possible to do so, the carriages rumbled along the length of downed trees or through decaying tunnels that occur naturally inside of them.

receptive audience for his thoughts, which melded Civil War–era patriotism with a call for stewardship of the wild landscape.

Shortly after the publication of King's articles, an exhibition that included some of the earliest photographs of Yosemite opened in New York. The mammoth plate and stereographic images by photographer Carleton E Watkins revealed an astonishing untamed wilderness complete with waterfalls and stone monuments. The exhibition turned into a critical success, and Watkins' work also caught the attention of California Senator John Conness, who purchased a set of the stereographic prints and who later played a key role in the preservation of Yosemite.

THE YOSEMITE GRANT

Meanwhile, Frederick Law Olmsted, the visionary landscape architect and designer of New York City's Central Park, brought his ideals to bear on Yosemite – he believed that government should play a role in preserving natural spaces that nourished the human spirit. Olmsted met with a San Francisco businessman named Israel Ward Raymond, who had become deeply concerned about the fate of Yosemite's trees. Raymond then wrote a letter to Senator Conness on February 20, 1864, proposing a bill that would grant Yosemite Valley and the Mariposa Grove to the State of California. Conness presented the bill to Congress, and on June 30, 1864, in the midst of the Civil War, President Abraham Lincoln signed the Yosemite Grant into law. The signing of the grant marked the first time that government had mandated the preservation and protection of a natural area for public use. Yosemite became the first state park in the world, and the foundation of what is now the national park system.

Unfortunately, the Yosemite Grant didn't manage to protect the new park from the greedy rabble. The conservationist language of Raymond's bill was nigh on heresy in the free-for-all of the gold rush and westward expansion. Hutchings and others in the tourist business believed they had a prior claim to the property. Along with small homesteaders and mining claimants in the surrounding region, they kept their concerns alive in the courts for decades to come.

THE WHITNEY SURVEY

Even at the height of the gold rush, there were those who speculated that El Dorado glittered with more than gold – that the mountains (and the entire state) held rich deposits of other minerals. In 1860 the newly appointed California State geologist, Josiah D Whitney, assembled a crew of scientists, surveyors, and cartographers to map out the locations of those resources.

The survey toured Yosemite in the summer of 1863 and the Kings Canyon and Mt Whitney regions the following summer. From these tours come vivid accounts of the Sierra scenery and society, of the naming of lakes, passes, and peaks, and of the scramble for first ascents. William Brewer's entertaining journal *Up and Down California* makes scaling a mountain sound like a Sunday picnic, while Clarence King's *Mountaineering in the Sierra Nevada* takes a considerably more dramatic tone. Both books are near the top of any good Sierra reading list.

THE NEW NATIONAL PARK

In 1889 environmentalist and writer John Muir took Robert Underwood Johnson, the publisher of *Century* magazine, on a camping trip to Tuolumne Meadows. There, by the campfire, the two hammered out a plan to save the larger watersheds of the Tuolumne and Merced Rivers from the sheep and the commercial interests that were pressing in on all sides. The plan drew upon the precedent set by Yellowstone, which was established as the country's first national park in 1872. Muir agreed to write some articles promoting the concept, which were published in *Century* the following summer, while Johnson wielded his considerable influence in Washington.

On October 1, 1890, Congress passed the Yosemite Act of 1890, creating Yosemite National Park, which encompassed the watersheds, though Yosemite Valley and Mariposa Grove remained under state jurisdiction, as had been established in the earlier grant.

Johnson realized that the creation of the national park might not be enough to protect Yosemite from the large and vocal contingent that saw the whole idea of public land as an affront to the Western ethic of free enterprise. He encouraged Muir to organize an advocacy association. This became the Sierra Club, chartered in 1892, with Muir as its first president. (For more on the Sierra Club, see the Discovering Environmentalism section, later.)

ARRIVAL OF THE ARMY

With the establishment of Yosemite as federal land in 1890, the Department of the Interior now had the responsibility of protecting the wilderness from its new owners – the public! The US Army was given the task and was well suited to it, in an era when soldiers routinely rode long distances on horseback through rugged country. Many of the soldiers who served in Yosemite felt that they had been assigned to paradise.

With precious little guidance from Washington and no apparent penalties to back up his efforts, acting superintendent Captain Wood set about guarding the park's resources. He encountered resistance from cattlemen and sheepherders, some of whom owned legal claims to plots within the park, and all of whom were accustomed to free-range grazing. Wood's men spent several summers chasing the herders through the park, using the toothless laws to convince them to herd elsewhere. The sheepherders were intimately acquainted with the Yosemite backcountry, and in pursuing them, the officers and troops rode into the most remote regions of the park.

During the army's tenure, highly skilled trackers blazed most of the current trails through the backcountry, creating maps with far more detail than those made by the Whitney Survey. They planted trout in the streams and lakes, educated visitors about trash disposal, and stood up against poachers and elite hunting parties alike in enforcing the ban on firearms in the park. And these forerunners of the national park rangers began the job that still remains one of the most important in wilderness management – fire education.

In 1906, after intense lobbying by John Muir and the Sierra Club, the State of California ceded Yosemite Valley and the Mariposa Grove to the national park. The Army promptly moved its headquarters from Wawona to Yosemite Valley. There it faced the challenge of bringing the 50-year-old culture of tourism (and nearly 10,000 annual visitors) in line with its then well-honed conservation policies. But the army was not destined to stay. In 1916 the establishment of the National Park Service relieved the Fourth Cavalry of its cherished Yosemite assignment.

Discovering Environmentalism

Tourist hordes have sometimes ridden roughshod over the park, but throughout Yosemite's history certain groups of visitors have ultimately proved essential in the fight to preserve the park's resources. These include visual artists, who have made Yosemite's

JOHN MUIR

Although his contributions and legacy reach far beyond the Sierras, John Muir is practically synonymous with Yosemite. When the Scotsman arrived in San Francisco in the spring of 1868, he set off on foot through the wildflowers of California's Central Valley to see Yosemite. He stayed only a short time, but the following year he returned to begin a monumental experiment in the observation of nature. He wandered, most often alone, into the highest realms of the Yosemite backcountry, taking only an overcoat, dry crusts of bread, and some tea. Though not a scientist by training, Muir looked at the natural world with a keen curiosity, investigating glaciers, trees, earthquakes, bees, and even the most plain-coated of the Sierra birds. His discoveries led him to argue with Josiah Whitney, the head of the California Geological Survey, who disbelieved Muir's contention that glaciers had helped to shape Yosemite's hall of polished granite.

LIBRARY OF CONGRESS

At first, Muir found employment as a sheep-herder in Yosemite, getting to know all too well the habits of the 'hoofed locusts' that were ruining the high country. Then he worked as a caretaker at Hutchings' hotel, disappearing frequently for his long walks into the wilderness. In 1880 he married and moved to Martinez (near San Francisco), but his association with the Sierra Nevada was undiminished by distance. From his prolific and florid writings on nature, one might see him as a poet among naturalists, but over time, his pen turned increasingly toward the political aims of the growing conservationist movement.

Muir's articles and lobbying efforts were the foundation of the campaign that established Yosemite as a national park in 1890. But despite his success with Yosemite National Park and his accomplishments with the Sierra Club, Muir was unable to save Hetch Hetchy Valley, which he believed rivalled Yosemite Valley in beauty and grandeur. He lost the battle in 1913, when Hetch Hetchy Valley was sacrificed to the water and power needs of a growing San Francisco. Despondent and outraged, Muir likened the damming of Hetch Hetchy to the desecration of a holy temple. He died in 1914, before the dreaded building of the O'Shaughnessy Dam in 1923 and the subsequent flooding of Hetch Hetchy Valley.

LET EVERYONE HELP TO SAVE THE FAMOUS HETCH-HETCHY VALLEY
AND
STOP THE COMMERCIAL DESTRUCTION WHICH THREATENS OUR NATIONAL PARKS

To the American Public:

The famous Hetch-Hetchy Valley, next to Yosemite the most wonderful and important feature of our Yosemite National Park, is again in danger of being destroyed. Year after year attacks have been made on this Park under the guise of development of natural resources. At the last regular session of Congress the most determined attack of all was made by the City of San Francisco to get possession of the Hetch-Hetchy Valley as a reservoir site, thus defrauding ninety millions of people for the sake of saving San Francisco dollars.

As soon as this scheme became manifest, public-spirited citizens all over the country poured a storm of protest on Congress. Before the session was over, the Park invaders saw that they were defeated and permitted the bill to die without bringing it to a vote, so as to be able to try again.

The bill has been re-introduced and will be urged at the coming session of Congress, which convenes in December. Let all those who believe that our great national wonderlands should be preserved unmarred as places of rest and recreation for the use of all the people, now enter their protests. Ask Congress to reject this destructive bill, and also urge that the present Park laws be so amended as to put an end to all such assaults on our system of National Parks.

Faithfully yours,

John Muir

November, 1909.

Read carefully pp. 20-21 and help to save the Park

LIBRARY OF CONGRESS

beauty accessible to politicians and others who have never set foot in the park, and outdoor adventurers, whose hands-on enjoyment of nature compelled them to try to save the Sierra from desecration.

SIERRA CLUB EXPLORERS

Since the advent of the Sierra Club in the 1890s, its members have sought to enjoy and preserve the wonders of the park – but ideas about how to do that have changed a lot since 1901, when William E Colby initiated the Sierra Club outings. The two- to four-week affairs, many in the Yosemite high country, were not exactly low-impact adventures (and the club would no doubt frown on them today). During outings, club members explored Yosemite en masse, while mule trains brought along elaborate camping gear, including tents, chairs, and a commissary to provide meals. Adventurers could scale mountains by day and listen to live classical music or distinguished lectures on nature and conservation issues by night.

There were many notable mountaineers among the club's charter members, the most famous of which was John Muir. Right behind were the LeContes. In 1870 Joseph LeConte, a University of California geology professor, was invited by some of his students to lead an extensive camping trip in Yosemite. Dubbed the "University Excursion Party," the group explored Yosemite Valley, climbed east to Tenaya Lake and Tuolumne Meadows, scaled Mt Dana, investigated some glaciers (in the company of John Muir), crossed the Sierra Crest, and descended to Mono Lake, where they roamed over the volcanic terrain.

In the 40 years that followed, LeConte's son, Joseph N, made many equally epic journeys. His 1889 expedition included the scaling of three of Yosemite's highest peaks: Mt Dana, Mt Hoffmann, and Mt Lyell. His journals and photographs from later expeditions revealed some of the most forbidding terrain of the High Sierra to the outside world.

Another notable character among the Sierra Club charter members, Theodore S Solomons came up with the idea of a route along the Sierra Crest from Yosemite Valley to Mt Whitney. This route, now known as the John Muir Trail, officially opened in 1916.

Norman Clyde also looms large in Sierra mountaineering history, both for the extensive terrain he covered and for his stamina and long career. Clyde's pack itself was legendary – cast iron skillet, fishing gear, a library of classic literature (in original languages), an axe, a firearm, extra boots, and several cameras. But even more memorable were his first ascents (over 200) and his role in rescues of lost and injured hikers. "The pack that walks like a man" as David Brower described Clyde, continued his Sierra ramblings up until 1970, when he was 85 years old.

After Clyde and others of his generation bagged all remaining first ascents in the Sierra, some Sierra Club members turned their attention to other frontiers, such as writing and conservation. Francis P Farquhar, a contemporary of Clyde's (with six first ascents under his own belt) and a longtime Sierra Club president, wrote the delightful and definitive *History of the Sierra Nevada* (1965), indispensable in the preparation of this brief account.

Farquhar's most potent successor as Sierra Club president was the tireless activist David Brower. Called "the Sierra Club's preeminent fang" by writer John McPhee, Brower began steering away from the club's charter directives as early as the 1930s by advocating low- (or no-) impact use of the wilderness. Although he was notoriously contentious, the club fell into line behind him as he waged his most memorable wars against the political lobbies that were pressing for more dams. After finally leaving the Sierra Club, he founded several powerful environmental protection organizations, including the Earth Island Institute, which he ran until his death in 2000.

YOSEMITE'S ARTISTS

While they might not call themselves environmental advocates, artists have often accomplished political ends by bringing the fragile spirit of the wilderness to the public's awareness. The artists who came to Yosemite with the first generation of tourists revealed a landscape of extraordinary beauty, even as the miners were tearing it apart in their lust to profit. From Thomas Ayres's illustrations to Carleton Watkins's photographs, their work played a crucial role in the bid to establish Yosemite as a national park.

In the mid-19th century, the Hudson River School and related movements in American art strived to capture the face of God in the wild magnificence of nature. A parallel trend in literature expressed a distinctly American spiritualism tied to the wilderness; some of the writers who explored such transcendental themes included Ralph Waldo Emerson, Walt Whitman, Emily Dickinson, and Henry David Thoreau. Into this intellectual moment, which flourished on the East Coast, came the first paintings of Yosemite by a recognized artist, Albert Bierstadt, in 1863.

At that time, San Francisco was becoming the epicenter for a distinctly Californian school of art. Inspired by the vistas that Bierstadt and the photographers were capturing in Yosemite, many other artists embraced the Sierra as a subject matter. Mountain landscapes by Charles Nahl, Thomas Hill, and William Keith soon adorned Victorian mansions in San Francisco and Sacramento, and painters became a regular fixture in the haunts of John Muir, who occasionally led groups of them on sketching expeditions into remote locations. Hill set up a studio at Wawona in 1884, beginning the tradition of resident artists and galleries in the park.

While the painters were often content to set up their easels in the meadows, the photographers became known for seeking out more inaccessible regions, even though, in the early years, they had to haul unwieldy equipment. It is perhaps no coincidence that many of Yosemite's photographers have also been capable mountaineers. As the recently departed photographer Galen Rowell said, Yosemite photography tends to be "a continuing pursuit in which the art becomes the adventure, and vice versa." Rowell followed in the

ANSEL ADAMS (1902–1984)

The best known of the photographer-mountaineers, Ansel Adams developed a level of craft not seen in the work of his predecessors. An early proponent of the idea that photography could adhere to the same aesthetic principles used by fine artists, he also became a strong advocate for the preservation of the wilderness, working on the frontlines of the growing conservation movement.

A San Francisco native, Adams first visited Yosemite with his family in 1916. He started his career as a pianist, but by mid-century he had discovered photography, centering his prolific and influential work in the Sierra. In 1929, he married Virginia Best, whose father's gallery in Yosemite Valley was the precursor to the Ansel Adams Gallery, found today in Yosemite Village.

In 1940, Adams held a photography workshop at the gallery with fellow photographer Edward Weston. This workshop began a tradition of photography education that continues to this day. Adams served on the board of the Sierra Club for several years and joined David Brower in educating wilderness trekkers in the ethic of low-impact wilderness travel.

footsteps of Sierra Club photographer-mountaineers LeConte and Clyde, and his mentor, the great Ansel Adams, but he also carried his camera while pioneering new routes up the faces of Half Dome and El Capitan. One of Rowell's lesser-known contemporaries is Howard Weamer, a ski-mountaineer who photographs the gorgeous face of the snow-covered high country while tending the ski trekkers' hut at Ostrander Lake each winter.

Tourism Evolves

The Yosemite tourists of the 19th century were a genteel yet hardy lot, considering the rigors of travel by mule or by carriage and the large and cumbersome bundles and trunks that accompanied any expedition into the park. They came stylishly dressed in waistcoats and long ruffled dresses, but in the earliest years they often had to make do with primitive hotel rooms where the walls might be nothing more than bed sheets.

Hotels came and went in the Valley's early years, changing names frequently as they changed hands. At one point near the end of the century there were nine hotels in operation, spread out through the Valley. Hastily erected of wood and canvas to house the ever-increasing hoards of tourists, many of the early hotels met their demise when sparks escaped from stoves, or when lanterns got too close to curtains.

Some visitors found "camping" to be a pleasant alternative – especially given the typically large and well-equipped tents that were common in the era. In 1899, when a night in the popular Sentinel Hotel cost $4, David and Jennie Curry established a camp with seven tents at the base of Glacier Point. At Camp Curry, for a mere $2 a day, campers were provided with a comfortable bed in a tent, bath and restroom facilities, and meals. The camp became immensely popular as families discovered that camping, Curry-style, made for an affordable summer vacation. What's more, Camp Curry offered an evening program of music, stunts, educational talks, and the nightly Firefall.

CARS & CROWDS

The first automobile came bumping and sputtering into Yosemite Valley in the summer of 1900. The dust had settled by the time two of its kin arrived two years later, but the cars were deemed to be unsuited to the park, and regulations were promptly issued against more of the same.

The new Yosemite Valley Railroad received a far more enthusiastic greeting when it chugged up to the park border five years later. Starting from the town of Merced, the rail line ran along the north bank of the Merced River. At El Portal, a stagecoach met park visitors for the steep climb up to the Valley. The railroad might have remained a vital part of Yosemite-area transportation, but a devastating flood in 1937 washed out the tracks. The railroad reopened the next year, but by then automobiles had become the most popular means of transportation into the park. Railroad service finally stopped for good in 1945.

Resurrection of the railroad remains a very popular but politically difficult idea. If it comes to pass, the tracks will be relaid along the old rail bed that can still be seen from across the river while driving on Hwy 140.

When the automobile ban was finally lifted in 1913, annual park visitation exceeded 12,000. Three years later, a serviceable dirt road opened through Tioga Pass, and the annual visitation figure spiked to more than 30,000. By 1922 it had surpassed 100,000, and by 1929 cars and campers had become even more of a menace to the meadows than John Muir's "hoofed locusts." In an effort to control the free-ranging automobiles, the

NPS PHOTOGRAPHS

park service dug ditches where the metallic beasts would get mired if they tried to drive off the road into the meadows.

GROWTH SPURTS & GROWING PAINS

In the early 1920s the National Park Service was just beginning to develop the concept of educating the park visitor. Ansel F Hall, the National Park Service's first naturalist, organized the Yosemite Museum Foundation to raise funds for the new Yosemite Museum. The museum opened in 1926, the same year as the new "All-Year Highway" (Hwy 140).

A year later Yosemite Valley culture got a good deal fancier when the luxurious Ahwahnee Hotel opened. A campground beside the new hotel was expunged so that the

THE FIREFALL

It sounds horrific to those schooled in the "leave no trace" wilderness ethic, but countless Valley campers still testify to the beauty and excitement of the Firefall. During its 88-year tradition, the Firefall was regarded as a sublime moment in the enchantment of a summer's evening. Even the echoing signal call to Glacier Point from the Camp Curry campfire, "Let the fire fall!" became a spine-tingling element of the tradition.

The Firefall originated around 1872, when a hotel was being built at the top of James McCauley's new 4-mile toll trail to Glacier Point. Perhaps as an advertisement for his enterprise, McCauley pushed his campfire off the cliff, creating a glowing waterfall of sparks that was so appealing the tourists in Yosemite Valley called on McCauley to repeat it. His sons made the Firefall into a family business, collecting $1.50 from each person who wanted to see it happen. When they found enough takers, a fire builder went up the trail to build a large fire of fir bark and push it off the cliff just after nightfall.

The McCauleys left Yosemite in 1897, but two years later David Curry reintroduced the Firefall as a way to draw business to his newly created Camp Curry. Apart from two brief hiatuses, one in 1913 and the other during WWII, the Firefall continued to hold a place in Yosemite evening activities until the National Park Service called a halt to it in 1968.

BEAR FEEDINGS

To this day, there is hardly a Yosemite visitor who does not consider a bear sighting to be part of the requisite experience. In the early years, bears and many other animals were valued as food and for their warm pelts. The ferocious grizzly was hunted to statewide extinction, but after hunting was banned in the park, the population of the peaceable black bear swelled.

But the garbage generated by tourists created a new and ill-adapted caste of bear. In the early 20th century, the park dumped its garbage onto theatrically lit bear-feeding platforms for the entertainment of Valley tourists, who came each night to photograph the bears as they consumed the inappropriate rations. The practice came to an end in the early 1940s, but by then the camp bears had become highly dependent on the easy pickings and went on to perfect their skills at raiding campgrounds and breaking into locked automobiles. The recent reeducation of visitors is beginning to pay off, and bears are once again becoming wary of human contact.

NPS PHOTOGRAPHS

well-heeled guests would not have to encounter grungy campers as they strolled out from the fashionable yet rustic stone fortress. But the Ahwahnee's wealthy guests were happy enough to embrace artists, especially the congenial Ansel Adams who organized the first Bracebridge Dinner in the Ahwahnee's spectacular dining hall. Adams wrote the script and even performed in the now annual Christmas pageant based on a sketch by Washington Irving.

Quite a different crowd took over the Ahwahnee during WWII, when the hotel became a naval hospital and the military covered the hotel grounds with hastily erected structures like a pool hall, bowling alley, two-cell jail, and a club for the enlisted men. Meanwhile, the army set up camps at Wawona and Badger Pass, and the California National Guard was stationed at Hetch Hetchy, under orders to protect the water supply.

Approximately 90,000 troops trained in Yosemite Valley during the war, while public visitation dropped significantly, to 40,000 in 1945.

The American art of the summer vacation blossomed after the war years, and campers rolled into the Valley in record numbers. Even the backcountry began to see crowds as the San Francisco Beat culture discovered backpacking. By the 1970s the Valley had become a dangerous place in summer, with frequent thefts, occasional murders, and clashes between hippies and park rangers, whom the hippies saw as authority figures in green uniforms. To manage the spiking visitation problems in the early '70s, the park service introduced one-way road patterns and free shuttle bus service, as well as a quota system for backcountry use.

Yosemite Today

In 1980, when annual park visitation neared 2,500,000, the Valley infrastructure included more than 1000 buildings – stores, homes, garages, apartments, lodging, and restaurants. The Valley floor was laced with approximately 30 miles of roadway used by more than 1,000,000 cars, trucks, and buses each year. With visitation projected to increase, the National Park Service decided to draw up its first General Management Plan.

The plan outlined goals aimed at preserving "the essence of wilderness" so that visitors could "step into Yosemite and find nature uncluttered by piecemeal stumbling blocks of commercialism, machines, and fragments of suburbia." It called for a reduction in traffic congestion through restrictions on private cars and an increase in public transportation. The ultimate goal – to prohibit all private vehicles from the Valley – became a point of considerable controversy.

In its effort to allow the natural processes of the park's ecosystems to prevail, the plan proposed the relocation of many commercial services outside the park and outlined numerous changes in the campgrounds, specifically where they have an impact on the river plain. To address overcrowding, the plan established visitor-use levels for different sights.

As the National Park Service tried to move forward, the agency had to make numerous changes to the plan, partly because of negative public response. By 1992 the plan got two amendments: a Concession Services Management Plan and a Final Environmental Impact Statement; these modified the recommendations regarding the number and mix of accommodations.

The flood of January 1997 brought a host of new concerns and greatly influenced the thinking about all development in the river's floodplain. The plan went into another stage of revision, and the resulting Yosemite Valley Plan was adopted on December 29, 2000. The new plan calls for restoration, protection, and enhancement of natural processes and cultural resources, a reduction in harmful environmental impacts (including those related to traffic congestion), and continued emphasis on creating effective park operations and high-quality visitor experiences.

Implementation of the plan continues to lag for several reasons. The park service must continue to study and understand the resources – both natural and cultural (eg, archeological sites) – and debate continues over the relative values of those resources, as well as over ideal visitor-use patterns.

Meanwhile, although the number of annual visitors has declined from its 4.2 million peak in 1996, people are still coming in droves. Plans for the future of the park must balance the needs of these visitors with the preservation of the natural beauty that draws them to Yosemite in the first place.

*Geologists call the Sierra Nevada a **tilted fault block** range – and it's a particularly impressive example at that, running more than 400 miles long and 40 to 60 miles wide, with 500 peaks over 10,000ft. Picture a tilted fault block as an iceberg listing to one side while floating in an ocean of earth crust. The iceberg itself is an immense body of granite known as a batholith (meaning "deep rock") that formed deep within the crust, then "floated" up and became exposed over millions of years. In fact, today we see only the tip of this batholith, and even that is obscured where older rocks (mostly metamorphic) still cling, like pieces of a torn mantle, or where newer rocks (mostly volcanic) have been added on top, like icing.*

YOSEMITE GEOLOGY

The Lay of the Land over Time

Around 225 million years ago, the area that is now the Sierra Nevada was a shallow sea lying off the coast of a young North American continent. Material from offshore island volcanoes, plus debris eroding from the continental landmass, was gradually filling this sea with layers of sediment at the same time the North American (continental) plate started drifting westward and riding over the leading edge of the Pacific (ocean) plate. This movement forced the edge of the Pacific plate down to depths where it melted into magma that later cooled to form the Sierra Nevada batholith. Today's Sierra Nevada and Cascade mountain chains mark the edge of this submerged, melting plate. The force of two plates colliding and crushing together also generated such enormous heat and

SHAKY GROUND

Uplift of the Sierra's batholith continues to occur along its eastern face, where a zone of recent geologic activity keeps life exciting for folks living between Mammoth Lakes and Lone Pine. In 1872 the eastern Sierra jerked upward 13ft in a single earthquake, and on a more incremental scale the Sierra crest is estimated to lift as much as 1.5 inches per century. The result of this skewed tilting is that the eastern face of the Sierra is now an abrupt wall rising up to 11,000ft high while the western face is a long gentle incline.

As uplift proceeds along the eastern face, rivers flowing down the west slope have picked up speed and cut progressively deeper canyons into the formerly flat, rolling landscape. Today, a total of 17 major river canyons mark the west slope and the rock that formerly filled those canyons now buries the Central Valley under 9.5 miles of sediment.

pressure that old sedimentary and volcanic rocks turned into the metamorphic rocks now found throughout the Sierra Nevada.

As it pushed over the Pacific plate, the North American plate buckled so strongly that it formed a proto–Sierra Nevada of folded rock that may have reached as high as 15,000ft. This building phase ceased about 130 million years ago, and the old mountains began a long erosional phase that reduced them to gently rolling uplands by 50 million years ago, leaving the then-flat batholith exposed on the earth's surface except for pockets of rock that remained from the old mountain range.

The Sierra Nevada batholith had formed from more than a hundred episodes of magma generation between 80 and 210 million years ago. Each magma event formed a discrete body of granitic rock known as a pluton (from Pluto, the Roman god of the underworld), each with a characteristic composition and appearance. Hikers can today trace these well-mapped plutons by examining the mix of minerals and the size of crystals within the rock matrix (see *Geologic Map of Yosemite National Park and Vicinity, California* by N King Huber).

Ten million years ago, the granite batholith began to lift and tilt or bulge upward between parallel sets of faults (cracks in the earth's crust). This led to increased erosion of old rocks, which were uplifted on the newly forming crest. Remnants of old rocks perched on top of granite ridges are called *roof pendants,* of which Mt Dana and the Ritter Range are fine examples. The batholith has continued to lift, reaching its current height an estimated two million years ago; since then, the counterbalancing forces of uplift and erosion have created an equilibrium that keeps the Sierra at more or less the same size.

From two million years ago until about 10,000 years ago, Ice Age glaciers covered portions of the Sierra Nevada in snow and ice. This glacial activity occurred in episodes of growing and retreating ice, much like waves on a beach, and the actual chronology and extent of the ice coverage are not completely known. The largest icefield, however, was a giant cap of ice that covered an area 275 miles long and 40 miles wide between Lake Tahoe and Yosemite. From high-elevation icefields, rivers of ice (glaciers) flowed down and scoured out rugged river canyons, simply enlarging some or beautifully sculpting others like Yosemite Valley.

After the Ice Age came a warm period when there were no glaciers in the Sierra, but about 99 glaciers and 398 glacierets (small glaciers or pockets of ice) have re-formed within the last 1000 years, during what's called the Little Ice Age. The largest are on Mt Lyell and Mt Maclure in the Yosemite region, and on the Palisades farther south.

The Geologic Story of Yosemite National Park by N King Huber captures the fascinating drama of Yosemite's landscape, while *Geology of the Sierra Nevada* by Mary Hill tells the larger story of the Sierra Nevada.

The Forces at Work

The fascinating tale of how Yosemite's rocks first formed is only the beginning of the geologic story – as soon as the rocks were exposed on the earth's surface, a host of new forces shaped them into what you see before you today. Hugely powerful Ice Age glaciers played the most dramatic role of all in the Yosemite region, but erosion and weathering have also done their part, as have lava and ash eruptions.

WHAT THE GLACIERS LEFT BEHIND

As a glacier flows downhill under its weight of ice and snow, it creates a distinctive collection of landforms, many of which remain once the ice has retreated or vanished. Yosemite National Park provides one of the clearest and most dramatic examples of glacial action.

The most obvious landform is the U-shaped valley (1) (Yosemite Valley is a classic), gouged out by the glacier as it moves downhill, often with one or more bowl-shaped cirques at its head. Cirques are found along high mountain ridges or at mountain passes called cols. From the summit of Mt. Hoffmann, you can look down the north face into a dramatic cirque and cirque lake.

Where an alpine glacier – which flows off the upper slopes and ridges of a mountain range – has joined a deeper, more substantial valley glacier, a dramatic hanging valley is often the result. In Yosemite, Bridalveil Fall (2) and Yosemite Falls (3) flow over the edges of hanging valleys. Hanging valleys and cirques commonly shelter hidden alpine lakes or tarns, such as those featured in so many hikes in this book.

The thin ridge that separates adjacent glacial valleys is known as an arête; the Ritter Range is an example. Where a glacier flows over a knob of bedrock it leaves a roche moutonnée or sheepback, elongated in the direction of the ice flow. Head to Lembert Dome in Tuolumne Meadows to see this glacial formation.

As a glacier grinds its way forward, it usually leaves long lateral moraine ridges along its course – mounds of debris either deposited along the flanks of the glacier or left by sub-ice streams within its heart (in the latter case, the debris mound is called an esker). At the end, or snout, of a glacier is the terminal moraine, the point where the giant conveyor belt of ice drops its load of rock and grit. Both high up in the hanging valleys and in the surrounding valleys and plains, moraine lakes may form behind a dam of glacial rubble. Yosemite Valley was once filled by such a lake.

GLACIERS

Most of the Sierra Nevada's landscape has been substantially shaped by glaciers. In fact, of all the forces that have contributed to the landscape of the Yosemite region, none have had greater impact than the relentless grinding caused by millions of tons of ice over two million years. Evidence of grinding is often right at your feet in areas where glaciers have worn granite surfaces down to a smooth, shiny finish. Along the road at Tenaya Lake, for example, flat granite shelves are so polished they glisten in the early morning light. In contrast, hikers to high alpine nunataks (peaks and plateaus that were too high to be glaciated) such as Mt Conness find rough-textured, sharp-edged, and jagged granite formations.

Glaciers arise in regions where snowfields fail to melt completely by summer's end. Over time, delicate snow crystals dissolve into tiny spheres that connect and fuse into solid ice. True glacial ice forms after hundreds of years, with the original snowflakes becoming nine times heavier and 500 times stronger in the process. These icefields develop in high mountain valleys where snowdrifts readily accumulate, and from there they flow downhill at the rate of inches or yards per day. The longest known glacier in the Sierra Nevada was a 60-mile tongue that flowed down the Tuolumne River Canyon about 20,000 years ago. In some valleys, the Sierra icefield reached up to 4000ft thick.

Hundreds or thousands of feet of ice created an unbelievable amount of pressure and shearing strength that completely altered the landscape. Massive boulders were easily plucked up and dragged along like giant rasping teeth on a file's edge. Smaller rocks and sand carried along the glacier's bottom acted like sandpaper that polished underlying bedrock. Every rock that was loose or could be pried loose was caught up and transported for miles.

Glaciers have the funny effect of rounding out landscape features that lie below the ice while sharpening features that rise above the ice. The same grinding force that smooths out valleys also quarries rocks from the base of peaks, resulting in undercutting that forms towering spikes. In Tuolumne Meadows, this effect is particularly dramatic – compare the smooth domes on the valley floor, like Lembert and Pothole, with the sheer spires of Cathedral and Unicorn Peaks.

ROCK ACTIVITY

The Sierra's granite owes its appearance not only to the tremendous sculpting power of glaciers but also to something far more subtle – its own internal properties. Granite tends to crack and separate along regular planes, often parallel to the surface. Everywhere you travel in Yosemite, you'll find evidence of this process at work.

At Olmsted Point along the Tioga Pass Rd, visitors can see a surrealistic view of vast granite walls peeling off like onion layers below Clouds Rest. This exfoliation is the result of massive rock formations expanding and cracking in shell-like layers as the pressure of overlying materials erodes away. Over time, sharp angles and corners give way to increasingly rounded curves that leave us with distinctive landmarks like Half Dome.

Weathering breaks granite down through a different process than glacial erosion or internal cracking, yet its effects are equally profound. Joints in the granite allow water to seep into deep cracks, where the liquid expands during winter's freezing temperatures. This pushes open cracks with pressures up to a thousand pounds per square inch and allows even more water to penetrate until eventually square-angled boulders break off from the parent formation. Edges and corners are further weathered over time to create rounded boulders. Finally, rain and exposure wear down granite's weaker biotite component, leaving an unstable matrix of pale minerals (quartz and feldspar) that crumble into fine-grained rubble called grus. Hikers walking on granite slabs might experience the unnerving sensation of slipping on tiny pebbles that roll like ball bearings – this is grus at an early stage. Grus later gathers underfoot along trails and basins, where it breaks down into soil in the presence of water.

In the western Sierra Nevada, granites are mostly fine-grained, with joints spaced fairly widely. As a result, rock formations tend to be massive structures shaped by exfoliation. In the eastern Sierra Nevada, granites are more likely to be coarse-grained and to have closely spaced joints. Here the process of water seeping into cracks and pushing rocks apart (called frost riving) results in characteristically jagged, sawtooth ridges such as those that form the Cathedral Range near Tuolumne Meadows.

Rocks: A Primer

The Sierra Nevada is one of the world's premier granite landscapes, yet the range includes more than just granite. To make things simple, we can divide the region's rocks into three main categories: prebatholithic, batholithic, and postbatholithic, which in this book correspond to metamorphic, granitic, and volcanic rocks.

Metamorphic rocks are older volcanic and sedimentary rocks whose structure has been dramatically altered by intense heat and pressure deep within the earth's crust. In the Yosemite region, these rocks predate the Sierra Nevada batholith. Fine examples of metamorphic rocks line Tioga Pass Rd between Tioga and Ellery Lakes, where seafloor sediments 500 million years old have been pushed up by the rising batholith and are now cast along the Sierra crest. These reddish, purplish, or greenish rocks are a distinctive change from the speckled grays of granite just to the west.

Granite is the popular label for a broad category of rocks that form when molten magma cools within the earth's crust (this same molten rock is called lava when it erupts or flows onto the earth's surface). Sierra Nevada granite actually consists of five separate minerals occurring in complex combinations that produce a characteristic salt-and-pepper appearance. With practice, hikers can learn to recognize these five minerals: quartz, which is a clear gray color; potassium feldspar and plagioclase feldspar, both clear gray when freshly exposed but chalky white after weathering; biotite, which consists of blackish hexagonal crystals that flake off in thin plates; and hornblende, which occurs in long, rod-shaped crystals of a dark green hue. Easily, the most striking set of granite examples can be found in Yosemite Valley itself.

Sierra Nevada granite actually consists of five separate minerals occurring in complex combinations that produce a characteristic salt-and-pepper appearance.

Chemically identical to other rocks that form deep within the crust, **volcanic rocks** change as they erupt on the surface as lava; this process injects gases into the liquid rock, giving it a pock-marked or bubbled appearance when it hardens, and it forces the rock to cool quickly. Rocks that have cooled deep underground (such as granite) do so very slowly, which leads to the formation of large, visible crystals; liquid rock exposed to air cools so quickly that crystals aren't able to form. Most of the Sierra's volcanic rocks have weathered away except for high, uplifted pockets. But it's still easy to see an example of volcanism in Yosemite: the Little Devils Postpile, along the Glen Aulin Trail west of Tuolumne Meadows, is a block of hard basalt that plugged a volcanic vent nine million years ago.

VOLCANOES

Between five and 20 million years ago, a series of lava and mud flows covered about 12,000 square miles of the Sierra Nevada north of Yosemite, with some volcanic activity extending south to the area now enclosed by the park. While much of this history has since eroded away, caps of old volcanic material still exist at Sonora Pass, an otherworldly landscape of eroding volcanic debris easily explored on several short hikes. Perhaps the most dramatic volcanic feature is the Dardanelles Cones, a resistant volcanic plug that towers like a foreboding castle over Hwy 108.

About three million years ago, the zone of volcanic activity shifted from the region north of Yosemite to the slopes east of the Sierra crest. Massive eruptions between Mammoth Lakes and Mono Lake created a series of calderas and volcanic mountains, including Mammoth Mountain itself. Mono Lake gained two islands and a small chain of hills on its south side during this period of activity, which is still ongoing; the landscape at Mono Lake has undergone dramatic volcanic changes as recently as 640 years ago.

The most familiar and popular landmark to form in the "current" era of volcanic activity is Devils Postpile, located west of Mammoth Lakes. Here a 600ft- to 700ft-deep lava flow filled a river canyon about 600,000 years ago, cooling so quickly that it formed one of the world's most spectacular examples of columnar basalt. The four-, five-, six-, and seven-sided columns are virtually perfect in their symmetry, evoking awe in all who view the formation.

The rawness and newness of these volcanic formations remind us how active and ongoing is the Sierra Nevada's evolution. Visitors only have to consider that Ice Age glaciers retreated a mere 10,000 years, not even enough time for soil to develop in most places. This is a remarkably young range, still jagged and sharp, still rising, still shaking!

Caps of old volcanic material still exist at Sonora Pass, an otherworldly landscape of eroding volcanic debris.

YOSEMITE NATIONAL PARK ASSOCIATION

The Sierra Nevada is a 400-mile-long, 14,000ft high monolith that dominates and protects California. And in one way or another the state owes much of its astonishing biological diversity to this lofty mountain range. Half of the state's 7000 plant species grow in the Sierra Nevada, while more than 400 animal species find permanent or temporary homes here.

THE GREATER
YOSEMITE ECOSYSTEM

A mountain range on the scale of the Sierra Nevada affects the natural world in a number of important ways. When the range reached its current height two million years ago, it created a towering wall that captures most of the cloud-borne water crossing eastward over California – dousing the west slope in water while shutting off the supply of precipitation to the east slope and the entire Great Basin desert farther east. But surprisingly, the wall also protects California from bitter winter storms blowing *west* out of the interior United States. Anyone visiting or living in California will appreciate the pleasant climate created by the Sierra Nevada – and humans aren't the only life-forms that have found refuge here. Relict plant species (the last of an otherwise extinct line) have managed to survive in the sliver of California that lies west of the Sierra Nevada, adding to California's incredible plant diversity.

To learn more about this rich realm of plants, animals, and habitats, pick up the fascinating books *Sierra Nevada Natural History* by Tracy Storer and Robert Usinger, *A Sierra Club Naturalist's Guide to the Sierra Nevada* by Stephen Whitney, and *Sierra Nevada: The Naturalists Companion* by Verna Johnston.

Life Zones

With nearly 14,000ft of elevational gradient along a gentle, well-watered west slope, and 11,000ft along a sheer, arid east slope, the Sierra Nevada encompasses a range of habitats virtually unrivaled in the world. It's not too hard to tell these habitats apart – they appear as distinctive bands of vegetation (plant communities) that you'll cross while traveling upslope over the Sierra Nevada. Each upward climb of a thousand feet is roughly equivalent to traveling north 300 miles, with corresponding changes in temperature, solar exposure, moisture and other environmental factors, which yields a different array of plants and animals the higher you go.

Biologically speaking, the Sierra Nevada begins where Central Valley grasslands give way to oak woodlands. This oak-dominated **foothill zone** ranges from 1500ft to 3000ft and features a classic Mediterranean climate of hot, dry summers and cool, moist winters. Here the basic unit of energy is the humble acorn, a rich source of proteins and carbohydrates that fuels an ecosystem comprised of animals large and small, ranging from tiny wasps to mice, woodpeckers, and mule deer. Dense thickets of shrubs known as chaparral sprawl along rugged canyon walls and rocky ridges at lower elevations, sometimes replacing or dominating the oak woodlands.

One big change you might notice as you ascend into the **mixed conifer zone**, from 3000ft to 6000ft, is the presence of moist, well-developed soils. Also, acorns largely give way to conifer seeds as the primary food source. The long growing season in this zone supports the highest diversity of species found in the Yosemite region. Summers are not so brutally hot as in the foothills, and a mix of tall, shading conifers and large oaks further cools the landscape down. Yosemite Valley is a particularly beautiful example of mixed conifer forest, with huge old conifers and oaks widely spaced around lush meadows.

In the **montane zone**, from 6000ft to 7500ft, winter snowpacks linger late in the season and result in short, cool summers. These conditions limit the number of species but still allow conifers to reach massive proportions. Look for red firs in cool, stately forests – a characteristic sight in the montane region.

In the **subalpine zone**, which runs from 7500ft to the timberline, hikers break out of the woods and find sweeping vistas of granite expanses speckled with twisted old trees and scattered pockets of forest. While powerful winds, bitter cold temperatures, and snow depths up to 18ft limit the development of trees, for a brief period in July and August this zone erupts in stupendous wildflower displays.

Only the hardiest hikers and backpackers ascend into the **alpine zone**. Lying mostly above 10,000ft and enjoying only a short, frost-free period, this zone supports arctic tundra rather than trees. Remarkably, 305 species of plants find home in this most extreme habitat, and nearly all of these produce colorful flowers.

Life Through the Seasons

Spring begins by February in the low foothills (but as late as July on alpine peaks of the Sierra Crest) with the first pushing of buds. Long before other songbirds arrive,

kinglets and vireos begin singing, while Anna's hummingbirds and great horned owls are already nesting. By March a combination of lingering rains and warming days set fields of brilliant green grasses on fire with constellations of colorful flowers.

In the mixed conifer zone, a significant change occurs in early April, when black oaks start unfurling their tender, pinkish leaves. This crop is immediately set upon by swarms of oak moths, whose caterpillars provide food for waves of migrating songbirds. Almost overnight the land comes alive with pungent wildflowers and humming bees, and birdsong fills the air. In Yosemite Valley, the beauty of this month is accentuated by the torrent of swollen waterfalls on all sides.

From the foothills to the upper mixed conifer zone, plant and animal activity peaks in April, May, and early June. In July and early August, the show retreats upslope into the subalpine and alpine zones, where wet meadows dazzle with wildflowers and the excited rush of hummingbirds. A number of low-elevation species move upslope to follow "spring," and August can be a particularly busy time, as warblers and songbirds with new youngsters fly up from the foothills and swarm around high mountain meadows.

September and early October are very pleasant months in the Sierra Nevada – a time of cooling temperatures, changing leaves, and few mosquitoes. Mammals of all stripes vigorously feed on dwindling crops of nuts, berries, and fruits before the cold sets in. After the first rains (or snows) in late October, the scene quiets down for a couple months, although a subset of animals remain active throughout the winter, including a handful of small, hardy birds like chickadees.

Animals Great & Small

Yosemite's rich wildlife ranges from lumbering bears and soaring birds to scampering lizards and fleeting butterflies, all scattered across a vast and wild region. In only a few places do animals congregate in large or conspicuous numbers. But if you can manage to be patient and alert, these virtues might indeed be rewarded with lifelong memories.

Birdwatchers, however, won't have to wait long – the Sierra Nevada boasts more than 300 species of feathered residents or visitors and hosts one of North America's great birding events, the arrival of nearly two million eared grebes at Mono Lake in late summer. Birdwatchers also can rely on the advice of two superb books: *Birds of Yosemite and the East Slope* by David Gaines and *Discovering Sierra Birds* by Edward Beedy and Stephen Granholm.

LIBRARY OF CONGRESS

Mammal enthusiasts will need *Discovering Sierra Mammals* by Russell Grater, while those favoring smaller critters can turn to *Discovering Sierra Reptiles and Amphibians* by Harold Basey. There are currently no guides to Sierra fish or insects.

LARGE MAMMALS

You'll probably see plenty of languid coyotes and deer in Yosemite Valley, but if you're hoping to spy any other large mammals in the park or its surrounding region, you're liable to go away disappointed. Another way of saying this, though, is that large mammals show up when you least expect it! Keep a look out for the following:

Mule Deer

The most common large mammals in the Sierra Nevada, mule deer dwell in all forest habitats below the timberline. Within the park, they have become remarkably unconcerned about human observers and tend to frequent the meadows of Yosemite Valley from late afternoon until sunset. White-spotted fawns first appear in mid- to late July, while tannish adults with big floppy ears become numerous in early winter, when deep snows push them out of the high country and they congregate below 5500ft. At all times, deer favor leaves and young twigs as a source of food, with *Ceanothus* shrubs being a perennial favorite. In late fall, deer feed heavily on acorns.

Mule deer

Bighorn Sheep

Magnificent and muscular bighorn sheep live on a handful of remote slopes above the timberline. Standing 3ft high at the shoulder and weighing well over 200lb, rams sport thick, curled horns that they use during the fall rut. Bighorn sheep have become extremely rare in the Sierra Nevada, with populations hovering around 100 individuals. Discreet hikers – or those with good binoculars – might catch a glimpse of small bands of the animals on the high slopes above Lee Vining, Bishop, or Lone Pine.

Black Bears

Arguably the animal people would most like to see (or most like to avoid) is the black bear. Weighing in at around 350lb (or in exceptional cases almost double that), bears can be formidable animals, especially since they can act fearless around people. Nothing compares to the anxiety you'll feel when encountering a bear on a remote trail or in your campsite at night, but you can take comfort from the fact that bears generally shy away from human contact. Whether climbing trees, poking under logs and rocks, or swimming in water, bears are basically big noses in search of food – and they'll eat almost anything. Strangely, bears often spend a considerable amount of time grazing like cows on meadow plants. Later in the summer, they switch over to berries and acorns, with insects (including yellowjackets) making up about 10% of their diet.

Black bear

For tips on how to avoid confrontations with bears, see p 67

Big Cats

Lucky and rare is the visitor who glimpses a **mountain lion** bounding off into the woods. Reaching up to 9ft from nose to tail tip and weighing as much as 190lb, this solitary and highly elusive creature makes a formidable predator; in the Sierra, mountain lions roam all forested habitats below the timberline in the hunt for mule deer. Humans are rarely more than a curiosity or nuisance to be avoided, although a few attacks have occurred in regions where encroachment by humans has pushed lions to their limits (mainly around rapidly growing suburban areas).

Mountain lion

Hikers are more likely to see the handsome **bobcat**, which looks like a scaled-up version of the domestic tabby, with a brown-spotted, yellowish-tan coat and a cropped tail.

Coyotes & Foxes

Wild members of the dog family include the ubiquitous coyote and its much smaller cousin, the **gray fox**. Both share the same grayish-brown coat and both have adapted to human habitats, becoming increasingly comfortable around roads, houses, and (of course) food left unguarded. You stand a good chance of seeing a coyote during the daytime, especially around meadows, where they go to feed on rodents. Foxes mainly come out at night; you might spy one crossing trails or roads. The coyote population has spread widely throughout the region, but foxes have stayed put in the low foothills of the west slope.

Coyote

SMALL MAMMALS
Chipmunks

Seven species of chipmunks live in the Yosemite region, divvying up or sharing habitat that ranges from sere sagebrush flats to dense forests to high alpine peaks. Trying to tell all the varieties apart is best left to experts, as all chipmunks share the same pattern of cinnamon, black, and white stripes running the length of their bodies. A favored food of many predators, chipmunks remain ever agile and alert even while intently collecting seeds, berries, or insects that they store in small caches.

Squirrels

The little **golden-mantled ground squirrel**, which lives above about 5500ft, is often mistaken for a chubby chipmunk, though it differs in numerous physical and behavioral ways. For one thing, ground squirrels have no stripes on their heads and shoulders (chipmunks are striped all the way to the tip of their noses). For another, ground squirrels spend the winter hibernating – so starting in late summer they become extremely focused on gaining weight. These bulging beggars will badger you relentlessly for food. However tempting, it is strictly forbidden to feed animals within the park and strongly discouraged elsewhere.

Chipmunk

A large cousin of the chipmunk, the bold **western gray squirrel** never hesitates to stamp its feet angrily on branches and scold human intruders. These pale gray rodents with a long, fluffy tail trailing behind tend to live in black oak forests at low to mid-elevations on the west slope. Above the zone of black oak, the smaller **Douglas squirrel**, or **chickaree**, recognized by its slender tail and rusty tone, makes its home in dark conifer forests up to the timberline.

Marmots

Among the largest rodents in the Yosemite region, the yellow-bellied marmot inhabits rock outcrops and boulder fields above 7500ft. Sprawled lazily like fat house cats on sun-warmed rocks, marmots scarcely bear notice until closely approached, at which point they jolt upright and send out shrieks of alarm to the entire marmot neighborhood. But that doesn't mean that they don't sometimes seek attention. Around popular viewpoints and roadside rests, they can become pesky and obese beggars, but this practice is becoming rare now that more park visitors obey regulations against feeding wildlife. Marmots have a great appetite – they must spend four to five months putting on a lot of pounds (an incredible 50% of their body weight is fat) before descending into a long, deep hibernation until the following spring.

Weasels

A tiny predator who strikes fear into the heart of every small animal, the long-tailed weasel is followed by shrill cries of alarm from birds and chipmunks wherever it travels. Long, slender, and extremely active, weasels search ceaselessly among logs and rocks for prey throughout the entire region.

Pikas

If you come across a pika, before you see it you're likely to hear its odd little "bleating" call, emitted from among jumbles of rocks and boulders. A careful search will reveal the hamster-like vocalist peering from under a rock with small beady eyes. Pikas typically live on talus slopes above 7700ft, especially in the realm of mountain hemlock, whitebark pine, and heather plants. If you're hiking up that high, you're bound to make the acquaintance of these unforgettable characters.

Pika

BIRDS

Whether you enjoy the aerial acrobatics of swifts and falcons over Yosemite Valley waterfalls, or the flash of brilliant warblers in oak woodlands, or the bright inviting lives of more than 300 other bird species found in the region, it goes without question that birds are one of Yosemite's wildlife highlights.

Small Birds

No other bird commands attention quite like the **Steller's jay**, found in virtually every forested habitat but most abundant around campgrounds, trailheads, and other human destinations. Flashing a shimmering cloak of blue feathers and an equally jaunty attitude, these noisy birds wander fearlessly among picnic tables and parked cars in pursuit of overlooked crumbs. One of their favorite tricks for stealing food from small birds is to swoop in on their feathered counterparts while perfectly imitating a hawk's scream.

Steller's jay

Another conspicuous bird, the small black-capped **mountain chickadee** is a perennial favorite with children because its merry song sounds like "cheese-bur-ger." You'll hear this song often in all forested areas above 4000ft.

In the highest mountain forests, campers and hikers can expect greetings from the raucous and inquisitive **Clark's nutcracker**, a hardy resident of subalpine forests that's easily recognized by its black wings and white tail. Groups of nutcrackers survive the winter by gathering and storing up to four million pine nuts each fall, burying the nuts in thousands of small caches that they memorize and dig up later for food.

In the high mountains, also keep your eyes open for the specialized **gray-crowned rosy finch**, a beautiful pink and gray bird found on alpine peaks. These finches feed almost entirely on insects that are swept up out of the lowlands by updrafts; the unfortunate bugs, numbed by the cold, fall out of the sky onto snowbanks.

The inveterate mountaineer John Muir greatly favored the **American dipper** (formerly known as a water ouzel) for its ceaseless energy and good cheer even in the depths of winter. This "singularly joyous and lovable little fellow," as Muir called the dipper, rarely leaves the cascading torrent of cold, clear mountain streams, where it dives to capture underwater insects and larvae. Look closely when you spot one of these slate-gray birds standing on a riverside rock – you might see the blinking flash of its whitish, translucent eyelids, which allow it to see underwater while diving.

Perhaps even more energized are the several species of hummingbirds that live in the Yosemite region. Fueled by a sugar-rich diet equivalent to a human eating 155,000 calories a day, hummingbirds take to flower-laden meadows like miniscule kamikazes. In mountain meadows above 4000ft, look for the tiny **calliope hummingbird**, recognized by its streaked or speckled throat; in the meadows and shrub thickets below 4000ft, expect to find the large, aggressive **Anna's hummingbird**, with its full hood of brilliant red feathers.

Great horned owl

Birds of Prey

While 11 species of owls live in the Yosemite region, including the common **great horned owl**, with its long, upright ear tufts, no other owl evokes the mystery of the nocturnal realm quite like that rare phantom the **great gray owl**. Easily Yosemite's most famous and sought-after bird, this distinctive owl stands 2.5ft tall. A small population (about 50 individuals) of these birds, residents of northern boreal forests, somehow survives in the park. These majestic owls have been spotted at Ackerson Meadow and Crane Flat, where they hunt around large meadows in the late afternoon.

You'll be fortunate if you see the **peregrine falcon**, a species that has climbed back from the brink of extinction and now is present in healthy numbers. This streamlined, fierce hunter with long, pointed wings and a black "moustache" mark on its cheek sometimes hangs around Yosemite's big walls.

AMPHIBIANS & REPTILES
Frogs & Toads

The Yosemite region is home to several unique amphibians, including its namesake **Yosemite toad**. This endemic, high-elevation toad used to abound in an area spanning 6000ft to 12,000ft, but in recent years it has mysteriously disappeared from many of its former haunts. At lower elevations, its close relative, the **western toad**, is still quite common and often observed moving along trails or through campgrounds at night. To

Peregrine falcon

identify a toad, look for a slow, plodding walk and dry, warty skin, which easily distinguishes them from smooth-skinned, quickly hopping frogs.

Another amphibian of the High Sierra is the scarce **mountain yellow-legged frog**, whose numbers have declined sharply in alpine lakes stocked with trout. This strong jumping and diving frog resides on lake margins. The abundant **Pacific treefrog**, in contrast, is a weak hopper that usually floats languidly on the water surface. Extremely widespread and diverse in their habitat preferences, treefrogs have the familiar "ri-bet" call that nearly everyone associates with singing frogs (thanks to Hollywood movies that use this frog in their soundtracks).

Yosemite toad

Salamanders

Oddest among Yosemite amphibians is the **Mt Lyell salamander**, first discovered in 1915 when accidentally captured in a mousetrap. A member of the web-toed salamander family, this granite-colored salamander resides on granite domes and talus slopes from 4000ft to 12,000ft, where it uses its toes and strong tail to climb sheer cliffs and boulders in search of food.

Lizards

The most abundant and widespread reptile in all of Yosemite is the **western fence lizard**, a 5- to 6-inch-long creature you're likely to see perched on rocks and logs or scampering across the forest floor. During the breeding season, dark-gray males bob energetically while conspicuously displaying their shiny blue throats and bellies.

Western fence lizard

Somewhat less common, or seemingly so because they live under forest floor debris, **southern alligator lizards** wiggle off noisily like clumsy snakes when disturbed. These 8- to 10-inch-long yellow-tan lizards reside from the lower foothills up into the mixed conifer zone.

Snakes

Among Yosemite's 10 or so snake species, **garter snakes** live in the widest diversity of habitats and are the snakes you're most likely to see. Two kinds of garter snake found in the region sport mainly black skin, with yellow or orange stripes running the length of their bodies. A third species, restricted to low to mid-elevation rivers, features a black checkerboard pattern on an olive-gray body.

One of the more beautiful snakes is the delicate **ring-necked snake**, most often seen crossing moist forest trails, where it searches for slugs, worms, and salamanders. Blue-gray on top, this snake has a coral-red belly and neckband that it displays by rolling over when disturbed.

No other snake elicits as much fear and curiosity as the **western rattlesnake**. Even if they're not rattling, you can quickly recognize rattlers by their bluntly triangular heads perched on remarkably slender necks. Rocky or brushy areas below 8000ft are the preferred haunts of this venomous though generally docile snake.

Western rattlesnake

FISH

The most widely distributed fish in the western Sierra is the **rainbow trout**. Formerly limited to the lower reaches of streams below insurmountable barriers (such as waterfalls), rainbow trout have been introduced into countless alpine and eastern creeks and lakes for sportfishing. In addition, three spectacular subspecies collectively called "golden trout" are found in the Kern River drainage of Sequoia-Kings Canyon National Park.

Further complicating the natural order of things, four nonnative trout – **brook trout, lake trout, brown trout**, and **kokanee** – have been successfully introduced throughout the Sierra Nevada. Introduced fish have had a devastating impact on aquatic ecosystems, especially in formerly fishless alpine areas, where fragile nutrient cycles and invertebrate populations have changed dramatically as a result.

INSECTS

Most visitors don't care to encounter the daunting variety of insects in the Sierra Nevada, except for a handful of conspicuous butterflies and other charismatic insects. Foremost among the large, showy butterflies are the six or so swallowtails. The **Western tiger swallowtail**, yellow in color with bold black bars and beautiful blue and orange patches near its "tail," follows stream banks from the lower foothills to subalpine forest. Restricted to the foothill zone, the stunning, iridescent blue **pipevine swallowtail** flits in large numbers along foothill canyons and slopes almost year-round.

Among butterfly-watchers, Yosemite is famous for the endemic **Sierra sulphur**, once highly sought by collectors because only one person knew the location of its home – a homesteader who collected specimens in secret and sold them to the world's museums. With the opening of Tioga Pass Rd in 1915, others learned that these small greenish butterflies live abundantly in the Tuolumne Meadows area, where their larvae feed on dwarf blueberry plants.

Western tiger swallowtail

Watchful observers in August will note a small white butterfly flopping lazily around the tops of tall pine trees. The **pine white**, as it's appropriately called, occurs in yearly outbreaks, which sometimes yield hundreds of butterflies. During another outbreak, the population of the **California tortoiseshell**, an orange butterfly with dark, ragged margins around its wing, can soar into the millions. At times, highways must be closed because the pavement becomes slick with dead tortoiseshells or because drivers can't see through the clouds of swirling butterflies.

One insect is hard to see, but its impact can be startlingly conspicuous. Only a quarter-inch in size, the moth known as the **lodgepole needle miner** appears every two years in late July or August. Swirling around lodgepole pine forests, these moths lay eggs that hatch into caterpillars that bore into the tips of pine needles. With a two-year life cycle, and millions of caterpillars occurring during a single outbreak, this species might kill 90% of the needles in an infected area and cause entire hillsides to turn orange with dying trees. The resulting stands of bleached dead trees are especially noticeable in the upper Tuolumne River watershed. While this event seems like something of a tragedy, the caterpillars do serve as a critical winter food supply for small songbirds and the dying trees provide a key link in several ecological processes.

Plant Life

The Yosemite region of the High Sierra boasts one of the richest selections of plants found anywhere in North America, in ecosystems that range from the Central Valley floor to alpine peaks and extend farther eastward into the Great Basin desert. Encompassing less than 1% of the state's land area, Yosemite National Park alone is home to 23% of the state's plant species. Richest of all is the Dana Plateau, which towers over Tioga Pass, where 1 square mile hosts 50% of all the alpine plant species in the entire range.

Because the park's territory spans a range of elevations, it's possible to find a zone of flowering plants from late March until the end of August, and taking time out to smell the flowers will definitely enrich your park experience. The exquisite new *An Illustrated Flora of Yosemite National Park* by Stephen Botti will enthrall wildflower aficionados, while the much smaller *Wildflowers of Yosemite* by Lynn and Jim Wilson and Jeff Nicholas should help more casual observers.

GIANTS' REALM

Although giant sequoias grow only on the west slope of the Sierra Nevada today, this was not always the case. Between five and 25 million years ago, their ancestors covered a vast area between what is now the Sierra Nevada and the Rocky Mountains. Migrating westward, possibly through low mountain passes, these trees got a foothold on the west slope of the Sierra Nevada just as the range began to achieve its current height. The formation of the Sierra Nevada isolated those sequoias on the west slope while at the same time creating a rain shadow that killed off the main population to the east. Giant sequoias survive today in 67 scattered patches or groves, three within the boundaries of Yosemite National Park. *A Guide to Sequoia Groves of California* by Dwight Willard tells you how to find the remaining populations of these great trees.

Lodgepole pine

Sugar pine

TREES

While flowers rise and fade with ephemeral beauty, trees hold their majesty for centuries and, thus, make an ideal study for the beginning nature enthusiast. Given a few simple tips, you can identify many of the region's prominent species and appreciate the full sweep of trees cloaking the landscape.

The **giant sequoia** is Yosemite's most famous tree and also the source of much legend and ballyhoo. Even information as basic as the trees' maximum height and width remains uncertain because loggers and claim-seekers who cut down many of the original giants found it beneficial to exaggerate record trees. The General Sherman tree of Sequoia National Park, 275ft tall and more than 100ft in circumference, is the species' largest known living specimen. Sequoias cluster in fairly discrete groves on the western slopes of the Sierra Nevada. You can recognize them by their spongy, cinnamon-red bark and juniper-like needles (reduced to small overlapping scales lying along the stem). Despite claims that these are the world's oldest trees, it's now thought that the longest they can live is 3300 years, far short of the age reached by bristlecone pines.

Pines are conifers whose needles appear in tight clusters, either two, three, or five needles per cluster. Named for its straight, slender trunk, the **lodgepole pine** features pairs of 1- to 3-inch-long needles, and globular cones that are less than 2 inches long. This is the most common tree around mountain meadows because the species has adapted to survive in water-logged soils or in basins where cold air sits at night (so-called frost pockets).

The **ponderosa pine**, with some examples of the **Jeffrey pine** mixed in, covers vast tracts of low to mid-elevation slopes. Three-needled clusters characterize both trees. Virtually identical in appearance, the two species do have distinct cones; on ponderosa cones, the spines curve outward, and on Jeffrey pines they curve inward. If you're unsure of the identification, simply hold a cone in your hand and remember the adage: "Gentle Jeffrey, prickly ponderosa." Jeffrey pines also claim the dubious distinction of being one of the world's few "gasoline trees," so named due to compounds in their sap that ignite explosively in wildfires.

Surely the prettiest pine is the **sugar pine**, which mixes freely with giant sequoias in the mixed conifer zone. This tree gets its uniquely elegant charm from long, broadly spaced branches with 1.5ft-long cones hanging from the tips. Look on the ground among fallen cones for needles in clusters of five.

The other characteristic five-needled pine of the Yosemite region, the **whitebark pine** lives in the subalpine forest, at the very upper limits of the timberline. Often wind-hewn and weather-beaten, these pines grow in fantastic forms that command the attention of photographers.

Among single-needled conifers, no other species covers so much terrain as the **red fir**, which dominates the forest between 6000ft and 8000ft. Uniform, dark stands of these stout somber firs stand out thanks to the chartreuse lichen growing on their trunks. Red fir forests feature more open space than other types of forest because the combination of shade, cold, and a short growing season preclude grasses and shrubs from growing there.

The wide variety of deciduous trees in the region includes the ever-popular **quaking aspen**, with its smooth, white bark and circular leaves. Every brief gust sets these leaves quivering on their flattened stems, an adaptation for shaking off sudden snowfalls that would otherwise damage fragile leaves. Aspens consist of genetically identical trunks arising from a single root system that may grow to be more than a hundred acres in size. By sprouting repeatedly from this root system, aspens have what has been called "theoretical immortality," and some aspens are thought to be over a million years old. In the Yosemite region, aspens grow mainly above 6000ft, but some have been planted as ornamentals in Yosemite Valley.

One of the most characteristic and important deciduous trees in Yosemite Valley and on the western slopes of the Sierra is the **black oak**. Grand old trees up to 80ft high and 4.5ft in diameter grow between 2000ft and 6000ft, and their immense crops of acorns serve as the main food source for many animals, including mice, pigeons, bears, and deer. Large, deeply indented leaves with spine-tipped lobes distinguish black oaks from other species.

SHRUBS

The term "shrub" is a somewhat arbitrary label that designates a woody plant with many stems, and sometimes it's hard to decide whether a plant is a tree or a shrub. For example, the **huckleberry oak**, one of Yosemite's most common shrubs, produces crops of miniature acorns, like its mighty cousins (which this small, ground-hugging oak scarcely resembles in any other way). The huckleberry oak abounds along many trails leading out of Yosemite Valley as well as along Tioga Rd, and together with **greenleaf manzanita** it forms a dense, nearly impenetrable habitat known as montane chaparral that carpets portions of the park around granite boulders and outcrops. Here bears, deer, rabbits, and many other animals find food and shelter not provided in nearby forests.

At lower elevations, montane chaparral gives way to foothill chaparral, which is characterized by **whiteleaf manzanita** and a number of ecologically important *Ceanothus* shrubs. The two manzanitas feature the same smooth, reddish bark and small, red, apple-like berries (manzanita is Spanish for "little apple"), but they differ in the color of their leaves. During late summer, the scat of animals like black bear, coyote, and fox are chock-full of partly digested manzanita berries – but you probably won't want to examine it too closely.

Poison oak

Ceanothus is a broad category of eight or more shrubs that provide a primary food source for mule deer and other animals. Deer favor the succulent young twigs while birds and rodents feast on the plants' seeds. Thriving between 1500ft and 6000ft, the tall *Ceanothus* known as **deer brush** puts out large displays of creamy white flowers. You can also recognize it by its leaves, which have three veins arising from the base.

An important food source for wildlife, eight types of **currant and gooseberry bushes** thrive in the region, all of which produce variously sweet and edible (though mainly spiny) berries. Some species have sticky leaves that are pungent when lightly rubbed.

One low-growing shrub in the rose family is so sticky and pungent that early miners gave it the name **mountain misery** because its resin accumulated on their boots and pants. (Fortunately this miserable name is increasingly being replaced by its musical Native American name, **kitkitdizze**.) This plant, with its lacy, fernlike leaves and large white flowers, forms extensive carpets under ponderosa pines at low elevations on the western slopes.

But no other shrub is as worthy of note as the maligned **poison oak**, which triggers an inflammatory skin reaction in many people who touch any part of the plant. If you'll be exploring the western slopes below 4500ft, learn how to identify – and avoid – this common trailside plant. The shrub is distinguished by its shiny, oaklike leaves that occur in groups of three. These leaves often take on various red and orange hues. Clusters of white berries appear by late summer and make a good meal for birds and rodents throughout the winter.

WILDFLOWERS

While Yosemite draws most visitors with its dramatic landscape, its floral displays are every bit as exquisite and spectacular. In the right season (based on elevation but ranging from late March into August), the meadows full of wildflowers are reason enough to journey to the region. You'll no doubt find your own personal favorites, but following is a list of some notable blossoms to get you started on your search.

At low elevations in early spring, when wildflowers carpet the hillsides of canyons like the Merced River below El Portal, you can't miss the brilliant orange of the **California poppy**, with its four large, floppy petals and finely indented leaves. One species on display is the California state flower, but another of similar appearance also grows in the region. At night and on cloudy days, poppy petals fold up and become inconspicuous.

Nearly every damp meadow between 5000ft and 7000ft hosts large patches of the dramatic, pinkish **Jeffrey shooting star**. The book *Wildflowers of Yosemite* exclaims that this species can "transform a moist landscape into a sea of beauty." Upon close inspection, this flower presents an odd face, with petals swept back to expose the flower's innards (highlighted with pretty maroon and yellow rings) to pollinators.

Prominent in the meadows of Yosemite Valley is the bright sunflower cousin **Bigelow's sneezeweed**. Standing chest-high, these plants sport yellow flowers with centers that look like dark-reddish Ping-Pong balls. They also feature long, narrow, ruffled leaves that clasp the stems at their bases.

At least 13 species of **Indian paintbrush** of varying colors and shapes grow in the region. Most are red or orange in color and seem somewhat hairy. Surprisingly, the flowers themselves are hidden and accessible only to hummingbirds (the plants' pollinators), while a set of specialized, colored leaves take on the appearance of petals. Paintbrushes are semiparasitic, often tapping into the roots of their neighbors to draw nourishment.

Lupine

While you're in Yosemite, you're bound to see the **lupine** – 20 species thrive here, and their masses of blue or purple flowers fill meadows and line roads and trails. All lupines feature leaves arranged in a circle like fingers on a hand, plus flowers like those found on peas (one petal raised as a banner to attract insects and two other petals enclosing the flower's reproductive structures). Their flowers have evolved a complex structure that facilitates pollination by bumblebees.

Mountaineers climb into a rarified realm rich in unique flowers, including one that has become symbolic of the High Sierra. **White heather** is a dense heath plant with beautiful nodding white bells for flowers. As an adaptation to the extreme mountain environment, its leaves have become tiny needles that lie closely overlapping along the stems. Though found throughout the Sierra Nevada, white heather abounds in the Yosemite region.

Sky pilot

If you need a single target flower to hunt for, one that's rare and mysterious like a distant peak, you couldn't make a better choice than the **Sierra primrose**. Confined to a handful of high subalpine slopes and peaks, this brilliant magenta beauty is a real find for the lucky hiker. Arising from clumps of toothed, succulent leaves, primroses sometimes grow in large patches sprawling across rocky slopes.

Highest and showiest of all is the aptly named **sky pilot**. Found only on summits over 11,000ft, this plant erupts into flagrant displays of blue flowers arranged in dense, ball-like clusters. After a long and grueling ascent, hikers to the highest peaks will better understand the name "sky pilot," a slang term for a person (eg, missionary) said to lead others to heaven.

FIRE!

Each year many thousands of acres of land burn in the Sierra Nevada. Some of these wildfires burn hot and fast, while others creep along slowly, but all play a natural and important role in the forests' life cycles. Foresters and land managers are increasingly reintroducing fire into the landscape after many decades of "Smokey Bear" type fire prevention (ie, stamping out fires as soon as they start).

Low-intensity fires thin out accumulated brush in the forest understory and leave nutrient-rich ash that stimulates plant growth. In the absence of fire, conifer seedlings become established and transform the nature of the forest environment, as they have in Yosemite Valley, where white firs and incense-cedars are replacing the more open pine and oak woodlands and obscuring the once-famous view.

Despite the potential value of forest fires, though, fire management should be left to the professionals. Visitors still need to practice extreme care with their own fires. Any flame can grow quickly out of hand, so it's imperative to clear away additional fuels around a campfire, to watch a fire at all times, to douse a fire thoroughly after use, and to obey specific regulations in regard to campfires.

LICHENS

Out of several groups of lesser known and mostly unappreciated plants, the lichens deserve some attention. Truly remarkable life-forms, lichens arise from an odd symbiotic relationship between fungi and algae and grow at a rate that can be measured in millimeters per century. These plants remain so overlooked that many species await discovery in the Sierra Nevada.

That said, several lichens have become an all-too-familiar and unavoidable part of the Yosemite experience. Take, for example, the ubiquitous **wolf lichen**, which grows as bits of chartreuse fluff that adorn nearly every mountain conifer in the region. This species has gone to town on red firs, festooning every trunk. Look closely and notice how the lichens stop abruptly at a line 5ft to 10ft off the ground – this is the height of the winter snowpack, below which the lichens can't grow. The only species of lichen that's known to be poisonous, wolf lichen takes its name from its former role as an ingredient in bait set out to poison wolves.

An equally flamboyant lichen, the **flame firedot** covers large patches of rock with intense coral-orange color – a particularly noticeable sight along foothill roads leading into Yosemite. It belongs to a type called crustose lichens, which grow flat against rock surfaces (actually insinuating themselves into the mineral matrix). Unlike flame firedot, many other species of crustose lichens come in muted shades of gray, brown, and black.

The **tree-hair lichen** (sometimes called "edible horsehair") can grow copiously on conifer and oak branches up to 8000ft. This species looks so much like clumps and knots of brown hair that one Native American myth holds that this lichen originated when trickster Coyote snarled his braid of hair in a tree and had to cut it loose.

Stresses on the System

With the discovery of gold in 1848, the natural world of the Sierra Nevada was forever altered by a rush of new settlers. Within a year, the number of ships entering San Francisco Bay jumped from four to 700 per year, and an estimated 150,000 to 175,000 people poured into the Sierra Nevada over the following decade. The stampede to find gold and profit at any cost had a devastating impact on both the Native Americans of the region and the landscape. In the gold-bearing region north of Yosemite, rivers were diverted, rocks moved, and entire hillsides washed away to reveal gold deposits. More than 1.5 billion tons of debris flowed downstream, with harsh consequences to aquatic ecosystems and watershed health.

Although the Yosemite region escaped largely unscathed, it was hit hard by a subsequent stampede that particularly appalled John Muir. This time, scores of sheep wreaked havoc – every year, ranchers drove six million sheep upslope to lush mountain meadows. In this profit-driven free-for-all, grazing rights went to whoever could get the most sheep to a meadow first. And the result? Sheep turned meadows into choking dustbowls by chowing down on fragile plants before they could flower and produce seeds. For a period in the late 1800s, the greatest danger to a "tourist" traveling in the Sierra Nevada was that his pack animals might starve to death because not a single blade of grass could be found. Even now, a hundred years later, the pattern of vegetation in the high mountains largely reflects this grazing history, with many hillsides still dry and barren or choked with species the "hoofed locusts" didn't like. Fortunately, the mountain environment is so extreme that few weed species took hold. However, the opposite is true of foothill slopes, where weed species introduced by the influx of sheep and humans now utterly dominate and choke out native plants.

John Muir's concern over destructive logging practices, especially those that felled his beloved giant sequoias, played an important part in the establishment of Yosemite National Park, but Muir didn't survive long enough to see the worst of what could happen. Industrial-scale logging took off after World War II, when gasoline-powered chainsaws, logging trucks, and heavy equipment were systematically brought into the hills with an intent to take everything that was profitable. Decades later, the debate over logging practices and their consequences remains far from resolved, though the scale of logging has been dramatically reduced in recent years. By now there's little disagreement that logging activities have been responsible for many forest fires or the conditions that create forest fires, that heavy equipment compacts soils for half a century or more, and that logging roads create long-term harm to watersheds – the question now is what level of destruction society is willing to tolerate for the sake of affordable wood products.

Without doubt, the greatest benefit the Sierra Nevada provides to the state of California is an abundant supply of fresh, clean water, and ironically the greatest harm to the Sierra Nevada has come from managing and collecting this precious water. Some have said that the building of Hetch Hetchy Dam in Yosemite broke John Muir's heart just before he died, and since then the damming of the Sierra's waters has only increased in pace and scale. In the last century, a virtual curtain of dams has been drawn across the face of the Sierra Nevada, eliminating spawning habitat for fish like salmon, whose population once numbered more than a million.

Now near extinction in the Sierra Nevada, salmon number only in the dozens or low hundreds during their spawning runs. Out of 40 species of fish native to the Sierra Nevada, only a few still boast healthy populations, while 22 have landed on the threatened and endangered species list or are under review for a place on the list. Native fish populations and aquatic ecosystems have been further decimated by the introduction (mostly for fishing) of 30 nonnative fish species that have come to dominate countless aquatic habitats.

Benign though they may seem, recreation and tourism also have an effect on the landscape. Each visitor inevitably contributes to the overall impact, whether through the smog or congestion of cars in Yosemite Valley, through campfire smoke and wood use, or through heavy foot traffic on popular trails – and in a park where thousands of acres are dedicated to visitor use, the cumulative effect can be big. From backpacking to tour-bus sightseeing, each type of tourist experience has its own consequences, but together they reshape a region that's being punished by too much love. Meanwhile, park personnel do all they can to preserve the experience of wilderness and nature for all visitors. Do your part to minimize your impact as much as possible – stay on trails, avoid trampling fragile areas, and respect other park regulations.

Yosemite National Park

General Yosemite Information

Yosemite National Park ☎ 209-372-0200
  W www.nps.gov/yose
Yosemite Valley Visitor Center ☎ 209-372-0299
Tuolumne Meadows Visitor Center ☎ 209-372-0263
Big Oak Flat Information Station ☎ 209-379-1899
Wawona Information Station ☎ 209-375-9531
Yosemite Medical Clinic ☎ 209-372-4637

YOSEMITE APPENDIX

Accommodations

National Park Reservation Service (campgrounds)
  ☎ 301-722-1257, 800-436-7275
  W www.reservations.nps.gov
YNP Campground Reservation Office (main)
  ☎ 209-372-8502
  W www.nps.gov/yose/trip/camping.htm
Wilderness Permit Reservations
  ☎ 209-372-0740
  W www.nps.gov/yose/wilderness
High Sierra Camps
  ☎ 559-253-5674
  W www.yosemitepark.com/html/accom_hisierra.html
Yosemite Concession Services (all other park lodging)
  ☎ 559-252-4848
  W www.yosemitepark.com
Yosemite West
  ☎ 559-642-2211
  W www.yosemitewest.com
The Redwoods in Yosemite
  ☎ 559-375-6666
  W www.redwoodsinyosemite.com

Transportation

Yosemite Visitor Shuttle
  ☎ 209-372-1240

Tuolumne Meadows Tour & Hikers' Bus
   ☎ 209-372-1240
Amtrak
   ☎ 800-872-7245
   W www.amtrak.com
Greyhound
   ☎ 800-229-9424
   W www.greyhound.com
Yosemite Area Regional Transportation System (YARTS)
   ☎ 209-388-9589, 877-989-2787
   W www.yarts.com

Tour Operators

Yosemite Concession Services
   ☎ 209-372-1240
   W www.yosemiteparktours.com
Yosemite Sightseeing Tours
   ☎ 559-877-8687
   W www.yosemitetours.com
Green Tortoise
   ☎ 415-956-7500, 800-867-8647
   W www.greentortoise.com
Incredible Adventures
   ☎ 415-751-7791, 800-777-8464
   W www.incadventures.com
VIA Adventures
   ☎ 800-842-5463
   W www.via-adventures.com

Activities

Badger Pass Ski Area
   ☎ 209-372-1244
   W www.badgerpass.com
California Department of Fish & Game
   ☎ 559-222-3761
   W www.dfg.ca.gov
High Sierra Hikers Association
   W www.highsierrahikers.org
Pacific Crest Trail Association
   ☎ 916-349-2109
   W www.pcta.org
Southern Yosemite Mountain Guides
   ☎ 800-231-4575
   W www.symg.com

Yosemite Guides
☎ 209-379-2231, 877-425-3366
Ⓦ www.yosemiteguides.com

Yosemite Institute
☎ 209-379-9511
Ⓦ www.yni.org/yi

Yosemite Mountaineering School
☎ 209-372-8344
Ⓦ www.yosemitemountaineering.com

Yosemite National Park Education Center
☎ 209-375-9505

Yosemite Outdoor Adventures
☎ 209-379-2321
Ⓦ www.yosemite.org/seminars

Useful Organizations

National Park Service
Ⓦ www.nps.gov

Sierra Club
☎ 415-977-5500
Ⓦ www.sierraclub.org

Yosemite Association
☎ 209-379-2646
Ⓦ www.yosemite.org

Yosemite Institute
Ⓦ www.yni.org/yi

Beyond Yosemite

Inyo National Forest
☎ 760-873-2400
Ⓦ www.r5.fs.fed.us/inyo/

Mono Lake Committee Visitor Center
☎ 760-647-6595
Ⓦ www.monolake.org

Sierra National Forest
☎ 559-297-0706
Ⓦ www.r5.fs.fed.us/sierra/

Stanislaus National Forest
☎ 209-532-3671
Ⓦ http://www.r5.fs.fed.us/stanislaus/

Tuolumne County Visitors Center
☎ 209-533-4420
Ⓦ www.thegreatunfenced.com

Yosemite Sierra Visitor Bureau
☎ 559-683-4636
Ⓦ http://www.yosemite-sierra.org/

Maps

Geologic Map of Yosemite National Park and Vicinity, California by N King Huber.
   Reston, VA: US Geological Survey, 1989.
Guide to Yosemite High Sierra Trails by Bob Roney.
   El Portal, CA: Yosemite Association, 1993.
Yosemite National Park and Vicinity Topographic Map. Berkeley, CA:
   Wilderness Press, 1999.
Yosemite National Park, California – Topographical Map. Washington, DC:
   National Geographic/Trails Illustrated, 1996.
Yosemite Road Guide. El Portal, CA: Yosemite Association, 1989.

Books

Lonely Planet's *Hiking in the Sierra Nevada* – John Mock and Kimberley O'Neil.
Lonely Planet's *California* – Andrea Schulte-Peevers, et al.

An Illustrated Flora of Yosemite National Park by Stephen J Botti.
   El Portal, CA: Yosemite Association, 2001
Bicycling America's National Parks: California by David Story and Dennis Coello.
   Woodstock, VT: Countryman Press, 2000.
Birds of Yosemite and the East Slope by David Gaines.
   Lee Vining, CA: Artemisia Press, 1992.
Camp 4: Recollections of a Yosemite Rockclimber by Steve Roper.
   Seattle, WA: The Mountaineers Books, 1994.
Discovering Sierra Mammals by Russell K Grater.
   El Portal, CA: Yosemite Association, 1987.
Discovery of the Yosemite by Lafayette Houghton Bunnell, MD.
   El Portal, CA: Yosemite Association, 1991.
Easy Access to National Parks: The Sierra Club Guide for People with Disabilities
   by Wendy Roth and Michael Tompane.
   Collingdale, PA: Diane Publishing Company, 1998.
Geology of the Sierra Nevada by Mary Hill.
   Berkeley, CA: University of California Press, 1975.
History of the Sierra Nevada by Francis P Farquhar.
   Berkeley, CA: University of California Press, 1976 (originally published in 1965).
Indian Life of the Yosemite Region by Samuel A Barrett and Edward W Gifford.
   El Portal: Yosemite Association, 1987.
Mountaineering in the Sierra Nevada by Clarence King.
   Lincoln, NE: University of Nebraska Press, 1997.
My First Summer in the Sierra by John Muir.
   Boston, MA: Houghton Mifflin Co, 1998 (originally published in 1911).
*Obata's Yosemite – The Art and Letters of Chiura Obata from His Trip to the High
   Sierra in 1927* by Chiura Obata. El Portal, CA: Yosemite Association, 1993.
Sierra Nevada Natural History by Tracy Storer and Robert Usinger.
   Berkeley, CA: University of California Press, 1972.
Sierra Nevada: The Naturalists Companion by Verna Johnston.
   Berkeley, CA: University of California Press, 2000.

The Geologic Story of Yosemite National Park by N King Huber.
El Portal, CA: Yosemite Association, 1989.
The High Sierra of California by Gary Snyder with Tom Killion (illustrator).
Berkeley, CA: Heyday Books, 2002.
The Yosemite by John Muir, with photos by Galen Rowell.
El Portal, CA: Yosemite Association, 2002.
Up and Down California in 1860-1864 by William Henry Brewer.
Berkeley, CA: University of California Press, 2002.
Yosemite by Ansel Adams. New York, NY: Bulfinch Press, 1995.
Yosemite Climbs: Free Climbs by Don Reid. Guilford, CN: Falcon Publishing, Inc,
1998.
Yosemite Climbs: Big Walls by Don Reid. Guilford, CN: Falcon Publishing, 1998.
Yosemite: Its Discovery, Its Wonders & Its People by Margaret Sanborn.
El Portal, CA: Yosemite Association, 1989.

Bookstores In and Near Yosemite

Yosemite Bookstore ☎ 209-379-2648
Yosemite National Park (6 locations)
Yosemite
Ⓦ www.yosemite.org
Operated by the non-profit Yosemite Association, with proceeds
benefiting the park.

Bishop Bookstore ☎ 760-872-2665
621 West Line Street, Suite 110
Bishop

Books Upstairs ☎ 209-274-6960
5 Main Street
Jackson

Mountain Bookshop ☎ 209-532-6117
Junction Center
13769-I Mono Way
Sonora
A great selection of books and a good resource for park information.
Say hello to Hobbes, the owners' dog, who is usually in the window.

Murphys Books ☎ 209-728-9207
178 Big Trees Road
Murphys

Sasha's Reading Room ☎ 209-728-2200
416 Main Street
Murphys

Spellbinder Books ☎ 760-873-4511
124 S. Main St
Bishop
The only full-service bookstore in Owens Valley, specializing in non-fiction,
California and Sierra history. Stop by, have a cup of coffee and browse.

ANNOUNCING
YELLOWSTONE &
GRAND TETON NATIONAL PARKS

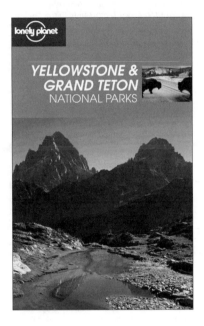

NEW TITLE

Yellowstone & Grand Teton National Parks

1 74104 116 3 Available April 2003
288 pp, 12 pp color, 25 maps
US$19.99 | UK£14.99
Bradley Mayhew, Andrew Dean Nystrom,
& Amy Marr

- from geysers to grizzlies, bison to bald
  eagles, this snappy guide introduces experts
  and tenderfeet alike to the wild and woolly
  wonders of both parks plus nearby
  attractions

- over 30 maps, including 1,200 miles of
  remote trails

- outdoor activities for all skill levels

- family-friendly travel tips

Lonely Planet Guides by Region

L onely Planet is known worldwide for publishing practical, reliable and no-nonsense travel information in our guides and on our Web site. The Lonely Planet list covers just about every accessible part of the world. Currently there are 16 series: Travel guides, Shoestring guides, Condensed guides, Phrasebooks, Read This First, Healthy Travel, Walking guides, Cycling guides, Watching Wildlife guides, Pisces Diving & Snorkeling guides, City Maps, Road Atlases, Out to Eat, World Food, Journeys travel literature and Pictorials.

AFRICA Africa on a shoestring • Botswana • Cairo • Cairo City Map • Cape Town • Cape Town City Map • East Africa • Egypt • Egyptian Arabic phrasebook • Ethiopia, Eritrea & Djibouti • Ethiopian Amharic phrasebook • The Gambia & Senegal • Healthy Travel Africa • Kenya • Malawi • Morocco • Moroccan Arabic phrasebook • Mozambique • Namibia • Read This First: Africa • South Africa, Lesotho & Swaziland • Southern Africa • Southern Africa Road Atlas • Swahili phrasebook • Tanzania, Zanzibar & Pemba • Trekking in East Africa • Tunisia • Watching Wildlife East Africa • Watching Wildlife Southern Africa • West Africa • World Food Morocco • Zambia • Zimbabwe, Botswana & Namibia
Travel Literature: Mali Blues: Traveling to an African Beat • The Rainbird: A Central African Journey • Songs to an African Sunset: A Zimbabwean Story

AUSTRALIA & THE PACIFIC Aboriginal Australia & the Torres Strait Islands • Auckland • Australia • Australian phrasebook • Australia Road Atlas • Cycling Australia • Cycling New Zealand • Fiji • Fijian phrasebook • Healthy Travel Australia, NZ and the Pacific • Islands of Australia's Great Barrier Reef • Melbourne • Melbourne City Map • Micronesia • New Caledonia • New South Wales • New Zealand • Northern Territory • Outback Australia • Out to Eat – Melbourne • Out to Eat – Sydney • Papua New Guinea • Pidgin phrasebook • Queensland • Rarotonga & the Cook Islands • Samoa • Solomon Islands • South Australia • South Pacific • South Pacific phrasebook • Sydney • Sydney City Map • Sydney Condensed • Tahiti & French Polynesia • Tasmania • Tonga • Tramping in New Zealand • Vanuatu • Victoria • Walking in Australia • Watching Wildlife Australia • Western Australia
Travel Literature: Islands in the Clouds: Travel in the Highlands of New Guinea • Kiwi Tracks: A New Zealand Journey • Sean & David's Long Drive

CENTRAL AMERICA & THE CARIBBEAN Bahamas, Turks & Caicos • Baja California • Belize, Guatemala & Yucatán • Bermuda • Central America on a shoestring • Costa Rica • Costa Rica Spanish phrasebook • Cuba • Cycling Cuba • Dominican Republic & Haiti • Eastern Caribbean • Guatemala • Havana • Healthy Travel Central & South America • Jamaica • Mexico • Mexico City • Panama • Puerto Rico • Read This First: Central & South America • Virgin Islands • World Food Caribbean • World Food Mexico • Yucatán
Travel Literature: Green Dreams: Travels in Central America

EUROPE Amsterdam • Amsterdam City Map • Amsterdam Condensed • Andalucía • Athens • Austria • Baltic States phrasebook • Barcelona • Barcelona City Map • Belgium & Luxembourg • Berlin • Berlin City Map • Britain • British phrasebook • Brussels, Bruges & Antwerp • Brussels City Map • Budapest • Budapest City Map • Canary Islands • Catalunya & the Costa Brava • Central Europe • Central Europe phrasebook • Copenhagen • Corfu & the Ionians • Corsica • Crete • Crete Condensed • Croatia • Cycling Britain • Cycling France • Cyprus • Czech & Slovak Republics • Czech phrasebook • Denmark • Dublin • Dublin City Map • Dublin Condensed • Eastern Europe • Eastern Europe phrasebook • Edinburgh • Edinburgh City Map • England • Estonia, Latvia & Lithuania • Europe on a shoestring • Europe phrasebook • Finland • Florence • Florence City Map • France • Frankfurt City Map • Frankfurt Condensed • French phrasebook • Georgia, Armenia & Azerbaijan • Germany • German phrasebook • Greece • Greek Islands • Greek phrasebook • Hungary • Iceland, Greenland & the Faroe Islands • Ireland • Italian phrasebook • Italy • Kraków • Lisbon • The Loire • London • London City Map • London Condensed • Madrid • Madrid City Map • Malta • Mediterranean Europe • Milan, Turin & Genoa • Moscow • Munich • Netherlands • Normandy • Norway • Out to Eat – London • Out to Eat – Paris • Paris • Paris City Map • Paris Condensed • Poland • Polish phrasebook • Portugal • Portuguese phrasebook • Prague • Prague City Map • Provence & the Côte d'Azur • Read This First: Europe • Rhodes & the Dodecanese • Romania & Moldova • Rome • Rome City Map • Rome Condensed • Russia, Ukraine & Belarus • Russian phrasebook • Scandinavian & Baltic Europe • Scandinavian phrasebook • Scotland • Sicily • Slovenia • South-West France • Spain • Spanish phrasebook • Stockholm • St Petersburg • St Petersburg City Map • Sweden • Switzerland • Tuscany • Ukrainian phrasebook • Venice • Vienna • Wales • Walking in Britain • Walking in France • Walking in Ireland • Walking in Italy • Walking in Scotland • Walking in Spain • Walking in Switzerland • Western Europe • World Food France • World Food Greece • World Food Ireland • World Food Italy • World Food Spain **Travel Literature:** After Yugoslavia • Love and War in the Apennines • The Olive Grove: Travels in Greece • On the Shores of the Mediterranean • Round Ireland in Low Gear • A Small Place in Italy

Lonely Planet Mail Order

Lonely Planet products are distributed worldwide. They are also available by mail order from Lonely Planet, so if you have difficulty finding a title, please write to us. North and South American residents should write to 150 Linden St, Oakland, CA 94607, USA; European and African residents should write to 10a Spring Place, London NW5 3BH, UK; and residents of other countries to Locked Bag 1, Footscray, Victoria 3011, Australia.

INDIAN SUBCONTINENT & THE INDIAN OCEAN Bangladesh • Bengali phrasebook • Bhutan • Delhi • Goa • Healthy Travel Asia & India • Hindi & Urdu phrasebook • India • India & Bangladesh City Map • Indian Himalaya • Karakoram Highway • Kathmandu City Map • Kerala • Madagascar • Maldives • Mauritius, Réunion & Seychelles • Mumbai (Bombay) • Nepal • Nepali phrasebook • North India • Pakistan • Rajasthan • Read This First: Asia & India • South India • Sri Lanka • Sri Lanka phrasebook • Tibet • Tibetan phrasebook • Trekking in the Indian Himalaya • Trekking in the Karakoram & Hindukush • Trekking in the Nepal Himalaya • World Food India **Travel Literature:** The Age of Kali: Indian Travels and Encounters • Hello Goodnight: A Life of Goa • In Rajasthan • Maverick in Madagascar • A Season in Heaven: True Tales from the Road to Kathmandu • Shopping for Buddhas • A Short Walk in the Hindu Kush • Slowly Down the Ganges

MIDDLE EAST & CENTRAL ASIA Bahrain, Kuwait & Qatar • Central Asia • Central Asia phrasebook • Dubai • Farsi (Persian) phrasebook • Hebrew phrasebook • Iran • Israel & the Palestinian Territories • Istanbul • Istanbul City Map • Istanbul to Cairo • Istanbul to Kathmandu • Jerusalem • Jerusalem City Map • Jordan • Lebanon • Middle East • Oman & the United Arab Emirates • Syria • Turkey • Turkish phrasebook • World Food Turkey • Yemen **Travel Literature:** Black on Black: Iran Revisited • Breaking Ranks: Turbulent Travels in the Promised Land • The Gates of Damascus • Kingdom of the Film Stars: Journey into Jordan

NORTH AMERICA Alaska • Boston • Boston City Map • Boston Condensed • British Columbia • California & Nevada • California Condensed • Canada • Chicago • Chicago City Map • Chicago Condensed • Florida • Georgia & the Carolinas • Great Lakes • Hawaii • Hiking in Alaska • Hiking in the USA • Honolulu & Oahu City Map • Las Vegas • Los Angeles • Los Angeles City Map • Louisiana & the Deep South • Miami • Miami City Map • Montréal • New England • New Orleans • New Orleans City Map • New York City • New York City City Map • New York City Condensed • New York, New Jersey & Pennsylvania • Oahu • Out to Eat – San Francisco • Pacific Northwest • Rocky Mountains • San Diego & Tijuana • San Francisco • San Francisco City Map • Seattle • Seattle City Map • Southwest • Texas • Toronto • USA • USA phrasebook • Vancouver • Vancouver City Map • Virginia & the Capital Region • Washington, DC • Washington, DC City Map • World Food New Orleans **Travel Literature:** Caught Inside: A Surfer's Year on the California Coast • Drive Thru America

NORTH-EAST ASIA Beijing • Beijing City Map • Cantonese phrasebook • China • Hiking in Japan • Hong Kong & Macau • Hong Kong City Map • Hong Kong Condensed • Japan • Japanese phrasebook • Korea • Korean phrasebook • Kyoto • Mandarin phrasebook • Mongolia • Mongolian phrasebook • Seoul • Shanghai • South-West China • Taiwan • Tokyo • World Food Hong Kong • World Food Japan
Travel Literature: In Xanadu: A Quest • Lost Japan

SOUTH AMERICA Argentina, Uruguay & Paraguay • Bolivia • Brazil • Brazilian phrasebook • Buenos Aires • Buenos Aires City Map • Chile & Easter Island • Colombia • Ecuador & the Galápagos Islands • Healthy Travel Central & South America • Latin American Spanish phrasebook • Peru • Quechua phrasebook • Read This First: Central & South America • Rio de Janeiro • Rio de Janeiro City Map • Santiago de Chile • South America on a shoestring • Trekking in the Patagonian Andes • Venezuela **Travel Literature:** Full Circle: A South American Journey

SOUTH-EAST ASIA Bali & Lombok • Bangkok • Bangkok City Map • Burmese phrasebook • Cambodia • Cycling Vietnam, Laos & Cambodia • East Timor phrasebook • Hanoi • Healthy Travel Asia & India • Hill Tribes phrasebook • Ho Chi Minh City (Saigon) • Indonesia • Indonesian phrasebook • Indonesia's Eastern Islands • Java • Lao phrasebook • Laos • Malay phrasebook • Malaysia, Singapore & Brunei • Myanmar (Burma) • Philippines • Pilipino (Tagalog) phrasebook • Read This First: Asia & India • Singapore • Singapore City Map • South-East Asia on a shoestring • South-East Asia phrasebook • Thailand • Thailand's Islands & Beaches • Thailand, Vietnam, Laos & Cambodia Road Atlas • Thai phrasebook • Vietnam • Vietnamese phrasebook • World Food Indonesia • World Food Thailand • World Food Vietnam

ALSO AVAILABLE: Antarctica • The Arctic • The Blue Man: Tales of Travel, Love and Coffee • Brief Encounters: Stories of Love, Sex & Travel • Buddhist Stupas in Asia: The Shape of Perfection • Chasing Rickshaws • The Last Grain Race • Lonely Planet...On the Edge: Adventurous Escapades from Around the World • Lonely Planet Unpacked • Lonely Planet Unpacked Again • Not the Only Planet: Science Fiction Travel Stories • Ports of Call: A Journey by Sea • Sacred India • Travel Photography: A Guide to Taking Better Pictures • Travel with Children • Tuvalu: Portrait of an Island Nation

LONELY PLANET

You already know that Lonely Planet produces more than this one guidebook, but you might not be aware of the other products we have on this region. Here is a selection of titles which you may want to check out as well:

California
ISBN 1 86450 331 9
US$21.99 • UK£13.99

Hiking in the Sierra Nevada
ISBN 1 74059 272 7
US$17.99 • UK£11.99

San Francisco
ISBN 1 86450 309 2
US$15.99 • UK£9.99

Los Angeles
ISBN 1 74059 021 X
US$15.99 • UK£9.99

Available wherever books are sold.

YOSEMITE INDEX

CLIMATE CHARTS

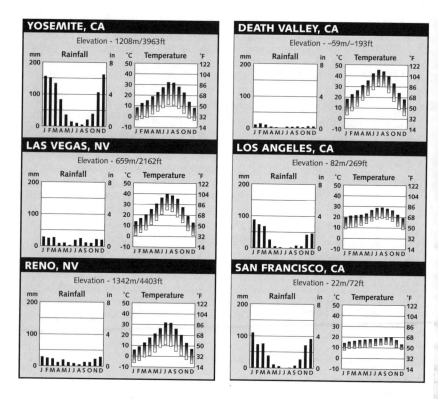

YOSEMITE, CA
Elevation - 1208m/3963ft

DEATH VALLEY, CA
Elevation - -59m/-193ft

LAS VEGAS, NV
Elevation - 659m/2162ft

LOS ANGELES, CA
Elevation - 82m/269ft

RENO, NV
Elevation - 1342m/4403ft

SAN FRANCISCO, CA
Elevation - 22m/72ft

LONELY PLANET OFFICES

Australia
Locked Bag 1, Footscray, Victoria 3011
☎ 03 8379 8000 fax 03 8379 8111
email talk2us@lonelyplanet.com.au

USA
150 Linden Street, Oakland, California 94607
☎ 510 893 8555, TOLL FREE 800 275 8555
fax 510 893 8572
email info@lonelyplanet.com

UK
10a Spring Place, London NW5 3BH
☎ 020 7428 4800 fax 020 7428 4828
email go@lonelyplanet.co.uk

France
1 rue du Dahomey, 75011 Paris
☎ 01 55 25 33 00 fax 01 55 25 33 01
email bip@lonelyplanet.fr
www.lonelyplanet.fr

World Wide Web: www.lonelyplanet.com *or* AOL keyword: lp
Lonely Planet Images: lpi@lonelyplanet.com.au